Prostitution, Polygamy, and Power

Prostitution, Polygamy, and Power

Salt Lake City, 1847–1918

JEFFREY NICHOLS

University of Illinois Press

URBANA AND CHICAGO

Library of Congress Cataloging-in-Publication Data
Nichols, Jeffrey, 1960–
Prostitution, polygamy, and power : Salt Lake City, 1847–1918 / Jeffrey
Nichols.
p.   cm.
Includes bibliographical references and index.
ISBN 0-252-02768-X (cloth : alk. paper)
1. Prostitution—Utah—Salt Lake City—History. 2. Polygamy—Utah—
Salt Lake City—History. I. Title.
HQ146.S27N525   2002
306.74'09792'258—dc21   2002000647

Contents

Illustrations follow page 82

Preface

THIS BOOK WAS born from a paper I wrote for Dean May's western history seminar at the University of Utah. While researching reaction to the posting of the 24th ("Colored") Infantry to Fort Douglas, I found evidence of a world only hinted at in the secondary literature. The local newspapers reported that some soldiers inevitably found their way downtown to patronize brothels and saloons. The papers wrote familiarly of white, African American, and Asian prostitutes; the long-lived network of houses where they worked; and the customers, policemen, and reformers with whom they interacted. Salt Lake City, the supposedly staid temple city of the Latter-day Saints, proved to have a regulated prostitution district like virtually all other American cities.

I returned to this trail some years after the seminar, expecting to write a relatively straightforward community study of prostitution. But I discovered Cornelia Paddock, Brigham Young Hampton, and the "Stockade" district, with their implications for the fight over polygamy and the struggle for political, social, and economic power in the city. I was hooked, and I made prostitution and polygamy the subject of my study.

I wish to express my deep appreciation to Edward J. Davies II, Robert A. Goldberg, Rebecca Horn, and James R. Lehning for their careful reading and useful and necessary suggestions and advice. I am especially grateful to my teacher, Dean L. May, who exhibited great patience while gently nudging me in new and better directions. I would like to thank the following scholars and others who assisted me with sources, connections, and advice: Thomas Alexander, Anne Butler, Sharon Carver, Kathleen Dalton, Craig Foster, Joan Iversen, John McCormick, Paula Petrik, D. Michael Quinn, Patricia Scott, John Sillito, and Sam Weller. Thanks also to Clark Secrest for his manuscript and sources, and Lieutenant Steve Diamond of the Salt Lake City Police Department for photographs. I am indebted to the descendants of Susan Free for their generosity and openness.

A number of archivists and librarians deserve special recognition. Ray Matthews and his colleagues at the Utah State Archives performed countless tasks of search, retrieval, and interpretation. The staff of the Marriott Library's Western History Division, Special Collections, and Manuscript Division were invariably helpful, especially Walter Jones. Rich Richmond of the Salt Lake County Recorder's Office and Doc Kivett at the City Recorder's Office allowed me full access to necessary materials. I would like to thank as well the staffs of the LDS Genealogical Library, the LDS Church History Library, the Utah State Historical Society, the Frances Willard Library, and the Social Welfare History Archives of the University of Minnesota.

Elizabeth Dulany was a patient and supportive editor throughout the long process of revision. Thanks to my colleagues at Westminster College for their tolerance of a seemingly never-ending process, and to my students for putting up with my many stories and asides about Salt Lake prostitutes. Melissa Coy Ferguson, Berkley Wilson, and Christina Podegracz, my research assistants, contributed greatly to the project; my office assistants, Jason Helme and Erin Helme, kept the rest of my professional life running smoothly. Of course, any errors are my responsibility.

And finally, thanks to Cheryl, with whom everything is possible.

Abbreviations

CA	Church Archives, Family and Church History Department, Church of Jesus Christ of Latter-day Saints, Salt Lake City, Utah
CHL	Church History Library, Family and Church History Department, Church of Jesus Christ of Latter-day Saints, Salt Lake City, Utah
FBC	First Baptist Church of Salt Lake City
JH	Journal History of the Church of Jesus Christ of Latter-day Saints
JWM	Manuscripts Division, J. Willard Marriott Library, University of Utah, Salt Lake City, Utah
SCP	Samuel C. Park Scrapbooks, Utah State Historical Society, Salt Lake City, Utah
SLCPC	Salt Lake City Police Court
SLCPD	Salt Lake City Police Department
SLCR	Salt Lake County Recorder
USHS	Utah State Historical Society, Salt Lake City, Utah

Prostitution, Polygamy, and Power

Introduction

"Mesdames Flint, Davis, Demarr, Lawrence, Noble and Grey were fined $99 each for keeping houses of prostitution. Of the twenty-four inmates of the houses of ill-fame, fifteen were fined $50 each."
—*Salt Lake City Daily Tribune,* 1 March 1885

"The complaints in each case are sworn to by B. Y. Hampton, the city license collector. Deputy Vandercook is charged with lewd and lascivious conduct with one Mrs. A. J. Field."
—*Tribune,* 22 November 1885

BOTH OF THESE NEWS items describe arrests for prostitution-related offenses in Salt Lake City, but the similarity ends there. The first article might have appeared in any western newspaper. It describes a typical periodic mass arrest of prostitutes and madams resulting in the payment of set fines, an unofficial licensing system that lasted for decades in many American cities. Prostitution in Salt Lake City and elsewhere was explicitly outlawed, but municipal authorities long tolerated and regulated the practice. Normally, only the women who sold sex faced legal penalties, not the men who bought it. The women who lived, worked, and sometimes died in Salt Lake City brothels contributed to the city's economic and social development despite the fact that most "respectable" citizens deemed them criminals.

The second item hints at a long and often bitter struggle for power. Since the Church of Jesus Christ of Latter-day Saints (LDS Church) announced to the world that its members ("Mormons") practiced polygyny (usually referred to as polygamy), non-Mormons ("gentiles") had condemned the practice and waged a campaign to abolish it.[1] By 1885 that campaign had resulted in the arrest of several prominent LDS officials and forced many others into hiding. Brigham Young Hampton, a Mormon, hoped to use prostitutes to entrap federal officials, thus proving that those officials were immoral, not the Saints. In this context, the targets were the male patrons of prostitutes.

These two news stories suggest the complex history of prostitution in Salt

Lake City. In many respects, Salt Lake resembled other western cities. Its settlers struggled to build homes, earn livings, raise families, and create community institutions. Their lives exhibited the limitless variety of human experience, but generally followed the patterns of settlement in other areas. Many of Salt Lake's inhabitants were undoubtedly not overly troubled by issues of theology or marital practice. The demands of daily life necessitated a degree of economic and social interaction across religious lines. By the early 1870s, gentile and Mormon residents had built a small business district where women and men sold goods and services, including sex. Most prostitutes' lives were probably similar to those lived elsewhere, and the city's other residents and municipal authorities often reacted to them in similar ways.

But Salt Lake City differed in important respects. The leaders of the LDS Church wielded great spiritual, social, economic, and political influence over their numerically dominant membership. And because of that influence, the city stood at the center of a conflict that ebbed and flowed for decades. A vocal minority of Mormons and gentiles competed for power in a variety of arenas, including economics, electoral politics, church pulpits, newspapers, and voluntary associations. The conflict drew national attention and resulted in unprecedented action by the federal government that eventually forced the Latter-day Saints to change some of their most distinctive practices.

This conflict shaped prostitutes' experiences and gave prostitution in Salt Lake City an additional significance. The most highly publicized aspect of the struggle concerned sexual morality. Many gentiles accused polygamous Mormons of violating Christian norms of family structure and sexual behavior. Gentile women especially condemned plural marriage because it institutionalized a double standard that allowed men to have multiple sex partners. In response, Mormons defended their church and their families and accused gentiles of immorality. Mormons argued that gentiles introduced prostitution, a sinful practice based on lust that degraded women and the family, into a previously pure and virtuous community of honorably married Saints. Prostitution quickly and enduringly became a mutual point of reference in the ongoing competition. At numerous significant junctures of the contest over polygamy, one or the other antagonist used prostitution to discredit its opponent.

The stakes in this public contest were great: economic and political power in the city and territory. The social significance was no less important. Prostitution and polygamy concerned the highly charged arena of human sexuality, and the contest had enormous consequences for the most intimate and fundamental aspects of individuals' lives. The contestants attempted to exercise control over women, whether prostitutes or plural wives, and over their customers, husbands, or lovers. The arguments sometimes seemed purely rhetorical, and those who struggled for power often seemed to ignore the actual people involved. But the results were quite real: women and men were arrested and jailed. Some lost their homes, livelihoods, or marriages or had their reputations ruined or their children's legacies endangered. Prostitutes, plural wives, and the men associated with them often found themselves buffeted by forces they could only partially control.

By the second decade of the twentieth century, the conflict between gentiles and Mormons had quieted, and their differences had narrowed. The LDS Church abandoned some of its most distinctive practices, especially communal economics and plural marriage, and consciously sought to accommodate to the larger American society. Gentiles and Mormons increasingly conducted business with one another and joined the same political parties and voluntary associations. Some united to fight regulated prostitution in a common reform effort that demonstrated a degree of reconciliation and recognition of shared values.

Morality did not cease to be contested in the early twentieth century, but divisions tended to be along generational and class rather than religious lines. As more young women worked and recreated in public, middle- and upper-class reformers feared that such newly independent behavior would lead those women into prostitution. The reformers demanded that the state intervene in young women's private lives and regulate venues where the sexes met. Mormon and gentile reformers alike welcomed the efforts of city, state, and federal governments to control the sexuality of young, mostly working-class women.

That reconciliation spelled trouble for prostitutes. As a consensus developed that prostitution should be abolished, the police forced women out of regulated brothels and into rooming houses and hotels, and onto the streets. Women continued to sell sex, but the end of regulation meant the loss of a certain degree of predictability, protection, and status. The law continued to hold them, not their customers, largely responsible for prostitution. Reformers had united to defend society from the alleged dangers of prostitution, but few seemed to care about the women involved or the conditions that drove them to sell sex.

An extensive and sophisticated historical literature on prostitution and reform has developed in the last three decades. Several works have particularly influenced this study. Ruth Rosen has studied the culture of prostitution in eastern cities in the early twentieth century, and she concludes that the change from regulation to abolition of restricted districts made prostitutes' lives even more difficult and dangerous.[2] Anne Butler has investigated prostitution in the West from the Civil War until about 1890. Her classifications by class, race, and ethnicity have proven applicable to this study, and she demonstrates the overwhelmingly bleak lives of most of the women who sold sex in the West.[3] Other scholars have contributed valuable studies of single western communities, including Jacqueline Baker Barnhart (San Francisco), Paula Petrik (Helena), Mary Murphy (Butte), and Marion Goldman (the Comstock Lode).[4] These scholars have convincingly proven what I found in Salt Lake City: prostitution was well known, openly regulated, and important to the growth of communities. Most women made the dangerous choice to sell sex because of financial difficulties and limited opportunities, and they faced exploitation by customers, brothel managers, and municipal authorities.

The responses to prostitution have also been extensively studied. Barbara Meil Hobson has shown how inequalities in gender, race, and class shaped policy in eastern cities, resulting in a coercive campaign against prostitutes in the Progressive Era.[5] Peggy Pascoe details the range of activities that middle-class reformers carried out across the West, from "rescuing" plural wives in Salt Lake City to freeing Chinese women held in virtual sex slavery in San Francisco, in a search for "female moral authority."[6] Paul Boyer provides a context for moral reform from the early nineteenth century into the Progressive Era. He argues persuasively that prostitution policy always reflected other contemporary concerns about American society.[7] Joanne Meyerowitz and Mary Odem demonstrate how young women's growing autonomy and economic independence around the turn of the twentieth century worried reformers and contributed to the campaigns against regulated prostitution and for state control of young women's sexuality.[8]

This study investigates prostitutes and the responses to them in Salt Lake City from its founding to the end of World War I. While it describes some women's experiences selling sex and the structure of prostitution in Salt Lake, it also investigates the roles prostitutes played in building a community. The terms "prostitute," "prostitution," and "reform" had complex and dynamic meanings across this time period, meanings shaped by gender, economics, religion, class, race, and power. Because of these contested meanings, prostitutes, prostitution, and reform could be put to many different uses. For poor women, selling sex could be a temporary expedient, a long-term source of livelihood, and/or an avenue of disease, abuse, and degradation. A few such women amassed considerable wealth and political influence, and some may even have attained a measure of social respectability for themselves or their families, but most prostitutes lived in poverty. To be labeled a prostitute meant incurring the fear and loathing of most other citizens. For women who sold sex, reform could mean arrest, public exposure, loss of money and freedom, or forced expulsion from their homes or from the city. Occasionally, reform meant expressions of sympathy or offers of "rescue." Prostitutes' lives were shaped extensively by the actions and policies of reformers. Prostitutes were among the least powerful residents of the city, but they were not simply passive recipients or victims: they accepted, rejected, evaded, or adapted to aspects of reform.

In the eyes of many middle- and upper-class Mormons and non-Mormons, prostitutes egregiously violated ideal moral codes and gender systems. Reform in this sense could mean the reinforcement of the respective moral code, which might be accomplished by "rescuing" individual prostitutes and converting them to "true" (or "true Mormon") women. For others, reform could mean using state power to abolish prostitution.

Prostitution had additional meanings and uses within the Mormon-gentile conflict. For many Mormon men, the presence of women selling sex was a galling symptom of their failure to maintain exclusive control over the city. Prostitution could stand for all of the unwelcome changes that gentiles supposedly brought to Zion, as well as "proof" of the immorality of those who condemned polygamy. Reform in this context could mean a return to Mormon hegemony and the enforcement of the LDS moral code and gender system. Mormons had additional reasons to condemn prostitution when some gentiles equated it with polygamy. Most Mormon women probably shared these views, at least publicly, although many welcomed the end of plural marriage.

Some gentile women activists defined prostitution and polygamy as two aspects of the same phenomenon: the exploitation of women by a patriarchal gender system. In similar fashion, a man betrayed a woman who then became a prostitute; a Mormon husband deceived a woman into becoming his plural wife; or a man seduced a single woman (although reformers believed such women shared different levels of responsibility). For these activists, then, reform could mean the abolition of prostitution, the overthrow of polygamy, the destruction of the LDS Church, the enforcement of a single sexual standard, or even the establishment of equality between men and women within the framework of separate spheres. While some gentile males genuinely shared this sense of moral outrage, others linked prostitution to polygamy as a convenient means by which to attack Mormon political and economic domination.

While the above considerations might seem to unite most citizens (except prostitutes) against prostitution, powerful factors resulted in its persistence. Most fundamentally, many men, Mormon and gentile, were willing to pay for sex. Some practiced a double standard of sexual morality that allowed them to use prostitutes while demanding chastity of other women in their lives. As for women, limited job opportunities and personal financial exigency (and for some, the opportunity to earn better money than in other occupations) meant there were always some women more or less willing to sell sex.

Prostitution also had a powerful economic constituency of gentiles and Mormons. Women and men who sold liquor and drugs, loaned money, provided legal counsel, or rented, sold, or leased rooms to prostitutes and their customers used their economic and political clout to defend their interests. A few madams became successful and influential businesspeople. Some business owners and municipal officials considered prostitution an inevitable or even welcome adjunct to a modern, prosperous city. Many men without any direct stake declared that prostitution, while morally reprehensible, was ineradicable and less dangerous when openly regulated. For municipal authorities and the police, prostitution could be an important source of revenue from fines and bribes.

For the members of this constituency, the proper policy toward prostitution was regulation. The city's political and economic elites developed a regulation policy that guaranteed customers access to sexual services while protecting profits, keeping social order, and allowing for easier policing and revenue collecting. Regulation also gave higher-status prostitutes a degree of economic and physical security. At the same time, prostitutes officially remained criminals, so individuals could be arrested or forced to move if authorities desired. Many prostitutes and madams skillfully adapted to or subverted this precarious system and used their mobility, anonymity, or personal, financial, and political contacts to stay in business. The police argued that regulation kept prostitution and its associated dangers localized and easy to control. The regulation of prostitution in Salt Lake City began under all-Mormon rule and continued without effective challenge until the campaign against the Stockade. During and after that campaign, which occurred in the midst of the national progressive campaign against regulated prostitution, many Mormons and gentiles in positions of power came to agree that "reform" meant abolition. Reformers decided that prostitutes were no longer necessary or desirable. Much of the legal apparatus that had been employed against polygamy was now turned against prostitution, with the result that women selling sex had to do so furtively and at even greater risk.

I see the history of prostitution as a lens through which we can view many changes in Salt Lake, including women's public activities; the city's physical and economic transformations; religious, ethnic, racial, and class relations; the construction and interpretation of gender systems and moral codes; and the relationship between citizens and the state. Salt Lake City's history can be better understood through analysis of the various uses and meanings of prostitutes, prostitution, and reform.[9]

Notes

1. I will use "Mormon," "Saint," and "Latter-day Saint" as synonyms. Similarly, "non-Mormon" and "gentile" will be considered equivalents.

2. Rosen, *Lost Sisterhood.*

3. Butler, *Daughters of Joy, Sisters of Misery.*

4. Barnhart, *Fair but Frail;* Petrik, "Capitalists with Rooms"; Mary Murphy, "Women on the Line"; and Goldman, *Gold Diggers and Silver Miners.*

5. Hobson, *Uneasy Virtue,* esp. pp. vii, 3–5.

6. Pascoe, *Relations of Rescue.*

7. Boyer, *Urban Masses and Moral Order in America.*

8. Meyerowitz, *Women Adrift;* Odem, *Delinquent Daughters.*

9. Little has been written about prostitution in Salt Lake City. Exceptions include McCormick, "Red Lights in Zion"; brief references in R. Snow, "American Party in Utah"; Schindler, "The Oldest Profession's Sordid Past in Utah," in *In Another Time,* pp. 178–81; and Alexander and Allen, *Mormons and Gentiles,* pp. 118, 148–49, 282.

1. "Celestial Marriage" vs. "Polygamic Lascivious Cohabitation"

THE ISSUES THAT DIVIDED Mormons and gentiles long predated the settlement of Salt Lake City. To many Americans, Mormon theology was presumptuous if not heretical, particularly because of its claims of a new scripture and the doctrine of continuous revelation through an anointed prophet, Joseph Smith, Jr. Some merchants resented the Saints for their exclusive trading practices. Their political opponents accused them of bloc voting, while others accused them of agitating Indians or tampering with slaves. To many gentiles, the tightly organized and hierarchical Mormons appeared deeply un-American in an era that revered the striving, competitive, self-made (white) male; the independent voter; the rugged individualist who rejected authority and demanded equality with others.

These issues led to a long period of conflict wherever the Mormons settled and ultimately to their self-exile in the Salt Lake Valley, which deeply affected the Saints by reinforcing their self-image as a chosen people subject to the hatred and abuse of unbelievers. The perceived persecution helped create a body capable of impressive cooperative achievements as well as long-term resistance to those they considered enemies. Many of the above issues resurfaced when non-Mormons began to settle in the Salt Lake region.[1]

The story of the settlement of the Salt Lake Valley is well known and will only be sketched here. The Saints welcomed the isolation of the valley because it allowed them to build their exclusive "Kingdom of God" with little interference. In effect, the civil and ecclesiastical governments of the region were the same: the LDS Church leadership. Salt Lake City's elected mayor and ward-based city council mirrored most contemporary American cities. City and territorial governments were all-Mormon (until 1888 and 1889 respectively), and generally acted in the LDS Church's interests and enforced its values.[2] The creation of the Territory of Utah in 1850, however, brought federally appointed judges and governors to Salt Lake City and marked the beginning of the long three-cornered contest between Mormons, the national government, and local non-Mormons for control of the territory.[3]

The Latter-day Saints' faith was central to all aspects of the new settlement; and marriage, the family, and certain gender roles were central to the faith. The sacred texts of the LDS faith—the Bible, the Book of Mormon, the Doctrine and Covenants, and the Pearl of Great Price—abound in prescriptions for proper family life, the roles of women, and the requirement of premarital chastity and marital fidelity. Worthy male members belonged to a universal lay priesthood, held all church governance offices, and exercised ultimate authority within their families.[4] Women had a subordinate but necessary role; together, righteous men and women sought to conceive and raise righteous progeny and achieve exaltation in the afterlife.[5]

The Saints held that sexual desire between man and woman was a positive gift from God, to be expressed only within marriage.[6] They shared with other Christians biblical strictures against sexual immorality. The Book of Mormon contains many similar moral prescriptions, which together constitute the "law of chastity."[7] The Doctrine and Covenants, which Saints believe contain divine revelations given to their prophet, also address sexuality.[8] LDS leaders supplemented these dictates with sermons and discourses.[9] Nineteenth-century Mormon doctrine revered the family, encouraged marriage, acknowledged necessary roles for women but subordinated them to male authority, valued the expression of sexuality but restricted it to the married state for purposes of procreation, and punished transgressions of the moral code. Few of these beliefs would have been surprising or unacceptable to other Christian Americans. The great difference, of course, lay in the Latter-day Saints' concept of "eternal" or "celestial marriage," defined in the nineteenth century as plural marriage.

The Saints were not alone in the Salt Lake Valley for long. Non-Mormons often stopped on their way to Oregon or California in the late 1840s and 1850s. A relative handful stayed, adapted to the Mormon community, and did not disrupt the Saints' hegemony.[10] The federal officials sent to the territory discovered that their authority was virtually nonexistent, much to their chagrin. Even the bloodless "Utah War" of 1857–59 did not appreciably shake the Mormon hierarchy's control, although it did demonstrate the federal government's willingness and ability to exert power over the territory.[11]

Substantial numbers of non-Mormons began to arrive in the 1860s. In 1862 Colonel Patrick E. Connor and his California volunteers established Camp

Douglas on the east bench of the city, creating a permanent army presence (and a steady source of customers for prostitutes). Connor, who deeply distrusted the Saints, felt he had a duty to attract "loyal" gentiles to the territory to counteract the Mormon majority. Accordingly, he encouraged mining in hopes of spurring a boom. The advent of the transcontinental railroad in 1869 eventually allowed both the transportation of tons of ore and the immigration of thousands of gentiles.[12] The railroad inaugurated an era which Leonard Arrington describes as a period of two separate, competitive economies: one consisting of nucleated, agricultural Mormon commonwealths, the other of gentile-dominated mining districts. From roughly 1869 to 1890, Utah society remained rather strictly divided between those "of the Kingdom" and those outside.[13]

Mid-nineteenth-century Christian Americans broadly shared the Mormon beliefs in the centrality of marriage, sexuality, the importance of family, and the proper role of women.[14] The rise of market capitalism and the physical separation of work and the home in the late eighteenth and early nineteenth centuries gradually led middle- and upper-class men and women to create the ideal of "separate spheres." While men were expected to operate in the competitive, striving, individualistic public sphere of wage work and politics, women were expected to remain in the home, creating a safe, pure, virtuous private refuge for their families. The home protected women from the public sphere, for whose rigors and corruption they were supposedly not suited, and made the best use of the "natural" attributes and talents that they did possess.

By the middle of the nineteenth century, these beliefs had crystallized into what historian Barbara Welter called the "cult of true womanhood," to which women were expected to aspire. A "true woman," according to Welter, was pious, pure, submissive, and domestic. Because she was virtuous, she might claim moral superiority over her husband, father, brothers, or sons. Marriage was the best and happiest state for a true woman, with motherhood a natural corollary. Individuals and families that followed these strictures (or at least appeared to) could consider themselves "respectable."[15] Of course, many women could not afford or did not aspire to this ideal state. Women who needed or wanted to work outside the home faced not only limited opportunities and low wages but also suspicions about their respectability.[16]

With the creation of women's sphere came new claims for the nature of women's sexuality. The female sex had traditionally been viewed as naturally lustful, and folklore as well as some accepted medical authorities held that women were possessed of stronger sexual appetites and capable of greater pleasure than men. By the middle of the nineteenth century, however, many authorities began to argue that women had no natural inclination for sex. For example, Dr. William Acton declared that "the majority of women (happily for them) are not very much troubled with sexual feelings of any kind."[17] Those authorities now considered men the passionate sex, a construction that allowed some men to argue for the importance of greater sexual license, including the patronage of prostitutes, to male health and happiness.[18]

Some historians maintain that the doctrine of separate spheres, while shutting women out of electoral politics and keeping most economically dependent, did provide them with certain power. The public and private spheres were, at least in theory, equally important and complementary. Historians John D'Emilio and Estelle B. Freedman argue that the separation of home and work altered the dominant meaning of marriage from an economic partnership whose main purpose was to produce children to an intimate relationship motivated by romantic love that provided companionship for husband and wife. Women could also exercise more control over their fertility through contraception, continence, abstinence, and abortion. Some women used their moral authority within their sphere to publicly demand curbs on men's sexuality.[19]

While the Mormon gender system was broadly similar to the non-Mormon, real differences existed. Mormon men continued to bear the ultimate responsibility and authority for the family's spiritual well-being. Mormon beliefs about the purposes of marriage, particularly that of raising righteous progeny, were more in keeping with the older conception of marriage. Historian Klaus Hansen suggests that Mormons may have stressed procreation as the primary purpose of marriage to counter gentile claims that male lust drove the Mormon leaders to institute polygamy.[20] The marriage of several women to a single man probably lessened the importance of romantic love as a criterion.

Compared to most other contemporary American women, especially in the middle and upper classes, Mormon women also tended to be more often present in public space. The demands of frontier life and the absence of husbands (whether on church missions or because they were with their other families) often forced women to take leadership roles within their families and communities. The network of LDS auxiliary organizations also provided Mormon women with opportunities to exercise leadership in the public sphere.[21]

Women who sold sex for money violated the tenets of true womanhood and Mormon womanhood alike. Prostitutes sold publicly what was supposed to be kept for marriage and shared only with a husband. Indeed, a frequent synonym for "prostitute" was "public woman." Historian Glenna Matthews notes that until around the turn of the century, "public man" was a term of high praise, while no positive connotation was attached to "public woman."[22] The discourse surrounding prostitution reveals much about nineteenth-century gender systems. Respectable people considered prostitutes "fallen women," a term evoking the biblical fall from grace. A prostitute "fell" just as a victim of seduction or an adulteress did; all three similarly violated the norms of virtuous true womanhood. A "fallen woman" might lose the protection of a father or husband, while an unmarried woman who lost her virginity was "ruined" (a term which suggests an economic aspect to virtue) and her chances for a desirable marriage were irreparably damaged.[23] Women who sold sex might also pollute the homes of the middle and upper classes. Men who patronized prostitutes exposed their wives or children to "loathsome diseases."[24] While some respectable people expressed sympathy for prostitutes, most probably regarded them with loathing and horror.

The obvious difference between Mormon and non-Mormon gender systems was polygyny, most often referred to as polygamy. Joseph Smith may have begun practicing plural marriage during the 1830s. A revelation of 12 July 1843 gave official sanction to the doctrine.[25] The Mormons continued to officially deny the existence of plural marriage until they were well established in Utah, by which time the majority had apparently accepted polygamy in principle if not in practice. Then, at a special Church conference in August 1852, Apostle Orson Pratt delivered a lengthy public defense of the practice that established the basic Mormon position for the next four decades.[26]

Pratt advanced arguments on a number of fronts. Most importantly for the Saints, he stressed that God commanded plural marriage, obligating Mormons to follow the practice or risk denying the faith. Pratt and the defenders who followed him emphasized the religious nature of plural marriage at least partly to claim protection for the practice under the establishment of religion clause in the First Amendment to the U.S. Constitution. The apostle also provided social arguments. He emphasized the sinful nature of the outside world, or "Babylon," from which the Saints had so recently escaped. Babylon abounded in sexual sins that plural marriage could prevent. Prominent among those sins was prostitution.[27]

This line of reasoning appeared again and again in Mormon sermons. Mormon leaders stressed the blessings of committed marriage and the loving, happy home, within which a pure woman could enjoy the protection of a good man and the joy of raising their children. They repeatedly contrasted the polygamous Mormon world, in which every woman had the possibility of achieving those worthy goals, with monogamous Babylon, where "surplus" women who could not find husbands were virtually forced into prostitution.[28]

Mormon arguments for plural marriage convinced few outside of their world. Polygamy offended and outraged many non-Mormons, who claimed it hurt the family, caused physical harm, and enslaved or prostituted women. An Illinois congressman summarized many of the arguments in an 1860 debate over a proposed antipolygamy bill: "I charge it to be a crying evil; sapping not only the physical constitution of the people practicing it, dwarfing their physical proportions and emasculating their energies, but at the same time perverting the social virtues, and vitiating the morals of its victims. . . . It is a scarlet whore. It is a reproach to the Christian civilization; and deserves to be blotted out."[29] Most opponents of polygamy charged that it fostered a broad and vague "immorality." Like Orson Pratt's public defense, these arguments stayed relatively consistent over time.[30]

Antipolygamists refused to credit Mormon claims that plural marriage was a legitimate religious practice. They often accused the LDS leadership of introducing and practicing plural marriage merely to gratify male lust, the same deadly sin that fueled prostitution. A typical attack charged that a libidinous Joseph Smith practiced concubinage through the "'sealing' process" and that the equally immoral Brigham Young gave institutionalized lust "the nature of a divine ordinance" by inventing the pivotal 1843 revelation after the fact.[31] The opponents of plural marriage also blamed it for a variety of social ills. One woman claimed that Mormon men discarded older wives for younger, more appealing women and practiced "the grossest of incest—the intermarriage of near relations." She cited other critics who blamed polygamy for keeping Utah in poverty.[32] Some medical authorities suggested that plural marriage was creating a "new race" of genetically damaged offspring.[33]

Polygamy also served as a surrogate for other concerns, especially for non-Mormons who sought a share of political and economic power in Utah. Many Mormons realized this and refused to accept gentile objections to polygamy at face value, contending instead that they served as a smokescreen to disguise efforts to break the Saints' control over Utah or to destroy their church. In the Mormon view, the antipolygamy "crusade" was merely a continuation of the persecutions that the Church had suffered for decades.[34] Most gentiles insisted that polygamy *was* the real issue. Charles Carroll (C. C.) Goodwin, editor of the *Salt Lake City Daily Tribune*, declared that the gentiles of Utah fought for "a higher civilization, a nobler manhood, a more exalted womanhood, a higher, deeper patriotism and a more profound regard for morals, for justice, for order and for law."[35] Some non-Mormon men, however, admitted that polygamy was not the most important issue. Fred T. Dubois, a longtime activist against polygamy and Utah statehood, later wrote that "those of us who understood the situation were not nearly so much opposed to polygamy as we were to the political domination of the church. We realized, however, that we could not make those who did not come actually in contact with it, understand what this political domination meant. We made use of polygamy, in consequence, as our great weapon of offense and to gain recruits to our standard."[36]

Mormon and gentile women, however, concentrated their arguments on plural marriage. Marriage was central to both gender systems. Married women's subordinate status in law and custom meant that their economic and social status and that of their children fundamentally depended upon the legitimacy of their marriages. Women also stressed family morality because society considered it part of their sphere. The female contestants employed the language of "domestic feminism": they emphasized the supposedly distinctive qualities of their sex and used their moral stature within the domestic sphere to define themselves as the guardians of true womanhood and the home.[37] Among the rhetorical weapons in their petitions, appeals, newspaper articles, and fiction was prostitution.

The federal government took no direct action against Mormon marriage until the Morrill Anti-Bigamy Act of 1862, but this law lacked an effective enforcement mechanism.[38] The federal government's interest in the Mormons' peculiar institution coincided with the beginning of the long power struggle between gentiles and Mormons in Utah. Brigham Young and other church officials responded to the influx of gentiles during the 1860s by attempting to strengthen the Saints' economic independence.[39] Although these efforts had their successes, the results were ultimately disappointing. A group of Mormon businessmen believed that such exclusive policies were harmful to the territory's economy. These men, known collectively as the New Movement or the Godbeites after one of their leaders, William S. Godbe, argued that the Saints should pursue a more open economic policy. The Godbeites aired their ideas in a series of publications, including the *Daily Tribune* newspaper.[40]

The Mormon leadership excommunicated or "disfellowshipped" most of the dissidents. Some Godbeites joined with gentile businessmen, professionals, and army officers to found the Liberal Party, which claimed to be the voice of the disfranchised Utah gentiles and the advocates of a progressive economic policy. Liberals complained of the Mormons' exclusive economic practices, their monopoly of political offices, and high taxes assessed upon gentiles. The Liberals opposed statehood for the same reason that Mormons desired it: statehood would mean greater political autonomy, with Mormons inevitably winning the lion's share of offices. Only through a continuation of territorial status, with the appointed federal officials that came with it, could Utah's gentiles continue to have some influence on politics and some protection from alleged Mormon abuses. Liberal candidates contested political offices with a marked lack of success until the late 1880s.[41]

The Godbeite/gentile alliance foundered in the early 1870s, mostly over the issue of polygamy (several of the Godbeites were polygamists) and the increasingly anti-Mormon stance of the *Tribune*. The paper's most strident criticism of the Mormons came between 1873 and 1883 under the editorship of Frederic Lockley.[42] In 1880, C. C. Goodwin joined the editorial staff. Goodwin, a committed Liberal, continued the criticism (albeit at a milder pitch) until the achievement of statehood inaugurated a period of reconciliation, roughly from the early 1890s until 1905.[43] Silver millionaire Thomas Kearns bought the paper in 1901 and revived its anti-Mormon stance as the organ of the "American" Party from 1905 to 1911. Thus, despite periods of peace, the *Tribune* served as the voice of the most determined and discontented gentiles in Utah for four decades. The Saints answered the criticism through their own outlets, including the LDS Church organ, the *Salt Lake City Deseret News* (*Evening* and *Weekly*), the *Salt Lake City Herald,* and other Mormon-owned or -influenced papers.[44]

A handful of gentile and Mormon female activists also conducted a public and often bitter struggle over polygamy. This struggle was part of "the search for female moral authority in the American West," in the course of which middle-class women battled perceived immorality and disorder.[45] Utah women contested suffrage, protection of the home, and the relative natures of plural marriage, slavery, and prostitution. Those fights brought some women out of their domestic circle, while others already involved in public activities used their organizations, contacts, and media access in the struggle, providing experience and developing tactics that some of them would use against prostitution in the coming years.

Most Mormon and gentile women in nineteenth-century Utah inhabited separate worlds. They shared some things: a subordinate position within patriarchal cultures; daily concerns such as child care and food preparation; and important cultural assumptions, including the proper role of women as wives and mothers within the domestic sphere. The spiritual, economic, and social exclusivity practiced by the LDS Church, however, and the existing antipathies between many non-Mormons and Saints, kept most women from making common cause within voluntary associations. Mormon and gentile women had little social contact, especially since Mormons had the active society of the ward and its auxiliary organizations. Plural marriage ensured that few women would cross the divide.[46]

Non-Mormon women were convinced that plural marriage was a prison for women, and that given the chance they would reject the practice. Indeed, many Mormon women were shocked and appalled by plural marriage; some left the faith because of their objections and became public advocates for its abolition.[47] Others suffered neglect, abuse, or loneliness, some more and some less quietly. For example, Abraham H. Cannon described an ugly scene between his uncle, Salt Lake stake president Angus Cannon, and Angus's wife Amanda: "We found Aunt Amanda, . . . who in her ungovernable rage said she was going to the U.S. Marshal's to have Uncle Angus arrested for marrying Dr. Mattie Paul Hughes." Joseph Marion Tanner virtually abandoned his second wife, Annie, who was forced to take household work to support their children.[48] Although Mormon leaders extolled polygamy as the highest form of marriage and nearly all of the high LDS officials married multiple women, reflecting both their spiritual authority and their relative ability to afford multiple households, the majority of rank-and-file Saints lived in monogamous relationships. While estimates vary, most scholars agree that between 10 and 20 percent of Mormon marriages before 1890 were polygamous.[49]

Mormons insisted that women were not forced into plural marriage but rather controlled the process: they could refuse to enter into plural marriages, while first wives could decide whether their husbands could marry others. Of course, Mormon women were subject to heavy pressure from husbands, neighbors, and LDS officials who exhorted them to "live their religion" by contracting plural marriages or risk denying their faith. Most women in polygamous marriages apparently accepted the difficult principle, either because they believed God commanded it or because they had little other choice.[50]

Some historians agree that plural marriage conferred certain benefits. When husbands were absent on church missions or with their other families, plural wives by necessity exercised a great deal of economic and social autonomy. The antipolygamy crusade also caused many women who had personal objections to the practice to close ranks behind the principle in defense of their religion and menfolk.[51] Many women, either on their own account or with the encouragement of the male LDS leadership or both, took action against the drumbeat of criticism. At a "mass indignation meeting" in the Mormon Tabernacle on 13 January 1870, women spoke out in favor of plural marriage.[52]

Less than a month later, the territorial legislature authorized woman suffrage, making Utah only the second territory to do so. Historians have traditionally argued that LDS officials granted women suffrage "to counter accusations that Mormon women were the downtrodden, ignorant slaves of the male hierarchy, to recruit the national suffrage organization to lobby against antipolygamy legislation pending in Congress, and to promote Utah's bid for statehood."[53] Historian Lola Van Wagenen argues that Mormon women themselves actively sought suffrage, as did some New Movement activists. Also, LDS women revived the Relief Society, an organization that carried out a variety of charitable and social programs, about this time. Such activities may also have helped to politicize Mormon women.[54] They gained a forum for their political and social views on 1 June 1872 with the first issue of the *Woman's Exponent,* the unofficial organ of the Relief Society. For almost four decades, the paper advocated women's rights while it defended the LDS Church and, until 1890, plural marriage.[55]

National activists welcomed woman suffrage in Utah, although sometimes for very different reasons. Non-Mormons initially believed that oppressed Mormon women would somehow "vote down" polygamy.[56] Elizabeth Cady Stanton and Susan B. Anthony came to Utah in July 1871 to congratulate Utah's women. Stanton lectured an overwhelmingly Mormon audience on the degrading effects of "polyandry, polygamy, monogamy, and prostitution," a speech which got her banned from the Tabernacle.[57]

Some gentile and ex-Mormon women associated with the New Movement and the Liberals also initially supported woman suffrage. Polygamy, however, split the alliance and turned some women from suffrage to antipolygamy activism. The most vocal of these activists was Cornelia Paddock. Paddock was born in New York in 1840. At twenty-eight she moved to Nebraska, where she married Alonzo G. Paddock, a mining man who had worked in Utah since 1858. They moved to Utah in 1870 and lived there until Cornelia's death in 1898.[58] The Paddocks were among the founding members of the First Baptist Church of Salt Lake City.[59]

Cornelia Paddock quickly became the leading female antipolygamist after hearing firsthand accounts of polygamy's horrors from Mormon friends and acquaintances: "All these women pour into my ears the story of their sufferings and their wrongs, and continue asking, 'Is there any hope for us?'"[60] Her Mormon informants included Sarah M. Pratt, first wife of Orson Pratt, who left her husband and the LDS Church when he sought to take other wives. Paddock eventually used their stories in her fiction.[61]

In February 1872, Paddock gave two public addresses condemning polygamy on social, health, and moral grounds. She helped write and organize a petition drive against the 1872 statehood attempt. The perceived anti-Mormon tone of the petition led many Mormon women to leave the alliance, just as the Liberal Party had split.[62] Cornelia Paddock became a favorite of the *Tribune,* contributing a series of articles. Male Liberals were delighted to have the support of a talented female writer who could bolster their arguments.[63]

The female opponents of polygamy organized after the Caroline Owens incident. Reportedly terrified by the prospect of life as a plural wife, Owens fled to a gentile woman's home on her wedding night. In response, in November 1878 a group of women launched the "Ladies Anti-Polygamy Society," with former plural wife Sarah Ann Cook its first president, gentile Jennie Froiseth vice president, and Cornelia Paddock secretary.[64] Supporters included two officers of the Woman's Christian Temperance Union (WCTU); Jennie Froiseth later helped found the Salt Lake chapter of the WCTU.[65] The society attacked plural marriage through meetings, petitions, and newspaper articles. Cornelia Paddock was one of the society's most active writers. Her pieces appeared less often in the *Tribune,* however. The male editors complained that Paddock expressed too much sympathy for Mormon women, whom the *Tribune* insisted "could not be permanently degraded unless they were parties to the injury; they could not be held slaves unless they were fitted for bondage."[66]

The split between the *Tribune* and Paddock illustrates gender differences in the antipolygamy fight. While men often used the issue as a pretext to fight Mormon hegemony, Cornelia Paddock and the Anti-Polygamy Society argued that polygamy violated the rights and dignity of women. Gentile women condemned the Mormon "hierarchs" as lustful despots who enslaved women for their own selfish purposes, including sex, labor, and political aggrandizement. Paddock appealed to the nation to save "multitudes of human beings in absolute thrall" in a land "tainted with treason and murder."[67] Paddock's opposition to polygamy was part of her larger concern for the equality of women and the defense of the Christian home, a concern that led her to espouse woman suffrage (with conditions) and to fight a variety of moral abuses including prostitution, the serving of minors in saloons, and the seduction of minor girls.

Paddock reached for a national audience in 1879 with *In the Toils; or, Martyrs of the Latter Days*, a novel which depicts the horrors of polygamy through the experiences of a woman and her daughter. After the women endure unspeakable hardships, including the loss of family members to Mormon murderers and "practices . . . on a par with those of the lowest portion of heathendom," General Patrick Connor rescues the kidnapped heroine.[68] The style of *In the Toils* and Paddock's other novel, *The Fate of Madame La Tour,* is derivative of earlier anti-Mormon novels, with their stereotypical depictions of the Mormons' "wily, insincere leaders, and the rabble of ignorant, fanatical followers."[69] These works, in turn, often draw on the captivity narratives of the eighteenth and early nineteenth centuries, especially anti-Masonic and anti-Catholic exposés.[70] Paddock, however, claimed "the characters . . . are real, the incidents are true," and that "scores of incidents . . . I have suppressed as unfit for publication."[71] Paddock's work gained her some national notoriety and a reputation as a knowledgeable voice within Utah.[72]

Paddock also expounds at some length about Utah's mineral wealth. The advent of the Pacific railroad, which brought gentile miners to Utah, was the "day of deliverance" and the "beginning of regeneration," but "the un-American aspect of the Territory, viewed from both a social and a political standpoint, deters American citizens from either making it their home or investing their money in its mines."[73] This emphasis upon economics is suggestive. Cornelia Paddock believed that economic modernization would bring "loyal" gentiles to the territory, "redeem" Utah from the Mormons, and make it prosperous and "American." Paddock and her activist colleagues may have shared personal concerns as well. Many non-Mormons found it difficult to make a living in the sometimes-hostile Utah atmosphere. The gentile women may have needed an influx of capital and development for their personal livelihoods. The Paddocks' fortunes were particularly tenuous. Alonzo Paddock worked at a variety of jobs, from supplying coal to the Utah penitentiary and gravel to a Salt Lake City school to clerking for the Utah Commission.[74] Cornelia's later struggles to finance her Rescue Home further suggest the family's precarious financial situation.

The Anti-Polygamy Society created its own print forum, issuing the first number of the *Anti-Polygamy Standard* on 1 April 1880, with the masthead slogan "'Let every Man have his own Wife, and Let every Woman have her own Husband'—1 Cor. 7:2." Jennie Froiseth edited the newspaper, which often featured Cornelia Paddock's writing. The society declared its stance in this first issue: polygamy was wrong because it kept woman in degradation and submission, instead of in the exalted position which a proper Christian marriage could bring her. Given the chance, the gentile activists believed Mormon women would gladly abandon the institution.[75] For almost four years, gentile and Mormon women argued through the pages of the *Standard* and *Woman's Exponent*. Both groups claimed to be the champions of the pure, Christian home presided over by the virtuous wife and mother.

The writers of the *Standard* drew on a powerful body of argument by equating polygamy with slavery. In their view, polygamy enslaved Mormon women, who needed and deserved the same vigorous action that had defeated slavery, since plural wives could not free themselves any more than the slaves could. The *Standard*'s writers blamed LDS men for polygamy, while espousing deep sympathy for their wronged sisters and defending their own right to "free" them. The society expressed "kindness and good will" toward Mormon women, and swore to "fight to the death that system which so enslaves and degrades our sex, and which robs them of so much happiness."[76]

The editors of the *Woman's Exponent* conducted a spirited defense using the same rhetorical weapons the Anti-Polygamy Society employed—the language of true womanhood: "Mormon women are not only virtuous, but chaste. The principle of plural marriage itself tends to the strictest chastity, and children born in this order of marriage, will, from antenatal influences, be purer in character . . . nowhere on the earth exist purer women than right here in Utah, those who have embraced this sacred order of marriage the world is so ready to condemn."[77] While the *Anti-Polygamy Standard* printed letters from women opposing polygamy, the *Exponent* published defenses from women who claimed they chose to enter polygamy and believed in it as a religious principle.[78]

In August 1880, the Anti-Polygamy Society became "The Woman's National Anti-Polygamy Society" and appealed to women throughout the country for support. This appeal paralleled the efforts of male Liberals to gain federal assistance against the Mormons through the pages of the *Tribune*.[79] Utah gentiles got the federal action they wanted. The Edmunds Act, signed into law in March 1882, put teeth into the Morrill Act. The Edmunds Act declared polygamy a felony and stripped polygamists of the franchise and eligibility for office and jury duty. The act further declared that any male who "cohabits with more than one woman" was guilty of a misdemeanor and could receive six months in prison and/or a three hundred dollar fine.[80] The act also created a commission with authority over elections within the territory. The five-man commission included Algernon Sidney Paddock, former senator from Nebraska and a cousin of Cornelia Paddock's husband Alonzo.[81] Perhaps influenced by Cornelia, A. S. Paddock quickly gained a reputation among Mormons as the commissioner most in favor of strict legal measures against the Saints.[82]

When the Edmunds Act brought the federal government into the antipolygamy effort, the Utah women changed their focus. The *Anti-Polygamy Standard* issued its last number in the spring of 1883 and a new activist helped steer the society in another direction. Angie Newman, a Vermont-born Methodist and ardent Republican, visited Utah in 1879, then returned to the territory as a full-time worker for the Methodist Episcopal Church's Woman's Home Missionary Society.[83] The "Home Mission" movement, mirroring the missions that sent thousands of Christians overseas, considered Utah prime territory in need of redemption.[84] Newman chose to make plural marriage her mission field. She determined that in the cause of killing polygamy, woman suffrage in Utah must be sacrificed. Along with Cornelia Paddock and the WCTU, Newman sponsored an antisuffrage petition drive that eventually contained a quarter of a million signatures when presented to Congress in June 1884.[85]

Newman proposed a new tool to fight plural marriage: a "rescue home." The idea of establishing "an Industrial Home, where the destitute and home-less women of Utah may find a refuge" attracted support from several evan-gelical Protestant ministers.[86] Cornelia Paddock backed the idea and expressed concern for the plight of women and children in polygamous families: "The man who cannot support one family in comfort certainly cannot support three or four; and men of this type, and of a type still worse,—drunken, brutal wretches, who, as a friend of mine once said, 'cannot be content with mak-ing one woman miserable for life,'—are among the most eager aspirants for the temporal blessings and eternal glories of celestial marriage."[87] Utah's antipolygamy women formed the Industrial Christian Home Association of Utah. Newman told Congress that "if the young Mormon females were of-fered avenues of escape from polygamy and its attendant evils, many of them would take advantage of such an opportunity."[88]

The proposed home would provide plural wives with security, protection, and training in domestic work and industry, in the hope that a "rescued" woman would build a loving Christian home with a nonpolygamous hus-band. The home received enthusiastic backing from Utah's gentile establish-ment, including federal appointees Governor Murray, the Utah Commission, Chief Justice of the Utah Supreme Court Charles S. Zane, U.S. Attorney Wil-liam H. Dickson, and U.S. Marshal Edwin A. Ireland, all actively involved in prosecuting plural marriage.[89] Congress authorized $40,000 for the home but also created an all-male Board of Control headed by the governor. The board members narrowly defined eligibility to receive aid, and the response was disappointing. While a substantial number of women and their children sought relief, many did not meet the strict criteria, while others disliked the home's moralizing atmosphere.[90] The LDS Church, of course, was outraged over the very purpose of the home and constantly ridiculed its problems. The *Woman's Exponent* predicted that only women who no longer had "the Holy Spirit abiding in them" would accept the offer of assistance.[91] When the home closed in 1892, the editor of the *Deseret Evening News* wrote that "we do not say that all the promoters of this so-called Industrial Home were guilty of falsehood or evil intent. The woman [Newman] who went to Washington with scandalous and salacious falsehoods in her mouth, in order to raise the funds for the building, was the chief deceiver and has never prospered for her filthy abuse of the people of this territory."[92]

Perhaps the filthiest abuse Mormons accused Angie Newman of spreading was to compare polygamy to prostitution. According to correspondents
who wrote to the *Woman's Exponent,* Newman gave a speech in Cincinnati
in 1883 claiming that in Mormon Utah, "every house is a house of prostitution" (a charge she denied making).[93] Newman later petitioned Congress,
declaring that "as the result of close personal investigation for ten years, I
assert the prostitution of the sacred office of motherhood, under the Mormon regime, has no parallel in any civilized country in the known *world.*"[94]
    This was not the first time that plural marriage had been compared to
prostitution. From the earliest hints of polygamy, some critics had likened
the two practices. John C. Bennett, an early apostate, charged that Mormon
leaders kept secret orders of prostitutes.[95] Ex-Mormon Sidney Rigdon interpreted Joseph Smith's murder as divine retribution for contracting "a whor-
ing spirit."[96] Several women who rejected overtures of plural marriage were
reportedly denounced as harlots.[97] Patrick Connor claimed that Mormon
Utah was "a community of traitors, murderers, fanatics, and whores."[98] At
least one unhappy plural wife drew a connection. Abraham Cannon's wife
Mina demanded a divorce and told him that "she considered herself in disgrace every day that she lived with me in polygamy, and she would as soon
be a prostitute as a plural wife."[99]
    Despite the Anti-Polygamy Society's professed solidarity with Mormon
women, gentile activists condemned one group. Prominent Mormons like
Eliza R. Snow, Emmeline B. Wells, and Sarah Kimball spoke and wrote force-
fully in favor of plural marriage; gentiles could hardly dismiss them as ignorant, naive, and blameless victims of lustful men.[100] The writers of the *Standard* contended that since these women had voluntarily abandoned their roles
as true women and encouraged other women to enter plural marriages, they
had virtually become brothel procuresses. The author of an unsigned piece
claimed to quote a young Mormon girl: "*I can only compare these women to
those dreadful characters which they say exist in the outside world, and whose
business it is to lure young girls to destruction. . . .* They are nothing but tools
of the priesthood, and while professing to be working for the elevation of
women, they are in reality doing nothing but seeking for new victims to gratify
the base passions of their infamous masters."[101] The *Tribune's* editor labeled
the editors of the *Exponent* "procuresses for the harems of the Mountain
Meadows Church."[102] The *Deseret Evening News,* in turn, used prostitution
to discredit the critics of polygamy. When antipolygamy activists met in November 1878 to form their organization, the Mormon newspaper claimed that
"several 'soiled doves' signed the petition. . . . Quite consistent. A loud outcry against a system established by the Almighty for the preservation of pu-

rity is likely, in the nature of things, to be echoed by the impure." The *Tribune* replied that the writer of that statement "should be horse-whipped in the streets by the husbands and brothers of the ladies whom he has so shamelessly slandered."[103]

While prostitution was one metaphor critics used for polygamy, the harem was a related (and perhaps more logical) one. Many antipolygamists declared that Mormon men had harems like the Ottoman Turks. The purported heroine of "Saved from the Mormons" described the marriage her father arranged for her: "My father had sold me, not because love for another had blinded his conscience, but from a base, sensual desire to increase the inmates of his harem."[104] Another author insisted that poor Mormon families who all lived in one room risked a "violation of virtue" because of their children's exposure to their father's "promiscuous indulgences" with his "harem."[105] The stereotype of the "lustful Turk" was a common one in anti-Mormon literature, and further identified Mormonism with un-American and un-Christian practice.[106]

Such stereotypes and accusations were deeply hurtful to LDS women, even those who objected to polygamy. Plural wives objected to their image in popular literature, but the antipolygamy crusade was a real threat. Some thought that plural wives were being treated like prostitutes or worse. One woman was imprisoned when she refused to name the father of her unborn child; other Mormon women claimed "the question was an insult and a vile insinuation of departed virtue, and yet were she a public prostitute, no such question would ever be asked."[107] Eliza R. Snow understood the danger to the economic and social status of plural wives and their children if their marriages were deemed illegal. In 1879, the U.S. Supreme Court issued its ruling in *Reynolds v. United States,* upholding the constitutionality of the Morrill Act and opening the door to effective prosecution. Snow wrote that the Supreme Court had in effect declared "let us cause thousands of honorable, loving wives to be stigmatized as prostitutes, and their offspring as bastards."[108]

The polygamy-prostitution equation was imperfect at best, and those who made it disagreed on a fundamental question: If polygamy was prostitution, which partner was the prostitute? Eliza R. Snow feared that if Mormon marriages were made illegitimate, then plural wives would be considered prostitutes. The members of the Anti-Polygamy Society called women like Snow "procuresses," again implying that plural wives were prostitutes. The *Tribune,* however, argued for Mormon men. The *Tribune* posed this parallel: "We will suppose a woman to have a circle of acquaintance, numbering say from two to twenty, with all of whom she may cohabit at stated intervals—would that not constitute her a prostitute? . . . Now, then, suppose a *man* under whatever pretext you please, religious or otherwise, indulges in sexuality to the same extent with a like number of women, does he not equally commit the crime of prostitution?"[109] On another occasion the *Tribune* straightforwardly called Mormon husbands "male prostitutes."[110] The *Deseret Evening News* responded that the real "prostitutes" were lascivious anti-Mormon men and referred to the *Tribune* as "the morning organ of male and female prostitutes."[111]

While the realities of Mormon polygamy were grim enough for some women, they were far removed from the brothel and harem stereotypes. Mormon authorities considered sexual sins—adultery, rape, incest, fornication—dangerous violations of their moral code. Of course, some Mormon men did violate the code, and not all were punished.[112] Polygyny itself granted men sexual license denied to women. Nevertheless, the LDS Church took its moral code seriously. The most common grounds for disfellowshipping in the nineteenth-century church was sexual misconduct.[113] Even C. C. Goodwin admitted in 1913 that "there were plural marriages among the Mormons, but the harem character didn't attach."[114]

Despite the prohibitions within Mormon doctrine, some prostitutes worked in Mormon communities. Joseph Smith took "active measures . . . to suppress houses and acts of infamy in [Nauvoo]."[115] Houses of prostitution were among the corruptions of Babylon that the Saints sought to escape by moving to the Salt Lake Valley, and they were largely if not wholly successful. President Jedediah M. Grant, the first mayor of Salt Lake City, admitted in 1856 that "some who profess to be 'Mormons' are guilty of enticing and leading girls to prostitution."[116] But most visitors to the Mormon capital in the 1850s and 1860s described its quiet, orderly nature. Such visitors, primed with stories about notorious marriage practices, may have expected an openly sensual atmosphere or a rowdy frontier town. Instead, they found well-ordered communities with few brothels, saloons, and other immoral "resorts."[117] Sociologist Stanley S. Ivins concluded that Mormon-majority communities before 1890 appeared "comparatively free from the evils of professional prostitution."[118] The surviving records suggest that the Mormons' claims were true: Salt Lake City had few prostitutes before the completion of the transcontinental railroad in 1869 and the influx of gentile men in the early 1870s.[119] Of course, the Mormons' near-exclusive presence in the Salt Lake Valley lasted for less than a quarter-century. It is entirely likely that tenacious and resourceful women would have found customers in Utah and that a brothel district would have developed without a gentile influx.

Mormon leaders warned against bringing prostitution to the Salt Lake Valley. In 1854, President Heber C. Kimball threatened consequences: "If ever it is allowed among this people, it will be when righteousness has ceased to dwell in their midst. It never can be allowed in this community in male or female, whether they belong to the Church or not; and we will wipe out such abominations, the Lord being our helper."[120] At the height of the "Mormon reformation" in 1856, LDS leaders often sermonized against immorality in startlingly violent language. Jedediah M. Grant, the major voice of the reformation, cautioned those who brought prostitutes to Utah that he would "make holes through such miserable, corrupting rascals."[121] Elder Orson Pratt suggested that prostitution in New York City and London could be eliminated by applying the biblical sentence of death to male and female sinners alike.[122] Some Mormons went beyond threats. Salt Lake City police captain Hosea Stout blandly noted in his diary in 1858 that a group of men entered another man's house "and dragged him out of bed with a whore and castrated him by a square & close amputation."[123]

The personal behavior of one federal official strengthened the Mormons' beliefs about depraved Babylon.[124] W. W. Drummond, appointed to the territorial judiciary in 1855, reportedly arrived in Utah with a prostitute-mistress.[125] Drummond also became embroiled in jurisdictional disputes with Mormons and was one of the "runaways" who persuaded President Buchanan to send a military force to the territory.[126] For many Mormons, these developments confirmed the linkage between the immorality of the outside world and its desire to persecute the Kingdom of God.

The "invasion" proved peaceful, but it brought unwanted elements. The U.S. Army established Camp Floyd about forty miles south of Salt Lake City.[127] Along with the troops came a handful of officers' wives and the usual camp followers and hangers-on, including sutlers, saloonkeepers, laundresses, and prostitutes, who established a makeshift town called Frogtown or Dobeytown (later Fairfield). One observer claimed "Frog town has a thousand or more inhabitants all gamblers or whore[s]."[128]

Prostitutes also gravitated to the edges of Camp Douglas when it was established in 1862.[129] One soldier in the territorial penitentiary managed to gain time with a prostitute and make a joke at Mormons' expense: "A well dressed female visited the Penitentiary with the view of having an interview with her purported husband. . . . Gen. Connor replied that [the soldier] had no wife, and asked the warden to describe the lady, which he did. The General replied, 'It's that old strumpet, Mrs. Hall, that keeps at the mouth of Dry Canon.' Next day the warden approached the prisoner, McCoy, with a view of reproving for suffering him to be deceived. The prisoner replied, 'Mr. Warden, you introduced her as my wife, and I understand that you Mormons have a way of marrying by proxy, and I accepted the ceremony.'"[130]

The Mormon leadership claimed to not find the advent of commercialized sex amusing. John Taylor fumed that "ministers and editors" who promised to civilize Utah and make it "American" had indeed brought some characteristic outside institutions with them, including prostitution and drunkenness.[131] Some Saints of the mid-nineteenth century produced and consumed alcohol, but LDS leaders condemned drunkenness and associated crime.[132] Their reactions seemed to correspond to the degree of control they exercised in the city. In 1852, when gentiles were rare and no serious challenge to Mormon hegemony had yet emerged, Ezra T. Benson declared that he would handle establishments selling whisky or tobacco by "temporal knocking" (evidently a physical assault upon these establishments).[133] After the arrival of federal troops, Erastus Snow declared "the Lord Almighty" would wield the sword that would wipe saloons out.[134] By 1871, Brigham Young acknowledged that saloons were well established on Main Street, but declared that he would never set foot in one.[135]

Mormon city officials sometimes moved decisively against objectionable establishments. In 1870, Paul Englebrecht, a gentile saloonkeeper, attempted to operate without a license. Jeter Clinton, the police justice, ordered the abatement of Englebrecht's saloon as a public nuisance. The all-Mormon police force broke open all the "fixtures and articles" in the saloon, dumped the liquor into the gutter, and precipitated a near-riot between gentiles and Mormons. Robert N. Baskin, a prominent Liberal attorney, initiated a lawsuit against Clinton and the police for treble damages.[136]

Englebrecht won his suit in the Third District court before Judge James B. McKean. The Englebrecht case was a minor one, as McKean's real target was Brigham Young's power. The judge was determined to enforce the Morrill Act but had found it impossible to obtain convictions before LDS-majority juries. He therefore ordered the U.S. marshal rather than the Mormon-dominated territorial attorney and probate court system to impanel juries. By this method McKean was able to seat gentile-dominated juries and obtain a number of convictions, including in the Englebrecht case. McKean then indicted Brigham Young for lascivious cohabitation. The city authorities, however, appealed the Englebrecht case to the U.S. Supreme Court. The court declared in April 1872 that McKean's juries were improperly chosen, and all indictments returned by them, including Young's, were overturned.[137]

The victory in the Englebrecht case may have emboldened Justice Clinton to take similar action against Commercial Street keepers of houses of prostitution. In 1870, one Kate Flint ran a brothel with three "inmates" in Corinne, the Box Elder County town that sprang up near where the Union Pacific and Central Pacific railroads had met just one year prior. A Corinne newspaper editor bragged that the town contained not a single Mormon.[138] By April 1872, Flint and a few other prostitutes had joined the influx of miners and railroad men south to Salt Lake City, and were keeping house on Commercial Street.[139]

The police arrested Flint and another madam, Cora Conway, and the women working in their brothels on 28 August 1872. Clinton found Flint and Conway guilty of keeping houses of prostitution and fined each fifteen dollars. The city attorney, however, noted that previous fines had not served to drive the women out of the city, and asked for abatement of their premises as nuisances. Clinton sent police officers to the brothels where they systematically demolished their furnishings.[140]

A crowd gathered to watch the demolition. The *Corinne Daily Reporter,* a paper often harshly critical of Mormons, claimed that "among the spectators Brigham Young the chief manager of prostitution, stood looking on grandly exempt from havoc touching the many stinking bagnios over which he is ruler."[141] A few men reportedly threatened to set fire to the street.[142] They may have been friends, relatives, or customers of the affected women, or may have simply been expressing sympathy for their plight. Some of them probably believed that prostitution was ineradicable and a necessary evil, if not a positive good. The *Deseret Evening News* flatly rejected such reasoning, claiming that congratulations for the police action had poured in from Mormons, who preferred "their sons to be husbands, not paramours; their daughters to be wives, not harlots; and while they live they will do all in their power to check such prostitution."[143] According to an anti-Mormon newspaper, Jeter Clinton advocated harsher action: "Now for these women, the low, nasty street-walkers . . . the low, nasty, dirty, filthy, stinking bitches—they stink— that will invite strange men into their houses and introduce them into their family circles. . . . They ought to be shot with a double-barreled shot-gun. That is my doctrine (pointing to a soldier), and when you see those street-walkers following behind such women, (God keep me from calling them women), take a double-barreled shot-gun and follow them, shoot them to pieces; and if you do not overtake them before they get to their haunts or dens, go in and kill them both."[144] This version of Clinton's "sermon" may have been published in response to his controversial abatement.

While Mormons thus insisted on differentiating between sinful prostitution and divinely sanctioned plural marriage, the *Tribune* insisted on their similarities. The gentile paper declared that the only difference between polygamy and prostitution was that the former involved multiple women and the latter multiple men, and that both constituted the same crime of "plural cohabitation."[145] The *Tribune* suggested that prostitution was preferable, and that "religious fanatics" taxed brothels to make up for tithing shortfalls by those living in "polygamic lascivious cohabitation."[146]

Kate Flint and Cora Conway had lost thousands of dollars' worth of furniture, bedding, and tableware in the raid. Their homes and those of their "inmates" were probably unlivable and their livelihoods disrupted, at the least. The abatements did not, however, drive the women from the city. Flint was back in business by December, and her house remained a fixture for fifteen years. The raid evidently hurt Conway more seriously, as she went on to work as a prostitute in other women's houses (including Flint's) rather than as a brothel keeper.[147]

Flint and Conway took advantage of the animosity between Mormons and gentiles to win redress. Both women sued Clinton and the police in the Third District court before Judge McKean. Mormon historian Orson Whitney wrote that Flint's suit represented a battle between good and evil. "Like its celebrated predecessor, the Englebrecht case, [the Flint case] was indicative of the struggle then going on in Utah between the opposing elements of vice and virtue,—the latter represented by the local civic authorities backed by the united sentiment of the majority of the people, and the former by saloon men, gamblers, and prostitutes, encouraged in their lawlessness by the anti-Mormon ring, and all but openly championed by officials of the Federal Government."[148] Flint and her lawyer Robert Baskin complained that she could not get a fair trial before any Mormon juror, since the defendants were all Mormons. She claimed the LDS Church specifically targeted her because she was "known as one who is opposed to the same, and has incurred its displeasure and hostility." She also complained that the police had wantonly destroyed her personal property, including her underwear, and had stolen or destroyed $1,000 in cash.[149] In March 1875, the court ruled that the warrant was defective and drew a pointed comparison between prostitution and plural marriage:

> If Kate Flint kept a house and it was proved that fifty men frequented it for purposes of illicit intercourse, and process could be issued and her furniture and household goods be broken up therefor[e], the same could be done with say John Smith, who might have in his house twelve women with whom he had illicit sexual intercourse. It would not matter whether or not he claimed that those women were his wives, the law allowed a man but one wife, and, had a justice of the peace the right to act as in the case of Kate Flint it would not alter the situation if Kate Flint claimed that the fifty or more men visiting her house were her husbands.[150]

Flint eventually won $3,400.00 and Conway $2,600.00, and the city council appropriated funds to settle the claims. Conway may have used the money to leave town, as her last arrest came nine days after the council voted to pay the two women.[151]

Kate Flint's defiance made her something of an enduring folk figure. Ann Gordge Lee was the disaffected plural wife of John Doyle Lee, who was convicted and executed for his part in the Mountain Meadows Massacre. She evidently turned the facts of the Flint story into a highly embroidered tale. Lee wrote a sort of autobiography sometime in the 1890s, full of fantastic accounts of her adventures and accusations of crimes committed by Brigham Young and other Mormons. She wrote that at some unspecified date, the Mormon leader ran a "percentage hoar house" and was upset by Kate Flint's competition. So, he sent some Mormon girls to infiltrate Flint's house and to covertly prepare for a raid. One of the girls tipped off Flint, who recruited soldiers from Fort Douglas to hide in the brothel. When the raiders burst in, the soldiers drove them off "badly beaten." Flint then stripped the clothes off the spies and drove them into the streets, but she dressed the tipster in stylish clothes and sent her to school in San Francisco. Flint then sued Young for $150,000, won, and claimed his personal property to settle the debt.[152]

Ann Lee was not the only one who remembered Kate Flint. Thirty years after her brothel was abated, the *Deseret Evening News* attempted to discredit "Mother" Jones, the labor leader, by suggesting that she had been a friend of Flint's.[153] Bernard De Voto, the journalist and historian who was born in Ogden, wrote in the 1920s that "Gentile Kate" bought Brigham Young's carriage and horses at auction after his death so that she could parade the streets and outrage the Saints.[154]

The city officials' bitter experience with Cora Conway and Kate Flint may have convinced them that the suppression of prostitution was a lost cause. Their unwelcome visitors proved they would fight hard to stay in business in the face of police power backed by a dominant church. Mormons continued to complain of the presence of prostitutes and other lawbreakers in Utah. Someone (probably Jeter Clinton) summed up the year in the police court record book: "This ends the year 1872 remarkable for the increase of crime of all kinds in this city owing to the influx of the so called Christians and the protection thrown around Every kind of vice by the Federal Officers backed up and sustained by the Government, Especially President Grant."[155]

Mormons turned to crime statistics in an attempt to discredit their critics. "Historicus" (Amos Milton Musser of the LDS Church Historian's Office) created a report in 1882 showing that Salt Lake police arrested seventy-seven inmates and twenty-one keepers of houses of ill fame, none of them Mormons. As for "Rape, Prostitution, Brothels, Lewd Conduct, Insulting Ladies, Exposing Person, Bigamy, Obscenity," the Mormons, 78 percent of the city, had committed only five such infractions, and the "Anti-'Mormons,'" 173. Musser failed to note, however, that the police force making the arrests was all-Mormon.[156] The lack of Mormons arrested for bigamy demonstrates the ineffectiveness of the antipolygamy effort to that date. Musser concluded that gentiles were thirty times more "base and wicked" than the Mormons, and he suggested that the figures be shown to the president and Congress.[157] Musser and others compiled similar figures for the years 1881, 1884, 1885, and 1890.[158] These reports, generally included in discourses delivered to Mormon audiences and published in LDS outlets, were likely ignored (or never seen or heard) by non-Mormons. Antipolygamy activists claimed that even a Mormon woman grew tired of church leaders distinguishing polygamy from prostitution, since "the systems are entirely similar, the only point of difference being that one is practiced under the cloak of religion, and the other is given its proper status and acknowledged to be a sin."[159]

The most successful phase of the campaign against polygamy began in the mid-1880s. The Utah Commission crafted a "test oath" to disqualify polygamous Mormons. While the Edmunds Act had created the misdemeanor "unlawful cohabitation" for any male who "cohabits with more than one woman,"[160] the commissioners added the phrase "in the marriage relation" to the test oath, words which nowhere appeared in the original legislation.[161] Outraged Mormons argued that Edmunds should be applied to all extramarital sexual activity, including fornication, adultery, and prostitution. The act would thus improve Utah's moral climate while disfranchising many lascivious gentiles. Instead, Mormons claimed, the commissioners inserted the "marriage relation" clause solely to target married Saints who in order to vote must "betake themselves to the streets as common prostitutes, and they mean to include at the polls, whoremongers and adulterers." Such reasoning was specious, if creative; Congress had undoubtedly meant to target polygamy, not general immorality.[162]

The law quickly created a martyr. Mormons complained that Feramorz Little, the ex-mayor of Salt Lake, was turned away from the polls by the registrar (his own son) because he had once been married to more than one woman. Next in line came the infamous Kate Flint and her inmates, who voted unmolested. The story became a staple of LDS discourses.[163]

The U.S. Supreme Court declared the test oath invalid in 1885, but it was already obvious that the oath was insufficient to impanel juries that would convict Mormons, mostly because relatively few of them lived in polygamy. Nor did the Edmunds Act disfranchise enough Saints to allow Liberals to seriously challenge the Mormon People's Party.[164] The 1884 arrival of Judge Charles S. Zane, who presided in the Third Judicial District and as chief jus-

tice of the Territorial Supreme Court, marked the beginning of the successful "crusade." Zane did not share the strong anti-Mormon sentiments of
some gentiles, but he was determined to make the Saints obey the law.[165]

Zane and his court officers developed techniques that allowed effective
prosecutions. U.S. district attorney William H. Dickson disqualified any potential grand juror who claimed to believe in plural marriage, which meant
in practice all believing Mormons. With the juror list exhausted by Mormon
disqualifications, Dickson continued to seat jurors under an open venire.
With non-Mormon juries in place, the federal judicial system could move
swiftly against polygamy. Zane and his colleagues began what Mormons
called the "judicial crusade" in the fall of 1884.[166] Orson Whitney described
the crusaders as a group consisting of "[the] governor, judges, attorneys,
marshals, editors, politicians, preachers, merchants, miners, allied with sa-
loon-keepers, gamblers, and bad characters in general, whose object was to
prosecute to the bitter end a 'holy war' against Mormonism."[167]

Most of the one thousand or so convictions in the federal courts were for
unlawful cohabitation, easier to prove than plural marriage. The arrest of Salt
Lake stake president Angus M. Cannon in April 1885 led the highest LDS
authorities, including President John Taylor and George Q. Cannon, to go
into hiding "on the underground."[168] The Angus Cannon case particularly
galled the Saints. In previous cases the prosecution had felt it necessary to
prove sexual intercourse between a man and his plural wives, which generally required wives' testimony. Dickson now argued that such proof was
unnecessary, since plural marriage and not extramarital sex was the avowed
target of the Edmunds Act.[169]

Mormons reacted to this latest blow with accusations of gentile hypocrisy in a "Declaration of Grievances and Protest" presented to President Cleveland in May 1885: "The Edmunds Law, which not only provides for the punishment of polygamy, but also cohabitation with more than one woman,
whether in the marriage relation or outside of it, is made to operate upon
one class of people only—the Mormons; and yet of the non-Mormon class
who transgress the law the name is legion. The paramour of mistresses and
harlots, secure from prosecution, walks the streets in open day. No United
States official puts a 'spotter' on his trail, or makes an effort to drag his deeds
of shame and guilt before a judge and jury for investigation and punishment."[170]

On 20 November 1885, federal officers arrested the highest-ranking Saint
to date, Apostle Lorenzo Snow. By that point, some Mormons had decided to go on the offensive. Salt Lake City police arrested U.S. Deputy Marshal Oscar Vandercook and brought him before Justice of the Peace Adam

Spiers, a Mormon, in the city police court. Vandercook was charged with lewd and lascivious conduct, a violation of city ordinance. Four other arrests quickly followed. A group of Mormon city officials and police officers had undertaken a project to turn the tables on their accusers. Brigham Young Hampton, the city license collector and former longtime police officer, led the effort. Hampton had been one of the officers who abated Englebrecht's saloon and Kate Flint's brothel and had faced charges resulting from both actions.[171]

Hampton claimed that citizen complaints led him to create a "citizens' committee" to detect and punish those guilty of lewd and lascivious conduct "Especially the Government Office Holders that are prosicuting and persicuting the Servants of God for keeping his laws of Marriage." Hampton hired two women, Fanny Davenport and S. J. Fields, and set them up in houses on West Temple Street, from which they attempted to attract the targeted customers. The houses were fitted with apertures in the doors and walls so that hidden policemen could witness "the beastile conduct."[172] Francis Armstrong, a Mormon merchant and city selectman, testified that he provided $500 of his own money to bankroll Hampton.[173] Hampton denied renting or furnishing the houses, but admitted that he paid the women some $300 to $400 "for detective purposes." He admitted offering Fields a "bounty" but claimed that the deal was $25 for "Mormon, Jew or Gentile."[174]

Altogether, Hampton claimed to have caught about a hundred men, including several government officials and one Protestant minister, but the larger fish avoided the bait. Only 5 percent of those "detected" were married Mormons "that were considered on the verg of aposticy for years past."[175] Mormons congratulated Hampton for his work in "balancing the scales" and proving to the world that the Edmunds act applied to "actual sinning of a sexual nature, as well as the assumed offenses of the 'Mormons.'"[176] The *Tribune,* however, ridiculed the plan, reflecting C. C. Goodwin's antipolygamy views and his support for regulated prostitution, if not male sexual license. Goodwin professed not to understand the logic behind proving that some men were "addicted to one of the common vices of humanity," since that in no way excused the immorality of plural marriage nor proved its divinity.[177] Although the *Tribune* insisted that LDS Church authorities must have directed and financed the "assignation fiends," the grand jury found no evidence to support the claim.[178]

Hampton's plan soon unraveled, with disastrous consequences. Vandercook's attorney obtained a writ of habeas corpus to bring his client before Judge Zane. Zane concluded that the warrant was invalid and discharged the marshal.[179] Mormons claimed bitterly that this ruling was entirely consistent with the moral hypocrisy of those who, like Zane, were using the legal process to destroy their Church.[180]

Zane dismissed the remaining cases brought under the municipal ordinance.[181] The city authorities did not give up, however; county sheriffs and deputies rearrested the four men under territorial statutes for resorting to houses of ill fame. They brought the men before Spiers in his capacity as Salt Lake County justice of the peace. Three of the men were found guilty but appealed to the third district court. The appeals brought an effective end to the police court prosecutions. Charles S. Varian, the prosecuting attorney, argued that no defendant had ever been charged under the territorial statute and refused to prosecute. He further argued that prosecutions could not be made on the basis of an unlawful conspiracy. Judge Zane dismissed the cases and directed the grand jury to prosecute all keepers of houses of ill fame. He made it clear that he believed polygamy and prostitution were comparable violations of the code of acceptable morality: "Polygamy and unlawful cohabitation and this class of crimes all tend to lust and lechery and lead men and women astray. . . . When a man that has a wife chooses to go to those houses or to marry and cohabit with other women he is instigated by lust and by lechery."[182]

By the time the prosecutions of the "L. and L.'s" (Hampton's shorthand for "lewd and lascivious") had failed, the grand jury had already indicted Hampton and his "detectives" for keeping houses of prostitution.[183] The grand jury reported that the police could not or would not provide sufficient information to indict any keepers other than Fields, Davenport, and Hampton.[184] The trial jury found Hampton guilty and Zane sentenced him to a year in the county jail.[185] His allies helped Fanny Davenport escape to Canada.[186]

The Brigham Hampton episode immediately entered the folklore of the Mormon-gentile conflict and served as fodder for charges and countercharges the combatants hurled in years to come. The Mormon press responded to the conviction with predictable outrage: "Mr. Hampton is to be punished for exposing the filthy practices of persons 'in sympathy with the prosecution' against 'Mormons.' The persons exposed, and whose guilt is not denied, are to be exempt from all punishment. And the people of Utah, looking upon such a travesty of justice as this, are expected to fall down on their knees and worship the law and its administrators."[187] A group of Mormon women referred to both the Hampton incident and Kate Flint in their memorial to the president and Congress protesting the crusade:

We see good and noble men dragged to jail to linger among felons, while debauched and polluted men, some of them Federal officers who have been detected in the vilest kind of depravity, protected by the same courts and officers that turn all their energies and engines of power towards the ruin of our homes and the destruction of our dearest associations. We see pure women forced to disclose their conjugal relations or go to prison, while the wretched creatures who pander to men's basest passions are left free to ply their horrible trade, and may vote at the polls while legal wives of men with plural families are disenfranchised.[188]

One unknown Mormon put the episode into song.

> They say that if the Mormons will polygamy deny,
> Like themselves take to houses of ill fame,
> They will call them friends and brethren and will take them by the hand;
> but in this, I think, they'll find they are lame.
>
> [Chorus]
> Murry holds the reins; the whip belongs to Zane;
> Old Ireland and his aid will go below;
> And old Dixon will do well to engage a case in Hell,
> For the road he is on will take him there, I know.[189]

On the other side, Angie Newman called the episode "a carefully constructed Mormon plot to blacken the character of Gentile residents."[190] Gentiles did not deny that some non-Mormon men had been caught with prostitutes, but they argued that polygamy was the greater evil. Newman, who styled herself a protector of the pure, maternally centered domestic sphere, presumably disapproved of prostitution, but she kept her public ire aimed at the Saints.

The *Tribune* dismissed the scheme as a "Desperate Attempt to Prove Polygamy No Worse than Prostitution"[191] and kept the Hampton "conspiracy" story alive. The paper noted that Francis Armstrong was to be the next Salt Lake City mayor, with Alfred Salomon his city marshal. Armstrong, it was claimed, would probably offer a "bounty" to every women who opened a brothel, while Salomon, one of those officers "peering through knot holes," had offered prostitutes municipal protection.[192] When reporting a brothel raid in May 1886, the paper noted that the city had found out from the Hampton episode that "there wasn't much money" in operating brothels, so they had given the women time "to lay up boodle enough to make it worthwhile to effect a capture."[193]

Such references became staples of anti-Mormon rhetoric in the coming years. Even the official LDS historian Brigham H. Roberts admitted that the Hampton incident was a "regrettable thing" perpetrated by "overzealous men."[194] The episode certainly proved damaging to the Saints' credibility.

While the scheme may have exposed a handful of gentiles as brothel patrons, anti-Mormons could point to the incident as "proof" that the LDS Church had operated brothels and that even Mormons considered polygamy and prostitution to be morally equivalent crimes.

The "judicial crusade" continued through autumn 1890. The events of that year, which included political victories by Liberals in Utah's two largest cities and the seizure of much of the LDS Church's property, eventually forced President Wilford Woodruff to issue his "Manifesto" which began a retreat from church-sanctioned plural marriages.[195] Although prostitution continued to be wielded occasionally as a rhetorical weapon in the Mormon-gentile conflict, other issues forced it into the background. But throughout this period, hundreds of other women with no direct stake in the conflict built a long-lived brothel district in Salt Lake City and sold sex to men of all descriptions.

Notes

1. Roberts, *Comprehensive History: Century I*, vols. 1–3 passim; Arrington and Bitton, *Mormon Experience*, pp. 44–64; May, *Utah*, pp. 42–63; and Alexander, *Utah, the Right Place*, pp. 78–91.

2. Morgan, *State of Deseret*; Hansen, *Quest for Empire*; Quinn, *Mormon Hierarchy: Extensions of Power*, pp. 226–325; and Campbell, "Government of Utah." For incorporation, see "An Ordinance to Incorporate Great Salt Lake City," "Salt Lake City Council Ordinances" (1851), Book A, "A Record of the City Council of Great Salt Lake City, Deseret," p. 50. For Salt Lake's government, see ibid., secs. 3, 5, 47. On LDS Church domination, see Tullidge, *History of Salt Lake City*, pp. 57, 77; Alexander and Allen, *Mormons and Gentiles*, pp. 51, 99; and Quinn, *Mormon Hierarchy: Extensions of Power*, pp. 262–301.

3. Firmage and Mangrum, *Zion in the Courts*, pp. 214–19.

4. Foster, *Religion and Sexuality*, pp. 128–30, 230–31.

5. Arrington and Bitton, *Mormon Experience*, pp. 185–205; Quinn, *Mormon Hierarchy: Extensions of Power*, p. 178; and Hansen, "Mormon Sexuality and American Culture."

6. See, for example, Erastus Snow, 1882, *Journal of Discourses*, 23:224. See also Raynes, "Mormon Marriages in an American Context."

7. *Encyclopedia of Mormonism*, s.v. "Chastity, Law of," lists the following references from the Book of Mormon: Alma 38:12, 39:35, 41:11; Jacob 2:28; and Moroni 9:9.

8. Examples include: Doctrine and Covenants of the Church of Jesus Christ of Latter-day Saints, 42:22–24; 76:103–5.

9. For example, see George Q. Cannon, 1873, *Journal of Discourses*, 16:145.

10. B. Madsen, *Gold Rush Sojourners*; Arrington, *Great Basin Kingdom*, 81–84; and Dwyer, *Gentile Comes to Utah*, pp. v–7.

11. On conflict, see Larson, *"Americanization" of Utah*, chap. 1 passim, chap. 4 passim; Lyman, *Political Deliverance*, chap. 1 passim; Dwyer, *Gentile Comes to Utah*, pp. 8–13, 41–43, 65–92, 137–40; Cresswell, "U.S. Department of Justice in Utah Territory"; and Cooley,

"Carpetbag Rule." For the Mormon point of view, see Roberts, *Comprehensive History*, 3:414–543, 4:181–557, 5: passim, 6:1–178; and Whitney, *History of Utah*, 1:389–727, 2: passim, 3:1292. On the "Utah War," see Moorman with Sessions, *Camp Floyd and the Mormons*; Furniss, *Mormon Conflict*; and Hibbard, "Fort Douglas," pp. 3–4.

12. B. Madsen, *Glory Hunter*. See also Arrington, "Abundance from the Earth"; Arrington, *Great Basin Kingdom*, pp. 201–5, 241–43; and Arrington, *Brigham Young*, pp. 348–50.

13. Arrington, "Commercialization of Utah's Economy," p. 3. On non-Mormon churches, see Dwyer, *Gentile Comes to Utah*, pp. 30–40; Lyon, "Evangelical Protestant Missionary Activities"; Lyon, "Religious Activities and Development in Utah"; Beless, "Episcopal Church in Utah"; Darling, "Cultures in Conflict"; and Reherd, *Outline History of the Protestant Churches of Utah*.

14. "Divided Passions: 1780–1900," part 2 of D'Emilio and Freedman, *Intimate Matters*.

15. Welter, "Cult of True Womanhood."

16. Kessler-Harris, *Out to Work*, pp. 49–72.

17. Acton, *Functions and Disorders of the Reproductive Organs*, p. 133; quoted in Degler, *At Odds*, p. 250. On women's perceived sexuality; see Degler, *At Odds*, pp. 250–53; Cott, "Passionlessness"; and D'Emilio and Freedman, *Intimate Matters*, pp. 56, 70.

18. D'Emilio and Freedman, *Intimate Matters*, pp. 141–45.

19. Ibid., pp. 56–84. On the domestic sphere and reform, see also Sklar, *Catharine Beecher*; Ryan, *Cradle of the Middle Class*; and Baker, "Domestication of Politics."

20. Hansen, "Mormon Sexuality and American Culture," p. 51. On Mormon and non-Mormon concepts of the domestic sphere, see Iversen, *Antipolygamy Controversy*, pp. 1–9.

21. May, *Three Frontiers*, pp. 136–40; Lobb and Derr, "Women in Early Utah," pp. 337–41; and Jeffrey, *Frontier Women*, pp. 214–37.

22. Matthews, *Rise of Public Woman*, p. 4.

23. A. Anderson, *Tainted Souls and Painted Faces*, pp. 2–3.

24. Walkowitz, *Prostitution and Victorian Society*, p. 4.

25. Van Wagoner, *Mormon Polygamy*, pp. 1–12, 56; K. Young, *Isn't One Wife Enough?*; Foster, *Religion and Sexuality*, pp. 123–80; Foster, *Women, Family, and Utopia*, pp. 123–69; and Ivins, "Notes on Mormon Polygamy."

26. Foster, *Religion and Sexuality*, pp. 199–204; Van Wagoner, *Mormon Polygamy*, pp. 82–86; and Bitton, "Polygamy Defended: One Side of a Nineteenth-Century Polemic," in *Ritualization of Mormon History*, pp. 34–53.

27. "Special Conference at Great Salt Lake City." See also Foster, *Religion and Sexuality*, pp. 199–204.

28. See, for example, Amasa Lyman, 1866, *Journal of Discourses*, 11:198; Brigham Young, 1866, *Journal of Discourses*, 11:257; George Q. Cannon, 1869, *Journal of Discourses*, 13:95; and Orson Pratt, 1869, *Journal of Discourses*, 13:183.

29. *Congressional Globe*, 36th Cong., 1st sess., 1860, 1514.

30. See, for example, Zane, "Death of Polygamy in Utah," p. 374.

31. Buel, *Metropolitan Life Unveiled*, 411.

32. Cook, "Face to Face with Mormonism," pp. 10–11.

33. Van Wagoner, *Mormon Polygamy*, p. 106.

34. Roberts, *Comprehensive History*, 6:135–40. See also Hardy, *Solemn Covenant*, pp. 41–60.

35. *Salt Lake City Daily Tribune,* 1 Sept. 1889.

36. Dubois, *Dubois's Making of a State,* p. 48; quoted in Lyman, *Political Deliverance,* pp. 38–39, n. 42.

37. D. Smith, "Family Limitation"; and Blair, *Clubwoman as Feminist,* pp. xii, 4–5.

38. Van Wagoner, *Mormon Polygamy,* pp. 107–9; Lyman, *Political Deliverance,* pp. 7–14; Larson, *"Americanization" of Utah,* pp. 8–65; Arrington and Bitton, *Mormon Experience,* p. 172; and Firmage and Mangrum, *Zion in the Courts,* p. 147.

39. Arrington, *Great Basin Kingdom,* chaps. 10 and 11; Arrington, Fox, and May, *Building the City of God,* chaps. 5–10.

40. Tullidge, *History of Salt Lake City,* appendix, pp. 9, 12–14; Erickson, "Liberal Party of Utah," pp. 1–24; and Malmquist, *First 100 Years,* pp. 6–19. See also Walker, "When the Spirits Did Abound."

41. Erickson, "Liberal Party of Utah," pp. 21–118; Tullidge, *History of Salt Lake City,* pp. 428–33; Lyman, *Political Deliverance,* pp. 14–15; B. Madsen, *Corinne,* pp. 101–12; Baskin, *Reminiscences,* pp. 23–27; and Arrington, *Great Basin Kingdom,* pp. 248–49.

42. Malmquist, *First 100 Years,* pp. 20–43.

43. Hulse, "C. C. Goodwin and the Taming of the *Tribune.*"

44. Malmquist, *First 100 Years,* pp. 66–252, McLaws, *Spokesman for the Kingdom.*

45. Pascoe, *Relations of Rescue,* pp. xvi, 32–72. On the women's antipolygamy movement, see Iversen, *Antipolygamy Controversy;* see also C. Cannon, "Awesome Power of Sex."

46. Derr, Cannon, and Beecher, *Women of Covenant,* p. 133.

47. For example, see F. Stenhouse, *Lady's Life,* and *"Tell It All";* and A. Young, *Wife No. 19.*

48. Abraham Hoagland Cannon Diaries, 1879–96 (hereafter "Abraham H. Cannon Diaries"), 5:55–56, 25 Dec. 1885, photocopy in JWM; Tanner, *Mormon Mother,* pp. 236–41. See also Jeffrey, "'If Polygamy Is the Lord's Order, We Must Carry It Out,'" chap. in *Frontier Women;* Goodson, "Plural Wives"; Charles, "Precedents for Mormon Women from Scriptures," p. 48; and Derr, "'Strength in Our Union,'" pp. 161–63.

49. Quinn, *Mormon Hierarchy: Extensions of Power,* p. 329; Van Wagoner, *Mormon Polygamy,* pp. 91–92; and Ivins, "Notes on Mormon Polygamy," pp. 170–72.

50. Tullidge, *Women of Mormondom,* p. 549; and Van Wagenen, "Sister-Wives and Suffragists," pp. 10–11.

51. Foster, *Women, Family, and Utopia,* pp. 202–9; Iversen, "Feminist Implications of Mormon Polygyny"; Lobb and Derr, "Women in Early Utah," p. 338; and Derr, Cannon, and Beecher, *Women of Covenant,* p. 136.

52. Van Wagenen, "Sister-Wives and Suffragists," pp. 17–22.

53. Beeton, "Woman Suffrage in the American West," p. iv. See also Alexander, "Experiment in Progressive Legislation."

54. Van Wagenen, "Sister-Wives and Suffragists," pp. 15–22; Beeton, "Woman Suffrage in the American West," pp. 41–44; and Derr, Cannon, and Beecher, *Women of Covenant,* pp. 86, 110–11.

55. Derr, Cannon, and Beecher, *Women of Covenant,* pp. 108–10. See also Van Wagenen, "Sister-Wives and Suffragists," pp. 110 and 143–44, n. 113; and Bennion, "*Woman's Exponent.*"

56. Beeton, "Woman Suffrage in the American West," p. 35.

57. Stanton, *Eighty Years and More,* p. 284.

58. *Tribune,* 27 Jan. 1898; Paddock, *Fate of Madame La Tour,* p. ix.

59. "Record and Roll Book of the Salt Lake City Baptist Church," p. 394, in FBC; "Minutes" of First Baptist Church, p. 3, in FBC; Reherd, *Outline History of the Protestant Churches of Utah,* pp. 651–52.

60. *Tribune,* 10 Sept. 1872.

61. Cornelia Paddock to Thomas Gregg, 3 Mar. 1882, Mormon Manuscripts and Broadsides, Chicago Historical Society, microfilm copy at USHS. On Sarah Pratt, see Van Wagoner, *Mormon Polygamy,* pp. 29–36, 41, 98–100; Paddock, *Fate of Madame La Tour,* p. ix.

62. Lyman, *Political Deliverance,* pp. 17–18; Hayward, "Utah's Anti-Polygamy Society," pp. 14–16; Van Wagenen, "Sister-Wives and Suffragists," pp. 101–11; and *Tribune,* 17, 23 Feb. 1872. For a general (and partial) discussion, see Sheldon, "Mormon Haters."

63. See, for example, *Tribune,* 1 June, 4 July, 10, 26 Sept. 1872; and Van Wagenen, "Sister-Wives and Suffragists," pp. 109–18.

64. *Tribune,* 8, 13, 27 Nov. 1878. Many were members of the Blue Tea Club, a non-Mormon literary society; see Blue Tea Club Record Book, Ladies' Literary Club Papers, p. 5, in JWM. See also Blair, *Clubwoman as Feminist;* Iversen, *Antipolygamy Controversy,* p. 28; Van Wagenen, "Sister-Wives and Suffragists," pp. 249–58; and Hayward, "Utah's Anti-Polygamy Society," pp. 17–28.

65. Van Wagenen, "Sister-Wives and Suffragists," p. 249. On the WCTU and polygamy, see Gusfield, *Symbolic Crusade;* Bordin, *Women and Temperance;* Blocker, *American Temperance Movements,* pp. 61–94; and Tyrrell, *Woman's World, Woman's Empire,* pp. 140–42.

66. *Tribune,* 31 Oct. 1876; Van Wagenen, "Sister-Wives and Suffragists," p. 185.

67. Paddock, *Saved at Last,* p. 5.

68. Paddock, *In the Toils,* p. 48.

69. Arrington and Haupt, "Intolerable Zion," p. 245.

70. Davidson, *Revolution and the Word,* pp. 206–10. See also "Mormonism and Fiction," part 2 of Givens, *Viper on the Hearth,* pp. 95–152; and Davis, "Some Themes of Counter-Subversion."

71. Paddock, *In the Toils,* p. 5.

72. The *New York Times* reviewed *In the Toils* (27 July 1879).

73. Paddock, *Fate of Madame La Tour,* pp. 226, 285, 291.

74. For the coal, see *Salt Lake City Herald,* 9 Feb. 1876, in JH, 7 Feb. 1876. For the gravel, see *Tribune,* 8 Dec. 1893. For the clerkship, see Polk, *Salt Lake City Directory* (1885–86).

75. *Anti-Polygamy Standard* 1, no. 1 (Apr. 1880). See also "The Discourse of Antipolygamy," chap. in Iversen, *Antipolygamy Controversy.*

76. *Anti-Polygamy Standard* 1, no. 1 (Apr. 1880). For similar expressions of sisterhood with Mormon women, see ibid., 2, no. 7 (Oct. 1881).

77. *Woman's Exponent* 12, no. 12 (15 Nov. 1883).

78. See, for example, the letter of Mary Teasdale, in *Woman's Exponent* 12, no. 14 (15 Dec. 1883).

79. *Anti-Polygamy Standard* 1, no. 5 (Aug. 1880).

80. Territory of Utah, "Edmunds Law," in Utah, *Compiled Laws* (1882), p. 110.

81. Grow, "Study of the Utah Commission"; Crofutt, *Crofutt's Salt Lake City Directory* (1885–86).

82. *Utah Journal,* 20 Oct. 1882, in JH, 12 Oct. 1882; *Salt Lake City Deseret Evening News,* 29 Sept. 1883, in JH, 29 Sept. 1883; and Whitney, *History of Utah,* 3:222.

83. Lender, *Dictionary of American Temperance Biography,* pp. 364–65.

84. Dwyer, *Gentile Comes to Utah,* pp. 30–40; and Pascoe, *Relations of Rescue,* pp. 6–22.

85. Van Wagenen, "Sister-Wives and Suffragists," pp. 387–89; Pascoe, *Relations of Rescue,* pp. 49–67; Dwyer, *Gentile Comes to Utah,* pp. 204–6; Larson, "Industrial Home for Polygamous Wives"; and Larson, *"Americanization" of Utah,* pp. 223–98.

86. Presbyterian Robert G. McNiece, Baptist H. G. DeWitt, and S. I. Carroll of the Methodist Episcopal church; *Tribune,* 30 Oct. 1885.

87. Paddock, "Industrial Home for Mormon Women."

88. *Tribune,* 8 May 1886. See also Iversen, *Antipolygamy Controversy,* p. 111; and Larson, *"Americanization" of Utah,* p. 56. For another lobbyist, see Field, "Mormon Monster," in CA.

89. Larson, *"Americanization" of Utah,* pp. 223–24.

90. Pascoe, *Relations of Rescue,* pp. 88–101; Larson, "Industrial Home for Polygamous Wives"; and Alexander, *Clash of Interests,* pp. 123–25.

91. *Woman's Exponent,* 1 Dec. 1886.

92. *Deseret Evening News,* 10 Mar. 1892.

93. For the accusation, see *Woman's Exponent,* 15 Nov. 1883; for the denial, *Woman's Exponent,* 1 Aug. 1884.

94. Newman, "To the Members of the Senate and House of Representatives of the 50th Congress," in CHL.

95. K. Young, *Isn't One Wife Enough?* p. 311; and Foster, *Religion and Sexuality,* p. 173.

96. *Latter Day Saints' Messenger and Advocate,* Jan. 1845, quoted in Van Wagoner, *Mormon Polygamy,* p. 72.

97. Foster, *Women, Family, and Utopia,* pp. 149–50.

98. B. Madsen, *Glory Hunter,* p. 65.

99. Abraham H. Cannon Diaries, 12:215–16, 8 July 1890.

100. Beecher, "Eliza R. Snow"; C. Madsen, "Mormon Woman in Victorian America"; and Derr, "Sarah Melissa Granger Kimball."

101. *Anti-Polygamy Standard* 2, no. 1 (1881).

102. *Tribune,* 17 June 1877. See also *Corinne Utah Tri-Weekly Reporter,* 25 Jan. 1870; *Tribune,* 13 Nov. 1878.

103. *Deseret Evening News,* 11 Nov. 1878; *Tribune,* 12 Nov. 1878.

104. "Saved from the Mormons."

105. Buel, *Metropolitan Life Unveiled,* pp. 483–84.

106. Givens, *Viper on the Hearth,* pp. 130–37; Arrington and Haupt, "Intolerable Zion," p. 247.

107. *Deseret Evening News,* 13 Mar. 1886.

108. E. Snow, "Decision of the Supreme Court of the United States in the Reynolds Case." See also U.S. Reports 98 (Oct., 1878), pp. 145–69; G. Cannon, *Review of the Decision of the Supreme Court of the United States in the Case of George Reynolds vs. the United States.* On the legal dangers for women, see C. Madsen, "'At Their Peril.'"

109. *Tribune,* 31 Aug. 1872.

110. *Tribune,* 14 Oct. 1886.

111. *Deseret Evening News,* 24 Nov. 1885.

112. For example, Frank J. Cannon was known by many to patronize Kate Flint's brothel. When the president of Sevier Stake disparaged Frank's character, his father George Q. Cannon threatened "to withdraw fellowship" (Abraham H. Cannon Diaries, 16:179, 25 Oct. 1892).

113. Firmage and Mangrum, *Zion in the Courts,* pp. 357–58.

114. *Salt Lake City Goodwin's Weekly,* 18 Oct. 1912, in JH, 18 Oct. 1912, 15.

115. Joseph Smith Journal, 14 May 1842, quoted in Roberts, *Comprehensive History,* 5:8, quoted in Barth, *Instant Cities,* p. 48.

116. J. M. Grant, 1856, *Journal of Discourses,* 3:234.

117. See, for example, Foster, *Religion and Sexuality,* p. 182; Burton, *City of the Saints, and Across the Rocky Mountains,* pp. 426–27, 508, 513, 519–20, 535; Twain, *Roughing It,* p. 89; Tuttle, *Reminiscences of a Missionary Bishop,* p. 110. See also Firmage and Mangrum, *Zion in the Courts,* pp. 359–60.

118. Ivins, "Notes on Mormon Polygamy," p. 176.

119. Police records apparently no longer exist from this period. City council minutes invariably refer to male criminals only; see, for example, "Salt Lake City Council Minutes," Book B, pp. 106–7, 15 Sept. 1858; and "Salt Lake City Council Minutes," Book D, p. 299, 16 Aug. 1864.

120. H. C. Kimball, 1854, *Journal of Discourses,* 7:16.

121. J. M. Grant, 1856, *Journal of Discourses,* 3:232. On the "Mormon reformation," see Peterson, "Mormon Reformation"; Arrington and Bitton, *Mormon Experience,* pp. 212–13.

122. Orson Pratt, 1859, *Journal of Discourses,* 7:251.

123. Stout, *On the Mormon Frontier,* 27 Feb. 1858, p. 653. See also Quinn, "Culture of Violence," in *Mormon Hierarchy: Extensions of Power,* pp. 241–61.

124. On federal officials in the territories, see R. White, *"It's Your Misfortune and None of My Own,"* pp. 172–73; Cresswell, "U.S. Department of Justice in Utah Territory"; and Cooley, "Carpetbag Rule."

125. A letter purportedly from Drummond's wife Jemima to her relatives identified the woman as Ada Caroll of Washington, D.C.; see *Deseret News,* 20 May 1857. See also Roberts, *Comprehensive History,* 4:200–206; Whitney, *History of Utah,* 1:577–85.

126. Tullidge, *History of Salt Lake City,* pp. 144–56; Arrington and Bitton, *Mormon Experience,* p. 165; Alexander, *Utah, the Right Place,* pp. 122–24; and Larson, *"Americanization" of Utah,* p. 17.

127. Moorman with Sessions, *Camp Floyd and the Mormons,* pp. 57–58; Hibbard, "Fort Douglas," p. 3.

128. R. W. Jones Diary, 1, 2 July 1859; quoted in A. Godfrey, "Housewives, Hussies, and Heroines," p. 168. See also "The Scourge of Gold: Fairfield," in Moorman with Sessions, *Camp Floyd and the Mormons,* pp. 59–80, esp. on brothels, p. 67.

129. Hibbard, "Fort Douglas," p. 28.

130. Rockwood, "Report with Extracts and a Concise History of Utah Penitentiary," USHS, pp. 19–20.

131. John Taylor, 1873, *Journal of Discourses,* 15:284; and 1879, 20:307.

132. See the brief discussion of prohibition in chap. 5.

133. E. T. Benson, 1852, *Journal of Discourses,* 6:248.

134. Erastus Snow, 1859, *Journal of Discourses,* 7:125.

135. Brigham Young, 1871, *Journal of Discourses*, 14:223.

136. Baskin, *Reminiscences*, pp. 32–35.

137. On McKean, see Alexander, "'Federal Authority versus Polygamic Theocracy.'" See also Firmage and Mangrum, *Zion in the Courts*, pp. 144–46; Larson, *"Americanization" of Utah*, pp. 65–77; and Arrington and Bitton, *Mormon Experience*, pp. 177–80.

138. U.S. Bureau of the Census, Ninth Census (1870), Box Elder County, p. 46, lines 37–40. On Corinne, see B. Madsen, *Corinne*, esp. pp. 11–14.

139. SLCPD, "Record Commencing July 7, 1871–June 8, 1875" (hereafter "Police, Record 1871–1875"), 8 Apr. 1872, pp. 84–85.

140. *Deseret Evening News*, 29 Aug. 1872, in JH, 29 Aug. 1872. For a petition against prostitution, see "Salt Lake City Council Minutes," Book F, p. 383, 16 July 1872; Flint v. Clinton et al., case no. 554 (3d dist. civil case files, 1877). For Flint's previous arrests, see "Police, Record 1871–1875," 8 Apr. 1872, pp. 84–85; 11 May 1872, pp. 94–95; 8 July 1872, pp. 124–25; 19 July 1872, pp. 130–31. For Conway, see 8 July 1872, pp. 124–25; 24 Aug. 1872, pp. 148–49.

141. *Corinne Daily Reporter*, 30 Aug. 1872.

142. *Herald*, 30 Aug. 1872, in JH, 30 Aug. 1872.

143. *Deseret Evening News*, 30 Aug. 1872, in JH, 30 Aug. 1872.

144. "Sermon Delivered by Dr. Jeter Clinton," *Mormon Expositor* 1, no. 1 (1875).

145. *Tribune*, 31 Aug. 1872.

146. *Tribune*, 30 Aug. 1872.

147. For Flint's brothel, see "Police, Record 1871–1875," 17 Dec. 1872, pp. 188–89; 16 Jan. 1873, pp. 200–201; 15 Apr. 1873, pp. 238–39; 8 Aug. 1873, pp. 298–99; 28 May 1874, pp. 540–41; SLCPD, "Record Commencing July 1, 1875–Oct. 23, 1878" (hereafter "Police, Record 1875–1878"), 8 Apr. 1876, pp. 98–99; 23 Dec. 1876, pp. 176–77; 5 May 1877, pp. 220–21; 27 Sept. 1877, pp. 260–61; 13 Apr. 1878, pp. 308–9; U.S. Bureau of the Census, Tenth Census (1880), Salt Lake County, Enumeration District No. 52, p. 204, lines 6–8; Historicus [Amos Milton Musser], "Offences in 1882"; *Tribune*, 2 June 1886; *Tribune*, 22 Aug., 10, 13 Oct. 1886. For the sale of Flint's property, see SLCR, "Deed Book 2Q," warranty deed, pp. 252–54, 7 Feb. 1888. For Conway as a prostitute in others' houses, see "Police, Record 1871–1875," 17 Dec. 1872, pp. 188–89; "Police, Record 1875–1878," 28 Dec. 1876, pp. 178–79; 5 May 1877, pp. 220–21; 27 Sept. 1877, pp. 260–61.

148. Whitney, *History of Utah*, 2:767–69.

149. Flint v. Clinton et al., case no. 554 (3d dist. civil case files, 1877). Flint claimed losses of $9,171.20.

150. *Deseret Evening News*, 15 Mar. 1875, in JH, 15 Mar. 1875.

151. Flint v. Clinton et al.; Conway v. Clinton et al., case no. 586 (3d dist. civil case files, 1877). See also Conway v. Clinton, 1 Utah 215 (1875). For the settlement, see "Salt Lake City Council Minutes," Book H, p. 103, 18 Sept. 1877; and *Tribune*, 21 Sept. 1877.

152. Ann Gordge Lee, "Autobiography." Two variants of this document exist, with almost identical versions of the Flint story; "percentage hoar house" is from the variant given a Salt Lake City policeman in 1915.

153. *Deseret Evening News*, 30 Apr. 1904.

154. De Voto, "Sin Comes to Ogden." This story could not be confirmed, but it contains some similar elements to Ann Lee's tale. Some people remembered Flint even long-

er. On 21 Nov. 1994, Floyd O'Neil, director of the American West Center, told the author that older members of the Westerners club in the 1970s recalled that in their youth, anyone who visited a prostitute was said to have "been to see Kate Flint."

155. "Police, Record 1871–1875," pp. 194–95.

156. Historicus, "Offences in 1882." On the all-Mormon force, see Gleason, "Salt Lake City Police Department," p. 67.

157. Historicus, "Offences in 1882."

158. John Taylor, 1882, *Journal of Discourses,* 23:58; John Taylor, 1884, *Journal of Discourses,* 25:303; "An Epistle of the First Presidency to the Church of Jesus Christ of Latter-day Saints in General Conference Assembled," Mar. 1886, in *Messages of the First Presidency,* 3:67; and First Presidency to A. Milton Musser, 28 Nov. 1890, in ibid., 3:200–201.

159. *Anti-Polygamy Standard,* 1, no. 2 (May 1880).

160. Grow, "Study of the Utah Commission," p. 66.

161. "Edmunds Law," sec. 3, in Utah, *Compiled Laws* (1888), p. 111.

162. Erastus Snow, 1882, *Journal of Discourses,* 23:301.

163. John Taylor, 8 Oct. 1882, *Journal of Discourses,* 23:257; and 11 Feb. 1883, ibid., 24:6; *Herald,* 16 Sept. 1882.

164. Larson, *"Americanization" of Utah,* pp. 99–104.

165. Alexander, "Charles S. Zane."

166. Ibid.; see also Larson, *"Americanization" of Utah,* pp. 104–10.

167. Whitney, *History of Utah,* 3:272.

168. Ibid., 3:358–63.

169. Firmage and Mangrum, *Zion in the Courts,* pp. 169–75; Whitney, *History of Utah,* 3:364–71.

170. Whitney, *History of Utah,* 3:381–83.

171. Others arrested included Charles E. Pearson, an attorney and former U.S. commissioner, attorney Samuel H. Lewis, detective Joseph Bush, and merchant W. H. Yearian. See Brigham Young Hampton Papers, 1870–1901 (hereafter "Brigham Y. Hampton Diary"), microfilm copy in CA. I have retained Hampton's spelling, punctuation, and grammar. Charles S. Varian, the prosecuting attorney, told his version in Baskin, *Reminiscences,* 223–29. See also Flint v. Clinton et al., case no. 554.

172. Brigham Y. Hampton Diary, p. 167. The women sent notes to the officials; for examples, see *Tribune,* 24 Nov., 4 Dec. 1885; and Baskin, *Reminiscences,* p. 225.

173. *Tribune,* 24 Dec. 1885.

174. *Tribune,* 23, 24 Dec. 1885.

175. Brigham Y. Hampton Diary, pp. 167–72.

176. *Deseret Evening News,* 23 Nov. 1885.

177. *Tribune,* 24 Nov. 1885.

178. *Tribune,* 24, 25 Nov., 4, 24 Dec. 1885; *Deseret Evening News,* 24 Dec. 1885, in JH, 24 Dec. 1885; Baskin, *Reminiscences,* p. 226; and Brigham Y. Hampton Diary, p. 167.

179. *Tribune,* 28, 29 Nov. 1885; Utah, Territory of, *Of Charters of Incorporated Cities, Compiled Laws* (1872), p. 696.

180. *Deseret Evening News,* 30 Nov. 1885.

181. *Tribune,* 1 Dec. 1885.

182. *Tribune,* 9, 12, 13, 15 Dec. 1885. Varian's statements and the jury charge are from 15 Dec. His argument against the criminal conspiracy is in Baskin, *Reminiscences,* p. 227.

183. *Tribune,* 8 Dec. 1885; Baskin, *Reminiscences,* p. 226; People v. Hampton, 4 Utah 258 (1886); and Third District criminal case files, case nos. 285, 286, 287, and 288. Separate counts were filed because of the doctrine of "segregation," established in unlawful cohabitation prosecutions but later disallowed, which permitted a defendant to be charged for each period of days spent with a plural wife (see Whitney, *History of Utah,* 3:414–17). These files contain no testimony. I have relied on newspapers and Hampton's unsuccessful appeal to the Utah Supreme Court, People v. Hampton.

184. *Tribune,* 20 Dec. 1885.

185. *Tribune,* 31 Dec. 1885; Baskin, *Reminiscences,* pp. 228–29; and People v. Hampton. Hampton's Mormon jailer allowed him to hold the key to his room and took him horseback riding and visiting friends, including "Faney Devenport." A police officer under indictment for cohabitation hid in his room on nine different occasions; Brigham Y. Hampton Diary, pp. 173–225. Hampton arranged a $1,000 mortgage at 10 percent to pay Davenport; Brigham Y. Hampton Diary, pp. 216, 225. For further arrests, see *Tribune,* 19 Jan. 1886; Hampton to George Q. Cannon, 6 Nov. 1886, copy in Brigham Y. Hampton Diary, p. 219; and Brigham Y. Hampton Diary, p. 221.

186. Brigham Y. Hampton Diary, pp. 187, 191.

187. *Deseret Evening News,* 30 Dec. 1885.

188. *Deseret Evening News,* 13 Mar. 1886, in JH, 13 Mar. 1886.

189. "In Defense of Polygamy," in Cheney, *Mormon Songs from the Rocky Mountains,* pp. 80–81. Cheney credits William H. Avery with the text and suggests the song is circa 1890. "Murry" is Gov. Murray; Ireland's "aid" is Oscar Vandercook; "Dixon" is William H. Dickson. Two variants of this song appear in Hubbard, *Ballads and Songs from Utah,* pp. 456–58.

190. Congress, Senate, *Woman Suffrage in Utah,* petition of Mrs. Angie F. Newman, 49th Cong., 1st sess., 8 June 1886, S. Misc. Doc. 122, copy in CHL.

191. *Tribune,* 24 Nov. 1885.

192. *Tribune,* 3 Feb. 1886.

193. *Tribune,* 30 May 1886. See also *Tribune,* 3 Feb. 1886, 23 Feb. 1890, and 10 Feb. 1900; *Salt Lake City Telegram,* 12 Dec. 1908.

194. Roberts, *Comprehensive History,* 6:158. For another Mormon version of the Hampton episode, see Whitney, *History of Utah,* 3:443–47.

195. On the "crusade," see Larson, *"Americanization" of Utah,* pp. 210–63; Lyman, *Political Deliverance,* pp. 41–149.

2. "Women of the Town"

PROSTITUTES AND MADAMS played an active and visible role in the public life of Salt Lake City. Several women began long careers managing brothels in the 1870s and 1880s, and more transient brothel prostitutes, saloon workers, crib workers, and streetwalkers started working in places where their successors could be found decades later. They built a network of prostitution venues, stratified along racial and class lines that reflected those of the surrounding community, that flourished for almost forty years. This chapter will detail the structure of prostitution, the places where women sold sex, the allies and supporters of prostitution, and the experiences of some women from the 1870s to approximately 1908.

Temple Block is the geographic center of Salt Lake City, and "ground zero" is the corner of South Temple (originally Brigham) Street and Main (originally East Temple) Street. North-south running streets are numbered beginning at Main, which is "0" longitudinally. East-west streets begin at South Temple, which is "0" latitudinally. As one moves away from ground zero, streets are numbered by 100s; for example, 200 North (or "Second North") is two blocks north of South Temple. Any spot in the city can be pinpointed by its north-south, east-west coordinates (see figure 1).

By the early 1870s, with the influx of gentiles and the gradual incorporation of Utah's products into outside markets, Salt Lake City had become a "commercial city" with a small business district concentrated on Main Street between 100 and 200 South Street. The location of this district, just one block south of the southeast corner of Temple Block, demonstrates the compact nature of the walking city of the 1870s.[1]

Women sold sex in locations that, in a physical and metaphorical sense,

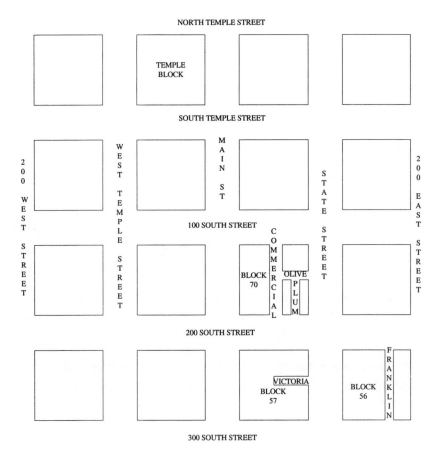

NORTH TEMPLE STREET

TEMPLE BLOCK

SOUTH TEMPLE STREET

WEST TEMPLE STREET

MAIN STREET

STATE STREET

200 WEST STREET

200 EAST STREET

100 SOUTH STREET

BLOCK 70

COMMERCIAL

OLIVE

PLUM

200 SOUTH STREET

VICTORIA BLOCK 57

BLOCK 56

FRANKLIN

300 SOUTH STREET

constituted the back side or underworld of this emerging business zone. One of the most persistent and best-known locations was Commercial (later Regent) Street. Commercial was one block long and fifty feet wide and ran north-south through Block 70 between 100 and 200 South. The street's situation made it contested ground. Since Commercial was a narrow street on the interior of a block, "disreputable" businesses were relatively less visible and obnoxious to passersby than they would have been on the outside streets of the block, yet still easily accessible to customers. Prostitutes, city authorities, and many businesspeople considered Commercial an ideal location for prostitution. Because of its centrality and proximity to the business district and Temple Square, however, Commercial Street property owners, municipal boosters, and reformers spoke frequently of its legitimate potential and demanded that prostitutes be removed. Despite these sentiments, which resulted in periodic "cleansings" of the street, the forces favoring prostitution held the upper hand and some women sold sex there until the 1930s.[2]

Madams and prostitutes established themselves in other long-term locales inside original city blocks. As the business district extended down Main Street to Third South in the 1880s, women began selling sex in Block 57, immediately south of Block 70. As on Commercial Street, brothels in Block 57 shared space with saloons, secondhand stores, restaurants, and other businesses.[3] Unlike the Commercial Street houses of prostitution, usually located in continuous-row buildings directly on the street,[4] the most persistent Block 57 brothels were detached dwelling houses in the center of the block, invisible from outside streets but easily accessible via narrow alleys. Franklin Avenue, which cut south through Block 56 from Second to Third South between State and Second East (one block east of Main), remained more residential than commercial throughout the period under study.[5]

Commercial Street and Franklin Avenue shared one characteristic that led many whites to consider them suitable for prostitution: they were the homes of racial minorities. In the late nineteenth and early twentieth centuries, white Americans across the nation instituted increasingly strict segregation and often violently repressed African Americans, Asians, and other ethnic groups. The high incidence of lynchings attests to the South's efforts to reestablish white supremacy over African Americans.[6] There is little reason to believe that racial attitudes in Salt Lake City differed from those in other northern cities. LDS leaders considered African Americans descendants of Ham and therefore ineligible for the priesthood or for marriage with Mormon women. Utah's territorial legislature legalized both African American and Indian bondage; slavery only ended when Congress barred it in the territories in 1862. Miscegenation was outlawed in 1852, and LDS leaders frequently warned their members against race mixing.[7] Mobs lynched a handful of African Americans in Utah between 1870 and 1925.[8] De facto residential segregation kept African Americans in distinct locations. By the 1890s, Franklin Avenue had become the center of the city's small African American population.[9]

The city's Asian inhabitants were also the object of severe prejudice and strict segregation. Throughout the West, whites resented the Chinese for allegedly depressing wages and feared their alien culture; as a result, Chinese were barred from emigrating to the United States in 1882. In Salt Lake, whites often associated them with vice, crime, and drug abuse.[10] Plum Alley, which paralleled Commercial Street some twenty feet to the east, was the center of Salt Lake City's tiny, overwhelmingly male Chinatown.[11] Many Chinese also lived and worked on Commercial, while at least one white woman managed a large brothel on Plum Alley in the 1890s.[12] A handful of Japanese immigrants began settling in the city after 1884, including some prostitutes on Franklin Avenue.[13]

The authorities considered Commercial and Franklin acceptable locales for prostitution, especially in its lower-status forms. Similarly, one reason municipal officials gave for moving prostitutes to the west side of town in 1908 was that neighborhood housed mostly immigrants.[14] By forcing or encouraging prostitutes and "less desirable" people to live together, the municipal authorities thought to keep white residential and business areas unpolluted by vice and crime (while still ensuring that prostitutes were available for white customers). Such segregation was common throughout the country. Historians Neil Shumsky and Larry Springer note that vice districts and "Chinatowns" were often co-located. Historian Ruth Rosen, who studied mostly eastern cities, notes that red-light districts were found commonly in poor sections of town, frequently where African Americans lived.[15]

Prostitutes worked in other places throughout the city. West Temple Street between First and Second South enjoyed a brief vogue as a brothel location in the mid-1880s and again in the mid-1890s.[16] Women also sold sex on Second South Street and near Fort Douglas.[17] The locales discussed above, however, were the most common areas for prostitution during the period studied. Customers could walk easily from one location to another, sampling the hospitality of each house. A supposed investigation by police and city councilmen in 1892 demonstrated this: in the course of the evening their party visited brothels on Commercial Street, Victoria Alley, Franklin Avenue, and Plum Alley within three contiguous city blocks.[18]

All three blocks contained a mixture of residential housing and commercial properties in varying proportions. Prostitutes and madams lived and worked alongside the owners, employees, and customers of a variety of legitimate businesses: tailor shops, gunsmithies, livery stables, breweries, locksmithies, cabinetmaking shops, barbershops, blacksmithies, confectioneries, drugstores, groceries, saloons, secondhand stores, cheap restaurants, and laundries, in addition to less savory "resorts": gambling halls, peep shows, and opium dens. This world was crowded, noisy, and busy, especially at night. Commercial Street at the turn of the century was particularly cosmopolitan.

> From a corner there comes the cry of "hot tamales," from another "chicken sandwich" floats on the wind; in a nearby mission there is the sound of a hymn, and this is mingled with a coarse song from a maison de joie nearby; the evangelists on the street are listened to when they can be heard above the roar of traffic and the music from the houses; Japanese, Chinese, negroes and white

mix together in a friendly way; occasionally from one of the saloons some tough who has aspirations to "run de place or doie," is seen to shoot out of a door— he doubles his fist, vows vengeance and then slides away; out from a dark and badly-scented alley comes a pale-faced man whose chief occupation in life is the burning of opium; Chinese merchants sit on their doorsteps and indulge in gossip and smoke after their day's trade is over; sad faces peer from the windows of shacks and watch the pedestrian as he ambles down the street; occasionally a female figure flits in from one of the side streets and is swallowed up in the darkness of Plum alley, and it needs not more than one guess from the uninitiated to tell where she has gone to.[19]

The women who sold sex in these locales were not there for excitement and entertainment. Scholars have studied and debated extensively the reasons some women turned to prostitution. At the turn of the twentieth century, Edward R. Seligman wrote *The Social Evil,* based on the influential work of the New York City vice commissions, completed in 1902. The commissions noted the existence of both "full-time" and "temporary" prostitutes. Seligman cited a number of possible factors that "impelled" women "to make a quasi-voluntary choice of prostitution as a means of livelihood," including poor wages, orphanhood, and "vicious" childhood influences. Seligman also claimed that certain women were "selfish," "greedy," or "hedonistic" and so entered prostitution because it paid better than respectable work.[20]

More recent scholars acknowledge the legitimacy of these factors (if not the moralizing tone Seligman attaches) but they emphasize economic necessity. Women's employment choices were severely limited, especially if they lacked education or had children to care for. Most women who turned to prostitution, whether full-time or occasional, did so because it seemed the best among their few alternatives. Some women sold sex occasionally between other jobs or before marriage.[21]

Economic prospects for a working-class woman in Salt Lake City in the late nineteenth and early twentieth centuries were not promising. Relatively few women worked outside the home at all: 18.5 percent of adult women in 1900, rising to 20 percent by 1910, slightly below the national averages. The largest single category of available employment in Salt Lake and the nation was domestic service, although by the first two decades of the twentieth century virtually as many women performed clerical work. Other common occupations included dressmaking, millinery, laundry, and candy manufacturing. A few Salt Lake women achieved professional status, the majority as nurses and teachers, and a number of female physicians worked in the city.[22] The most widely available work offered poor wages. A "servant girl" working in a private home in 1880s Salt Lake City could expect to earn perhaps

$3.00 a week, and some people would only hire girls of their own religion.[23] A brothel prostitute might earn ten times that amount.[24]

The evidence from Salt Lake City supports financial necessity, sometimes to the point of crisis, as the leading reason some women resorted to selling sex. Women's stories depict their desperate circumstances as they struggled to keep themselves or their families afloat. Rose Watkins told the city court that she turned to prostitution after her father died, leaving the family nothing and forcing her mother to take in washing. When her mother became ill and Rose lost her (unspecified) job, she began selling sex.[25] Alma Baxley feared she might be forced to become a prostitute. She claimed that her "fall" had been "effected" in Dallas, and that she had come to Salt Lake City to work as a domestic but that "stories of her former disgrace gained circulation here, and she lost her place. . . . as a final effort to avoid the inevitable" she called on the police for help.[26] About a third of likely prostitutes in the Stockade told the census enumerator that they were or recently had been out of work, sometimes for the entire previous year. One brothel alone contained a stenographer, two clerks, a telephone operator, a nurse, and a waitress, all unemployed.[27] Dogney Lofstrom entered the Stockade in 1911 after losing her laundry job during a strike.[28] When "rescue" workers offered one woman help finding "honest work," she replied "I can't support my child with the wages paid girls for honest work in this city."[29]

The *Tribune* characteristically provided "life histories" of prostitutes that indicted Mormonism rather than financial exigency. One unnamed 16-year-old purportedly was "the scion of a Mormon house . . . [and] a good illustration of the beauty of Mormon education and training. . . . Her father has been to the Pen, and her mother, a polygamous wife, is now living as the mistress of another man."[30] The *Tribune* claimed that a Mormon upbringing, which exposed a girl to the immoralities of polygamy while offering her more opportunities to be in public, specially suited her to prostitution: "As soon as night comes she wants to be in the streets, for *that is what she has been accustomed to all her life*. So trained and with her passions abnormally excited by her teachings from childhood, a great many of them know no such thing as virtue from almost childhood."[31]

The numbers of prostitutes working in Salt Lake City during this time period cannot be stated with anything approaching certainty. This is a function of both the incompleteness and the inaccuracy of records, and also of the vagaries of the terms "prostitute" and "prostitution." While some women were full-time prostitution workers (i.e., madams and their brothel workers), others sold sex as a temporary expedient or a supplement to other work.

Nevertheless, some clues can be found. Police arrested three to five brothel keepers and five to sixteen "inmates" on an irregular basis from 1872 through 1878.[32] About five or six keepers and twenty-five to thirty prostitutes were arrested from 1880 through 1891.[33] A raid in April 1891 produced ten keepers and fifty-two inmates.[34] Those approximate numbers remained through about 1894.[35] By 1903, nearly one hundred women were being arrested and fined on a monthly basis.[36] By mid-1908, when city officials were planning the Stockade district, eight housekeepers and about 130 prostitutes were on the arrest books.[37]

The women enumerated above worked in the well-known brothels and undoubtedly represent only a portion of women who sold sex. An unknown number of full- and part-time prostitutes escaped arrest, while some women arrested in brothels were probably servants. Other people occasionally offered their own estimates. Mary Grant Major, who helped found a "rescue home" for prostitutes, guessed in 1892 that there were nearly a thousand "fallen women" in Salt Lake.[38] ("Fallen women," of course, was a blanket term and might include mistresses and victims of seduction; in this context, Major seems to refer only to prostitutes.) J. Golden Kimball, an LDS leader, claimed in 1896 that "there are 500 girls who are public prostitutes in Salt Lake City some of these are dau[ghters] of Latter day Saints."[39] A reformer in 1902 suggested "there are at least 500 people who depend upon this nefarious business for a livelihood."[40]

As in other cities, contemporary opinion divided women involved in commercialized sex into five rough categories, from highest to lowest status: brothel operator or owner/operator (madam), brothel prostitute, saloon or dance hall worker, crib worker, and streetwalker.[41] The boundaries between these categories were fuzzy, and some women changed status, usually downward. While the physical venue where prostitution occurred had much to do with a woman's perceived status, her personal characteristics also mattered. Some women could not hope to inhabit the upper strata because of their race, advanced age, or drug or alcohol abuse. Prostitutes, municipal authorities, and the general public collaborated to create this status hierarchy, and all acknowledged its existence. The police and the public were usually much more tolerant of the madams and higher-end brothel prostitutes than they were of crib women or streetwalkers, who were often nonwhite. These women were understood to belong to different strata, and it was worthy of remark when police raids brought them together: "An almond-eyed beauty from the land of the Mikado fraternized with an ebony-hued damsel whose ancestors dwelt on the banks of the Kongo, and the sturdy Teuton swapped neighbor-

hood gossip with an erstwhile grisette of Paris. . . . The inmates of the gilded palace of sin and the brothels of 'Darkest Africa' met for once on a common level, and a great deal of jolly badinage was indulged in by all."[42]

The most elaborate brothels were known as "parlor houses" for the central parlors where women and customers socialized. The owners and operators of parlor houses were the highest-status, most visible, and best-known
representatives of the "sporting class." Through the period under discussion,
the great majority of brothel operators and many owner/operators were white
women. For them, prostitution offered a chance to use entrepreneurial tal-
ent and ambition to carve out comfortable livings in an economy that offered few other outlets. A handful succeeded in earning substantial amounts,
especially through the appreciation of real estate; and at least one, Dora
Topham, wielded considerable political power. Madams funded the construction of the brothel district through mortgages and loans from some of the
city's most prominent and ostensibly respectable bankers and businessmen,
both gentile and Mormon.

The heyday of the independent female brothel keeper lasted from the 1870s
until the establishment of the Stockade, although a few women continued
to run houses outside that district. Three women, Kate Flint, Emma DeMarr,
and Sadie Noble, owned and operated parlor houses in Salt Lake City for
years, and after their retirement, other women continued to run the brothels the three established. Their persistence and centrality makes it important
to examine their lives and careers in some detail.

Kate Flint ran a brothel with three women in Corinne in 1870; the census
describes her as twenty-three years old and Irish-born, although a census
taker ten years later recorded that she was born in Tennessee to Tennessee-
born parents.[43] Flint ran brothels on Commercial Street in Salt Lake City in
the 1870s. In March 1880, her husband D. Frank Connelly bought a rectan-
gular lot in Block 57, the narrow northern end of which opened on Second
South Street, and immediately deeded it to Flint. On that lot she opened what
seems to have been the first brothel in Block 57.[44] Connelly purchased an
adjoining lot two years later and turned it over to his wife as well. Connelly
bought both lots from David F. Walker of the prominent Walker Brothers
banking firm, which also helped to finance the purchase of the first lot.[45] The
roundabout purchases may have provided cover for Flint or the Walkers, since
she was already a notorious figure.

Until autumn 1886 or early 1887, when the now-widowed Flint apparently abandoned the business, she operated a brothel on her Block 57 property.
The likeliest location, based on its relative seclusion and proximity to other
long-term brothels, was a two-story adobe building at 42 or 44 east Second

South, set some one hundred feet south of Second South Street in the interior of the block and accessible by a narrow alley (see figure 2).[46] Flint sold the property in 1888 for $25,000 and apparently retired from the business, moving to Social Hall Avenue a few blocks away. Tenants in her former properties operated brothels through at least 1899.[47]

Emma DeMarr, whose given name seems to have been Matilda Turnross, proved one of the most enduring and financially successful owner/operators.[48] Evidence suggests she was born in Sweden around 1860 and emigrated to the United States in 1873.[49] By 1876 she seems to have been working in Emma Davis's Salt Lake City brothel.[50] Emma and "Alvie," her sister, operated a brothel in Bellevue, Idaho, in 1882. The sisters returned to Salt Lake

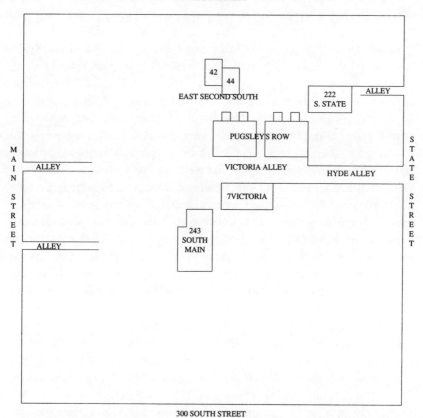

Figure 2. Block 57 brothels, ca. 1895 (locations approximate). Other buildings are not shown for clarity. Based on "Fire Insurance Map of Salt Lake City, 1895," newspapers, and arrest records.

City in autumn of that year with over three thousand dollars in joint earnings. Less than a month before Kate Flint obtained her second Block 57 lot, the sisters bought a plot of land that included a two-story adobe house near the center of the same block, where they started a brothel.[51]

Alvie (née Christina Elvitina Turnross) married in 1883 and evidently left the management of the brothel to Emma. Three years later, however, Christina filed suit charging that her older sister had defrauded her of her share in the property. Emma skillfully (if not ruthlessly) defeated Christina and established sole control over the brothel. Emma convinced the court that no formal partnership had existed between the sisters, that Christina had signed over her interest to Emma, and that the bulk of the purchase money for the property was Emma's. Emma even convinced their brother to forge a letter, purportedly from their mother, misrepresenting Christina's age as several years older than it actually was to prove that she was competent to sign over her share.[52]

Emma DeMarr purchased surrounding lots until she owned a keyhole-shaped plot stretching east from Main Street to the center of Block 57 where stood the adobe dwelling house, no. 243 south Main Street, accessible from Main via an alley.[53] In 1888, DeMarr married Charles V. Whiting, a saloon-keeper and restaurant operator.[54] Emma and Charles embarked on a variety of financial ventures over the next decades, using the Block 57 property as a cash cow for other transactions. The Whitings repeatedly mortgaged part or all of that property, raising money to invest in other real estate.[55]

The brothel at 243 south Main Street was the heart of Emma's business. For thirty years she maintained ownership and she or women to whom she leased it ran the brothel almost continuously.[56] Emma gave up personal management sometime after 1887 (perhaps in conjunction with her 1888 marriage), but she and Charles continued to live there until at least 1898.[57] Emma resumed personal management in the mid-1890s, perhaps because she needed more income; by 1900, Ida Walker was running the house and the Whitings had moved elsewhere.[58]

Emma DeMarr Whiting was the dynamic financial partner in her marriage. Her name nearly always appears before Charles's in property records, and she continued to conduct extensive business in her name alone.[59] Emma left the brothel business entirely and reaped a financial windfall in 1909, selling all of her Block 57 property for $120,000 to William Montague Ferry (W. Mont Ferry), a prominent mining operator and future Salt Lake City mayor, and his wife Ednah. The Ferrys financed the purchase with an $80,000 mortgage from Emma Whiting.[60]

Within two weeks after purchase, however, the Ferrys conveyed the property via special warranty deeds at the same price to two banks.[61] Why W. Mont Ferry transferred ownership of this valuable property so quickly is not clear. It is possible (but unlikely, given 243 south Main's long history) that he did not realize he was buying a brothel, and when that realization came, moved to distance himself from it. The political context suggests a related explanation. In autumn 1909, Ferry was an American Party candidate for reelection to the city council and a member of the police and prison committee. The *Salt Lake Herald-Republican,* a bitter opponent of the Americans, attacked the party for sponsoring the Stockade. The newspaper charged that the Americans were illegally registering "women of the under world" and that "a piano player in a disorderly house at the rear of 243 Main street" had been fraudulently chosen an election judge. Ferry may have feared the political fallout from public knowledge of his ownership of that prominent brothel. Ferry won reelection ten days after he conveyed the Block 57 property; by 1915, he was mayor. Among his more controversial policies as mayor was support for regulated prostitution.[62]

Women continued to sell sex at 243 south Main until at least November 1910, one year after Ferry transferred the property. When the police raided the house in February 1911, they reported finding it empty, and the Sanborn map for 1911 labels the building "vacant." Competition from the Stockade, combined with police harassment of brothels located outside the restricted district, may have contributed to its abandonment.[63]

By the time of her death in 1919, Emma DeMarr Whiting had amassed a substantial fortune. She left Charles the bulk of her estate of about $145,000, nearly all in securities (more than $1,500,000 in 2000 dollars); at Charles' death in 1928, he left an estate worth about $231,000. Any residual family tension from the legal wrangling over 243 south Main had apparently eased by the time Emma executed her will in 1914. The childless Emma left $5,000 to her sister Christina and another $5,000 to her brother, along with $3,000 to each of her brother's three children. She had less close ties with her family in Sweden; her sister there, whose married name she apparently mistook, was only to receive $3,000.[64]

Sadie Noble was another Salt Lake City woman known to have made the transition from brothel prostitute to parlor house owner/operator. She was born Susan Norton on 19 November 1854 in Boston.[65] "Saddie Noble" worked as a prostitute in another woman's Salt Lake brothel in 1880. By 1882 she ran her own house, apparently at 137 south West Temple Street in Block 69 (one block west of Commercial Street). Noble closed that house after a police crackdown in May 1886; her employees and piano player were said to be leaving for Butte, Montana.[66]

Sadie Noble traveled east about this time, apparently for personal reasons. At some point in the 1880s she married John Finley Free, a saloonkeeper and ex-Mormon whom she had known since at least 1883. She gave birth to a daughter in Clinton, Iowa, in July 1887. By December 1887, the Frees were back in Salt Lake City.[67] They embarked on a flurry of real estate dealings. "Susie Free," as she now called herself, sold her Block 69 property in 1889, most of it (including 137 south West Temple) to *Tribune* owner/publisher Patrick H. Lannan for $33,500. She also extended Lannan a mortgage for $13,500. The Frees then bought and sold a number of other properties throughout the city.[68]

Like Emma DeMarr Whiting, Susie Free retreated from daily brothel operations, although she continued to own buildings used for prostitution. In March 1892, she leased a brothel on South Temple Street to Jessie Blake, who had worked at 243 south Main and who had since become a well-known madam. In December Blake fled the city, reportedly owing "several moneylenders . . . in the neighborhood of four or five thousand dollars." She probably owed Susie Free money, as "the house which she run [*sic*] is said to be now run by its owner, who used to be known among the sporting fraternity as Sadie Noble."[69]

The Frees suffered financial reverses in the early 1890s that forced them to sell several lots for back taxes. Both Emma DeMarr Whiting and Susie Free may have been hurt by the general business panic that began in 1893. The depression hit Utah particularly hard because of its dependency on outside markets for its agricultural and mineral products, and that undoubtedly hurt the prostitution business as well; with unemployment hovering at perhaps 25 percent, customers had less disposable income.[70]

The ripple effects from the panic lasted through the decade and may well have disrupted the two madams' finances. Emma Whiting and Susie Free probably resumed management of their brothels to earn and save more money. Susie Free also mortgaged her brothel furniture five times in just over two years, raising over three thousand dollars overall, but she was forced to watch its sale for just $137.50 in 1895 when she was unable to repay a loan from the Deseret Savings Bank.[71] That sale marked the end of "Sadie Noble's" career, and indeed her existence apart from "Susie Free," who lived another half-century. Kate Flint apparently offered the Frees temporary refuge at her home on Social Hall Avenue.[72]

Kate Flint, Emma DeMarr, Sadie Noble, and other women laid the foundations for a long-lived prostitution district. Flint's and DeMarr's houses stood less than 150 feet apart in the interior of Block 57. Others established brothels and cribs nearby where women sold sex for years. Victoria Place (or Alley) ran east-west through Block 57 from State Street to Main (by 1911, only the eastern end was still open). Twelve feet wide at its State Street entrance, then opening to about twenty-five feet, the alley allowed discreet access to the brothels and dwellings in the interior.[73] A row of adobe tenements on the north side of Victoria Place (known as "Pugsley's Row" for its longtime owner, Philip Pugsley) midway between Flint's and DeMarr's houses, contained crib women as early as September 1885.[74] Pugsley sold the property in 1899 to Joseph J. Snell, and women continued to rent cribs there until at least 1916.[75] Various women operated a brothel on the south side of the alley at no. 7 Victoria Place, less than ten feet from 243 south Main, from 1897 until at least mid-1912.[76] Another major brothel stood some twenty-five feet northeast of Pugsley's Row and operated from at least 1892 through 1911. Customers reached this house, which bore the address 222 south State Street ("The Three Deuces"), from State Street via a short, six-foot-wide alley.[77]

Taken together, this handful of buildings and the women who worked in them constituted a prostitution district—localized, invisible from outside the block, accessible only by narrow alleys, but in the heart of downtown—which thrived for decades. While prostitutes also worked on Commercial Street, Franklin Avenue, and other nearby locales, their activities on those streets brought more scrutiny, economic competition, and subsequent turnover. The Block 57 buildings were the most permanent part of Salt Lake City's demimonde. Their owners equipped, furnished, and sometimes built them for prostitution; and the authorities knew and approved of them. These buildings served as nodal points in a network through which scores of madams and hundreds of women passed, some staying to work only for days or weeks, others staying for years, still others leaving but returning later. While some madams owned their brothels outright, they were the exception; most madams rented or leased their properties from others. A few examples illustrate this durable network and provide evidence of both the lucrative potential of the brothel business for some and its transient nature for most.

At least one would-be madam seems to have resorted to fraud upon a dying woman in an attempt to acquire her brothel. Sometime before November 1891, Emma DeMarr leased no. 243 south Main Street to Minnie Barton. Barton fell mortally ill, setting off a complex and sordid battle over her possessions. According to the *Tribune,* she summoned her friend Martha Turner to her deathbed since "more than once [Barton had] abandoned the gilded halls of dissolution and vice, and, raising her eyes upward, declared that henceforth she would lead a pure life. . . . she would go to the house of Martha Turner in Chicago, and remain there until the weakness of the flesh overcame her good resolutions."[78] Turner claimed that about ninety minutes before Barton died on 20 February 1892, the madam signed over to Turner bank accounts, securities, furnishings, and personal belongings worth over twelve thousand dollars, as well as her leasehold interest in the brothel and its "piano, groceries, provisions, wines, [and] liquors." Turner swore that Barton had assigned her the property in return for $1,000 and the nursing she had lavished on her dying friend.[79]

Subsequent events cast serious doubt upon this melodramatic tale. Since Barton died intestate, her estate's administrator challenged the transfer, claiming that she was much too ill to voluntarily assign her property to Turner. Martha Turner won in the Third District court, but the Utah Supreme Court overturned the decision, finding that she and another woman, Helen Smith, had used "crafty, avaricious, and selfish" means to coerce Barton into signing over her belongings.[80]

Helen Smith, better known as "Helen Blazes," was also present at Barton's deathbed, and Barton's death may have launched her long career as a Salt Lake City madam. On 18 April 1892 (less than two months after Barton's death) Helen Smith borrowed $1,500 from Martha Turner, secured by the furniture at no. 243 south Main, which Smith had purchased. Helen Blazes ran the brothel for the next two years.[81] Turner may also have tried to run a brothel after Barton's death; the Third District grand jury indicted "Mattie Turner" on 21 May 1892 for keeping a house of prostitution at an unspecified location. The case was dismissed, probably because Turner had already left town.[82] Helen Blazes, however, managed a series of brothels within the Salt Lake City network for years and became one of the city's best-known madams. She moved to Franklin Avenue in 1894 when the police forced all prostitutes there (by unlikely coincidence to no. 243). In 1895, Blazes took over Sadie Noble's former house at 166½ west South Temple. By 1897, she was firmly established at 7 Victoria Place and ran that house until 1908.[83]

Other women also rotated throughout the network. Ida Walker kept houses in Salt Lake City from 1891 through at least 1906; she successively managed 22 Commercial Street, 222 south State Street, 243 south Main Street, and 222 south State again.[84] While little direct evidence remains to explain why madams moved so often, some plausible reasons can be advanced. Police or citizen pressure might force women to change venues or leave town. Retirement or death created openings, as we have seen. Some madams may have wanted a larger or smaller and less expensive house. When one madam left a desirable location, another could "move up" from a less desirable house. Brothel owners like Emma DeMarr wanted experienced women managing their profitable houses. Survival, let alone success, in the network required women to have entrepreneurial know-how, political and diplomatic skills, and an ability to adjust to changing circumstances.

Some madams neither retired with a small fortune like DeMarr, nor settled their debts and retired like Sadie Noble, nor operated successfully for years like Helen Blazes. Dozens of other women operated on the edge of disaster. Jessie Blake fled the city in 1892, leaving behind unsatisfied creditors.[85] Essie Watkins suffered many setbacks—legal, personal, and financial—that resulted in her hasty departure. Though she was reportedly once the madam of "the leading flash house of Dallas," scandal and legal bills forced Watkins to leave that city for Salt Lake, where she was running a house by mid-1893. When one of her women killed a customer in 1894, her brothel came under heightened police scrutiny. Watkins moved to Franklin Avenue with other women in 1894, but she was forced off that street with the others at the end of the year. In early 1895, she moved into the *Salt Lake Times* building on Commercial Street, but the Brigham Young Trust Company and the police almost immediately forced her out.[86]

Watkins found anchorage in Kate Flint's old house at 44-46 east Second South, but trouble arose there too. The multiple moves, which probably resulted in the loss of chattel property, and constant legal pressure were undoubtedly expensive. Watkins mortgaged various items seven times in two years, ranging from her elaborate furnishings to her "Cleveland 'Ladys' Bicycle," and at one point borrowed eight hundred dollars from her mother. In October 1897, she was convicted of obtaining money under false pretenses for claiming the property of one of her prostitutes. The police raided her Commercial Street brothel in December, claiming that she had not paid her regular fine for three months. Before the month ended, Watkins had left the city. Henry Dinwoodey, a furniture dealer to whom she owed over one thousand dollars, reportedly claimed her property.[87]

While the madam-prostitute system obtained in the best-known houses, men were arrested occasionally for keeping houses of prostitution. These were often husbands accused of forcing or allowing their wives to prostitute themselves. Other men owned or managed rooming houses or hotels. This class of arrest was particularly common following police crackdowns on the regular houses that forced prostitutes to find other lodgings and especially after the Stockade closed in 1911. Men caught with known prostitutes were sometimes charged with keeping. At least two men, Philip Pugsley and Joseph J. Snell, owned and rented cribs for years. Throughout this time period, however, women largely controlled the prostitution business in Salt Lake City.[88]

Madams transacted extensive business with a broad spectrum of bankers and businessmen, who thus developed a direct interest in the success of their operations. Bergen DeMott, a farmer, and Samuel A. Merritt, an attorney (and future city attorney), both loaned money to Kate Flint.[89] Henry Dinwoodey

was a Mormon and a member of the city council committee that recommended settling Flint's case against Jeter Clinton in 1877. He loaned her $500 three
years later.[90] Susie Free was particularly involved with the city's elite, Mormon,
Jew, and gentile. Many of these transactions had nothing directly to do with
Free's brothel properties, and it is possible that some people she dealt with
did not know she was a madam, especially since most transactions occurred
during her hiatus from active management. Free conducted business with
William H. King, an LDS attorney and future U.S. congressman and senator;
Frederick H. Auerbach, a prominent Jewish merchant; Louis C. Karrick, a
gentile banker and later member of the city council's police committee; and
William S. McCornick, owner of the city's largest independent bank and the
first gentile on the city council.[91] A more common way that women raised
money was to mortgage their furniture. The Freed Furniture and Carpet
Company executed dozens of chattel mortgages with madams, allowing them
to use furniture, kitchen utensils, linens, glassware, paintings, and other items
while paying for them on time.[92] These transactions indicate that while society might condemn prostitution, many citizens were willing to conduct business with prostitutes.

Although madams left behind far more records than prostitutes did, many
details of their lives remain shadowy, and the information that can be found
is often contradictory. Many basic facts about their lives such as given names,
marital status, birthplace, and date of birth cannot easily be determined. Much
of this confusion was deliberate, as madams sought to protect their identities,
keep families ignorant of their profession, or hamper authorities in their prosecutions. While some women blurred their pasts, they also worked to construct
alternate identities for the brothel and beyond. Many madams used two names,
one for brothel business and the other for legitimate life. Thus in 1885, "Mrs.
D. F. Connelly, wid[ow]" lived at 46 east Second South, while "Mrs. Kate Flint,
wid." lived at no. 44.[93] "Helen Blazes" and "Helen Smith" (once "Mrs. Helen
Blazes Smith") both lived at 7 Victoria Court.[94] One woman apparently created different birthdates and birthplaces and current addresses for her two
identities, "Catherine Fairchild" and "Kitty Hicks."[95] Some madams used their
pseudonyms for legitimate business; "Sadie Noble" transacted real estate deals
involving thousands of dollars.[96] Dora B. Topham (whose real name is uncertain) evidently called herself or was variously known by at least five names
during her life. Two of her identities became well known: Topham and her alter
ego, Belle London, both became notorious. Topham/London evidently wanted
to leave her infamy behind; by 1920, she had become "Maxine Rose."[97]

Emma DeMarr engineered perhaps the most complete makeover. Her sister swore in 1886 that Emma's maiden name was Turnross, and her brother

filed a deposition under that surname; but Emma swore she was born De-Marr (and won the case).[98] She may have been establishing a legal basis for an alternate identity while laying the economic foundation for her future. From 1880 (and perhaps earlier) until her marriage in 1888, she was "Emma DeMarr." Bits of evidence suggest she may also have successfully left behind her notorious past and attained respectability. In 1890, a grand jury indicted her for keeping a house of prostitution at 243 south Main, but the case was dismissed because DeMarr had leased the brothel to another woman. The prosecutor cited the "defense of landlord" provision that protected owners of property from prosecution.[99] In 1893, a prostitute denied a floor seat in the Salt Lake Theater complained that "the Madame of two forty three" was sitting in the parquette. That brothel belonged to Emma Whiting but was then being managed by Helen Blazes. Was the woman in the theater Blazes or Whiting? A year later, the *Deseret News* reported a small fire at 243 south Main, which it described as "formerly occupied as a 'sporting' house"; now "Mrs. Emma Whiting" owned it.[100] Had Emma Whiting so successfully left Emma DeMarr behind that she fooled the district attorney, theater ushers, and a reporter? The former madam sought to memorialize permanently her rise to respectability, leaving money in her will for a handsome monument at her gravesite.[101]

The women who actually performed sex for hire within the brothels were the "inmates" (the police and newspaper term) or simply the "girls" (generally used among themselves and their madams). Each brothel housed between two and twelve women; most commonly four to seven.[102] The women who worked and lived in the fancier "parlor houses" were at the top of the hierarchy, although they lived a far more tenuous existence than their madams and were much less persistent over time. Like many madams, prostitutes moved from house to house and city to city to escape personal conflicts or legal harassment.

The women in the lower classes were even more transient. Their lives and careers pose problems for a historian, as they are difficult to identify in directories, property, or probate records. Just as with madams, much of this obscurity was deliberate, as mobility and anonymity were useful tools for prostitutes; some of it was a function of the brevity of their prostitution careers. The sources in which they do occasionally appear, especially newspapers and police and court records, can give the researcher a skewed picture. Prostitutes appear in those sources almost solely for criminal or other negative reasons: as subjects of arrests; as perpetrators or victims of crime or violence; or as victims of suicide, overdose, or other grisly deaths. While these harsh possibilities were real enough, the nature of the sources almost precludes knowledge of any positive outcome. For example, a woman leaving the brothel for a respectable job or marriage would leave little trace.[103] The quality of these sources is also dubious; police court reporters or desk sergeants often showed little interest in accurately recording names (especially since prostitutes often used pseudonyms), ages, nationalities, or the like.[104]

With these caveats in mind, some information about these women can be tentatively advanced. The women of the well-known brothels that can be identified in the census were young, averaging twenty-three years of age, and all identified themselves as white. Nearly two-thirds of them were native born of native parents; of those foreign born or with one or both foreign parents, nearly all had Canadian or western European backgrounds. About one in ten was married, and about one in eight had children.[105]

A few women are known to have made the transition from prostitute to madam, including Emma DeMarr, Sadie Noble and Jessie Blake; most madams probably began as prostitutes. "Housekeeper" was an intermediate step between prostitute and madam. A madam might hire a trusted woman to manage the house when she was absent or wanted to leave day-to-day management.[106] May Hart moved up from a virtually penniless prostitute in Emma Davis's house in 1886 to a housekeeper in Ogden in 1889. By 1891, she was running a brothel on Franklin Avenue.[107]

Some women probably left the brothel through marriage. Stella Holmes, the "star boarder at Hattie Wilson's," was reportedly courted by a "wealthy miner" who plied her with "frequent and heavy orders of champagne, moonlight drives and the usual etceteras." The couple married in Ogden, but a deputy marshal "disturbed the pleasures of the honeymoon by ruthlessly seizing the fair Stella's trunk on a claim for $56, which Mary Miller, a colored woman and a housekeeper at one time in the employ of Hattie Wilson, claims is due her for money advanced and services rendered."[108]

Race and ethnicity of both the prostitutes and their customers played a key role in perceived status. The prostitution hierarchy reproduced the racial biases of society. The fancier parlor houses were all-white and most likely served an all-white clientele. Nonwhite prostitutes nearly always appear in lower-status houses. A handful of Chinese prostitutes were arrested in the 1870s, but apparently none after the 1890s.[109] African American women were arrested for prostitution throughout the period under study.[110] Japanese women began appearing in the 1890s, always within all-Japanese houses.[111] The great majority of women arrested as prostitutes, however, were white. Mixed-race houses were rare, although Essie Watkins, a white madam, did employ at least two black women in her Franklin Avenue brothel in 1894.[112] That unusual circumstance may have resulted from the forced move to Franklin; some white madams may have hired women they otherwise would not, and some African American prostitutes were already working on that street. Crossing the color line could cause a white parlor worker to lose caste; accusations of such behavior could lead to violence. Bessie Johnson, who worked in the plush "Palace," provoked a fight when she taunted "Miss Midget" (née May Brown), a prostitute in another brothel, for working in a house "frequented by negroes and Chinamen."[113]

Drugs caused some women's slide down the status hierarchy. Opiate use, a common habit in the late nineteenth century (made easier by the proximity of Chinatown), could be a prostitute's downfall.[114] One madam reportedly fired two women because "they were wont to seek the seclusion of the joint of the celestial washee-washee man and engage in hitting the pipe."[115]

Below parlor house women were saloon or dance hall workers, crib workers, and streetwalkers. These categories were fluid; an individual woman might, at various times, work in more than one venue. The city's saloons provided ready customers. Women in parlor houses often had ties of economics and affection with saloon denizens. At least two prominent madams married saloonkeepers, and parlor houses shared neighborhoods, buildings, and patrons with saloons. Saloonkeepers often put up bond money for prostitutes and their customers.[116] The saloon itself was in theory an all-male province. Respectable women did not frequent saloons, and parlor house women probably did not need to, as customers came to them and could get alcohol in brothels. The saloons' all-male status was established in law. Women could not be employed in them as musicians or performers; in 1891, the city barred women altogether after 9 P.M., and in 1901, when saloons could operate around the clock, women were barred between 7 P.M. and 7 A.M.[117]

Despite this official prohibition, prostitutes often solicited men in saloons. One paper complained of a place where "one or more fallen females, representing the lowest order of their class, conduct their calling on the premises, dividing the financial proceeds with the saloon."[118] Women were arrested frequently for such activity.[119] Some saloons featured partitions or curtained booths where women could solicit or perform sex acts.[120] Saloonkeepers were sometimes accused of encouraging or coercing women into prostitution.[121] A shorter-lived venue was the variety theater on Franklin Avenue in the early 1890s, where women sold drinks and sometimes sex.[122]

The women who worked in cribs were perceived to stand well below parlor house prostitutes in the status hierarchy. One paper claimed the residents of Victoria Alley cribs were so degraded as to be unsexed: "Having the forms and faces of women, they have no other attributes of their sex."[123] Given their work, this may seem a strange remark, but this writer obviously means that crib women did not display gender-appropriate behavior. As employed by Salt Lake City newspapers, "crib" was an elastic term: it could refer to anything from a single tiny room used only for prostitution to a small house in a minority neighborhood.[124] The simple presence of foreign-born or women of color may have led the newspapers and police to label a locale a "crib." Some so-called crib workers lived and worked in dwelling houses that resembled humbler versions of the parlor house, with a designated keeper and two to four prostitutes. Many of these smaller brothels were located on Franklin Avenue, particularly in the dwelling houses at its southern end. Examples included the houses operated by African American, Japanese, and French women on Franklin in the 1890s and 1900s, each housing two or three women. Some of these contained prostitutes of various races; Nellie Davis, an African American keeper on Franklin, apparently had some white inmates.[125] Other houses apparently had no designated "keeper"; those arrested at these locations were lumped together as "inmates."[126]

Some prostitutes may have worked alone by preference, since it meant greater independence than the parlor house: they could accept customers when they wanted or needed to, and they could keep all their earnings instead of sharing with a madam. Women who solicited on the streets earned the label "streetwalker" or "night walker."[127] The blatantly public and unregulated nature of such women's actions was particularly obnoxious to citizens and the municipal authorities. Those identified as streetwalkers often suffered from alcohol or drug abuse, and they evoked responses of pity, contempt, and fear in the newspapers. The death of a white streetwalker elicited the comment that "she has for years been regarded as the lowest of the degraded class, of which she was a member."[128] Perhaps even lower were the women who sometimes operated on the edges of Fort Douglas. One soldier claimed that "women, who are known as sage-hens, are in the habit of frequenting the brush on the reservation near the quarters of the men . . . one has utilized an abandoned pigpen for a bedroom for weeks at a time."[129]

Gender, race, and class biases in contemporary society make the men who patronized prostitutes even more difficult to identify than the prostitutes themselves. Because women were held largely responsible for prostitution, police seldom arrested customers and identified them even less often. Men of color, those who patronized crib workers, and those accused of other crimes were arrested but often identified in arrest records or newspapers only as "John Doe." These men may have refused to give names, but it is likelier that the police or newspapers were protecting them. Those who were named were invariably working class: miners, railroad workers, laborers, saloon employees, and the like. Men of all classes undoubtedly patronized prostitutes; working-class men would have had great difficulty affording parlor house women. The police particularly targeted and newspapers named black men caught with white prostitutes.[130] White men who patronized black prostitutes, on the other hand, almost never had their identities revealed.[131]

One possible customer who left a brief record was John Held, Jr., a Salt Lake native who went on to fame as a Jazz Age cartoonist. Held recalled with relish (but without self-revelatory details) his youthful visits to the brothels of Ada Wilson, Helen Blazes, Belle London, and others, which were furnished with "mirrored ballrooms and red plush." Held claimed he learned the song "Frankie and Johnny," a version of which he later illustrated, from the "colored piano player" in Helen Blazes's house.[132]

Evidence of other customers is rare. Higher-status customers obviously existed, but they received preferential treatment from the police and courts. The diary of Abraham H. Cannon, an LDS Apostle and son of George Q. Cannon, provides a glimpse of a few brothel patrons. On 18 March 1885, Abraham learned that his half-brother Frank J. Cannon "was in Kate Flint's establishment and that his associations with that notorious prostitute are well know[n] to several police officers."[133] Frank, twenty-six years old at the time and married (monogamously), continued to carouse in saloons and brothels for at least the next four years, interspersed with periods of repentance and sobriety. Abraham protected him from scandal and apparently settled an embarrassing debt Frank owed Kate Flint.[134] The all-Mormon city police also protected Frank, since he was evidently never arrested for a prostitution-related offense.[135] Abraham also noted that three lesser-known Mormons pardoned in 1886 from the territorial penitentiary immediately got drunk and visited a brothel, where one assaulted a prostitute.[136]

Relations among women in the brothel district were complex and often troubled. Prostitutes and madams may have felt a sense of "sisterhood," as Ruth Rosen terms it. She suggests that these women felt a kinship based on their participation in an illegal but lucrative business that violated and mocked conventional social mores. They shared a subculture with its own rules, conventions, and traditions, and sometimes looked out for and protected one another. But their experiences were almost certainly more often bleak than positive.[137]

Parlor house women worked, ate, and slept in the larger houses. Several brothels employed servants and cooks, often Chinese men or black men and women. Prostitutes paid their madam a fixed weekly sum for board ($16 a week in one house in 1886). Many houses also employed musicians, usually piano players ("professors"), at least one of whom was married to a prostitute and resided in the house with her.[138] Other people sometimes lived in the houses. Emma and Charles Whiting, for example, lived at 243 south Main Street while Minnie Barton actively managed the brothel.[139] Some of the larger brothels may have kept rooms for husbands, lovers, or other roomers. The "Big V" on Plum Alley, for instance, had six bedrooms downstairs and ten upstairs, but no more than seven women at a time were arrested from that house.[140]

The larger houses' locations were well known, if discreet. Madams often listed their addresses in city directories, but nothing overtly identified these addresses as brothels and they did not appear in the business listings. Some madams, however, were bolder than others. Ada Wilson and Helen Blazes had elaborate business cards made up to advertise their establishments.[141] In 1901, some Commercial Street brothels featured "flaring electric signs." Wilson, a flamboyant character who seemed to enjoy flaunting her occupation, paraded the streets in a dogcart drawn by a Hackney pony; by 1907, she traveled by chauffeur-driven automobile. She listed her brothel, "The Palace," in bold-face in the 1899 city directory (with no further identification). Both Elsie St. Omar and Ada Wilson sent engraved invitations to scores of prominent citizens upon the "grand openings" of their brothels. Wilson sent invitations to the city attorney and high officials of the LDS Church.[142]

Parlor houses were elaborately furnished and decorated. Several houses received guests in two parlors, decorated with thick carpets, tapestries, oil paintings, and silk-covered sofas and chairs (and many spittoons). Gussie Foote kept a "Light Green Parrot named Judah with [a] yellow head."[143] The professor or one of the women might play or sing at a customer's request.[144] Cigars and alcohol were staples; Helen Blazes's high-end houses served wine only, while the majority offered beer and whiskey, although many had no liquor license.[145] At least one brothel boasted a ballroom. A typical bedroom in one of Sadie Noble's brothels contained a black walnut bedstead, dressing case, wash stand, and wardrobe; a patent rocker; an oak chair; a towel rack; a zinc heating stove; a window shade with a pair of lace curtains and black curtain pole; a brussels carpet; a seven-piece toilet set; a box spring mattress, two feather pillows, one pair of blankets, and one quilt.[146]

A reporter purported to describe a parlor house visit in 1916:

> Into the parlor one is ushered with all due ceremony, everyone from the colored attendant to the landlady beaming graciousness.
> The gay tones of "raggy step" greet one's ears as the nickel-a-tune piano does its duty. Perhaps a "professor" conducts the orchestra and pounds out a melody. . . .
> Cleo approaches patronizingly and queries as to how her "dear" is tonight and if he won't join her in a bottle of beer.

How much? One dollar—and the sight of a dollar automatically removed all liquor restrictions and a bottle of the amber liquid immediately made its appearance and two tiny glasses clinked while the visitor held "Gladys" on his lap and drinks to her health and she to his.

And with each drink the siren grows bolder and the visitor more gullible.

And then the dance sets up and if the visitor be a disciple of Terpsichore he whirls his companion around the floor a dozen times or so, until the tune ends and both conveniently flop down into the soft lap of a lounge, and Cleo nestles close to her "man," while a display of lingerie and hose and ankles stirs the blood. . . .

And as the display of lingerie and ankles, amorous caresses and the liquor get in their work, she nestles still closer and whispers an invitation. . . .

A moment later the room is minus two occupants.[147]

The opulence of the larger brothels testifies to the profits they generated. Madams earned money from liquor sales, plus room and board payments and often a percentage of each prostitute's takings. Prostitutes, however, shared little in this generous income. The records are virtually silent about some basic economic realities of the Salt Lake City brothel business: for instance, prices charged for sexual services, the number of customers that each woman might have in the course of a night or week, and the percentage of income that went to the madam. Parlor houses in eastern cities charged five to ten dollars per customer, while "middle-class" houses might charge one dollar, and women in shacks or cribs fifty cents. While parlor house women might only entertain one customer, the lower-class prostitute could see as many as thirty men per night. Five dollars was a standard price for a night of sex in western brothels in the late nineteenth century.[148] Whatever the prices charged, it is almost certain that most brothel women were not earning substantial sums. Many owned little more than the contents of a trunk and had to rely upon their madams for bail or money to purchase food or clothing. Women sometimes supplemented their meager earnings with theft. A Victoria Alley prostitute named Tillie Williams, for example, was twice convicted of robbery, one time of her Chinese laundryman and the other of a Mexican customer.[149] Madeline Mortimer was accused of stealing $92 in cash and a $450 check (not endorsed) from a customer, but only served fifty days for keeping a house of prostitution.[150] A "panel worker" could hide behind a removable panel in a closet or wall and rob a customer after he fell asleep or passed out. Estella King was accused of panel work, but the grand jury failed to indict her, probably because the customer refused to testify.[151] The frequency of theft of clothing, jewelry, and other items of value further testifies to prostitutes' general impoverishment.[152]

Crib workers lived an even more precarious existence far different from the posh surroundings of the parlor houses. A murder in 1902 offered a rare glimpse into Joseph J. Snell's cribs: "He harbors at the present time fifteen women of the town. . . . Each of these women occupies one room, the furniture of which, consisting of a small stove, a washstand, a chair and a bed, are furnished by Joseph J. Snell. The tenant furnishes her own bedclothing and other linen, and also light and heat. There are no sanitary arrangements in the buildings and no conveniences." One woman detailed her expenses:

> We have to make at least $5 a day, but that isn't so hard to do. If a girl can't make that much money she had better get off the row, for Snell don't want her. . . .
> To make any kind of a decent living, I have to take in more than $100 a month. Snell takes $60 for rent, the city takes $10 for fine, coal and light cost me from $8 to $10, board is $20, and then I have to dress myself and have spending money for cigarettes and beer.[153]

If fifty cents per crib customer is an accurate figure, this woman had to service at least ten men each day, six days a week, to earn her "decent living."

Parlor house madams, dependent upon their women to generate income, provided a greater degree of protection and assistance than crib owners. Madams were usually willing and eager to post bail or appearance money to keep prostitutes out of jail.[154] Emma DeMarr even "went out to try and rustle up the amount necessary" to bail another housekeeper out of jail.[155] Prostitutes themselves probably felt a similar sense of mutual dependence, and sometimes friendship. Of sixty-three women arrested in a mass raid in 1891, four could not afford to pay their fines; other women contributed to free them.[156] A number of tearful prostitutes brought flowers to one woman's funeral.[157] Ada Wilson, the keeper of the "Palace," even adopted the four-month-old baby of one of her women.[158]

Relations among madams and prostitutes were not always close, of course. Disputes sometimes led women to move from one house to another. When two of Emma DeMarr's employees for whom she had filed bonds failed to pay their court costs, they were "delivered up by the fickle Emma to the police."[159] Helen Blazes claimed to have paid dressmaking and boarding bills totaling $400 for two women, and she attached a diamond and a trunk for the return of the money and had the women arrested. One of the women left Blazes's house shortly afterwards, perhaps as a result of this dispute, and moved to another brothel; by July 1899, she was working in a third house.[160] When May Hart could not pay her $50 fine, her husband convinced Emma DeMarr to pay it—with the understanding that Hart would move to DeMarr's house. DeMarr also loaned Hart $34 and gave her two weeks' free board. The madam's altruism had its limits, though: Hart charged that De-Marr sold her trunk, wardrobe, and canary bird to another woman, but De-Marr won the ensuing lawsuit.[161] Ruth Rosen concludes that a madam could be "both friend *and* exploiter of her 'girls.'"[162]

Disputes were not always settled in the courtroom. Prostitutes frequently faced violence at the hands of customers, husbands, lovers, madams, and each other. Men sometimes punched, kicked, or stabbed prostitutes.[163] Drunken or disgruntled customers broke furniture or ripped up upholstery, carpets, and curtains with knives; one man completed his destruction of Hattie Wilson's parlor by "acting the beast" (presumably, urinating or defecating).[164] Minerva Reeves tried to shoot her sister Juanita, a fellow inmate of 243 south Main Street, allegedly because Juanita refused to entertain a male friend of Minerva's.[165] Essie Watkins led another woman and two customers in an early morning attack on the women of Ida Walker's "Three Deuces" for unknown reasons.[166] When Bessie Johnson taunted Miss Midget about black and Chinese patrons, Midget and a customer beat Johnson so badly that she was hospitalized.[167] Lena Carter, who worked in several Salt Lake brothels, was murdered by her husband, who then killed himself.[168] Madams were not immune. When Edna Prescott ordered a drunk out of her brothel, he knocked her unconscious with a rock.[169] Emma DeMarr Whiting claimed that her drunken husband Charles beat her severely and called her "a bitch, a damned whore and [oddly] a damned son of a bitch."[170] Sometimes brothel patrons experienced violence. Nellie Ogden stabbed to death Charles "Kid" Mason after he beat and kicked her.[171] Cora Thomas shot her soldier husband to death when she found him at breakfast with two suspected prostitutes.[172]

Physical violence was perhaps the worst hardship that prostitutes faced, although not the only one. Women faced many consequences of their sexual activity; Ada Wilson's adopted child demonstrates one. Nineteenth-century women had a range of contraceptive technology of questionable efficacy to choose from, including rubber condoms, womb veils, and douches. Folklore has always maintained that professional sex workers had special knowledge of and access to contraceptive methods.[173] What Salt Lake prostitutes actually used is a matter of speculation, since the records are silent. Some may have used commonly available patent medicines containing traditional emmenagogues, such as pennyroyal.[174] When these methods failed, doubtless some women turned to abortionists.[175]

Sex workers also faced the danger of venereal diseases, especially syphilis and gonorrhea, for which treatments of the time were largely ineffective.[176] Infection rates for prostitutes ran as high as 70 to 80 percent in some cities, and Salt Lake prostitutes were certainly not immune. The body of a streetwalker who died in police custody reportedly "was a most repulsive sight, as it was marked with syphilitic sores which made the undertaker's men handle it very gingerly."[177] Dora Topham, the Stockade manager, employed a doctor to examine prospective prostitutes for infection before hiring them. She also operated a "hospital" for her employees, both in Ogden and in Salt Lake City.[178]

Prostitutes often sought temporary escape from the violence and degradation of their lives in alcohol and drugs. Alcohol was easily available in nearby saloons and in their own brothels, cribs, and rented rooms. All classes of prostitutes used alcohol, and hundreds of them were arrested for drunkenness over the years. The lower classes were especially reported to indulge in other substances. The "morphine fiend" was a stock police court character.[179] Two well-known streetwalkers were accused of "stealing furniture from their lodgings with which to buy opium, whisky, cocaine and tobacco."[180] Busts of opium houses frequently yielded prostitutes among those indulging.[181] A raid on Victoria Alley found "morphine, cocaine and opium fiends, as well as inveterate drunkards" of both sexes.[182] Nellie Conley, one of the women who stole from Helen Blazes, was committed to the state insane asylum, reportedly as a result of morphine use.[183]

Drugs could also provide a permanent solution to a prostitute's misery. From 1885 to 1908, at least nine Salt Lake City prostitutes killed themselves, while twenty other women attempted suicide, including two madams. Women most commonly chose morphine, easily obtained from drugstores; others used chloroform, laudanum, or carbolic acid. The papers claimed that shame over a misspent life or unrequited love caused most prostitute suicides.[184] One madam, however, reportedly tried to kill herself when relatives in the East discovered her profession and took custody of her child.[185] Some of these "suicides" may have been accidental. A woman may have attempted to induce miscarriage with opiates and taken too large a dose.[186]

The women who created, lived, worked, and sometimes died in the prostitution district did not do so in isolation. They had to negotiate the terms of their work with the municipal authorities, elected officials and especially the police. They also had to cope with citizen pressure and respond to reform efforts. Prostitutes and authorities came to a mutual accommodation that allowed women to sell sex while the authorities defined them as criminals and maintained a great deal of control over their activities.

Notes

1. See Marilyn Reed Travis, "Social Stratification and the Dissolution of the City of Zion in Salt Lake City," esp. chap. 4, "The Commercialization of Zion"; Alexander and Allen,

Mormons and Gentiles, pp. 87–91; and Boyce, "Historical Geography of Greater Salt Lake City," pp. 52–82. On the "commercial city," see Warner, *Urban Wilderness,* pp. 88–91.

2. "Fire Insurance Map of Salt Lake City, 1884," sheet 8. On the persistence of prostitution on Regent Street, see McCormick, "Red Lights in Zion," p. 181.

3. "Fire Insurance Map of Salt Lake City, 1884," sheet 13.

4. See, for example, buildings labeled "F.B." ("female boarding") on Commercial Street; "Fire Insurance Map of Salt Lake City, 1898," sheet 103. See also "Fire Insurance Map of Salt Lake City, 1895," sheet 41.

5. "Fire Insurance Map of Salt Lake City, 1884," sheet 14; "Fire Insurance Map of Salt Lake City, 1889," sheet 41; "Fire Insurance Map of Salt Lake City, 1898," sheet 113; "Fire Insurance Map of Salt Lake City, 1911," sheet 238.

6. On race relations at the turn of the century, see Newby, *Jim Crow's Defense,* pp. 4–15; Brown, *Strain of Violence,* pp. 151, 209, 214–18; Williamson, *Crucible of Race,* pp. 327–45; Painter, "Race and Disfranchisement," chap. in *Standing at Armageddon;* and Brands, "Plessy v. Crow," chap. in *Reckless Decade.*

7. Bringhurst, *Saints, Slaves, and Blacks,* pp. 3–14, 98, 129; Bush, "Mormonism's Negro Doctrine"; and Embry, "The LDS Church and African Americans," chap. in *Black Saints in a White Church.*

8. Gerlach, "Vengeance vs. the Law"; Gerlach, "Ogden's 'Horrible Tragedy'"; Gerlach, "Justice Denied"; and Quinn, *Mormon Hierarchy: Extensions of Power,* p. 259.

9. *Salt Lake City Herald,* 9 Apr. 1901; Coleman, "History of Blacks in Utah"; and Coleman, "Blacks in Utah History." For African Americans on Franklin, see U.S. Bureau of the Census, Thirteenth Census (1910), Salt Lake County, Enumeration District No. 144, sheets 8A and 8B. In 1870, 118 "colored" people were counted in the city; see table 22, "The Table of Sex," in U.S. Bureau of the Census, Ninth Census (1870), vol. 1: *Population and Social Statistics,* pp. 606–7. By 1890, 218 lived in the city; in 1900, 278; and 1910, 737; see table 2, "Composition and Characteristics of the Population for Cities of 25,000 or More," in U.S. Bureau of the Census, Thirteenth Census (1910), *Abstract,* p. 592.

10. See, for example, *Salt Lake City Daily Tribune,* 14 Apr. 1890; Edwin G. Straub to the editor, *Tribune,* 1 Sept. 1890; and *Herald,* 27 Mar. 1891. See also Barth, *Bitter Strength;* R. White, *"It's Your Misfortune and None of My Own,"* pp. 282–84.

11. The census counted 222 Chinese in Salt Lake City in 1890; table 17, "Population by Sex, Nativity, and Color, for Places of 2,500 Inhabitants or More," in U.S. Bureau of the Census, *Compendium of the Eleventh Census* (1890), part 1: *Population,* p. 577; and 193 in 1910; table 2, "Composition and Characteristics of the Population for Cities of 25,000 or More," in U.S. Bureau of the Census, *Thirteenth Census* (1910), *Abstract.*

12. Conley, "Pioneer Chinese of Utah,"; Liestman, "Utah's Chinatowns"; and Cheng, "Chinese." See also "Fire Insurance Map of Salt Lake City, 1884," sheet 8; "Fire Insurance Map of Salt Lake City, 1889," sheet 31; "Fire Insurance Map of Salt Lake City, 1898," sheet 103; and "Fire Insurance Map of Salt Lake City, 1911," sheet 235. For the Plum Alley brothel, see *Tribune,* 7 July 1892, 23 Jan. 1893.

13. Papanikolas and Kasai, "Japanese Life in Utah"; Kasai, "Japanese." The 1890 census lists 4 Japanese in Utah, none in Salt Lake County; table 17, "Population by Sex, Nativity, and Color, for Places of 2,500 Inhabitants or More," in U.S. Bureau of the Census, *Compendium of the Eleventh Census* (1890); in 1900, 22 were counted in Salt Lake City; in 1910, 345; and in 1920, 403; see table 7, "Indians, Chinese, and Japanese, for Counties and for

Cities of 25,000 or More," in U.S. Bureau of the Census, *Fourteenth Census* (1920), vol. 3: *Population,* p. 1033. For Japanese prostitutes, see SLCPD, "Arrest Register, 1891–94" (hereafter "Arrest Register, 1891–94"), 20 May 1891, p. 34.

14. *Herald,* 10 Dec. 1908.

15. Shumsky and Springer, "San Francisco's Zone of Prostitution"; and Rosen, *Lost Sisterhood,* p. 79.

16. *Tribune,* 2 Feb. 1895.

17. McCormick, "Red Lights in Zion," p. 181; *Tribune,* 24 Mar., 17 Nov. 1892, 14 June 1899.

18. See *Tribune,* 7 July 1892; and chap. 3.

19. *Tribune,* 15 Oct. 1900. See also Hoop, "Recollections of Fort Douglas."

20. Seligman, *Social Evil,* pp. 5–10.

21. Hobson, *Uneasy Virtue,* pp. 85–103; Rosen, *Lost Sisterhood,* pp. 137–62; Butler, *Daughters of Joy, Sisters of Misery,* p. 126; and Petrik, "Capitalists with Rooms."

22. U.S. Bureau of the Census, *Thirteenth Census* (1910), vol. 4: *Population: Occupation Statistics,* p. 37. See also Miriam B. Murphy, "Working Women of Salt Lake City."

23. Dudden, *Serving Women,* pp. 219–22; Sutherland, *Americans and Their Servants,* pp. 102–20; Katzman, *Seven Days a Week,* app. 3, "Servant Wages," pp. 303–14; and Salmon, *Domestic Service,* pp. 88–89. On women's work, see Kessler-Harris, "Women's Choices in an Expanding Labor Market," chap. in *Out to Work;* on low wages as cause of prostitution, see pp. 103–7. For Mormons hiring only Mormons, see *Salt Lake City Deseret Evening News,* 6 Jan. 1885; for Mormon girls in gentile homes, see *Tribune,* 26 May 1887, 17 May 1888.

24. Hobson, *Uneasy Virtue,* pp. 96–98.

25. *Tribune,* 28 Jan. 1905.

26. *Tribune,* 16 Mar. 1900.

27. U.S. Bureau of the Census, Thirteenth Census (1910), Salt Lake County, Enumeration District No. 120, sheets 13A, 15A, 15B.

28. *Salt Lake City Herald-Republican,* 23 July, 7 Aug. 1911.

29. *Herald,* 8 Feb. 1896.

30. *Tribune,* 22 June 1886.

31. *Tribune,* 26 May 1887.

32. "Police, Record 1871–1875"; "Police, Record 1875–1878."

33. *Tribune,* 28 Feb. 1885, 7 Feb. 1891.

34. *Tribune,* 1 May 1891; "Arrest Register, 1891–94," p. 28, 30 Apr. 1891.

35. SLCPD, "Arrest Register, 1891–94," p. 56, 7 Aug. 1891; p. 79, 28 Oct. 1891; p. 110, 18 Mar. 1892; p. 285, 13 Mar. 1894; p. 330, 17 Aug. 1894; p. 340, 17 Sept. 1894; p. 348, 17 Oct. 1894; p. 357, 19 Nov. 1894.

36. *Herald,* 22 July 1903.

37. Salt Lake City Court Criminal Division, "Minute Book, 1908," passim; *Herald,* 4 May 1908.

38. *Herald,* 13 Dec. 1892; *Tribune,* 17 Dec. 1892.

39. Levi J. Taylor Diary, microfilm copy in CA, 20 Sept. 1896.

40. *Herald,* 11 Feb. 1902.

41. Butler, *Daughters of Joy,* p. xvii.

42. *Tribune,* 1 May 1891.

43. U.S. Bureau of the Census, Ninth Census (1870), Box Elder County, p. 46, line 37; U.S. Bureau of the Census, Tenth Census (1880), Salt Lake County, Enumeration District No. 52, p. 204, lines 6–8.

44. SLCR, "Abstract Book A 10," p. 81, line 8, 24 Mar. 1880; line 9, 24 Mar. 1880. (All succeeding "Abstract Books," "Mortgage Books," "Deed Books," etc. in these notes are from SLCR; that identifier will be omitted.) See also Polk, *Salt Lake City Directory* (1896).

45. "Abstract Book A 10," p. 126, line 15, 1 May 1882; line 17, 1 May 1882. For the first lot, see "Mortgage Book H," deed of trust, pp. 858–62, 24 Mar. 1880. The Walkers left the LDS Church in the 1860s; see Tullidge, *History of Salt Lake City*, pp. 52–58; Bliss, *Merchants and Miners*, pp. 49–272 passim; and T. Stenhouse, *Rocky Mountain States*, pp. 623–25.

46. Crofutt, *Crofutt's Salt Lake City Directory* (1885–86); *Tribune*, 17 Mar. 1887; "Fire Insurance Map of Salt Lake City, 1884," sheet 13; and "Fire Insurance Map of Salt Lake City, 1889," sheet 42. For D. F. Connelly's estate, see Probate Court for Salt Lake County, "Probate Record Book O," p. 80.

47. For the sale, see "Deed Book 2Q," warranty deed, pp. 252–54, 7 Feb. 1888. For continued prostitution, see *Herald*, 22 Jan. 1895; *Tribune*, 3, 4 July 1899.

48. "DeMarr" is the most common spelling and will be used throughout this study. The name also appears as "DeMar," "Demarr," "Demar," "De Mar," and "De Marr."

49. Salt Lake City Death Records, register and burial permit P-1368, lists a birth date of 14 Mar. 1861 in Sweden. The 1900 census lists a birth date of Mar. 1863 in Sweden of Swedish parents, and an immigration date of 1873 (U.S. Bureau of the Census, Twelfth Census [1900], Salt Lake County, Enumeration District No. 54, sheet 4, line 88). A birth date of 1858 would accord with both the 1880 census and DeMarr's and Charles V. Whiting's marriage license, Salt Lake County Probate Court, U.T., Record of Marriage Certificates, license no. 430, filed 19 June 1888.

50. "Miss Emma Le Mar" appears in "Police, Record 1875–1878," 17 July 1876, pp. 128–29. See also U.S. Bureau of the Census, Tenth Census (1880), Salt Lake County, Enumeration District No. 52, p. 198, lines 1–2.

51. For the sisters' earnings, see Christina E. T. Johnstone v. Matilda Turnross, alias Emma DeMar, no. 6528 (3d dist. civil case files, 1887). For the purchase of the property, see "Abstract Book A 10," p. 126, line 127, 10 Apr. 1882; "Abstract Book A 10," p. 186, line 3; and "Deed Book X," warranty deed, pp. 537–38, 6 Feb. 1884.

52. Johnstone v. Turnross. For the deed assigning "Alvie's" interest to her sister, see "Deed Book V," warranty deed, pp. 318–20, 24 Mar. 1883; for the suit, see "Liens and Leases etc. Book D," notice of lis pendens, pp. 585–86, filed 24 Apr. 1886.

53. "Abstract Book A 10," p. 148, line 34, filed 26 Nov. 1883; warranty deed, p. 230, line 5, filed 19 Aug. 1886. See also "Fire Insurance Map of Salt Lake City, 1884," sheet 13, and "Fire Insurance Map of Salt Lake City, 1889," sheet 42.

54. Marriage License No. 430, Record of Marriage Certificates.

55. See, for example, "Deed Book Q," trust deed, pp. 478–81, 19 Aug. 1886; "Leases and Liens Book J," lease, pp. 514–16, filed 1 Apr. 1890; "Mortgage Book 3I," mortgage, pp. 309–10, filed 20 Aug. 1892; "Mortgage Book 5M," mortgage, p. 559, entry no. 186760, filed 14 Oct. 1904.

56. For DeMarr at 243 South Main Street, see Crofutt, *Crofutt's Salt Lake City Directory* (1885–86); and Polk's *Salt Lake City Directory* (1890, 1891–92, 1896, 1897, 1898). For the

brothel, see People et al. v. Emma Whiting, case no. 832 (3d dist. criminal case files, 1891); *Tribune,* 23 Jan. 1893; and *Herald-Republican,* 9 Feb. 1911.

57. See Historicus, "Offences in 1882"; and *Tribune,* 19 May 1887. No further evidence was found until she was indicted for leasing no. 243; People et al. v. Emma Whiting, case no. 832. For the Whitings elsewhere, see U.S. Bureau of the Census, Twelfth Census (1900), Salt Lake County, Enumeration District No. 54, sheet 4, lines 88–89; Polk, *Salt Lake City Directory* (1901); and *Deseret Evening News,* 27 Aug. 1919.

58. Evidence of financial difficulties includes "Liens and Leases Book R," assignment of goods and chattels, pp. 74–75, filed 30 Jan. 1893; "Deed Book Q," trust deed, pp. 478–81, 19 Aug. 1886; and "Deed Book 3J," release of trust deed, pp. 133–34, filed 3 Sept. 1892. DeMarr reappears as a brothel keeper in 1894; see "Arrest Register, 1891–94," passim, and SLCPD, "Arrest Register, 1896–98" (hereafter "Arrest Register, 1896–98"), 15 Nov. 1895. For Ida Walker, see U.S. Bureau of the Census, Twelfth Census (1900), Salt Lake County, Enumeration District No. 54, sheet 4, line 77; and Polk, *Salt Lake City Directory* (1900–1905).

59. For example, see "Deed Book 3R," deed, p. 287, filed 30 Sept. 1890.

60. For the sale of the property, see "Deed Book 7X," warranty deed, entry no. 255912, p. 127, filed 9 Oct. 1909. For the mortgage, see "Mortgage Book 6H," mortgage, entry no. 256111, p. 467, filed 14 Oct. 1909. For the release, see "Mortgage Book 9O," release of mortgage, entry no. 436983, 21 July 1920.

61. "Deed Book 6K," special warranty deed, entry no. 269113, p. 411, 22 Oct. 1909; and "Deed Book 8U," special warranty deed, entry no. 281543, pp. 210–11, 22 Oct. 1909.

62. For Ferry as councilman, see Polk, *Salt Lake City Directory* (1908). For accusations against the Americans, see *Herald-Republican,* 16 Oct. 1909 and 13 Sept.–2 Nov. 1909, passim; quotes from 16 Oct. For Ferry's election, see *Herald-Republican,* 3 Nov. 1909. On Ferry as mayor, see Alexander and Allen, *Mormons and Gentiles,* pp. 166–72, and chap. 5 of this study.

63. For the last evidence of prostitution, see *Herald-Republican,* 5 Nov. 1910; *Herald-Republican,* 9 Feb. 1911; "Fire Insurance Map of Salt Lake City, 1911," sheet 237; and "Liens and Leases Book 2Y," lease, entry no. 303718, pp. 114–18, 5 Dec. 1912. For brothels outside the Stockade, see chap. 4.

64. Estate of Emma Whiting, "Salt Lake County Probate Record Book 78," p. 35. Emma listed the name of her sister as "Wilman"; the settlement indicated it was "Willmer." Estate of Charles V. Whiting, "Salt Lake County Probate Record Book," p. 691, no. 15449.

65. Commonwealth of Massachusetts, Office of the Secretary of State, "Copy of Record of Birth," Susan Norton, no. B 000897, date of birth 19 Nov. 1854.

66. U.S. Bureau of the Census, Tenth Census (1880), Salt Lake County, Enumeration District No. 45, p. 92, line 14; Historicus, "Offences in 1882." For the brothel, see "Deed Book V," warranty deed, pp. 54–55, 17 Feb. 1883; Crofutt, *Crofutt's Salt Lake City Directory* (1885–86); "Fire Insurance Map of Salt Lake City, 1884," sheet 9; "Liens and Leases Book D," mechanics' lien, p. 13, 12 Jan. 1884; and *Tribune,* 1 Mar. 1885; 30 May 1886. For the closure, see *Tribune,* 22 June 1886.

67. For John F. Free, see Polk, *Salt Lake City Directory* (1890). Free witnessed some of Noble's business transactions; see "Deed Book V," warranty deed, pp. 54–55, 17 Feb. 1883. For the child, see State of Iowa, Department of Health Records and Statistics Division, "Certification of Birth," Free, state file no. 23-87-264, date of birth 27 July 1887. Property

records after mid-1887 refer to "Susie M. Free formerly Sadie M. Noble"; see "Mortgage Book U," deed of trust, pp. 356–60, 15 Dec. 1887.

68. For the sale of the Block 69 property, see "Deed Book 2V," quit-claim deed, pp. 203–4, filed 11 June 1889; and "Deed Book 2W," deed, pp. 495–96, filed 31 Aug. 1889. For the mortgage to Lannan, see "Mortgage Book 2F," mortgage, pp. 74–76, filed 2 Sept. 1889. For examples of the Frees' dealings, see "Deed Book 2H," multiple deeds, pp. 285, 290–93, filed 23 July 1889; "Deed Book 3A," deed, pp. 24–25, filed 11 Sept. 1889; "Deed Book 3K," deed, pp. 30–31, filed 6 Mar. 1890; "Deed Book 3T," warranty deed, p. 585, filed 23 June 1891.

69. *Tribune*, 22 Dec. 1892. For the lease, see "Liens and Leases Book Q," lease, pp. 174–75, filed 8 Mar. 1892. For Blake at 243 south Main, see "Arrest Register, 1891–94," p. 79, 28 Oct. 1891; for other arrests, see p. 111, Mar. 18 1892; p. 139, 13 July 1892; p. 164, Oct. 15 1892.

70. See *Tribune*, 5 Aug. 1893; Arrington, "Utah and the Depression of the 1890s"; and Arrington and Alexander, *Dependent Commonwealth.*

71. For evidence of financial problems, see "Liens and Leases Book N," notice of lien, pp. 289–90, filed 24 Oct. 1891, released 4 Apr. 1893, "Grantee Index M"; "Grantor Index O," tax sale, filing 79005, filed 23 Jan. 1894; "Grantor Index X," tax sale, filing 125233, sale of 27 Dec. 1895, filed 31 Oct. 1898; "Grantor index X," tax sale, filing 125149, sale of 10 Jan. 1894, filed 31 Dec. 1898. For Susie Free's chattel mortgages, see "Chattel Mortgage Book G," pp. 9–11, 2 Mar. 1893; ibid., pp. 289–92, 29 Aug. 1893; ibid., pp. 542–44, 15 Feb. 1894; "Chattel Mortgage Book I," pp. 110–13, 10 Oct. 1894; "Chattel Mortgage Book J," p. 271, 13 July 1895. For the furniture, see The Deseret Savings Bank v. Susie M. Free, case no. 12972 (3d dist. civil case files, 1894).

72. For Noble's last arrests, see *Tribune*, 2 Oct. 1894; and "Arrest Register, 1891–94," p. 364, 17 Dec. 1894. For the Frees and Flint on Social Hall Avenue, see Polk, *Salt Lake City Directory* (1896); and "Fire Insurance Map of Salt Lake City, 1889," sheet 17. For her death, see *Deseret Evening News*, 20 July 1948.

73. The eastern part was also known as "Hyde's Alley." Polk, *Salt Lake City Directory* (1897); "Fire Insurance Map of Salt Lake City, 1911," sheet 237.

74. *Tribune*, 3 Sept. 1885. For "Pugsley's Row," see Crofutt, *Crofutt's Salt Lake City Directory* (1885–86); and Polk, *Salt Lake City Directory* (1907).

75. For Pugsley's purchase, see "Abstract Book A10," quit claim deed, p. 126, line 22, filed 19 May 1882. For the sale to Snell, see "Deed Book 5Y," warranty deed, p. 245, executed 11 Nov. 1899, filed 9 Nov. 1900. For prostitution in Snell's buildings, see *Herald*, 20 Dec. 1902; *Herald-Republican*, 23 Sept. 1916; and chaps. 3 and 5.

76. For the building, see "Liens and Leases Book V," lease, entry no. 109393, executed 29 Sept. 1896, filed 19 Feb. 1897. For prostitutes at no. 7 Victoria, see "Helen Blazes" in Polk, *Salt Lake City Directory* (1897–1908); "Arrest Register, 1891–94," passim; and Helen Smith v. H. J. Robinson et al., case no. 11444 (3d dist. civil case files, 1911). For other women arrested at 7 Victoria, see *Herald-Republican*, 26 May 1911.

77. *Tribune*, 10 Sept. 1892; U.S. Bureau of the Census, Thirteenth Census (1910), Salt Lake County, Enumeration District No. 145, sheet 2B, line 77; and Salt Lake City v. Edna Prescott, No. 2979 (3d dist. criminal case files, 1912).

78. *Tribune*, 22 Apr. 1893. For the lease to Barton, see People et al. v. Emma Whiting, case no. 832.

79. Salt Lake City Death Records, Death Certificate No. C 3070 lists cause of death as

"Bright's disease"; the Utah Supreme Court decision "syphilitic degeneration of the kidneys"; see Turner v. Utah Title, 10 Utah 61 (1895). The brothel's contents are in the latter.

80. Martha Turner v. Wells, Fargo & Company, No. 10326 (3d dist. civil case files, 1893); Martha Turner v. Union National Bank, No. 10330 (3d dist. civil case files, 1893); Martha Turner v. Union National Bank, No. 10415 (3d dist. civil case files, 1893); and Martha Turner v. Utah Title Insurance and Trust Company, No. 10493 (3d dist. civil case files, 1893). See Turner v. Utah Title for the Supreme Court's reversal.

81. For Turner and Blazes, see "Chattel Mortgage Book D," trust deed, pp. 522–24, 18 Apr. 1892. For Blazes at 243 south Main, see *Utah Gazetteer* (1892–93); "Arrest Register, 1891–94," p. 357, 19 Nov. 1894.

82. People v. Mattie Turner, case no. 919 (3d dist. criminal case files, 1892).

83. For Blazes on Franklin Avenue, see Polk, *Salt Lake City Directory* (1894–95); *Tribune,* 22 Dec. 1894. For Noble at 166½ west South Temple, see *Tribune,* 22 Dec. 1892; 2 Oct. 1894; for Blazes at that address, see Polk, *Salt Lake City Directory* (1896). See also Helen Smith v. H. J. Robinson et al.

84. For Walker at 22 Commercial, see *Tribune,* 21 Apr. 1891; for 222 south State, see *Utah Gazetteer* (1892–93), and Polk, *Salt Lake City Directory* (1896, 1897); for 243 south Main, see U.S. Bureau of the Census, Twelfth Census (1900), Salt Lake County, Enumeration District No. 54, sheet 4, line 77; and Polk, *Salt Lake City Directory* (1901–5); for her move back to 222 south State, see Polk, *Salt Lake City Directory* (1906). For arrests, see "Arrest Register, 1891–94," passim; SLCPC, "Book of Miscellaneous Offenses, 1891–93," passim; Salt Lake City Court Criminal Division, "Minute Book, 1905," passim.

85. *Tribune,* 22 Dec. 1892.

86. For Watkins in Dallas, see *Tribune,* 6 Jan. 1894. For the murder, see *Tribune,* 2 Jan. 1894; and People v. Nellie Ogden, case no. 1116 (3d dist. criminal case files, 1894). For Watkins on Franklin, see Polk, *Salt Lake City Directory* (1894–95). For Watkins in the *Times* building, see *Tribune,* 15 Jan. 1895.

87. For Watkins at 44–46 east Second South, see Polk, *Salt Lake City Directory* (1897). For the mortgages, see "Chattel Mortgage Book E," p. 601, 25 Feb. 1895; "Chattel Mortgage Book J," p. 390, filed 13 Apr. 1895; "Chattel Mortgage Book K," p. 347, filed 30 Dec. 1895; "Chattel Mortgage Book E," p. 628, entry no. 104754, filed 11 July 1896; "Chattel Mortgage Book K," p. 397, entry no. 104789, filed 13 July 1896. For the bicycle, see "Chattel Mortgage Book J," p. 192, filed 5 June 1895. For her mother, see "Chattel Mortgage Book I," pp. 586–89, filed 8 Feb. 1897; see also *Tribune,* 1 Sept. 1897. For Watkins's last arrest, see SLCPC, "Book of Miscellaneous Offenses, 1897–99," p. 101, no. 1959, complaint filed on 29 Nov. 1897. For her departure, see *Tribune,* 26 Dec. 1897.

88. For men arrested for involving their wives, see *Tribune,* 15 June 1886; *Deseret Evening News,* 20 July 1888. For men with prostitutes in their homes or rented rooms, see *Tribune,* 26 Mar. 1892, 17 June 1892. For male rooming house or hotel keepers, see *Tribune,* 13 Apr. 1887, 3 Mar. 1898.

89. For DeMott, see "Mortgage Book T," mortgage, pp. 357–59, filed 14 Sept. 1887; and *Deseret Evening News,* 18 Oct. 1932. For Merritt, see "Mortgage Book T," mortgage, pp. 17–18, filed 16 July 1887; and Polk, *Salt Lake City Directory* (1890).

90. For Dinwoodey and Flint, see "Mortgage Book I," mortgage, pp. 139–41, 12 Aug. 1880;

25 May 1881. For the committee, see "Salt Lake City Council Minutes," Book H, p. 103, 18 Sept. 1877.

91. For the deal with King, see "Deed Book 3T," warranty deed, p. 585, filed 23 June 1891. On King, see Alexander, *Mormonism in Transition,* pp. 10, 29, 32, 45, 55, 86. For the deal with Auerbach, see "Deed Book 3C," deed of trust, pp. 90–93, filed 29 June 1891. On Auerbach, see also Alexander and Allen, *Mormons and Gentiles,* p. 68. For the deal with Karrick, see "Deed Book 2V," deed, pp. 203–4, filed 11 June 1889. For Karrick as councilman, see Polk, *Salt Lake City Directory* (1890); *Utah Gazetteer* (1892–93). For the deal with McCornick, see "Mortgage Book 2W," marginal release of mortgage, p. 407, 25 Sept. 1891. On McCornick, see Bliss, *Merchants and Miners,* pp. 208–9; and Alexander and Allen, *Mormons and Gentiles,* pp. 13, 91, 99, 103, 105, 129.

92. For example, see "Chattel Mortgage Book D," pp. 227–28, 2 Nov. 1891.

93. Polk, *Salt Lake City Directory* (1885–86).

94. Ibid. (1901–8) lists "Helen Blazes" and "Helen Smith." "Smith, Mrs. Helen Blazes" appears in *Utah Gazetteer* (1892–93).

95. For Catherine Fairchild, see U.S. Bureau of the Census, Twelfth Census (1900), Salt Lake County, Enumeration District No. 65, sheet 9, line 63; for Kitty Hicks, see U.S. Bureau of the Census, Twelfth Census (1900), Salt Lake County, Enumeration District No. 55, sheet 1, line 82. "Mrs. Kittie Fairchild" lived at 58 Commercial Street in 1897 (Polk, *Salt Lake City Directory* [1897]); "Kitty Hicks" lived there in 1898 (Polk, *Salt Lake City Directory* [1898]). See also *Herald,* 13 Mar. 1909; and Catherine C. Fairchild v. Milton A. Fairchild, case no. 5052 (3d dist. civil case files, 1902).

96. See n. 68 above.

97. Adora Long, Dora Hughes, Dora Topham, Belle London, and Maxine Rose. Ethel Topham's death certificate names her mother as "Adora Long," born Kentucky; State of California Department of Health Services, Certificate of Death no. 86-174183. "Dora B. Hughes" married Thomas Topham, Jr., on 1 May 1890 in Ogden; see Weber County Record of Marriage Certificates, license no. 1330, filed 1 May 1890. Thomas's vital information matches that in his obituary, *Ogden Standard,* 19 Nov. 1906, and the marriage date accords with census records below. "Dora Topham" and "Belle London" appear in scores of 1911 newspaper articles. "Maxine Rose," head of household, lived with her "daughter" "Ethel Topham," whose information matches Ethel's in other censuses; and "boarder" Thomas Matthews, "lawyer," in California; see chap. 4 and U.S. Bureau of the Census, Fourteenth Census (1920), San Francisco County, Calif., Enumeration District No. 92, sheet 1A, lines 7–16. "Maxine Rose's" age, birthplace, and parents' birthplaces match Dora Topham's in U.S. Bureau of the Census, Twelfth Census (1900), Weber County, Enumeration District No. 187, sheet 8, line 1.

98. See Clos Adolf Reinholt Turnross's deposition, 1 Apr. 1887 (Johnstone v. Turnross).

99. People et al. v. Emma Whiting; Brigham Young Hampton Papers, 1870–1901, microfilm copy in CA. For the law, see "An Ordinance Relating to Houses of Ill-fame and Prostitution," Book C, *Salt Lake City Council Ordinances* (1877).

100. For the theater, see Nellie Kingsley v. Salt Lake Dramatic Company, case no. 11774 (3d dist. territorial civil case files, 1893); for the fire, see *Deseret Evening News,* 6 July 1894, in JH, 6 July 1894.

101. Estate of Emma Whiting, p. 35; Estate of Charles V. Whiting, "Salt Lake County Probate Record Book," p. 691, no. 15449.

102. For "inmate," see for example *Tribune*, 1 Mar. 1885. No brothel listed more than twelve inmates. In August 1894 three brothels contained twelve women, probably resulting from crowding women onto Franklin Avenue. For twelve inmates, see "Arrest Register, 1891–94," p. 330, 17 Aug. 1894; for the average size, see same source, passim.

103. On the difficulty in tracing prostitutes' lives after prostitution, see Hobson, *Uneasy Virtue*, pp. 104–8.

104. The police often listed inmates by the madam's last name; e.g., "Cora Blazes et al." worked in Helen Blazes's brothel; Salt Lake City Court Criminal Division, "Minute Book, 1908," 21 Jan. 1908, p. 29.

105. This tentative statistical profile is based on sixty-four women identified as brothel prostitutes in the federal censuses of 1870, 1880, 1900, and 1910 (other than those in the Stockade; see chap. 4). No woman appears twice. Mean age was 23.06. Of those who reported their own and their parents' birthplaces, 62.3 percent claimed to be native born of native-born parents (N=53); no statistically significant change occurred over time. Of twenty women who were foreign-born or had at least one foreign parent, only one—a Japanese—was not of Canadian or western European background. Of those reporting a marital status, 89.3 percent claimed to be single or divorced (N=56), and 12.8 percent reported having children (N=64). See also Rosen, *Lost Sisterhood*, pp. 138–54; Hobson, *Uneasy Virtue*, pp. 88–93.

106. See, for example, *Tribune*, 2, 3 June 1886.

107. For Hart as inmate, see *Tribune*, 15 Aug. 1886. For Hart in Ogden, see Ogden Police Court, "Justice's Docket, 1889," 14 Aug. 1889, pp. 386–87; *Tribune*, 26 Sept. 1889. For Hart on Franklin, see "Chattel Mortgage Book D," pp. 227–28, 2 Nov. 1891; and "Arrest Register, 1891–94," p. 56, 7 Aug. 1891.

108. *Tribune*, 2 Nov. 1891.

109. "Police, Record 1871–1875," 23 May 1872, pp. 104–5; 25 Aug. 1872, pp. 148–49; 11 Mar. 1873, pp. 220–21; 8 Aug. 1873, pp. 300–301. Evidence after 1873 is scant; see *Deseret Evening News*, 19 Mar. 1879; 15, 18 July 1890; and *Tribune*, 16 July 1890; 5 Aug. 1895. On Chinese prostitutes elsewhere, see Hirata, "Free, Indentured, Enslaved"; Tong, *Unsubmissive Women*.

110. The earliest record of a woman identified as African American arrested for prostitution is in "Police, Record 1871–1875," 22 Apr. 1873, pp. 242–43.

111. "Arrest Register, 1891–94," passim.

112. For Watkins and black women, see "Arrest Register, 1891–94," p. 331, 17 Aug. 1894; and p. 271, 22 Dec. 1893.

113. *Herald*, 10 July 1901; SLCPC, "Book of Miscellaneous Offenses, 1899–1901," no. 1681, 9 July 1901.

114. Mary Murphy, "Private Lives of Public Women," pp. 198–200.

115. *Tribune*, 10 Sept. 1891.

116. See the "Fire Insurance Map of Salt Lake City" for 1884, 1889, 1895, 1898, and 1911 for the proximity of brothels and saloons. For an example of saloonkeepers posting bond, see *Tribune*, 10 Oct. 1886.

117. On saloon culture, see Noel, *City and Saloon;* West, *Saloon on the Rocky Mountain*

Mining Frontier; and Hathaway, "History of the American Drinking Place." For the ban on women performers, see Utah, *Compiled Laws* (1876), pp. 600–601. For the ban on women in saloons after 9 P.M., see *Herald*, 19 Mar. 1890. For the ban between 7 P.M. and 7 A.M. see *Tribune*, 4 Jan. 1901.

118. *Deseret Evening News*, 27 Sept. 1890.

119. See, for example, *Tribune*, 6 Jan. 1887, 10 July 1892, 16 Feb. 1899.

120. For partitioned saloons, see *Herald*, 18 Dec. 1907. No explicit evidence of sex in saloons was found, although Ruth Rosen suggests that it occurred; see Rosen, *Lost Sisterhood*, p. 84.

121. See, for example, *Tribune*, 26 July 1905.

122. *Tribune*, 8 Dec. 1891.

123. *Herald*, 19 Dec. 1902.

124. The small rooms in the Stockade were called "cribs" ("Fire Insurance Map of Salt Lake City, 1911"), as were adobe "tenements" ("Fire Insurance Map of Salt Lake City, 1889") on Victoria Alley (see *Herald*, 19 Dec. 1902) and small dwelling houses on Franklin Avenue (*Tribune*, 2 Nov. 1891).

125. Davis is described as "colored" and her inmates as "American" in "Arrest Register, 1891–94," p. 338, 9 Sept. 1894.

126. For Franklin, see "Fire Insurance Map of Salt Lake City, 1884," sheet 14; "Fire Insurance Map of Salt Lake City, 1889," sheet 41; "Fire Insurance Map of Salt Lake City, 1898," sheet 113; "Fire Insurance Map of Salt Lake City, 1911," sheet 238. For French "cribs," see *Tribune*, 2 June 1892; for Japanese women, see "Arrest Register, 1891–94," p. 34, 20 May 1891; and *Tribune*, 10 Dec. 1897; for African American women, see *Deseret Evening News*, 10 Nov. 1890. For "inmates" but no "keeper," see "Arrest Register, 1891–94," passim.

127. *Tribune*, 9 June 1886.

128. *Tribune*, 15 Apr. 1888.

129. *Tribune*, 24 Mar. 1892. One nickname for a brothel near a post was "hog ranch"; Butler, *Daughters of Joy*, p. 8.

130. For examples of "John" or "Joe Doe" arrests, see *Tribune*, 2 June 1886; "Arrest Register, 1891–94," p. 343, 27 Sept. 1894; and *Tribune*, 2 Oct. 1894. For working-class patrons, see "Arrest Register, 1891–94," passim. For examples of nonwhite men with white women, see "Arrest Register, 1891–94," p. 114, 26 Mar. 1892; p. 215, 30 Apr. 1893; p. 219, 10 May 1893.

131. See *Deseret Evening News*, 12 Aug. 1910.

132. For the "mirrored ballrooms," see Held, *Most*, p. 100. For "Frankie and Johnny," see Shelley Armitage, *John Held, Jr.*, p. 5.

133. Abraham H. Cannon Diaries, 5:92–3, 18 Mar. 1885, photocopy in JWM.

134. Ibid., 5:118–19, 9 May 1885. Abraham Cannon made no further mention of Flint, but detailed Frank's drunkenness and periodic repentance; see 5:124, 21 May 1885; 5:134, 5 June 1885; 5:206–7, 31 Dec. 1885; 6:31–2, 3 Mar. 1886; 11:78, 8 Aug. 1889; 13:211–12, 12 Jan. 1891.

135. Frank Cannon lobbied for Utah statehood and served as territorial delegate to Congress and as one of Utah's first U.S. senators. On lobbying, see Lyman, *Political Deliverance*, pp. 131–32. On his political career, see pp. 200–202, 257–58, 282–83. On his conflict with the LDS Church, see K. Godfrey, "Frank J. Cannon"; and chap. 4 of this study.

136. Abraham H. Cannon Diaries, 7:52–54, 24, 25 Apr. 1886.

137. Rosen, *Lost Sisterhood,* pp. 102–7.

138. Chattel mortgages often list kitchen equipment; see, for example, "Chattel Mortgage Book D," p. 227, 2 Nov. 1891. For servants, see U.S. Bureau of the Census, Tenth Census (1880), Salt Lake County, Enumeration District No. 45, p. 92, lines 10–11. For housekeepers, see *Tribune,* 2 June 1886. For piano players, see U.S. Bureau of the Census, Twelfth Census (1900), Salt Lake County, Enumeration District No. 54, sheet 4, line 82; Held, *Most,* p. 99.

139. Polk, *Salt Lake City Directory* (1891–92).

140. For the "Big V" (No. 5 Plum Alley), see "Chattel Mortgage Book F," pp. 105–7, 25 June 1892. For arrests, see "Arrest Register, 1891–94," p. 135, 25 June 1892; p. 156, 13 Sept. 1892; p. 202, 17 Mar. 1893; p. 228, 15 June 1893; p. 250, 29 Aug. 1893.

141. Held, *Most,* p. 99.

142. For signs, see *Herald,* 6 Mar. 1901. For the dogcart, see Held, *Most,* pp. 99–100. For the automobile, see Thompson v. Wilson et al., case no. 9432 (3d dist. civil case files, 1908). For "The Palace," see Polk, *Salt Lake City Directory* (1899). For St. Omar's invitations, see *Tribune,* 23 Aug. 1890; for Wilson's, see Foster, "Open Letter to Angus M. Cannon," and chap. 3.

143. "Chattel Mortgage Book I," filing number 99657, pp. 376–78, filed 19 Nov. 1895.

144. *Tribune,* 7 July 1892.

145. For wine at Blazes's, see Held, *Most,* pp. 99–100. For alcohol and cigars, see *Tribune,* 29 Apr. 1885. For liquor without a license, see "Police, Record 1875–1878," 24 Nov. 1875, pp. 52–53; *Tribune,* 7 July 1892; and *Tribune,* 19 Feb. 1895.

146. "Chattel Mortgage Book G," pp. 9–11, 2 Mar. 1893. For other lavish furnishings, see the inventory at the "Big V," "Liens and Leases book P," bill of sale, pp. 340–41, filed 27 May 1892.

147. *Herald-Republican,* 17 Sept. 1916.

148. On eastern brothels, see Rosen, *Lost Sisterhood,* pp. 86–98; on western, see Butler, *Daughters of Joy,* pp. 59–61.

149. SLCPC, "Book of Miscellaneous Offenses, 1899–1901," no. 199, 2 June 1899; State v. Tillie Williams, case no. 684 (3d dist. criminal case files, 1901); *Tribune,* 8 June 1907; SLCPD, "Criminal Record, 1892–1920," p. 334, 6 June 1907.

150. SLCPD, "Criminal Record, 1892–1920," p. 98, 26 Sept. 1894; *Herald,* 27, 28 Sept. 1894.

151. SLCPD, "Criminal Record, 1892–1920," p. 113, 14 Jan. 1896; *Tribune,* 27 Aug., 2 Oct. 1895, 14 Jan. 1896. For other "panel workers," see *Tribune,* 22 June 1891, 15 Apr. 1892.

152. For prostitutes with little more than a trunk, see *Tribune,* 15 Aug. 1886, 8 Aug. 1891. For brothel theft, see *Tribune,* 19 Jan. 1899; *Herald,* 11 Apr. 1902.

153. *Herald,* 18, 19 Dec. 1902.

154. See, for example, Kate Flint; *Tribune,* 2 June 1886.

155. *Tribune,* 26 June 1886.

156. *Tribune,* 2 May 1891.

157. *Tribune,* 27 Apr. 1897.

158. *Tribune,* 4 Feb. 1899; Salt Lake County Probate Court, "Estate Registers Book F," no. 2884, p. 406.

159. *Tribune,* 19 May 1887.

160. *Tribune,* 24 Aug. 1893 and "Arrest Register, 1891–94," p. 249, 24 Aug. 1893. Cecil Gray

(née Nellie Conley) moved to Malvina Beauchamp's brothel; see "Arrest Register, 1891–94," p. 250, 29 Aug. 1893; then to the "Three Deuces"; *Tribune*, 12 July 1899.

161. *Tribune*, 15 Aug. 1886.

162. Rosen, *Lost Sisterhood*, p. 88.

163. See, for example, *Tribune*, 27 Feb., 27 Apr. 1892.

164. *Tribune*, 17 Jan. 1892.

165. SLCPD, "Criminal Record, 1892–1920," p. 290, 22 Jan. 1906; *Tribune*, 23, 25 Jan. 1906; *Deseret Evening News*, 23 Jan. 1906.

166. *Tribune*, 20 Mar. 1894; SLCPC, "Book of Miscellaneous Offenses, 1893–5," p. 133, 20 Mar. 1894.

167. *Herald*, 10 July 1901.

168. *Tribune*, 25, 26, 27 Apr. 1897.

169. *Herald*, 11 Nov. 1906.

170. Emma M. Whiting v. Charles V. Whiting, case no. 1873 (3d dist. civil case files, 1897).

171. Ogden was sentenced to three months for involuntary manslaughter. People v. Nellie Ogden, case no. 1116; *Tribune*, 28 Dec. 1893, 2, 3, 5, 6, 9 Jan., 27 Feb. 1894.

172. Thomas was acquitted on mental grounds; State v. Cora Thomas, no. 246 (3d dist. criminal case files, 1897); *Tribune*, 9, 12 June, 26, 27, 28, 30 Oct. 1897; *Herald*, 9 June 1897; and *Deseret Evening News*, 9 June 1897.

173. Himes, *Medical History of Contraception*, pp. 181–94; Gordon, *Woman's Body, Woman's Right;* Reed, *Birth Control Movement*, pp. 3–39; McLaren, *History of Contraception*, pp. 184–91; and Tone, "Contraceptive Entrepreneurs" and "Black-Market Birth Control," chaps. in *Devices and Desires*. The index of Duke, *CRC Handbook of Medicinal Herbs*, lists thirty-eight herbal substances with claimed abortifacient value. See also Rosen, *Lost Sisterhood*, p. 99.

174. Such products were frequently advertised in Salt Lake newspapers; see *Tribune*, 1 Jan. 1890.

175. I found no abortion cases that specifically labeled the woman a prostitute. One woman arrested for "keeping a house of assignation" was labeled "abortionest"; see "Police, Record 1871–1875," 16 Apr. 1873, pp. 240–41. For abortion arrests, see "Police, Record 1871–1875," 31 May 1874, pp. 412–13; *Tribune*, 20 Jan. 1893; *Tribune*, 30 Nov. 1895; *Herald*, 8 Jan. 1903.

176. Brandt, *No Magic Bullet.*

177. *Tribune*, 19 Mar. 1890; *Deseret Evening News*, 19 Mar. 1890. The death certificate does not cite the condition. Salt Lake City Death Records, death certificate no. 15877, p. 397. On other cities, see Rosen, *Lost Sisterhood*, p. 99.

178. *Herald-Republican*, 28 Sept. 1911; State v. Topham, no. 2710 (3d dist. criminal case files, 1911).

179. *Tribune*, 2 July, 21 Aug. 1887.

180. *Tribune*, 19 Jan. 1888.

181. See, for example, *Tribune*, 6 May 1888; SLCPC, "Book of Miscellaneous Offenses, 1899–1901," no. 1542, 14 May 1901.

182. *Herald*, 5 Sept. 1907. See also Finnegan, *Poverty and Prostitution*, pp. 125, 145.

183. *Tribune*, 12 July 1899; U.S. Bureau of the Census, Twelfth Census (1900), Utah County, Enumeration District No. 211, sheet 3, line 30.

184. For suicides, see *Tribune,* 12 June 1887, 4 June 1889, 27 Aug. 189, 16 Mar. 1891, 4 Feb. 1892, 30 Aug., 3, 27 Dec. 1893, 4 Apr., 22 May, 16 Aug. 1894, 7 Sept. 1896, 9 June 1897, 11 June, 19 July, 10 Oct. 1898, 29 July 1900; *Herald,* 3 Mar., 23 May 1901, 13 Mar., 4 May, 18 Sept. 1902, 7 May 1903; and *Tribune,* 17 Mar. 1904. The madams were Grace Fuller; see *Herald,* 27 Jan. 1908; and Cleo Starr; see *Herald,* 6 June 1908.

185. *Herald,* 27 Jan. 1908.

186. Mary Murphy, "Private Lives of Public Women," p. 205, n. 29.

Madeline Mortimer, 1894. Arrested for grand larceny, she pleaded guilty to keeping a house of prostitution. Courtesy Salt Lake City Police Department Museum.

Nellie Davis, 1894. She was a brothel keeper on Franklin Avenue and was found guilty of abducting a woman for the purposes of prostitution but won on appeal because the woman was "not of previously chaste character." Courtesy Salt Lake City Police Department Museum.

Estella King, aka Annie Cleary, 1896. Police arrested her as a "panel worker" in a brothel; she was convicted of vagrancy. Courtesy Salt Lake City Police Department Museum.

Minerva Reeves, 1906. Committed to the industrial school in 1903 and accused of attempting to burn it down. In 1906 she was convicted of attempting to kill her sister and fellow inmate at 243 south Main Street. Courtesy Salt Lake City Police Department Museum.

Tillie Williams, aka English Laura, 1907. She worked on Victoria alley from 1897 to 1901 and served a five-year term for robbery; she was convicted of petty larceny in 1907. Courtesy Salt Lake City Police Department Museum.

The Brigham Young Trust Company building, 1891. From 1897 through 1908, Ada Wilson operated the "Palace" brothel on an upper floor. Used by permission, Utah State Historical Society.

The editor, ca. 1915. Charles Carroll (C. C.) Goodwin edited the *Salt Lake City Daily Tribune* from 1880 to 1901 and his own papers afterward. He favored regulated prostitution and condemned plural marriage. Used by permission, Utah State Historical Society.

The policeman, ca. 1895. George A. Sheets served on the Salt Lake police force for decades and arrested hundreds of prostitutes. He was among the police and city council party in Hattie Wilson's brothel in 1892. Used by permission, Utah State Historical Society.

The mayor, 1909. John S. Bransford served as mayor from 1907 to 1911. He led the city government's efforts to build and protect the Stockade. Used by permission, Utah State Historical Society.

The madam, ca. 1908. Dora B. Topham, aka Belle London, managed the Stockade until her 1911 conviction for pandering. Used by permission, Utah State Historical Society.

The Stockade's north entrance, 1911. Used by permission, Utah State Historical Society.

The Stockade's cribs under construction, 1908. Used by permission, Utah State Historical Society.

3. "The System in Vogue"

HISTORIAN GUSTIVE LARSON labeled the LDS Church's long, grudging, and uneven retreat from plural marriage, political domination, and cooperative economic practices the "Americanization of Utah."[1] One aspect of the "Americanization" of Salt Lake City was prostitution policy. Responses to prostitution, shaped by economics, partisan politics, the Mormon-gentile conflict, and the actions of women who sold sex, sometimes overlapped, contradicted, or reinforced each other. While some people worked to abolish prostitution, powerful forces ensured the creation and maintenance of a regulationist policy much like those in other American cities. Accommodation between Mormons and gentiles contributed to broad agreement on regulation. The state developed formal and informal policies in accordance with contemporary gender, race, and class hierarchies. The policy of regulation began in the 1870s under all-Mormon governments and became more open and systematic under the mixed administrations that governed the city after 1890.

Prostitutes and prostitution served many important roles in the community. Many citizens profited from prostitution economically or politically or otherwise favored it. Prostitution remained illegal, however, and the "public reenactment of guilt and conviction" represented by periodic arrests and fines stigmatized madams and prostitutes as criminals no matter how useful, necessary, or profitable they might have been to the community.[2]

Regulation did not satisfy everyone. Individuals and groups sometimes condemned the presence of prostitutes in their neighborhoods and demanded their removal, without addressing the larger issue of regulation. Citizens formed temporary organizations to demand action in response to specific incidents through techniques of public pressure such as mass meetings, petitions, sermons, and lobbying of city officials.

Other reformers, especially women, used those techniques but also took more direct action, forming permanent organizations to address a variety of municipal problems, including prostitution. Some reformers founded "rescue homes" where "fallen women" could be saved through immersion in a domestic, Christian environment. Especially after 1890, some organizations included gentiles and Mormons, a sign of easing tensions after the Woodruff Manifesto. Detente was tenuous, however, and old antagonisms resurfaced. While some prostitutes welcomed the aid of reformers, others resisted rescue for a variety of reasons. Antiprostitution efforts did not seriously affect official policy. City officials and many male citizens continued to favor regulation for pragmatic reasons; and the creation of the Stockade in 1908 marked its fullest expression.

The legal system formed the basis of prostitution policy. When the city was founded in 1847, the Latter-day Saints hoped that voluntary adherence to the church's moral teachings would maintain social order. Failing that, ecclesiastic authorities established church courts for violations of church law or disputes between members.[3] They also wrote civil ordinances (purportedly for the valley's few gentiles) punishing vagrancy, disorderly conduct, adultery, and fornication.[4] The legislature of the provisional State of Deseret also crafted a criminal code outlawing disorderly assembly and prescribing severe penalties for extramarital sex.[5] Those ordinances, which applied to males and females, demonstrated the Saints' emphasis on chastity and may also have been intended as a refutation of accusations of the immorality of polygamy. Women selling sex could be prosecuted under these broad laws. Nineteenth-century American law defined a prostitute as a vagrant with employment that offended public decency and morals, thus a type of "disorderly person." A prostitute, a keeper of a house of prostitution, a hanger-on or dependent of such a house, or a customer could be charged with vagrancy. "Disorderly houses" were defined as public nuisances that endangered public morals because dangerous persons gathered in them. As a type of disorderly house, a brothel was a public, physical, and moral nuisance.[6]

Salt Lake City municipal authorities did not specifically outlaw prostitution until 1858, probably because it did not seem necessary to do so. A code adopted that year subjected anyone who enticed an unmarried female "for the purpose of prostitution" to a ten-year prison term, a ten thousand dollar fine, or both.[7] Keeping a house of prostitution could bring a ten-year sentence and/or a five thousand dollar fine. Inveigling or enticing any female "before reputed virtuous" to a house of ill fame could earn fifteen years and/

or a fifteen thousand dollar fine. Neither inmates of houses of ill fame, street-walkers, nor customers received specific mention.[8] This draconian code was a product of its time. The LDS Church was in the midst of a "reformation" to reignite spiritual fervor, and the 1858 ordinances may have been meant to reinforce the LDS moral code. A greater factor was probably the impending approach of "Johnston's Army," which threatened to bring hundreds of soldiers and their supposed vices to the city.[9]

Municipal prostitution laws continued to evolve, gradually achieving the form that governed through the early 1900s. In 1860, city authorities proscribed prostitutes, owners, and keepers of houses of prostitution but dramatically reduced penalties from the 1858 code.[10] In 1877, the city council passed a single ordinance that applied to owners, agents, guardians, or lessees of properties used for prostitution, as well as to keepers, inmates, and those who "resorted" to brothels.[11] Similar territorial statutes also applied, but these were seldom invoked.[12]

Four categories of law enforcement officials shared responsibility for enforcing the law within Salt Lake City: U.S. marshals, territorial (later state) marshals, county sheriffs, and the city police. The police and the municipal ordinances they enforced were by far the most important instruments of law for prostitution-related offenses.[13] The force, like contemporary forces in other cities, was far from professional. Its primary responsibility was to maintain order by controlling the "dangerous classes": vagrants, gamblers, drunks, and prostitutes.[14] In most cities, appointments were political plums awarded to supporters, with police receiving "on the job" training from experienced colleagues. The political and social realities in Salt Lake City affected the makeup and duties of the force. Until 1890, the department was all Mormon, and its duties included protecting Saints from the antipolygamy crusade of the 1880s.[15] The great majority of prostitution-related cases were decided in the "police court," presided over by a justice of the peace—until 1890, usually an LDS bishop. The police justice dispensed summary justice—fines and short terms in the city jail—for misdemeanors under municipal ordinances.[16]

To LDS city officials, the "dangerous classes" usually meant non-Mormons. Saints were subject to the oversight of their LDS neighbors, ward members, and church authorities, and they blamed gentiles for most of the city's crime. The soldiers, camp followers, miners, railroad workers, and even allegedly lascivious judges who came to the city seemed to represent both a threat to the Kingdom and a more prosaic threat to municipal order.[17] A. M. Musser's partisan investigations into comparative morality also claimed to prove that the disorderly classes were non-Mormon.[18] Subsequent scholars have agreed that gentile men were disproportionately responsible for crime. Rootless young men lacking the social controls of family or church drank and broke laws in other western towns, particularly those dominated by cattle, mining, or lumbering. These men also patronized prostitutes throughout the West.[19] While it is plausible that gentiles committed a disproportionate number of crimes, the Mormon-dominated police and lower court system also helped ensure that non-Mormon criminals were punished while Saints were sometimes protected.

By the 1870s, then, a body of law forbade all aspects of prostitution and a system was in place to enforce it. LDS Church authorities, who commanded the allegiance of the majority and dominated government, continued to warn against prostitution. Persons selling or buying sex, female and male, faced legal proscription and societal condemnation. On paper, prostitution was strictly prohibited and its penalties were gender-neutral.

In practice, however, city authorities, business interests, and average citizens established a modus vivendi with prostitution in the 1870s for a number of reasons. Some Mormons undoubtedly joined in the national consensus that prostitution should be regulated rather than abolished. Civil and religious authorities across the country outlawed and condemned prostitution yet allowed it to flourish nonetheless. The *Salt Lake City Herald,* mostly Mormon-owned and -edited, noted "the evil has not been suppressed in any country or in any age of which we have record. It may be checked in places, but it cannot or at least has not been stopped." The editor called for periodic fines.[20] Like the members of any other faith, Mormons sometimes ignored their spiritual leaders' teachings or broke laws for their own benefit. As shown in the previous chapter, some Saints patronized prostitutes or conducted business with them.

The backgrounds of some municipal officials also changed. Instead of the high LDS officials who had traditionally held the office, the four mayors from 1876 through 1890 were prominent Mormon businessmen. Historians Thomas G. Alexander and James B. Allen suggest that the selection of these men to govern the city indicated that LDS Church leaders acknowledged that the city was becoming more commercial and that bankers and merchants had joined them among the city's elite.[21] Although they were loyal Saints and often acted in the interests of their church,[22] they may have viewed abolition as impractical, impossible, or unwise from an economic standpoint. The influx of soldiers, miners, railroad workers, and others who sometimes patronized prostitutes may also have helped convince authorities that fighting vice was a losing proposition.[23] The expensive failure to abate Kate Flint's and Cora Conway's brothels had burned city officials badly and probably discouraged further abolition efforts.

The embarrassment of B. Y. Hampton's 1885 "city brothel" scheme probably further dissuaded Mormon city officers from action against prostitution, although Francis Armstrong, who helped fund Hampton, launched an eradication drive during his term in 1886. That attempt only strengthened the arguments for regulation. The *Herald*'s editor applauded the action but implied that regulation was the best that could be hoped for. He asked "that prostitution shall be driven out of sight and made odious; . . . that prostitutes shall be prevented from parading on the streets, painted and bedecked so as to excite the gross passions of men and envy of silly girls."[24] The *Tribune*'s C. C. Goodwin argued that the raid was misguided and would only serve to scatter "dissolute women" through the city's residential districts, a common theme of the regulationist camp.[25] Goodwin was still reminding Mormons of Armstrong's failure seventeen years later and still advocating regulation.[26]

The increasingly intense pressures of the antipolygamy "crusade" in the 1880s may also have relegated the control of prostitution to a minor concern. The LDS authorities and the city administration were instead concerned with what President Wilford Woodruff called "the temporal salvation of the church."[27]

Another major consideration had nothing to do with the polygamy conflict. Gendered power played an obvious role in the establishment and continuation of regulation. Those who benefited most from regulated prostitution—sexually or financially—were male. There is little evidence that any women other than prostitutes and madams favored regulation. The relatively few respectable women, gentile or Mormon, willing to express an opinion about prostitution nearly always condemned the exploitation of women by lustful or greedy men, even if they did not always explicitly condemn regulation or call for abolition. But since men wielded far greater economic and political power, women's voices were long drowned out. Gender inequities also guaranteed that male patrons would be arrested far less often than female prostitutes. Many men implicitly felt they had the right to patronize prostitutes without endangering their own respectability.[28] C. C. Goodwin agreed that frequenting brothels did not damn a man: "A man who has vices may be a strictly honest man in business and may be a patriot who would on demand cheerfully lay down his life for his country. Such a man, despite his vices, is a first-class citizen."[29]

Whatever the mix of reasons, a policy of official toleration (if not quite regulation) was firmly in place by the early 1870s. The fragmentary evidence that remains shows that police arrested women on an irregular basis from 1872 to 1890 for various prostitution-related offenses, with months-long periods of no arrests. Despite laws against patronizing brothels, very few men were arrested. The Mormon municipal authorities had decided that although laws against prostitution were on the books, they would not be strictly enforced. And although patronizing prostitutes was a crime, few men would face consequences. The women who sold sex would bear nearly all of the legal responsibility, as well as the condemnation of respectable society. But the persistence of some women over time indicates that they successfully adapted to the policy.[30]

Regulation reflected a widespread nineteenth-century belief that prostitution could not and should not be eradicated.[31] The most influential advocate of regulation, French physician Alexandre-Jean-Baptiste Parent-Duchatelet, proposed three principles to prevent the contamination of society:

1. Prostitutes must be confined to an enclosed milieu invisible to respectable society.
2. The municipal authorities must constantly supervise the milieu.
3. The milieu must be hierarchized and compartmentalized to prevent the mixing of age groups and classes.[32]

Many European and American cities adopted elements of this system, sometimes called "reglementation."[33] In general, authorities unofficially segregated prostitutes in a specified area and regulated them through periodic arrests and fines. In some cities, health officials examined prostitutes and quarantined the ill. Supporters argued that regulation kept respectable residential and business areas free of an evil that could not be eradicated in any event. Crime and drunkenness, which inevitably came along with prostitution, were likewise restricted and minimized. Some advocates argued that regulation protected "true women" by providing naturally licentious males with an alternative outlet for their uncontrollable passions. A Salt Lake City chief of police, for example, declared that "if it were not for the presence of houses of prostitution in this city, it would be unsafe for women to walk the streets alone after dark."[34] While most of the city's police chiefs, especially during the Mormon era, probably maintained at least a pretense of favoring abolition, a few stated publicly that they favored a well-regulated district, and after the early 1870s, all followed regulationist policies.[35]

The advocates of regulation dominated well into the twentieth century, but they did not convince everyone. "Regulationists" carried on a running argument with "abolitionists," those who favored eradication. The toleration of prostitution and male sexual license in general came under harsh criticism in the early nineteenth century, especially from evangelical women. A group of New York City women fought the sexual double standard and advocated the abolition of prostitution in the 1820s and 1830s. Historian Carroll Smith-

Rosenberg cites this movement as a protofeminist attack upon patriarchy through the issue of male sexual license. These moral reformers sought to foment a sense of female solidarity against male exploitation.[36]

Such campaigns had limited impact. By mid-century, medical authorities had entered the debate, generally on the side of regulation.[37] Activists launched renewed attacks upon regulation in England and America in the 1870s and 1880s, and some medical authorities began to side with these "new abolitionists."[38] When the British Parliament enacted statutes providing for the sanitary inspection of prostitutes at military depots, Josephine Butler led a successful campaign against the legislation on grounds that it formalized the double standard and ignored men's responsibility for prostitution.[39] Susan B. Anthony and others successfully fought attempts to implement officially regulated prostitution in New York City in the 1860s and 1870s. When the city of St. Louis instituted a formal policy of regulation in 1870, temperance advocates helped to defeat the experiment.[40] Mormons observed the St. Louis experiment and claimed that it indicated the folly of compromising with evil. The *Deseret News* reprinted a letter from a St. Louis physician that declared the utter failure of the experiment in decreasing disease, raising the general morality of the community, or lessening "the number of clandestine prostitutes."[41] Despite such opposition, however, informal regulation was the rule in most American cities.

An incident that began in Salt Lake City in 1890 demonstrates the real targets of prostitution laws and helps explain the attraction of regulation to many officials and businessmen, Mormon and gentile. Brigham Young Hampton, now a private businessman, erected a building on Commercial Street on land leased from the Brigham Young Estate. Hampton leased the building to Louis Bamberger, one of four German Jewish brothers prominent in real estate and mining, who subleased it to Elsie St. Omar, who opened a brothel.[42]

In September 1891, Judge Charles Zane of the Third District court instructed the grand jury to indict keepers of houses of prostitution.[43] Hampton claimed that the officers of the Brigham Young Trust Company (now managing parts of the estate) decided to sacrifice him to the authorities. All of the sublessees agreed to cancel the objectionable leases, including St. Omar, even though she had spent "several hundred dollars" outfitting the building as a brothel. Hampton declared that the madam "was a hundred times more Considerate than my Should be friends and I think in the day of Judgment She will out Shine Many of the B.Y.T.Co."[44] Despite the cancellation, Hampton was indicted for keeping a house of prostitution; the same grand jury also returned an indictment against Emma Whiting for leasing no. 243 south Main to Minnie Barton.[45] Hampton faced prosecution by the same district attorney, Charles S. Varian, before the same judge who had sentenced him to a year in prison in 1885.

Varian dismissed both cases, however. According to Hampton, Varian declared "the Fact is these Gentlemen and Lady had nothing to do with the places."[46] Owners of property used in prostitution could escape prosecution through the "defense of landlord" provision. If the owner could prove that he had "diligently used the power which the law gives him to suppress the improper use of the building or tenement," no charges would result.[47] Property owners seldom faced legal action if there was a manager (i.e., a madam) to prosecute instead. By limiting legal action to madams—"fallen women" practicing an outlawed profession who were relatively powerless and who could count on little public sympathy—authorities accomplished two tasks. They could tell the community that they were punishing prostitution and at the same time protect a (usually male) property owner from an embarrassing prosecution that might bring retribution against the authorities or damage the city's reputation. Such property owners often wielded substantial social, political, and economic power. Prosecuting landlords for keeping houses of prostitution might have cast a pall over the city's business climate.[48] In general, only madams and the owners of particularly "disorderly" houses were in danger of arrest. In this case, the "defense of landlord" provision protected a Mormon businessman and even Emma Whiting, who as Emma DeMarr had been one of the city's most notorious madams. Except for the brief period in the mid-1890s when she took back the active management of her house, DeMarr owned a brothel until 1909, apparently without facing further legal action.

The dismissal pleased Hampton, but his bitterness against the trust company only increased. The company's officers included some high officials in the LDS Church: First Counselor George Q. Cannon was president of the company; Apostle Brigham Young Jr. was vice president; and alternate member of the High Council of the Salt Lake Stake Spencer Clawson was treasurer.[49] The company's ownership of this building did not become a matter of public comment at this time, but brothels became a public issue and a matter of contention within the company in coming years. Elsie St. Omar continued to manage houses and played a peripheral role in a municipal scandal.

The involvement of some Mormons with prostitution illustrates a larger phenomenon. Economic cooperation between gentiles and Mormons began before political accommodation. The advent of railroads and large-scale mining enterprises helped integrate Utah's economy into national markets. Most LDS businessmen abandoned their cooperative and exclusive business practices for capitalist enterprises, often in partnership with gentiles. Leading busi-

nessmen organized the Salt Lake Chamber of Commerce in 1887 as a self-consciously nonsectarian body.[50] The shared interest in the economic growth of
the city helps explain the appeal of regulated prostitution. Regulation made
good business sense whatever an individual's religious or moral principles. A
well-regulated district helped protect real estate values by keeping prostitution
confined. Within the district itself, prostitution and its allied businesses—
saloons, restaurants, stores, boardinghouses—often earned healthy profits.
Landlords and merchants often charged prostitutes higher rents and prices
than they did other citizens. Cora Conway testified that merchants "charge us
women more than they do any body else—They charge us two prices. They
make us pay more than they do any body else. Every body knows that."[51]
Owners of property already surrounded by brothels sometimes argued that
they had little choice other than to rent to prostitutes. Many businessmen of
all creeds or none thus came to favor regulation for self-interested reasons.

The only women who received the full "benefits" of regulation—de facto
licensing, minimal harassment, and a degree of official protection that helped
women earn a reasonably predictable living—were the keepers of parlor
houses located within the acknowledged limits of the prostitution district and
conducted in an "orderly" fashion. Women on the lower rungs of the hierarchy, those who seemed to be acting like prostitutes outside of the district,
or those inside who violated the rules often found themselves the targets of
legal action. Regulation was never formalized; when citizens sometimes complained of prostitution, the police used existing laws to crack down on women
who might be allowed to work undisturbed in quieter times.

Effective regulation depended on establishing geographic boundaries.
Women who sold sex outside of the boundaries discussed in chapter 2 were
subject to prosecution. The chief of police noted in 1897 that ten recently
arrested women were "of the kind who start houses of ill-fame anywhere and
everywhere in the city. We have notified them, time and again, that they must
obey the restrictions set upon them by the police to remain in stated places."[52]

Women continued to bear nearly all of the responsibility and risk for prostitution. In 1886, police arrested thirty-six women as "inmates," fifteen as
"keepers," and only eleven men as "resorters." (Women were also occasionally arrested for resorting to a house of prostitution.) The 1890 report listed
twenty-eight arrests for keeping, eighty for "Residing in house of ill-fame,"
and seven for resorting. The 1891 report listed sixty-six arrests for keeping,
fifteen for "Prostitution" (presumably streetwalking), and 299 for residing;
no category even appears for "resorting." In 1904, 115 cases appeared in the
city court for keeping, 743 for "Prostitution," and only nine for resorting.[53]
The police did sometimes target the men who lived with and profited from

prostitutes with the goal of forcing them out of the city. City authorities considered the "cadets," "pimps," "macquereaux," prizefighters, piano players,
bartenders, and others who sometimes lived in brothels as actual or potential criminals. As with prostitutes, African Americans among this class of men
were especially liable to arrest.[54]

The usual method of regulation was to arrest women on a periodic basis.
The women deposited bail money to guarantee their appearance in court.
When the cases were called a few days later, the women did not appear and
their bonds were forfeited. The bonds/fines varied; the quarterly rate assessed
in 1891 was $50 for keepers and $25 for inmates; in June 1893, the police justice switched to a monthly assessment of $17 and $8.50 respectively.[55] The
system was especially regularized in 1897–98, when keepers were assessed
monthly between the twenty-second and twenty-ninth day of each month.
Keeping a house of ill fame could bring a fine of $25–$100, residing in such
a house, $10–$50, and resorting, $10–$20; the fines evidently varied by the
length of time since a woman had been assessed. The police probably did not
even have to visit the well-known brothels; it seems likelier that the madam
or her agent brought the money to the police station. If an offender could
not pay, she might be locked in the city jail at the rate of one day per dollar.[56] If the authorities wanted to force a woman out, she could be "vagged"—
arrested for vagrancy—and given a "floater"; that is, released on her promise to leave town.[57]

Whether they supported regulation or not, everyone involved understood
this system was de facto licensing. Prostitutes argued that paying the fine
protected them from arrest for the rest of the period. Louise Dreyfus protested to the court in vain that "I have ze license, I pays ze fine every month."[58]
The same judge released another woman because she had "'paid the money
regularly demanded by the city for the conduct of her business.'"[59] The press
frequently referred to the "license"; for example, twelve Japanese women paid
"the regulation license fee."[60] The Third District grand jury condemned in
1891 "the system in vogue of virtually licensing gambling houses and houses
of prostitution, by collecting from them regular quarterly fines, serving as
an incentive to these violators of the law to ply their avocations with greater
avidity."[61] Upon taking office in 1896, Mayor James Glendinning denounced
the custom "to compel the payment of a monthly license."[62]

Women charged with prostitution-related offenses did not always submit
tamely. Those who could afford an attorney and the time often took their
chances and demanded a trial before a jury that might include friends or
customers.[63] Conversely, the authorities preferred a rapid process and sometimes tried to deny women their legal rights. The city tried to avoid jury tri-

als, since they cost $10 to $20 each to prosecute (as of 1891) and tied up the court's time. One police justice maintained that persons appearing in police court were not entitled to a jury trial, but the Third District court quickly overruled.[64] Populist newspaper editor Warren Foster accused one justice of imposing harsher sentences upon those requesting jury trials.[65] Prostitutes were, of course, not always successful before juries. May Hart demanded a trial and was found guilty and fined about three times what an initial guilty plea would have cost.[66] Ida Walker quixotically demanded a trial for keeping a brothel after having paid fines on a regular basis for months; she lost and paid $50 plus $12 court costs.[67]

The municipal authorities frequently resorted to cosmetic measures that protected respectable sensibilities while keeping prostitution profitable and available. In 1891, for example, Franklin Avenue prostitutes were reportedly told that "hereafter they will not be allowed to parade the avenue dressed in a go-as-you-please or any other style; that they are to conduct themselves in a more decorous manner than heretofore, and that they must refrain from indulging in gymnastic and linguistic exercises in the back yards of the harems."[68] Three years later, the chief of police ordered window blinds on that street be kept down; a few months later, he barred piano playing. In 1901, the mayor ordered Commercial Street women to vacate ground floors of buildings, lower their blinds, and douse their electric lights.[69]

While regulation offered a measure of security to brothel keepers and prostitutes, they were still highly vulnerable. The authorities might raid a house they considered particularly disorderly until the women moved or capitulated to regulations. General crackdowns, although temporary, forced many to leave the city. The high mobility rate of some madams, and especially of prostitutes, testifies to their predicament. Women who followed regulations, however, earned praise and perhaps even respect. One official noted that some brothels "are under such perfect control that if a man is robbed in one of them the stolen property can be recovered within one hour's time." He claimed that a "sporting man" who lost a diamond stud complained to the police, who went to the madam; she quickly obtained the gem from the offending woman.[70] A murder in a Victoria Alley crib elicited the chief of police's wistful comparison to Helen Blazes's orderly resort across the street.[71] In turn, cooperative women could call on the police for help with larcenous employees or abusive patrons. When two of Blazes's employees left for Denver with $400 she had advanced them, a Salt Lake detective brought them back to face prosecution.[72] When a salesman tried to wrench a ring off Lillie Evans's finger, the irate madam woke the police justice and obtained a warrant for his arrest.[73]

The lower classes could not count on the limited benefits that parlor house women received. The same authorities who supported regulation vigorously prosecuted streetwalkers and (sometimes) crib workers.[74] Streetwalkers could receive brutal treatment. A policeman arrested Maggie Cope, a white streetwalker, and was leading her to jail when she stumbled and fell. "The officer thought it was merely a drunken stupor, and stopping a cart, dumped the woman into it. On reaching the City Hall she was found to be dead." The coroner ruled she died of "apoplexy."[75]

The regulation of prostitution also illustrates racial realities in Salt Lake society. Arrest records make clear official racism. While the "nationality" column in the arrest registers was usually left blank for prostitutes, African American women were often labeled "nig" or "coon." Police identified one woman only as "A China Woman." Japanese surnames were almost never recorded; instead, the police named them, for example, "Minnie Jap" or "Lottie Jap."[76] The posting of the 24th Infantry, an all-black unit, to Fort Douglas in 1896 sparked white Utahns to express concerns about race mixing and drunken black soldiers accosting white women.[77] The unit's white officers worried about the kind of houses which some of the soldiers frequented. Acting on complaints from the fort, the police ordered the temporary closing of most cribs on Victoria and Franklin Avenues. Japanese women were allowed to sell sex as they did "not admit the [black] soldiers to the houses."[78]

Police justice John B. Timmony used his powers to enforce the racial hierarchy by levying particularly stiff fines against white prostitutes found with black clients. A white woman who worked near Fort Douglas admitted she was a prostitute but "pleaded that she drew the color line. The evidence introduced, however, proved differently." She received ninety days in jail at a time when brothel inmates were normally fined between $10 and $25.[79] The same judge sentenced a "husky negro" found with a white prostitute to ninety days, although other customers were rarely prosecuted.[80] The *Tribune* noted approvingly "the vigorous war being waged by the police department against the white women who associate with colored men and women is beginning to have its effects."[81]

Regulating brothels was relatively straightforward, as police could easily identify and fine the women of the established houses. Because brothels shared space with a wide variety of "legitimate" businesses and homes, however, many other women worked or lived in or passed through the district. As more women moved into the workforce, lived without the supervision of fathers, brothers, or husbands, or took advantage of new opportunities for commercial recreation, they expanded women's presence in public and complicated the distinction between "respectable" and "disorderly" behavior.

The definition of prostitution as a form of vagrancy meant that prosecution depended largely upon a woman's "general reputation." Those women arrested as keepers or inmates of houses of prostitution were usually arrested for their reputed status, not a specific act. The prosecution of a disorderly house likewise relied largely upon testimony as to its reputation.[82] Such reliance meant that the appearance and behavior of women living and working in the business district were constantly subject to police scrutiny. By the standards of the "separate spheres," a respectable woman had no business on the street without a male escort. Her presence alone in public could bring charges and label her a fallen woman. Police often arrested a woman because the officer thought she looked or behaved like a prostitute: she was walking the streets alone, entering a saloon, wearing certain clothing, or talking to men on the street. Unlike male brothel patrons, once a woman lost her positive public reputation it was probably gone for good. It is likely that not everyone was equally concerned about a respectable reputation, although the nature of the sources makes it difficult to determine the reactions of those outside the elite. Many working-class women obviously cared about threats to their reputations, but some prostitutes and their friends, neighbors, and families were probably less concerned with middle- and upper-class notions of "respectability." They could empathize with or overlook the difficult circumstances that could drive a woman to selling sex.[83]

Many women fought hard to defend their reputations. A woman allegedly found drunk in a saloon and arrested for prostitution "proved that she was a married woman and lived at home with her husband and her eight children, and that she was a respectable woman, having only stepped into the saloon on a business errand."[84] Officer Benedict Siegfus arrested Louise Coleman for vagrancy when he found her in a hotel doorway at five o'clock in the morning. Siegfus "considered it his duty to arrest her for being out on the street at that hour without an escort." Coleman indignantly insisted that she had been attending a ball and became separated from her escort. She was awaiting a streetcar back to Fort Douglas, where she worked as a domestic, when Siegfus "made a very indecent proposal to her." Coleman's employer and other officers testified that she "bears an excellent reputation" and threatened to prosecute Siegfus.[85]

Siegfus and other police officers evidently had reputations for overzealousness, and their testimony did not ensure a conviction. At a trial for a mother and daughter, Siegfus testified that the mother "is a prostitute, . . . I have seen her soliciting on the street." The furious woman screamed that Siegfus was a liar and attacked him. When she calmed, she "swore positively that she earned an honest living by taking in washing, and that her daughter did likewise by hiring out as a servant." The judge believed her against the testimony of three police officers.[86] Another officer arrested a woman for soliciting because he had seen her on the street talking to men and "Mrs. Wilson, a notorious character" (probably Ada Wilson). The woman angrily told the court "if a woman could not walk up the streets of this city without being molested and insulted by policemen, then she wanted to know it." The judge dismissed the charges and noted that "prostitution was a serious charge to bring against a woman, and it should not be brought unless there was ample proof to sustain it."[87] Slandering a woman's reputation could be a criminal act. One man was fined $5 "for the pleasure of calling a respectable woman 'chippy.'"[88] Once a woman was labeled a prostitute to the court's satisfaction, however, her reputation could not easily be restored. Dora Topham, the Stockade manager, understood that "my reputation as a pure woman is gone. If I give this up there is nothing left for me to do. Nobody would believe in me. Nobody would help me."[89]

Reputation and ethnicity collided in the reporting of one woman's multiple arrests for prostitution. Under the headline "A Naughty Little Jap," the *Tribune* noted that "Miss Kimma . . . claims to be the wife of a Second South Street restaurant keeper and of 18-carat virtue." When a jury acquitted her, she became "The Japanese Woman" and "the wife of a respectable restaurant-keeper." Several weeks later, the police "had their revenge for they caught the woman in a corner and arrested her." The woman forfeited $50 for prostitution and selling liquor without a license.[90]

Appearance and reputation circumscribed many aspects of prostitutes' lives. Theater owners tried to segregate prostitutes from other patrons. In 1893, the doorkeeper of the Salt Lake Theater refused entrance to the parquette section to several women holding tickets because they were "of character not at all doubtful."[91] He offered them seats in the balcony or a refund, but the women refused. Among them were Malvina Beauchamp, the manager of the "Big V," and her employee Nellie Kingsley. The manager wrote Beauchamp that "women of the class to which you belong have been admitted to the theatre, and their language and conduct have been such as to offend our patrons." Beauchamp and Kingsley sued the theater for violating the 1875 Civil Rights Act and initially won $100 each, but lost on appeal.[92] Such incidents proved the dilemma of judging respectability by appearance. The theater's treasurer noted that a lady of "conspicuous appearance" whom he had judged a prostitute turned out instead to be "the wife of a prominent citizen."[93] Some respectable women were apparently beginning to wear clothing or use cosmetics popularly associated with prostitutes.[94]

Regulation sometimes served political purposes. The turn of a new year frequently brought crackdowns, especially under a new administration. For example, in 1896 incoming mayor James Glendinning denounced licensing and ordered city authorities to conduct waves of arrests and levy stiff fines.[95] The *Tribune's* C. C. Goodwin spoke again for regulationists: "the proposed drastic remedies will simply delocalize the evil, but in so doing it will be scattered from Camp Douglas to beyond the Jordan."[96] Glendinning quickly returned to a regulationist stance. The party (political and/or religious) out of power frequently accused incumbent administrations of profiting from prostitution. The city earned substantial sums from prostitutes, gamblers, and drunks: in 1889, for example, police court revenues totaled nearly $28,000; in 1895, over $16,000.[97] The issue was often colored by Mormon-gentile antagonism; in 1886, the *Tribune* referred to periodic fines as "tithing the harlots."[98]

Prostitutes played another role in electoral politics. Utah women had exercised the franchise since 1870 (with the exception of 1887–96), so candidates actively sought their votes. Several campaigns allegedly depended on the strength of prostitutes' votes, especially the ward-based campaigns for city council. Mormons complained that Kate Flint and her women voted while respectable but polygamous Saints could not. Mormons also claimed that brothel patrons voted Liberal in 1890 and that prostitutes would have if they could. At the state constitutional convention in 1895, the prominent Mormon Brigham H. Roberts claimed that if suffrage was granted to women in the new constitution, the only women who would vote were "the brazen, the element that is under the control of the managers and runners of saloons. . . . The refined wife and mother will not so much as put her foot in the filthy stream." Suffragists (including Mormons) were outraged and Roberts was easily outvoted.[99]

Parties sought or coerced prostitutes' votes while condemning their opponents for doing the same. Madam Kitty Hicks reportedly told the Republican *Tribune* in 1899 that "a very prominent young Democrat" promised that under the Democrats "the houses will be allowed to run all right, and the town will continue to be wide open."[100] The Democratic *Herald* returned the favor two years later, charging that Republican mayor Ezra Thompson had promised prostitutes a wide-open town.[101]

Two politicians allegedly based their careers on the brothel and saloon. R.[obert] Bruce Johnson, an African American saloonkeeper, reportedly mobilized prostitutes, vagrants, and drunks for the Republicans in the 1890s and early 1900s and for the "Americans" after 1904. His opponents acknowledged his clout, once calling him the "boss of the white slaves" (meaning those whose votes he controlled rather than women coerced into prostitution). Johnson was accused but apparently never formally charged with renting rooms to prostitutes on several occasions.[102]

Martin E. Mulvey, a white saloonkeeper, allegedly rode brothel and saloon votes into office, where he protected regulated prostitution. Mulvey ran saloons on Commercial, State, and Main Streets, all locales where prostitutes worked, and won election to the city council from the fifth ward in 1896 as a Democrat.[103] Mulvey joined the American Party, won reelection, and was instrumental in creating the Stockade.[104]

While regulation was firmly entrenched by the late 1870s, the details of prostitution policy often caused controversy. This was especially true in the turmoil of the 1880s, when the polygamy campaign still raged and gentiles struggled for a share of political power. The Liberal victory in the municipal election of 1890 both strengthened regulation and indirectly launched the first tentative reform efforts against prostitution.

The influx of gentile voters, and the disfranchisement of polygamous Mormons and all women under the Edmunds and Edmunds-Tucker Acts respectively, resulted in roughly equal numbers of eligible Mormon and gentile voters and allowed the Liberals in 1890 to narrowly win the mayoralty and a majority of the council.[105] The *Tribune* claimed that the win was a triumph for women: "Twice ten thousand women, who are bound in the toils of Mormonism, will, while kissing their babies to sleep to-night, thank God that the cup they were forced to drink, will be dashed from their children's lips."[106] Gentiles who had long complained of Mormons' exclusive business practices planned to modernize the city and boost it as a regional economic power. Mayor George Scott's administration launched an ambitious program of improvements, including long-delayed upgrading of water systems, sewers, and streets. Ironically, Commercial Street, already well known as a prostitution district, was the first street paved.[107]

The loss of political dominance in their temple city was another in a series of blows that threatened to destroy the LDS Church's temporal hegemony. The perceived moral hypocrisy of the Liberals made the loss harder to bear. Mormons insisted that the Liberals, despite their high-minded denunciations of Mormon "lawlessness," had the backing of the disorderly element. The *Herald* claimed that "every prostitute" and virtually every brothel customer, saloonkeeper, drinker, gambler, and criminal was a Liberal; "and what is more, a large percentage of those who lead the Liberal forces and decry Mormon morals are themselves steeped in lewdness."[108] The *Deseret Evening News* called the *Tribune* "the organ of the prostitute, rumseller and blackleg" and reminded its readers that the *Tribune* had written that "billiard halls, saloons, and houses of ill-fame are more powerful reforming agencies here in Utah than churches and schools, . . . anything to break the shackles [young Mormons] were born in."[109]

The Liberals insisted that as monogamists they would foster a purer moral atmosphere, but they made it clear that they would regulate prostitution.[110] Liberal law enforcement seemed to prove Mormons' worst fears. Although women could not vote in 1890, prostitutes probably did favor the Liberals, who made no pretense of abolishing their livelihoods, and by several accounts more women began to openly sell sex in Salt Lake. Although it is difficult to determine if or how many more prostitutes worked during the Liberals' term, the number of saloons showed a proven increase from seventy to over one hundred.[111]

While gentiles applauded the Liberals' infrastructure improvements, the perceived laxity of law enforcement alienated even some of their staunchest supporters. When a "Citizens' Mass meeting" was called in December 1890 to protest the deteriorating moral climate, the *Tribune* grudgingly conceded that conditions warranted the move.[112] The "law and order" reformers included Protestant clergymen, attorneys, businessmen, and other professionals, many of them Liberals. The chairman declared "it is a slander on the people of this city for licenses to [be] granted on the supposition that the people have no objection to the running of brothels right under our noses." The editor of the *Deseret News* stated that Mormons "also were ready to range themselves on the side of decency, and order," an offer that generated applause. Although women probably attended, their presence was not noted and apparently none spoke. Attorney Frank B. Stephens claimed that the police only arrested prostitutes because they could not vote and called for the arrest of male owners and patrons.[113] A committee drafted a petition to the city council complaining that Liberals were "imperiling the cause of morality." Not surprisingly, the petition did not include Stephens's endorsement of a single moral standard, although it called on the government to "enforce promptly and thoroughly the laws."[114]

Reformers were most concerned, however, with saloons being open on Sundays. Temperance activists, including many of the "law and order" petitioners, demanded the city "enforce the laws as they exist"; brothels were an afterthought. These reformers did not call for the eradication of prostitution or the prohibition of alcohol, nor did they form a permanent organization. They wanted the city to use its coercive power against the "disorderly classes" and "disorderly resorts" for the benefit of its respectable citizens.[115]

The Franklin Avenue Variety Theater was a particular target. Reformers worried that the new theater would feature bawdy entertainment and drunken crowds. Its proprietor obtained a theater license after promising not to sell liquor.[116] The theater's success was immediate; opening night saw hundreds of people turned away. The *Herald* sniffed "in the house was a riff raff miscellaneous assemblage. . . . Cowboys, tin-horners, higher-toned gamblers and the rag tag and bobtail element generally swarmed, smoked and spit. There was not a female visage to be seen off the stage."[117]

Despite promises, the proprietors won a saloon license after a long struggle. Opponents saw the theater's female employees as a dire moral threat.[118] Complaints poured in to the police and the papers about the women who sold drinks and sex. One man reported that a "box nymph" robbed him of $10.[119] Another man complained "a young woman lost to shame" tried to get "money to commit vice and crime." He added that "such institutions as the Novelty Theater are on par with the practice of polygamy, and each apparently has its thugs. I have no harsh words for the poor women who are the victims in both institutions."[120] Citizen pressure finally convinced the council to revoke the saloon's license and the theater soon went under. Ironically, when authorities forced prostitutes onto Franklin Avenue in 1894, madams converted the theater into a large brothel.[121] Dissatisfaction in Liberal ranks with Mayor Scott's lax policies may have contributed to his replacement in 1892 by Robert N. Baskin, an attorney and prominent anti-Mormon activist, as their candidate for mayor.[122]

Most reformers and municipal authorities did not have much daily interaction with prostitutes, but beat patrolmen did. Policemen in the "tenderloin" naturally spent time in its businesses in the course of patrolling (and sometimes off-hour recreating); long-term officers undoubtedly knew dozens of prostitutes on sight. Some policemen used their authority to abuse and exploit women. The control of prostitution in the early 1890s exacerbated tensions within the police department, leading to violence, public scandal, and changes in the department's leadership and its control by the municipal government.

The first controversy surrounded Captain William B. Parker. Officers complained of his harsh discipline, profane language, and alleged favoritism. Hattie Wilson, who ran a Franklin Avenue brothel, claimed that a drunken Parker came to her house after midnight on 4 July 1891 and demanded to be entertained on the piano. As only one girl "was at leisure" (who apparently couldn't play), Parker left but returned minutes later when he heard singing. Two prostitutes and an unnamed male patron corroborated that Parker attempted to drag the thinly dressed Wilson to police headquarters and that another detective struck the patron when he tried to interfere. The testimony of the women and the "resorter" carried little weight. Parker was cleared, but the council abolished the office of police captain, apparently as a back-door means of removing him. A few months later Parker accosted one of his accusers, patrolman George Albright, and attempted to shoot him; when his gun misfired, Albright drew his own weapon and killed Parker, an action that was ruled self-defense.[123]

Albright had his own connections that provide insights into prostitutes' vulnerability, their relationship with the authorities, and the strength of reg-ulation; they also give a rare glimpse inside Salt Lake brothels. A woman named Rose Miller claimed in June 1892 that while she had worked in Sadie Noble's and Minnie Barton's brothels, Albright tried to make her his private mistress. When she refused, he threatened her life and forced himself on her several times over the course of months.[124] Police arrested Miller and anoth-er woman as inmates of a house of prostitution just after her accusations appeared. Their landlady, the well-known Elsie St. Omar, was charged with keeping a brothel.[125] St. Omar pleaded not guilty, claiming that she "had gone there to live in a private house, as some of her relatives were coming and she didn't want them to know of the life she had been leading."[126] Miller and the other woman insisted they were no longer prostitutes, and Miller now swore that three other policemen had also abused her. The charges against the other woman were dismissed, but St. Omar and Miller were found guilty.[127]

The trials of Elsie St. Omar and her boarders drew large, curious crowds, as was often true of prostitution cases. Mayor Robert Baskin found the testi-mony of a night on the town by city councilmen troubling and conducted his own investigation.[128] He found that several councilmen decided on the night of 17 June to investigate Rose Miller's charges. At Elsie St. Omar's house, they discovered reporters from the *Times* and the *Deseret Evening News* interview-ing Miller. Someone produced beer, and two councilmen joined the interview. A reporter told them "Marshal [Ed] Janney was with some of his men at a house of prostitution on Franklin avenue having a general good time." The councilmen proceeded to Hattie Wilson's house at 53 Franklin. The madam was evasive but eventually admitted the councilmen and reporters.

The marshal was in a parlor with a police officer, detective George Sheets, police justice Frederick Kesler, and a deputy sheriff from Wyoming. Janney explained that the Wyoming lawman was searching for a witness in a murder case and thought she might be in a Salt Lake brothel. Janney had invited the others to join the search, which began in "the variety theater" (probably the People's Opera House on Commercial Street) and moved on to no. 243 south Main Street, then run by Helen Blazes, where they questioned the women. The officers then moved to an unnamed location on Commercial Street, and from there went to Hattie Wilson's, where the councilmen surprised them.

The police party was in "a parlor where the floor is bare, no bedroom or beds or lounges there, only settees, and there was a woman playing a piano." "There was dancing going on and music" while women passed in and out. Kesler was reportedly stretched on a couch smoking a cigar when the councilmen entered and "said in a smiling and joking way, 'I plead guilty to the charge and will fine myself $25.00.'" Chief Janney remarked "we are caught" and worried aloud that the councilmen might do something "to injure him." The officials spent fifteen or twenty minutes drinking beer and dancing with the women, although the officials swore that the dancing was chaste.

Janney suggested the combined party proceed to Malvina Beauchamp's "Big V" on Plum Alley, where "we were looking up some business, and I said you will miss nothing if you go, you can hear a girl there that is a very fine singer." One councilman went along "first, for the curiousity [sic], the other to see what I could see." The party danced and drank beer at the Big V and enjoyed the singer. Beauchamp had an electric call button system, and "some one would say more beer, and then a woman would shove a button." The patrolman, noting that "our business often takes us to such places," asserted knowledgeably that "women order beer as men come in, and if no one pays for it then they usually call it on the house." The party broke up when several councilmen expressed concern that Chief Janney was becoming drunk.

Baskin reiterated three questions: how much did the men drink (and who paid)? Did anyone touch the women? And why had he learned of the "investigation" through the papers? One councilman admitted that "we were having a jolly good time, cracking jokes. . . . It was mutually understood and agreed that none of us would open our mouths." Only once did Baskin express legal concerns about the brothels: "You knew they were outlawed institutions? You took no steps to punish them?" The answers were negative. The mayor's position was clear: he had no objection to well-regulated brothels but felt "it is scarcely proper for members of the City Council to participate in a drunken revelry at a house of ill-fame at 1 and 2 o'clock in the morning."[129]

Mayor Baskin fired Chief Janney, Detective Sheets, and the patrolman; Albright followed a few weeks later. The new chief immediately revised department rule five, which read "officers . . . must not in uniform enter a saloon, except in the discharge of their duty." The words "gambling house, or house of ill fame" were inserted between "saloon" and "except."[130] No real harm was done Janney and Sheets, as both were later rehired as patrolmen;

Sheets would eventually become chief.[131] The mayor censured the councilmen and Kesler, but he had no power over the council and that body appointed the police justice, so the council itself decided their fates. A select committee concluded "this body has no authority to take any action" against the councilmen. The police committee (which included one of the censured councilmen) reported that "no excuse can be given for [Kesler] . . . his conduct was against the honor and dignity of his high and responsible position and was open to censure." The council eventually replaced Kesler. His behavior may have been particularly embarrassing to Mormons as his father was a longtime LDS bishop.[132]

This minor episode offers some intriguing insights, but the women's viewpoint is missing. The mayor did not question them and seemed little concerned with their role. Hattie Wilson's attempt to protect the officers suggests that they were frequent visitors, and the councilmen's behavior must have also reassured her. We can only speculate on the thoughts of Malvina Beauchamp and her "girls" when two reporters (taking notes?), the chief of police, a patrolman, the police justice, and four council members entered their parlor to talk, joke, drink, and dance. The evidence suggests that the madams were gracious but cautious. Elsie St. Omar and Hattie Wilson initially claimed to have no beer, probably because they had no liquor license. The women were by all accounts restrained, decorous, and modestly dressed; no one admitted to soliciting or being solicited for sex. The authorities' evening out must have been a topic of much discussion among women in the brothel district. The comfortable presence of Chief Janney and Justice Kesler—the two officials with the most power to suppress their business—could only have convinced prostitutes and madams that orderly parlor houses were in little danger.

The authorities ignored Rose Miller's accusations in the flap over the events of 17 June. A prostitute stood virtually no chance of proving rape, especially against a policeman. A rape charge depended upon a woman's refusal of consent to an act of sex, considered impossible behavior for a prostitute.[133] Miller's other charges, which constituted stalking by later standards, were not statutory offenses in the late nineteenth century. Albright's abuse did arouse some backhanded public sympathy for Miller: "No matter how low the woman may be, how vile her occupation, the imposition practiced upon her by ALBRIGHT through threats of violence show him to be infinitely lower and viler."[134] The problem was solved to the authorities' satisfaction by Albright's dismissal, but none of the other officers Rose Miller accused were punished. Miller was arrested fifteen months later for keeping a brothel.[135]

The Liberals' opponents tried to make political capital of this incident, but many people dismissed it out of hand. A former Liberal member of the police committee claimed that he had made "similar tours of investigation in the interest of the city" and that if the mayor had complained, he would have told him "to take a trip to the regions where his Satanic majesty presides and where his imps hold high carnival."[136] The councilmen may have also avoided public censure because two were Democrats (and Mormons) and two Liberals, making it difficult for the partisan press to charge impropriety.[137] The *Herald* suggested that Baskin should have expected such things, since "the Liberal victory was celebrated by drunken orgies in every brothel in this city." The paper continued to express support for regulation, however, as long as the worst houses were suppressed.[138] Baskin did direct the police to close saloons on Sunday (a rule often flouted) and to raid gambling houses and several small brothels. Significantly, he took no action against parlor houses, including any of the houses visited on 17 June.[139]

Although the brothel-hopping incident received much press, reform groups expressed little interest. Four weeks after it became public, another mostly Liberal group of "law and order" reformers met. The speakers, again all male, emphasized Sunday saloons with only one mention of houses of ill fame. Frederick Kesler, still clinging to his seat, attended; he was criticized not for his behavior on 17 June but rather because he "virtually offers a bribe to lawbreakers through the imposition of such trifling fines as to make his administration of justice a public farce."[140]

The police controversies led the territorial legislature to create a Board of Police and Fire Commissioners in 1894. The council and mayor appointed two members each, but the board was to be completely independent. O. J. Salisbury, a gentile banker, chaired the first board, which included Nelson A. Empey, bishop of the LDS Thirteenth Ward, which encompassed the prostitution district.[141] The board did not alter prostitution policy. Orderly brothels continued to be regulated, while the city government sometimes responded to citizen pressure to deal with particularly obnoxious houses.

By the time of the councilmen's night out, substantive changes were well under way in the city. The early 1890s were a period of great transition, as LDS Church leaders and members sought to adjust and accommodate to the nation's economy, society, and political establishment.[142] The capitulation on polygamy drew the most attention. President Wilford Woodruff issued his so-called Manifesto on 25 September 1890, counseling Mormons not to enter into plural marriages. Although some gentiles found the statement ambiguous and remained suspicious, and some Mormons continued to contract plural marriages, most accepted that the manifesto meant the beginning of the end of polygamy and the federal authorities eased their "crusade."[143]

The lessening of tensions extended to politics as well. The People's Party and the Liberals disbanded, and activists organized branches of the national parties that included Mormons and non-Mormons. Robert Baskin left the Liberals and received the backing of a nonpartisan citizen's committee, including many Saints, and won reelection as mayor in 1893.[144] LDS Church authorities consciously retreated from politics, although their occasional interference sparked fierce reaction from political activists across the religious spectrum.[145] Economic accommodation, already well under way, also picked up steam. The LDS Church sold or privatized most of its business concerns, including a street railroad, a gas company, and Zion's Co-operative Mercantile Institution (ZCMI), and solicited outside investment in many financial enterprises.[146]

Reformers also found some common ground. For example, temperance work, including a newly energized branch of the Woman's Christian Temperance Union (WCTU), attracted interest across religious lines. The speakers at a temperance rally in July 1892 included Protestant ministers who opposed polygamy, but also many Mormons.[147] Historian Carol Cornwall Madsen cites these activities as among the first that united reformers during what she calls the "Decade of Detente."[148] Members of Mormon and gentile women's clubs founded the Utah Federation of Women's Clubs in 1892. Detente was not immediate or complete, of course. When a mixed group of women assembled the Utah display for the Women's Pavilion at the Columbian Exposition in 1893, Cornelia Paddock contributed copies of her anti-Mormon novels.[149]

Many reform efforts were temporary and limited in scope. In 1892 Mary Post and twenty-five others petitioned the city council to remove "the immoral class of tenants from Franklin Ave." so that residents "would be able to rent their houses and be able to pay the city taxes on the same."[150] Such petitions posed a dilemma for the authorities, who did not want to lose the votes of respectable property owners. On the other hand, regulation's supporters argued that brothels had to be located somewhere. The Franklin Avenue houses were established, localized, and relatively orderly. When residents there complained of prostitution, those complaints did not carry much weight with city hall, since most residents were working-class and many were African American. Any crackdown on Franklin would force prostitutes elsewhere, and people who perhaps wielded greater economic and political clout would complain of the influx.

This particular petition, however, fit Mayor Baskin's plans to "make this the best governed city in the Rocky mountain region" (and perhaps counter charges of Liberal immorality).[151] The police notified prostitutes that they had a week to leave Franklin.[152] The police complained, however, that the move was a mistake. When a gambler and a hack driver reportedly "carved themselves into pieces" over a prostitute living on State Street, the police captain was not surprised: "This, . . . is the result of driving the women of the town off Franklin avenue. They are located in the business blocks all over the city, and are almost absolutely beyond police control. It is almost impossible for us to make a charge of prostitution stick against the women that are doing business in these blocks. They ought all to be kept on one street, where they could be watched and controlled."[153] Franklin Avenue remained a location of choice for authorities, and in early 1894 they ordered the police to force all prostitutes back. That campaign, which included the unusual step of arresting "every man found resorting to the dens that are maintained in respectable localities," was reportedly successful by summer 1894, but the move aroused new complaints.[154]

Just after the 1892 cleansing of Franklin Avenue, some citizens began to look beyond police action and the techniques of mass meetings, speeches, sermons, and petitions. A group of reformers sought to change the behavior of individual women. An evangelical revival meeting inspired several ministers and laypersons to create a rescue mission.[155] Their council, dominated by evangelical male Protestants, included Sarah Reed, a Presbyterian and WCTU officer. Reed proposed maternalist solutions to prostitution. She first suggested the need for a police matron at the city jail, explaining that female prisoners (mostly prostitutes) "are cared for by men entirely, and deprived of the attention and care that only the sympathetic nature of a good Christian woman can give."[156] Reed further proposed "a home for fallen women. . . . There is now no place where such women coming out of the jails can go for reformation."[157]

This proposed method of rescue had deep roots. Since the early nineteenth century, those women and men who had helped to construct the "cult of true womanhood" had stressed women's potential to do for society what they did for the home: make it clean, pure, moral, and safe. Women used their most widely respected role—that of mother within the home—to justify their participation in moral reform efforts. Middle-class Protestant women sought to address the perceived disorder and immorality of the western United States by establishing "home missions," including the Industrial Christian Home for plural wives in Salt Lake City.[158] Although that institution was not particularly successful, antipolygamy activists could claim victory over the last of the "twin relics of barbarism" in 1890.[159] With the apparent solution of that problem, which had monopolized the reform energies of Utah's activist gentiles, some reformers were ready to apply similar techniques to other moral problems.

Some of the same persons who had fought polygamy—clubwomen, missionaries, evangelical Protestant ministers and their wives—now turned their attention to prostitution. The presence of those particular reformers or their successors, the similarity between the Industrial Christian Home and Reed's proposed home for fallen women, and the emphasis placed upon a proper "Christian" atmosphere appear to have discouraged the participation of more than a few Mormons who might otherwise have joined the effort.

In late 1892, the rescue mission issued a prospectus for its "rescue home." Mary Grant Major, a director, stressed female solidarity and the responsibility that Christian women bore for their "sisters."[160] Like the directors of the Industrial Christian Home, Major and her colleagues believed in the redemptive power of a pure, Christian, maternal, domestic atmosphere upon a woman who had been sinned against, whether by a Mormon husband, a seducer, or a brothel procurer. Some men agreed that a good mother's influence was the best hope for saving fallen women. LDS Elder John Henry Smith, speaking in favor of rescue work, stressed a mother's responsibility to keep her daughters pure. Mayor James Glendinning asked a rescue worker about the mothers of girls in the home; the worker replied that "many of them had no mothers, and that others who had mothers would be better off if they didn't have."[161]

The home found a suitable location in late February 1893. Dr. Helen Ritchie offered the rental use of her house and agreed to serve as matron of the "Anchorage." Mary Grant Major boasted that "for the first time in the history of this city, there stands within it a home from whose door no destitute woman shall be turned. Within that home waits a kindly Christian woman with sympathy and help. . . . The home will be open alike to destitute or fallen, those who have taken but one wrong step or those who have sunk to the blackest depths, yet who have found room for repentance. The thought has been to refuse no one whom God would receive."[162] From the home's inception, funding was tenuous; the mission relied mainly on contributions raised in Protestant churches.[163] The directors suggested that an appropriate source would be the fines collected from prostitutes. By using that money for rescue purposes, the city could cleanse itself of the sin of profiting by women's immorality and exploitation. While the proposal to use fine money for "saving many others from the horrors of such an existence" gained some support, the city council considered such a use illegal but eventually appropriated $100 per month.[164]

The executive committee included women with strong evangelical Protestant connections, including Sara McNiece, an officer of the WCTU and wife of a Presbyterian minister and antipolygamy activist. Their petition laid out the home's purposes: to provide "an avenue of escape from [prostitutes'] life of shame" and "a thorough reformation and change of heart and life." The home would accomplish two goals: "reform these degraded women and at the same time protect society by diminishing their number."[165]

To judge by the petition's language, the home's founders seemed ambivalent toward the women they intended to save. The founders expressed sympathy for their "fallen" sisters but it is not clear whom they held responsible. What little rhetoric survives hints that they believed a fallen woman had been betrayed by a lover, a brothel procurer, or a negligent or abusive parent, but they also blamed that woman for having "taken but one wrong step." The rescuers' ideology of true womanhood implicitly assumed that no women would enter a brothel voluntarily.[166] Fallen women had to be "sav[ed] . . . from themselves" and prove "worthy of . . . a future of respectability and honesty." The founders were certain that a complete break from the past and immersion in their version of middle-class true womanhood were the proper and necessary antidotes to the "life of shame" that would inevitably lead to an early death.[167]

The daily operation of the rescue home combined voluntary with coercive elements.[168] As originally envisioned, admission was voluntary and women could leave at any time, but the executive committee and the matron strictly supervised those who chose to enter. The "inmates," as they were sometimes called,[169] had to divorce themselves completely from their past lives. They were not allowed to send or receive letters without going through the matron. The rescuers instructed inmates in domestic industries—"sewing, cooking and other useful accomplishments"—so that they could "earn an honest living." The directors sought to reestablish a fallen woman's status as a true woman who could work in a proper home and eventually marry a respectable man. Like the antipolygamy activists, the antiprostitution reformers assumed that all women aspired to marry, raise children, and manage a home.[170]

The authorities had a different view of the home's purpose and contributed to a change in its character. The city council referred the original petition to the police committee, perhaps indicating from the outset that the council envisioned a penal use.[171] The authorities used the home as an alternative to imprisonment, especially for young women who might still be "saved" but who would be further degraded by incarceration. Within months of its opening, the police justice "committed" an "incorrigible maid" to the home. Another woman found drunk was offered her choice of the home or jail.[172] Also rescued was seventeen-year-old Maggie Stewart, who was reportedly born in Pittsburgh and abandoned by her mother at fourteen months, then adopted by a "Samaritan" who made her "the drudge of the household." After her adopted mother's death, Maggie spent three years in an orphan's asylum before her birth mother "reclaimed" her and brought her to Butte, Montana. For unspecified reasons "then began the downward march on the path which has for its goal shame and degradation." Maggie came to Salt Lake City and worked in a variety theater until police arrested her for prostitution. The directors of the rescue home negotiated her release and brought her, "friendless, penniless and ill," to the Anchorage "where she will be tenderly cared for and nursed back to health and strength."[173] The police justice dismissed a charge of prostitution against another woman on whose behalf the rescue workers "endeavor[ed] to secure a home."[174] The U.S. attorney ordered the release of two other girls ("white, though not of the lily order") arrested for fornication with black men and brought them to the home.[175]

These women's fates are unknown, but others resisted the rescuers' ministrations. A tearful nineteen-year-old named Annie Ricker told the police justice that she would give up prostitution if she could find a job to support herself and her young brother and sister. She was placed in the home, but that night a rescue worker complained that Ricker "was creating a disturbance there, and requested that she be removed forthwith." By the time the police arrived, she was gone.[176]

Stories like Annie Ricker's obscure the fact that many women probably welcomed the home's assistance. A pregnant or ill unmarried woman might have few alternatives, especially if she was a penniless prostitute. Although the home's records apparently no longer exist, periodic newspaper reports indicate that at least several dozen women received much-needed childbirth services, vocational training, or medical care. The rescuers focused most of their attentions on young, presumably more easily redeemable women, although there were exceptions. Sallie Davis, a twice-married homeless woman frequently arrested for drunkenness and prostitution, reported that the mission twice tried and failed to reform her.[177]

The home continued to evolve throughout its existence. In early 1899, a city ordinance "authoriz[ed] the chief of police to send any unfortunate females that may be sentenced by the police justice, to the Woman's Home or confine them in the city jail." The ordinance was interpreted to mean that a runaway from the home could be incarcerated in the city jail.[178] In six years, the home had metamorphosed from a private, voluntary reformatory to a quasi-penal institution subject to municipal oversight where women could be coerced to stay. By the time that change had occurred, the rescue home had experienced severe financial troubles and a change in management.

The home had the bad luck of being founded at the outset of the worst economic depression the nation had known. The panic of 1893 heavily damaged Utah's economy and increased competition for charitable dollars. In

November a relief committee was created to help the poor, ill, and unemployed. Rev. R. G. McNiece, president of the rescue mission, reminded citizens that the new committee, although worthy, was a temporary expedient. The rescue mission did not merely feed people or provide them with work; its goal was to "reclaim the fallen and the lost."[179]

The relief committee, however, attracted more attention and more prominent citizens. Perhaps because of its purely secular nature, the committee included gentiles and Mormons, including some former opponents. Its "visiting committees" included Mormons Emmeline B. Wells, editor of the *Woman's Exponent,* and Emily S. Tanner Richards, a longtime suffrage advocate and wife of a prominent LDS Church attorney. Non-Mormons included Isabel Cameron Brown, a former member of the Industrial Christian Home Association; the rescue home's Mary Grant Major; and Cornelia Paddock, the antipolygamy activist. The presence of former antagonists in the polygamy debate in the same organization demonstrates the extent to which "detente" prevailed in 1893 and the ability of women to cooperate once polygamy seemed settled.[180]

In October 1894, a group of "Christian ladies" led by Cornelia Paddock moved to revive the rescue home, which had foundered some months earlier, probably from lack of funding.[181] Paddock was elected president of the "Woman's Home Association of Salt Lake City" (WHA). The other officers included more old enemies. Dr. Ellen B. Ferguson was chosen first vice president and later served as secretary. Cornelia Paddock and Ellen Ferguson seem unlikely allies, and the reasons for their cooperation are not clear. Ferguson, a convert to Mormonism, helped found Deseret Hospital and was a longtime suffrage advocate and president of the Woman's Suffrage Association.[182] Ferguson and Paddock apparently knew one another as suffrage allies and as opponents in the polygamy debate; the *Anti-Polygamy Standard* had attacked the LDS physician when she spoke publicly in defense of plural marriage.[183] Both women had experience with public activism and an interest in public morality, and had long advocated a single sexual standard and the prosecution of brothel patrons.[184] Ferguson told a WHA meeting that "every fallen and disgraced woman in this city is the sister of those present. . . . This work of rescue devolves upon women, but the men should come forward and give of their means to assist them."[185] Other WHA officers included Mary I. Tisdale, later president of the Central Christian Church's Ladies Aid Society, and Mrs. Winfield S. Hawkes, a WCTU member and wife of the Congregational minister.[186] While Ferguson left the WHA within the year, Tisdale and Hawkes remained active for the next four years.

The WHA divided its reform targets into two categories. The first included those destitute, homeless, or unemployed through no fault of their own; the second, "fallen women." Cornelia Paddock and her coworkers expressed divergent attitudes toward these groups, reflecting the Victorian dichotomy between true and fallen women. Women in the first category remained "respectable" because their shortcomings were economic; they had committed no moral transgression. Fallen women, however, were at least partially responsible for their condition, and WHA rhetoric did not distinguish between prostitutes and women who had been seduced. Paddock described fallen women as "erring girls" and "hapless ones" "groping in the darkness of immorality." She evinced concern for "the miserable condition of these outcasts" who deserved a "share in the divine compassion that caused our elder brother to sweat great drops of blood."[187]

Unlike her criticism of lustful Mormon men, Paddock did not publicly condemn the male customers, landlords, or seducers of these women. Nor did she publicly advocate legislative or police remedies for prostitution, let alone the kind of federal intervention she had championed in the 1880s. While antipolygamy activists had sometimes compared plural marriage with prostitution, Paddock did not invert the comparison, at least publicly. The WHA concentrated on individual women who wanted to reform (although some minors were involuntarily committed to its care). Neither Paddock nor other WHA members apparently took an explicit stand on prostitution policy, although it can be inferred that they favored abolition.

The WHA initially attracted wide support. An early meeting attracted about one hundred people, including Protestant clergy and Mormon authorities. Rev. William D. Mabry, First M.E.; Rev. Hawkes; Wilma Burton of the Davis Deaconess Home, M.E.; and LDS elder John Henry Smith spoke for rescue. Burton complained that many women lacked necessary domestic skills: "There are women in this city who cannot properly cook a beef steak; neither do they understand the use of the needle. [Fallen women] should be instructed in these directions, in order that they may make good housewives." Mabry, Hawkes, and Smith advocated a single moral standard for men and women, a central tenet of WCTU and LDS rhetoric (although non-Mormons long had difficulty accepting the latter's sincerity, given polygyny). The speakers condemned the police and city authorities for indifference in the face of the "ruin" of young girls.[188]

The rescue home received a boost from a December 1894 appearance by General William Booth, the founder of the Salvation Army, before a large crowd in the Mormon Tabernacle. Booth argued for vigilance to protect the morality of young people but Christian charity for those who had fallen. The WHA also benefited from its shared membership with local women's organizations. Deaconess Wilma Burton and WCTU president Helen Tibbals addressed the Woman's Suffrage Association and its president, Ellen B. Ferguson, on the city's morality. Reformers created a joint committee to lobby the Board of Police and Fire Commissioners for a police matron.[189]

Meanwhile, the police were responding to citizen complaints about prostitutes on Franklin Avenue. Twenty-six "respectable women" asked that prostitutes again be moved from that street in October 1894. The police responded with a raid that netted five housekeepers and fifty-seven inmates.[190] A similar petition followed from a Dr. F. Gardiner and sixteen others.[191] Chief Arthur Pratt preferred the women stay where they were: "To keep the prostitutes where they are now probably is an injustice to fifty persons, whereas to remove them to some other quarter would undoubtedly be extremely repugnant and equally unjust to 500 or more residents and taxpayers." Wherever they ended up, Pratt wanted prostitution "within restricted limits, properly patrolled."[192]

Pratt was correct that any movement would bring new complaints. Owners of Commercial Street property counterpetitioned that an influx of what they euphemistically called the "present residents of Franklin avenue" would cause "great damage and almost irreparable injury." The most important signatory was the Brigham Young Trust Company. The trust company's attorney argued before the Board of Police and Fire Commissioners for the suppression of prostitution but found little support. All of the commissioners and Chief Pratt responded that suppression would only scatter fallen women, but they disagreed on where they should be segregated. Two commissioners suggested the district be moved out of the heart of the city, while two others favored keeping in women where they were.[193]

The trust company petition coincided with yet another from Franklin Avenue. These petitioners, however, profited or sought to profit from prostitution. They asked that the city "not remove our present tenants" since "much money has been spent by us for improvements on our property on this street within the last six months with the understanding that this matter was finally settled." Dr. Gardiner had apparently experienced a change of heart (or tenant) since he joined this new action. The landlords may have realized that prostitutes paid better than other tenants.[194]

Despite the above petitions, the authorities ordered all prostitutes off Franklin Avenue by 1 January 1895. This forced move, the third in sixteen months, probably caused women to lose rent payments, furniture, and other property. The collector of water rates shut off service to several women who refused to pay water taxes until they found "undisturbed anchorage" elsewhere.[195] The cautious commissioners denied they told police to force the women *to* any

particular location. Chief Pratt claimed he "ordered at least a dozen of the leading ones" to stay off Commercial Street and advised many to leave town.[196]
Commercial, however, was the logical destination and at least two madams
quickly moved there. Essie Watkins moved to the former *Times* building with
six women, and Gussie Blake came to Commercial with five more. Their presence was particularly embarrassing for some city authorities. Chief Pratt was
part-owner of the *Times* building, while Blake secured property belonging to
a bank whose president, O. J. Salisbury, was a former president of the Board
of Police and Fire Commissioners. The attorney for the Brigham Young Trust
Company complained that the company had spent $60,000 to refurbish a
building on Commercial and was having difficulty finding respectable tenants.

The dispute reopened old antagonisms. The *Tribune* recalled that the company had long rented to prostitutes, while the Mormon press emphasized the
presence of prostitutes in gentile-owned buildings.[197] The women themselves
were caught in the crossfire. Watkins, Blake, and their women were arrested;
within a week, Watkins moved to a former Kate Flint property, where she stayed
for two years. The experienced Essie predicted no change in prostitution policy: "I am not going to do any business until this affair blows over, . . . but when
houses open again I shall open and try to make money again. I imagine that I
will have to remain quiet for about three months, and then everything will go
on as usual. Till then I am going to live decent."[198] Watkins returned to operate briefly on Commercial Street in late 1897.[199]

Gussie Blake was more persistent and faced more determined legal action.
A U.S. marshal charged her with keeping a house of prostitution and selling
liquor without a license. Blake was convicted of the liquor violation, but she
continued to operate, leading the Brigham Young Trust Company to swear
out more complaints. The pressure was evidently successful, as Blake disap-
peared from the records.[200]

The latest "cleansing" of Franklin Avenue resulted in a temporary decline
in the number of prostitutes and the relocation of some women.[201] As usual,
the discreet and orderly houses in Block 57 were unaffected. The cautious
Helen Blazes remained on Franklin and was arrested in early February. Blazes
told the police justice that she was "simply awaiting there until such time as
the matter of the demi-monde's destination is decided." She eventually settled into Sadie Noble's former house at 166½ west South Temple before establishing her long residence at 7 Victoria Place.[202]

Throughout this time, the Woman's Home Association also struggled to
find a home. Cornelia Paddock complained that the WHA had searched for
nine months and interviewed the owners of some thirty houses but had been
unable to find one who would rent a building. She must have been frustrat-

ed by her inability to offer refuge to displaced Franklin Avenue women. In the interim, the WHA proposed to open sewing rooms for destitute women and extracted a promise from the laundry association to employ women from the association in preference to other applicants.[203] A year later, Paddock reported that financial troubles continued to hinder the association in "caring for erring girls," but some women had been helped. "Sixteen fallen girls have been sent to us to be cared for, or have come of their own accord"; eight were sent to Ogden to the "Home of [or "for"] the Friendless," a WCTU-run rescue institution; two were "earning their own living in respectable places"; four were "returned to their friends"; one "of unsound mind" was turned over to county authorities; and one was "under our care in this city." The report did not specify whether these "erring girls" were prostitutes or simply unmarried pregnant women.[204]

The rescue effort received a boost only days after this report. Charles Nelson Crittenton, a wealthy evangelist who helped found a chain of homes for unwed mothers named for his deceased infant daughter Florence, addressed some four thousand in the Mormon Tabernacle. Crittenton claimed a 25 to 30 percent success rate in reforming fallen women. He donated $500 to an Ogden woman and the "Home of the Friendless" became part of the National Florence Crittenton Mission.[205]

The WHA operated in association with the bolstered Ogden home, which served all of Utah, and Paddock became a member of the Ogden organization. The Salt Lake organization finally established its own "rescue station and home of the friendless" by April 1896.[206] Paddock appealed frequently for material assistance, but emphasized the spiritual as well. She explained to one audience that education and training, while important, could not save fallen girls; only "a touch of the divine hand" could do that. One girl had been taken from jail and "saved" before dying, while another whose mother had "sold her into a life of shame and iniquity" had been healed in body and soul and sent to California to keep her away from her mother.[207]

Despite funding problems, the rescuers actively sought out subjects. Paddock attended the trial of two girls under sixteen charged with soliciting and volunteered to place them in the Ogden home, to which all agreed.[208] Some women, however, showed no inclination to accept the promise of respectability training. Paddock and another woman attended the trial of fifty-eight women arrested in a mass raid. The judge announced that "the ladies were present to offer homes and respectable employment to all who would abandon their life of sin," but there were no takers.[209] One woman, the mother of a ten-month-old child, complained that the rescue workers could not offer a job that would support her family and chose jail instead, evidence to a reporter of "the total depravity of some of these unfortunate sisters of sin."[210]

At her trial, Bertha Brown was defiant to the point of appearing "enfeebled" in mind and morals. She told Paddock "I'll be of age in one month, . . . and then I'm going to be a thoroughbred, see!" The judge, however, committed her to the care of the WHA. Brown's experience further demonstrated the dual (if not contradictory) nature of the rescue home. When she became violent and attempted to run away, the matron turned her over to the police. Paddock emphasized that "we have no bolts or bars to keep any girl, but we generally find the law of kindness strong enough to hold those who are brought to us. Moreover, we never let any girl go. If we find it impossible to keep her, we turn her over to the authorities."[211]

Little evidence exists of what motivated these women to reject the WHA's aid, but economics are the likeliest explanation. Despite prostitution's dangers, it did hold out the promise of substantial earnings. Some women may also have preferred the relative freedom and independence of brothel life compared to the domestic sphere. Historian Ruth Rosen notes that prostitutes often expressed contempt for respectable culture and a preference for their own.[212] Some women may have chosen the madam's version of maternalism over the strict isolation and discipline offered at the rescue home.

The WHA continued to struggle with a low profile and public indifference, in spite of Paddock's appeals. A handful of Sisters of the Good Shepherd came to Salt Lake City in late 1896 to found a Magdalen Home "to care for and protect poor, frail, misguided and misdirected girls who have no homes and who are ostracized by the world." The *Herald*, perhaps indicating Mormon antipathy toward Cornelia Paddock, claimed "no such institution has before been established in our midst." Little further evidence of this home has been found.[213]

Paddock and other reformers sought also to prevent women from "falling." A number of overlapping reform efforts began in Salt Lake City in the 1890s and gained momentum in the new century. Some continued the tradition of Protestant evangelical-based moral reform, while other avowedly secular groups advocated environmental changes to solve the city's perceived problems. These reform efforts were part of the vast, amorphous national reform climate known as "progressivism."[214]

The unwillingness of the Board of Police and Fire Commissioners to suppress prostitution inspired one reform effort. Former chief of police Arthur Pratt's effort to regain his office sheds light on the workings of the board and the class bias of chastity policing. Mayor Glendinning fired Pratt in 1896, reportedly because of his "failure to enforce the laws against gambling and prostitution" and his refusal to divulge the names of two rendezvousing lovers arrested two years earlier. Detectives observed the two in a hack several times and finally arrested them. Pratt sent the woman home since she was "the wife of a well-known business man, a woman of prominence in social circles, ... [and] the mother of a family."[215] Such consideration was seldom extended to working-class lovers and certainly not to prostitutes.

The ex-chief took legal action to compel his reinstatement. Pratt testified that from its inception until 1896, the majority of the board had ordered him to regulate rather than suppress vice. Even when the board, at Glendinning's urging, ordered the crackdown of February 1896, some members came to Pratt and requested that he refrain from total suppression. Three commissioners consistently opposed abolition, especially Worden P. Noble, who told Pratt he "wanted [brothels] to run; did not want to live in a town that did not have them; he said he owned over $150,000 worth of property, and it would ruin the town if they did not have them." Commissioner Frank B. Stephens, who had earlier expressed sympathy for prostitutes and advocated the arrest of customers and owners, supported the crackdown on gambling but not prostitution.[216] The Utah Supreme Court reinstated Pratt in 1897.[217]

The Pratt controversy sparked debate about prostitution. Rev. Frank Lockwood, M.E., declared that officials told him "it was the policy of the city simply to divide with these women their revenue." The disgusted minister urged the creation of a "civic federation, or a good citizens' league" to combat prostitution.[218] The police chief responded that regulation kept the city "freer from the outward evidence of vice than almost any other city of its size in the country." The police board chairman boasted that Salt Lake was "the best regulated city of its size in the country, ... you will never see women of bad character plying their calling, and show me another city of this size where such is not the case."[219]

Other clergymen took up Lockwood's call for a campaign against vice.[220] Reformers founded the Salt Lake City Municipal League, "an influential, nonpartisan, non-sectarian association, embracing all the forces that are now laboring to advance the municipal, philanthropic and moral interests" through "investigation, publication, agitation and organization, together with the exercise of every moral influence needed." The league's officers crossed religious lines and included veterans of both sides of the polygamy debate. The reluctant president, Henry W. Lawrence, was a businessman and an ex-Mormon.[221] City attorney William McKay stated that the league needed to convince two members of the police board, Louis Cohn and Worden Noble, that they were wrong about brothels being "an absolute necessity in this city from a business standpoint."[222]

The commissioners voted to extend all assistance to the league but pointedly asked that body to make formal charges backed by proof of corruption or malfeasance. McKay challenged the board to explain its policy toward Ada Wilson's plush new "Palace" brothel, which had opened a few months before in a Brigham Young Trust Company building on Commercial Street. The city attorney claimed to have received an invitation to a "grand opening ball," but despite his complaints to the board, the house was still running. McKay claimed the only change made in the Palace's debut was the transformation of the "grand opening ball" into a "reception."[223] Heber J. Grant and other high-ranking LDS officials also received Ada Wilson's invitations to her opening ball. According to Anthon Lund's diary, they were "astonished to find that they *had been* [emphasis mine] in a regular whore-house." Lund's phraseology is intriguing; did the Palace appear so respectable they did not know it was a brothel?[224]

The Palace caused consternation within the trust company as well. According to the *Tribune,* since its successful campaign against Gussie Blake and Essie Watkins the company had attempted to rent or lease only to legitimate businesses, with few takers and a resultant financial loss. The directors decided to strike the "moral clause" from its leases, which stated that the company could break the lease if a tenant carried on immoral or illegal business. Company president George Q. Cannon and two directors argued against this change but were outvoted. The building was subleased to Ada Wilson. Wilson reportedly spent $15,000 to fit out the building as a brothel; B. Y. Hampton claimed (improbably) that it was the biggest west of New York. The building had some unlikely tenants. The Palace shared the second floor with the Gospel Relief Mission; by 1905, the relief mission had moved to another ex-brothel: no. 5 Plum Alley, formerly Malvina Beauchamp's "Big V."[225]

The Palace became grist for the Municipal League. Rev. Lockwood complained that five hundred invitations had been issued to the opening, "scores of these to boys under 18, requesting their presence from 8 in the evening to 4 in the morning."[226] Two years later, Populist-turned-Socialist Warren Foster scolded LDS Salt Lake Stake president Angus Cannon for ignoring the brothel.[227] Another minister reported that when Wilson heard that the city's ministers were condemning her, she snapped "let the preachers be damned."[228] The madam's arrogance was justified: she knew that her prominent landlords would protect her from sporadic reform efforts, and indeed her house ran openly for the next decade.[229]

Supporters of regulation argued that if prostitution was abolished, women who wished to reform had no place to go. Cornelia Paddock challenged that assumption, writing in 1897 that the rescue home had already "received and cared for thirty-four women and girls belonging to the class of which these papers say that the Christians of Salt Lake will not lift a finger to help them." The home was always crowded, and Paddock noted that the WHA could care for more women if it could afford a larger house. The Municipal League recognized her efforts; by April 1897, she was serving on its philanthropic committee.[230]

From its inception, the league proposed to enter politics. One female member appealed to women to bring "the home influence" to bear as a purifying agent in politics.[231] The Populist Party nominated Henry W. Lawrence for mayor on a platform containing league priorities, including the "rigid enforcement of all laws" concerning prostitution, but the nonpartisan John Clark won the city in November 1897.[232] Clark promised to end the "miserable failure" of the Board of Police and Fire Commissioners, which was allowed to expire on 1 January 1898. Control of the police reverted to the mayor and council, who continued to practice regulation. The Municipal League lost public support and faded before being revived in the early 1900s.[233]

Cornelia Paddock and other activists continued their quieter efforts. "Social purity" advocates across the country fought perceived immorality on a number of fronts. For example, they waged a campaign to raise the age of consent for women.[234] Utah's legislature raised its age from fourteen to eighteen in 1896 at the urging of lobbyists, including Emmeline B. Wells.[235] Paddock used the new law to pursue legal action against a man accused of fathering a child with a sixteen-year-old orphan who took refuge at the WHA home.[236] Paddock also fought the saloon. She told an audience that alcohol was "the worst factor in the ruin of young girls" and called on mothers to prevent their daughters from "buying beer, entering Chinese joints or risking other perils of life."[237] In a case that may illustrate divergent cultural values between immigrants and a native-born evangelical Protestant, Paddock stopped a child on the street with a pail of beer. A saloonkeeper admitted selling it to the minor but argued that the child's father, a Polish Jew, had told him to sell the child beer. The saloonkeeper was fined $25 and had to post a bond.[238]

Most of Paddock's energies were devoted to rescue work. In September 1897, she reported that seven children had been born at the WHA Home since May. Paddock noted that sickness was so rampant that "our station has been a veritable hospitable [sic]." The WHA received free medical care from Drs.

Luella Miles, James N. Harrison, and John A. Hensel.[239] Cornelia Paddock's work, however, was cut short. She died on 26 January 1898 after an operation for uterine cancer. Ironically, her death raised the profile of the WHA and probably extended its life. Eulogists noted that she had often carried on the rescue work almost alone, and remorse over this fact seemed to contribute to an outpouring of support, although some Mormons still resented her antipolygamy activism.[240] Shortly after her death, two workers from the national WCTU helped raise over $200 for the home.[241] They gave two presentations on social purity in the assembly hall, one each to women and men. Emmeline B. Wells presided at the women's meeting, and the speakers included Lulu Loveland Shepard, a schoolteacher and local WCTU officer who would become increasingly involved in purity reform. The speakers emphasized the importance of continuing Paddock's efforts in the face of municipal indifference.[242]

The WHA renamed its house "The Cornelia Paddock Rescue Home" and chose Anna C. Plummer, a schoolteacher and wife of a surgeon, as its new president. The rescuers petitioned the council's police committee for an increase in the monthly appropriation from $50 to $100 (the appropriation had been halved during the financial panic). Newly restored chief of police Arthur Pratt spoke highly of the home "as an adjunct to the department, as a place where young girls and other women not hopelessly lost could be sent without having to go to jail." The committee appropriated $75, with the proviso that the chief be granted the power to commit juvenile offenders to the home.[243] By early 1899, the home's directors were reporting a sounder financial picture. The home had cared for twenty girls, experienced five births, one death, and one marriage, and placed seven girls in respectable homes in the previous ten months.[244]

Just as the home seemed to gain a secure footing, it began to experience a different kind of trouble. Neighbors complained to the council about "scandalous actions," including the correspondence between "two youths of respectable families" and "a tough young inmate, planning as to her future actions when she should be released." A councilman suggested that the home, which was "in one sense, a place of detention," be moved away from densely populated areas and kept isolated and guarded.[245] Fifteen-year-old Bertie Todd, committed to the home after her mother complained of her "incorrigibility," testified to the bad influence of some women: "I never knew how bad girls could become until I entered the home. There is vulgarity everywhere and some of the girls at the home ought not to be allowed to live. For myself, I'd rather go to jail, the penitentiary or the Reform school rather than to return to the home. My godmother has promised to take good care of me, and I am willing to work as hard as I can, but please don't send me back there." Bertie was released and allowed to live with her godmother.[246]

The home's directors sought "better and more isolated quarters" in the southeastern part of the city, but each proposed site drew criticism from residents. One exasperated minister complained "there is room enough for houses of prostitution, which bring these girls into lives of shame, but there is no room for a home which would surround them with Christain [sic] influences; with environments which would be entirely wholesome."[247] Rev. William Paden concluded that the home "must find a community that was so respectable that rescuing the lost would not hurt it, or a community so disrespectable that rescuing the lost would not hurt it." He suggested that as the first option seemed to be failing, Commercial Street would meet the second. A home there would not only save individual women but would also "drive the evil from the street." The WHA was unable to find a suitable location, however, probably due to the high rents that prostitutes and other businesspeople could pay.[248]

Not all citizens approved of the WHA's mission. One man suggested that "falling" was permanent, unforgivable, and genetic. Rescue homes put "a premium on illegal motherhood. . . . The soiled offender knows she will be cared for, a good home will be found for her offspring with its hereditary dower of vile tendencies, and she, in spite of all that is done for her, will return, renovated and refreshed, to her paths of vice." Better that the money be used for (unspecified) preventive measures.[249]

Some reformers agreed that prevention was the best solution. While the WHA searched for a home, the local WCTU promoted social purity. Several WCTU members supported the WHA, including Sarah Reed and Lulu Shepard. The Salt Lake WCTU called for the arrest of prostitutes' customers rather than the "one-sided morality" that punished only women. Their demand echoed the national organization's call for a single sexual standard, the "white life for two" which Frances Willard advocated.[250] A WCTU committee that met with Chief of Police Thomas Hilton made little headway, eliciting instead a defense of the double standard and regulation. The reformers complained that only women had been arrested in a recent wine room raid; Hilton responded that they were all fallen women there to "roll" drunken men. When the WCTU women suggested publishing the names of men found with prostitutes, Hilton appealed to their mutual Christianity: such a course would only bring shame and disgrace to "wives and little ones." To the union proposal that houses be abolished, the chief advocated instead the "isolation and

concentration" of brothels. Hilton concluded patronizingly that the reformers' "hearts were all right, but their ideas were not practical."[251]

The WCTU was interested in more than rescue work in 1899. At the social
purity meeting, Shepard also condemned the election of Brigham H. Roberts to Congress. Roberts was known to have plural wives, and some gentiles
(and some Mormons) argued that his election violated the Woodruff Manifesto and the conditions for Utah statehood. The House of Representatives
eventually denied Roberts his seat, and the controversy eased. Shepard's
stance portended her future anti-Mormon activities and made problematic
her cooperation with Mormon reformers.[252]

The rescue home never did find a suitable location. Former police justice
W. W. Gee opened his own house to the WHA in January 1900, but that
brought another petition for removal. One opponent declared that the home
was a bad influence on his children and grandchildren and vowed to protect
them from women whose "own parents could not keep them in the straight
and narrow path" and who were now being cared for by women with "mis-
taken ideas." Supporters crashed the opposition meeting to argue the home's
merits. Henrietta Gee, the judge's wife, drew on well-worn arguments when
she declared it "ridiculously inconsistent of men to protest at the presence
of a Rescue Home when those same men were married to four women and
spending their time begetting illegitimate children."[253]

By June 1900, the WHA had new quarters. This time angry neighbors not
only petitioned the council, garnering 243 names, but threatened to have the
home abated as a nuisance. While the city attorney rejected such a prosecution unless proof was offered of its lewd nature, the action forced yet another move. In December the WHA abandoned the effort and turned over
its effects to the Salvation Army. That organization had little better luck.
Citing continued opposition, Charlotte Mathis, the officer in charge, announced the home's closure in 1902. Mathis regretted the loss of the institution that had helped many women to be restored to their families, find
work, or make "noble, self-sacrificing wives." The redeemed women "ma[d]e
good Christians who are zealous in trying to bring the happiness of a pure
life to others."[254]

The failure of rescue demonstrated the continued strength of regulation
and was in fact ironically consistent with the city's policy toward prostitution. The neighbors of the rescue home did not see a pure, Christian, maternal refuge, but rather a disorderly resort full of fallen women that threatened
to corrupt their children and injure their property values, and they demanded
that it be segregated and strictly regulated. The rescue home did not even

provide the economic benefits that brothels did. The brothel district stayed and prospered, while Salt Lake City's rescue home faltered.[255]

The failure of rescue also demonstrated the relative impotence of voluntary actions. Despite widespread publicity, support from many community leaders, and their own hard work, antiprostitution reformers were chronically underfunded and able to reach only a handful of the many women who needed or wanted their help. Although voluntary associations continued to attempt to influence conditions, reformers increasingly turned to the state to solve the city's moral problems.

Prostitution continued to be a matter of sporadic concern. In late 1902, a miner named Daniel Ryan was found dead in an outhouse on Victoria Alley. Authorities concluded that a pair of African American crib women accidentally killed Ryan with a dose of morphine in a robbery attempt. Reporters and reformers flocked to the alley and were aghast to discover conditions on the street that had been the heart of the prostitution district for three decades.[256] They expressed the same mix of condemnation and sympathy that rescuers offered fallen women. One reporter found a "babel of blasphemy, a sink of debauchery" "redolent of the stained souls of the inmates."[257] The presence of young boys particularly horrified the respectable. One prostitute supposedly preferred youths since "it takes no morphine in beer or rough treatment to get [the money]; they give up easily and are glad of permission to enter my house."[258] A few people, however, sympathized with the women driven to sell sex in such wretched conditions. One observer condemned the cribs' owner, Joseph J. Snell, and the city for extorting rent and fine money respectively.[259]

Lulu Shepard and the WCTU spearheaded an investigation of the alley, supported by the Ministerial Association, which represented the city's Protestant clergy, and the LDS Church. LDS president Joseph F. Smith appointed businessman B. F. Grant and John Hansen, city editor of the *Deseret Evening News,* to a "moral purity" committee which included Frank B. Stephens and other prominent gentiles. The committee found that conditions were indeed bad, although perhaps not as bad as the papers claimed.[260]

Joseph Snell counted on the authorities' regulation policy to protect him. He noted that with neighbors like Helen Blazes at 7 Victoria, Ida Walker at 243 south Main Street, and the women of 222 south State, he could hardly expect to rent to respectable tenants.[261] Snell failed to mention that police regularly arrested those women but never him. Remarkably, even with attention focused on the alley, no reformer publicly condemned those other brothels steps from Snell's cribs. Mayor Ezra Thompson defended regulation: "If those dives must exist in the city, it is better to have them all bunched together and under strict police supervision."[262] Lulu Shepard's investigation proved in vain; between the strength of the regulation interests and renewed Mormon-gentile antagonism, Victoria Alley was soon forgotten. Five years later, Snell still rented cribs and still defended himself by pointing to other brothels. Complaints from neighbors, and from the crib workers themselves concerning high daily rents, led the police to close five of "the most disreputable resorts" (a move that would have scarcely improved the crib women's lot).[263] Despite a murder, publicity, investigations, sermons, and petitions, women were still selling sex in Snell's cribs in 1908.[264] Instead of suppression, police captain John B. Burbidge proposed a new and stricter version of the regulationist system:

> There is no question but that these women should be removed from the district which they now occupy. . . . The only thing that prevents this being done is the fact that we have no place to put them. Although they are violating the law and could be punished for their offense and, I suppose, be prevented from plying their trade, such a course would be impracticable in a city the size of Salt Lake. . . . We are now searching for a place to which we can remove these women. They should be removed from Commercial street and Victoria alley to some place centrally located in order that it might be well policed and at the same time far enough away from the respectable business center.[265]

A few months later, city authorities acted on Burbidge's suggestion.

Notes

1. Larson, *"Americanization" of Utah*.

2. Hobson, *Uneasy Virtue*, p. 47. On regulation, see Pivar, *Purity Crusade*, pp. 13–17; Haller and Haller, *Physician and Sexuality in Victorian America*, pp. 238–42; and D'Emilio and Freedman, *Intimate Matters*, pp. 111–16.

3. Firmage and Mangrum, *Zion in the Courts*, pp. 214–16.

4. Appendix B: "Ordinances of the High Council," in Morgan, *State of Deseret*.

5. Territory of Utah, *Territorial Ordinances of Utah* (1851), sec. 20, 24; in Morgan, *State of Deseret*, pp. 216–17.

6. Mackey, *Red Lights Out*, pp. 28–121.

7. "An Ordinance in Relation to Offences," Book A, *Salt Lake City Council Ordinances* (1858), part 1, sec. 9.

8. "An Ordinance in Relation to Offences," Book A, *Salt Lake City Council Ordinances* (1858), part 2, sec. 14.

9. Peterson, "Mormon Reformation"; Quinn, *Mormon Hierarchy: Extensions of Power*, pp. 142, 181, 246, 249. This code was adopted 20 Mar. 1858, two days after the decision was made to abandon Salt Lake City. See Arrington and Bitton, *Mormon Experience*, p. 168.

10. "An Ordinance Relating to Houses of Ill-fame and Prostitution," Book B, *Salt Lake City Council Ordinances* (1860), sec. 1.

11. "An Ordinance Relating to Houses of Ill-fame and Prostitution," Book C, *Salt Lake City Council Ordinances* (1877), sec. 1, 3.

12. Utah, *Compiled Laws* (1876), sec. 138, 166. See also Mackey, *Red Lights Out*, p. 123.

13. See Campbell, "Governmental Beginnings," p. 154; Gleason, "Salt Lake City Police Department," p. 13; "An Ordinance Authorising a City Police," Book A, *Salt Lake City Council Ordinances* (1851); Book A, *Salt Lake City Council Ordinances*, p. 31; "An Ordinance Authorizing a City Police and Defining the Duties of Policemen," Book B, *Salt Lake City Council Ordinances* (1860); Salt Lake City, *Great Salt Lake City Charter and Amendments, Revised Ordinances* (1875), sec. 5; and "An Ordinance in Relation to the Police," Book C, *Salt Lake City Council Ordinances* (1884). See also Alexander and Allen, *Mormons and Gentiles*, p. 107; and Carpenter, *Souvenir History of the Salt Lake Fire Department*, table 21, p. 95.

14. Monkonnen, *Police in Urban America*, p. 10.

15. Gleason, "Salt Lake City Police Department," pp. 63, 217; Abraham H. Cannon Diaries, 5:133, photocopy in JWM. On police training, see Monkonnen, *Police in Urban America*, pp. 1–11.

16. Similar courts existed throughout the nation; see Mackey, *Red Lights Out*, p. 76.

17. Tullidge, *History of Salt Lake City*, pp. 241–42. See also "Salt Lake City Council Minutes," Book B, pp. 106–7, 15 Sept. 1858.

18. Historicus, "Offences in 1882."

19. See Gleason, "Salt Lake City Police Department," pp. 19–33; Alexander and Allen, *Mormons and Gentiles*, pp. 52–55, 66. On disorderly young men throughout the West, see Dykstra, *Cattle Towns*, pp. 239–92; R. White, *"It's Your Misfortune and None of My Own,"* pp. 328–32.

20. *Salt Lake City Herald*, 22 Jan. 1879, in JH, 22 Jan. 1879.

21. Alexander and Allen, *Mormons and Gentiles*, pp. 132–33.

22. For example, see Abraham H. Cannon Diaries, 11:140–42.

23. For example, see Brigham Young, 27 Aug. 1871, *Journal of Discourses*, 14: 224–5.

24. *Herald*, 5 June 1886.

25. *Salt Lake City Daily Tribune*, 9 June 1886.

26. *Salt Lake City Goodwin's Weekly*, 3 Jan. 1903, in JH, 3 Jan. 1903.

27. Diary of Wilford Woodruff, 25 Sept. 1890, quoted in Arrington and Bitton, *Mormon Experience*, p. 183.

28. D'Emilio and Freedman, *Intimate Matters*, pp. 79–80, 111–15.

29. *Tribune*, 15 Nov. 1889.

30. In the late 1870s, for instance, police arrested thirty-six women for "keeping a house of ill fame," twelve for "prostitution," fifty-four for "being the inmate of a house of ill fame," four for "lewd and lascivious conduct," one for "renting a house for prostitution," and one for "lewd and lascivious conduct and prostitution." Police arrested four men for "keeping," five for "prostitution," one for being an "inmate," six for "renting," and eight for "lewd and lascivious conduct and prostitution." No men were identified as patrons. "Police, Record 1875–1878." For similar patterns, see "Police, Record 1871–1875," Salt Lake City Fifth Precinct Court, "J. P. Docket Book, Feb. 1880–Jan. 1884"; Salt Lake City Fifth Precinct Court, "J. P. Docket Book, July 1886–Oct. 1890." This study does not address same-sex prostitution. The context suggests that many men arrested as "prostitutes" were prob-

ably patrons. D. Michael Quinn discovered clear evidence of male prostitution in Salt Lake City; see *Same-Sex Dynamics,* pp. 316–20.

31. Pivar, *Purity Crusade,* pp. 13–17.

32. Parent-Duchatelet, *De la prostitution,* 2:513; quoted in Corbin, *Women for Hire,* p. 4. See also Harsin, *Policing Prostitution in Nineteenth-Century Paris,* pp. 96–130; and Corbin, p. 9.

33. For example, see Gibson, *Prostitution and the State in Italy,* pp. 13–37.

34. *Tribune,* 23 Feb. 1898.

35. See, for example, *Tribune,* 26 Jan. 1904; *Herald,* 7 Sept. 1907. On police and prostitution, see M. Haller, "Historical Roots of Police Behavior," p. 316; Fogelson, *Big-City Police,* pp. 20–21; and Harring, *Policing a Class Society,* pp. 191–95.

36. Smith-Rosenberg, "Beauty, the Beast, and the Militant Woman," in *Disorderly Conduct,* pp. 109–28; Hobson, *Uneasy Virtue,* pp. 51–76.

37. D'Emilio and Freedman, *Intimate Matters,* pp. 143–50; Smith-Rosenberg, "Abortion Movement and the AMA, 1850–1880," in *Disorderly Conduct,* pp. 217–44; Sanger, *History of Prostitution;* Hobson, *Uneasy Virtue,* pp. 86–100; Acton, *Prostitution Considered,* cited in Walkowitz, *Prostitution and Victorian Society,* pp. 42–47.

38. Pivar, *Purity Crusade,* pp. 88–99.

39. Walkowitz, *Prostitution and Victorian Society,* passim.

40. Pivar, *Purity Crusade,* pp. 50–56; Burnham, "Social Evil Ordinance"; Wunsch, "Social Evil Ordinance."

41. *Salt Lake City Deseret Evening News,* 26 Apr. 1876, in JH, 26 Apr. 1876.

42. Brigham Y. Hampton Diary, pp. 241–42. Hampton is wrong on the facts or the chronology; he says he leased to Bamberger on 1 Aug., but the lease from Bamberger to Elsie Anderson (alias St. Omar) was executed on 12 July 1890; see Salt Lake County Recorder, "Lease and Lien Book L," lease, pp. 299–301, filed 14 July 1890. For Elsie St. Omar's career as a madam, see *Tribune,* 23 Aug. 1890; and SLCPD, "Arrest Register, 1891–94," 7 Feb. 1891, 3–4; 30 Apr. 1891, 28; 7 Aug. 1891, 56; 28 Oct. 1891, 79; 21 June 1892, 134.

43. Brigham Y. Hampton Diary, pp. 241–42, and *Tribune,* 15 Sept. 1891.

44. Brigham Y. Hampton Diary, p. 242. See also "Liens and Leases, Book O," lease, pp. 540–41, 10 Nov. 1891; and People et al. v. Brigham Y. Hampton, case no. 830 (3d dist. criminal case files, 1892). For the company, see Brigham Young Trust Company Records, file no. 853, Corporation Files, Salt Lake County Clerk.

45. People v. Hampton, case no. 830; People et al. v. Emma Whiting, case no. 832 (3d dist. criminal case files, 1892).

46. Brigham Y. Hampton Diary, p. 240.

47. "An Ordinance Relating to Houses of Ill-fame and Prostitution," Book C, *Salt Lake City Council Ordinances* (1877), sec. 3.

48. See, for example, *Tribune,* 9 Nov. 1889, 31 Jan. 1897.

49. Brigham Y. Hampton Diary, pp. 241–48; Brigham Young Trust Company Records.

50. Arrington, "Commercialization of Utah's Economy"; and Alexander, "Temporal Kingdom," chap. in *Mormonism in Transition.* On the Chamber of Commerce, see Arrington, Fox, and May, *Building the City of God,* p. 333.

51. Conway v. Clinton et al., case no. 586 (3d dist. civil case files, 1877). For high rents, see *Tribune,* 28 Nov. 1894.

52. *Tribune,* 3 June 1897.

53. For 1886, see *Tribune,* 16 Feb. 1887. For 1890, see *Tribune,* 28 Jan. 1891. For 1891, see "Annual Reports of the Officers of Salt Lake City, Utah Territory, 1892," p. 136; *Tribune,* 1 Jan. 1892. For 1904, see "Annual Reports of the Officers of Salt Lake City, 1904," pp. 29–30.

54. For crackdowns on men, see Salt Lake City v. Victor La Grasle, case no. 679 (3d dist. criminal case files, 1901); *Tribune,* 3 Feb. 1901; *Herald,* 30 Oct. 1901, 29 Apr. 1903. For black men, see *Tribune,* 7 Feb. 1900; *Herald,* 1 May 1903. Some accused the police of trying to force out black voters associated with R. Bruce Johnson; see *Herald,* 4, 12 Aug., 5 Sept. 1903.

55. For quarterly assessment, see SLCPD, "Arrest Register, 1891–94," pp. 1–228, passim; for monthly, see pp. 228–464, passim.

56. SLCPD, "Arrest Register, 1896–99," passim.

57. See, for instance, *Salt Lake City Herald-Republican,* 16 Jan. 1912.

58. *Tribune,* 7 Sept. 1898.

59. *Tribune,* 2 June 1899.

60. *Tribune,* 9 June 1891.

61. *Tribune,* 8 Dec. 1891.

62. *Tribune,* 29 Jan. 1896.

63. See, for example, the jury trials won by Irene Mudd and Mary Langary, SLCPC, "Book of Miscellaneous Offenses, 1893–5," pp. 130–32, 10 Mar. 1894.

64. *Tribune,* 22, 23 May 1891.

65. *Salt Lake City Living Issues,* 15 Oct. 1897.

66. *Tribune,* 1, 5, 6, 9, 10, 11 Dec. 1891.

67. SLCPC, "Book of Miscellaneous Offenses, 1893–5," p. 272, 14 Aug. 1894; and "Arrest Register, 1891–94," passim.

68. *Tribune,* 30 Aug. 1891.

69. *Tribune,* 24 Apr., 21 Aug. 1894; *Herald,* 6, 7 Mar. 1901.

70. *Tribune,* 28 Mar. 1897.

71. *Herald,* 15 Dec. 1902.

72. *Herald,* 25 Aug. 1893.

73. *Herald,* 10 Oct. 1901.

74. *Herald,* 11 May 1892, 7 Aug. 1907.

75. *Tribune,* 19 Mar. 1890; *Deseret Evening News,* 19 Mar. 1890; Salt Lake City Death Records, death certificate no. 15877, p. 397.

76. "Arrest Register, 1891–94" and "Arrest Register, 1896–99," passim. "Miss No Name" was arrested on 2 Aug. 1894, and described as "Am < Cold" (American Colored) and a "sport," a common all-purpose designation for prostitutes, gamblers, and vagrants of both sexes. For "A China Woman," see "Police, Record 1871–1875," 11 Mar. 1873, pp. 220–21. An example of the casual attitude that reporters and policemen took toward names: "Zula Ashbury," "Zula Azhburg" ("Arrest Register, 1891–94," p. 271, 22 Dec. 1893); "Zella Ashberry" ("Arrest Register, 1891–94," p. 245, 7 Aug. 1893); "Zella Ashbury" (*Tribune,* 9 Aug. 1893); "Lulu Ashburg" (*Tribune,* 23 Dec. 1893); "Zulu Ashley" (*Tribune,* 6 Nov. 1894); "Zula Ashburg," People v. Nellie Davis, case no. 1190 (3d dist. criminal case files, 1895); and "Zula Anderson" (*Herald,* 16 Jan. 1895); all are likely the same African American woman.

77. *Tribune,* 20, 23 Sept., 22 Oct. 1896.

78. *Tribune,* 10 Dec. 1897. On the 24th Infantry, see Clark, "History of the Twenty-Fourth

United States Infantry Regiment in Utah"; and Nichols, "African-American Soldiers and Civilians in the News."

79. *Tribune*, 20 June 1899.

80. *Tribune*, 3 June 1899.

81. *Tribune*, 29 Dec. 1898.

82. Mackey, *Red Lights Out*, pp. 31–76, 143–54.

83. Matthews, *Rise of Public Woman*, pp. 3–4; D'Emilio and Freedman, *Intimate Matters*, pp. 130–37.

84. *Tribune*, 22 Oct. 1892.

85. *Tribune*, 18 Dec. 1890.

86. *Tribune*, 17 Jan. 1893.

87. *Tribune*, 9 Sept. 1899.

88. *Tribune*, 28 May 1890.

89. *Herald*, 1 July 1909.

90. *Tribune*, 2 Feb., 20, 21 Mar. 1893.

91. *Tribune*, 3 Mar. 1893.

92. Quote from Kingsley v. Salt Lake Dramatic Company, case no. 11774 (3d dist. civil case files, 1893); Beauchamp v. Salt Lake Dramatic Company, case no. 11780 (3d dist. civil case files, 1893); and *Tribune*, 7 Mar., 9, 23 Apr. 1893.

93. *Tribune*, 5 Mar. 1893.

94. Peiss, *Cheap Amusements*, p. 66.

95. *Tribune*, 7 Feb. 1896. For other examples, see *Tribune*, 7 Feb. 1891; 25 Feb. 1894; 4 Jan. 1895.

96. *Tribune*, 7 Feb. 1896.

97. *Annual Message of the Mayor with the Annual Reports of the Officers of Salt Lake City, Utah, for the year 1889*, p. 92; *Annual Message of the Mayor with the Annual Reports of the Officers of Salt Lake City, Utah, for the year 1895*, p. 42. Police court clerk Charles B. Glenn insisted that the fines were not licenses and were handled properly (*Tribune*, 2 Nov. 1891), but Glenn absconded with about $900 in fines (*Tribune*, 15, 18 Jan. 1893).

98. *Tribune*, 10 Oct. 1886.

99. Utah Constitutional Convention, 1895, *Official Report of the Proceedings and Debates*, 2:469. See also Ivins, "Constitution for Utah," pp. 103–6; and J. White, "Woman's Place Is in the Constitution."

100. *Tribune*, 6 Nov. 1899.

101. *Herald*, 3 Nov. 1901.

102. For Johnson as "boss of the white slaves," see *Herald*, 27 Oct. 1903. See also *Herald*, 6 Jan., 28 Oct. 1903. For Johnson as an "American," see *Herald*, 5 Oct. 1907. For accusations of Johnson renting rooms to prostitutes, see *Herald*, 21 Dec. 1902. For Johnson's saloons, see Polk, *Salt Lake City Directory* (1896–1907). See also *Tribune*, 12 Aug., 19, 28 Dec. 1893.

103. For Mulvey as saloonkeeper and councilman, see Polk, *Salt Lake City Directory* (1896, 1897, 1906, 1907). For Mulvey as a Democrat, see *Tribune*, 31 Oct. 1903, in JH, 31 Oct. 1903.

104. *Herald*, 20 Aug. 1907; see chap. 4.

105. Alexander, *Utah, the Right Place*, pp. 198–99; Alexander and Allen, *Mormons and Gentiles*, pp. 99–100.

106. *Tribune,* 11 Feb. 1890.

107. Alexander and Allen, *Mormons and Gentiles,* pp. 100, 108–23; "An Ordinance Levying the Tax and for the Assessment of Property on Both Sides of Commercial Street, in Paving District No. 1 of Salt Lake City, for the Purpose of Paving Said Street," Book C, *Salt Lake City Ordinances* (1890); *Herald,* 1 July 1890; *Deseret Evening News,* 11 Nov. 1890. A local legend holds that Liberals paved Commercial Street so that wives would not spy the telltale red dirt of the street on their husbands' shoes and trouser cuffs.

108. *Herald,* 21 July 1889.

109. *Deseret Evening News,* 16 July 1885, quoting *Tribune,* 6 Mar. 1881. The *Tribune* claimed to be quoting a Mormon.

110. *Tribune,* 9 Aug. 1890.

111. Alexander and Allen claim thirty new brothels opened; see *Mormons and Gentiles,* p. 118. The source of this estimate is uncertain. See also Erickson, "Liberal Party of Utah," p. 121. For numbers of saloons, see Polk, *Salt Lake City Directory* (1890–92).

112. *Tribune,* 29 Dec. 1890.

113. See *Tribune,* 30 Dec. 1890; Polk, *Salt Lake City Directory* (1890).

114. "Salt Lake City Council Minutes," Book M, pp. 368–69, 30 Dec. 1890.

115. *Tribune,* 13 Jan. 1891.

116. *Salt Lake City Times,* 26 Nov. 1890; and Utah, *Compiled Laws* (1876), sec. 153.

117. *Herald,* 16 Dec. 1890; *Tribune,* 16 Dec. 1890. On variety theaters, see Nasaw, *Going Out,* pp. 13–14, 18.

118. *Times,* 5 Jan. 1891. For the license fight, see *Tribune,* 30, 31 Dec. 1890; *Herald,* 1 Jan. 1891; *Tribune,* 7, 22, 31 Jan., 4 Feb., 18, 25 Mar., 14 Oct., 8, 16 Dec. 1891.

119. *Deseret Evening News,* 3 July 1891; *Tribune,* 4 July 1891. See also Johnson, "That Guilty Third Tier," p. 578; Nasaw, *Going Out,* pp. 13–14.

120. *Tribune,* 21 Nov. 1891. See also *Tribune,* 2 Dec. 1891.

121. *Tribune,* 25 Feb. 1894. See also "Fire Insurance Map of Salt Lake City, 1895," sheet 41. The People's Opera House similarly failed; see *Tribune,* 4 Aug., 16 Oct. 1892; 3 Mar., 7 June 1893.

122. Baskin, *Reminiscences; Tribune,* 8 Feb. 1892; and Erickson, "Liberal Party of Utah," p. 122.

123. *Tribune,* 2 Sept., 27 Nov. 1891; "Salt Lake City Council Minutes," Book N, p. 127, 1 Sept. 1891.

124. *Deseret Evening News,* 18 June 1892. "Rosa Miller" was arrested on 7 Dec. 1871 ("Police, Record 1871–1875," pp. 50–51) and "Rose Miller" on 30 July 1872 (pp. 138–39), but she does not appear from 1875 to 1878; the context of the 1892 incident suggests this is a different woman.

125. *Deseret Evening News,* 22 June 1892; *Herald,* 23 June 1892; and *Tribune,* 22 June 1892. For Elsie St. Omar's previous arrests, see SLCPD, "Arrest Register, 1891–94," pp. 34, 7 Feb. 1891; p. 28, 30 Apr. 1891; p. 56, 7 Aug. 1891; p. 78, 28 Oct. 1891.

126. *Herald,* 28 June 1892.

127. *Tribune,* 28, 29 June 1892; People et al. v. Elsie St. Omer, whose real name is Elsie Anderson, case no. 366 (3d dist. criminal case files, 1892); People et al. v. Rose Miller, case no. 369 (3d dist. criminal case files, 1892).

128. *Tribune,* 20 Apr., 28, 29 June 1892.

129. *Tribune,* 7 July 1892.

130. *Tribune,* 6 July 1892; "Salt Lake City Council Minutes," Book O, p. 41, 5 July 1892; *Tribune,* 1 Jan. 1893.

131. For the firing of the police officers, see *Tribune,* 6 July 1892. For Janney's firing, see *Tribune,* 1 Oct. 1892. For Sheets's reappointment, see *Tribune,* 17 Aug. 1892. For Janney's reappointment, see Polk, *Salt Lake City Directory* (1897).

132. For "no authority," see *Tribune,* 13 July 1892; for "no excuse," see *Tribune,* 10 Aug. 1892. See also *Tribune,* 11, 24 Sept., 6 Oct. 1892; and Kesler's obituary, *Tribune,* 14 Jan. 1935.

133. Butler, *Daughters of Joy, Sisters of Misery,* pp. 111–12.

134. *Times,* 20 June 1892.

135. *Tribune,* 24 Sept. 1893. "Rose Miller" appears in the 1900 census as the keeper of a boardinghouse in Mercur City, Tooele County (U.S. Bureau of the Census, Twelfth Census [1900], Tooele County, Enumeration District No. 146, sheet 6, line 81).

136. *Deseret Evening News,* 7 July 1892.

137. *Herald,* 9 Feb. 1892.

138. *Herald,* 25 June 1892.

139. *Tribune,* 11, 12 July 1892; "Arrest Register, 1891–94," p. 139, 142–43.

140. *Tribune,* 2 Aug. 1892. See also *Deseret Evening News,* 2 Aug. 1892; *Herald,* 2 Aug. 1892.

141. Polk, *Salt Lake City Directory* (1894–95); and *Tribune,* 12, 20 June 1894.

142. See Alexander, "Mormon Revolution," chap. in *Things in Heaven and Earth;* Alexander, *Mormonism in Transition;* Mauss, "Mormons as a Case Study in Assimilation," chap. in *Angel and the Beehive;* and Quinn, *Mormon Hierarchy: Extensions of Power,* pp. 325–41.

143. On reaction to the Manifesto, see *Tribune,* 8 Oct. 1890; Van Wagoner, "Interpreting Woodruff," chap. in *Mormon Polygamy;* and Alexander, *Things in Heaven and Earth,* pp. 268–70.

144. Lyman, *Political Deliverance,* pp. 150–84, 255; Shipps, "Utah Comes of Age Politically," p. 94; *Tribune,* 29, 30 Oct., 8 Nov., 19 Dec. 1893.

145. See Quinn, *Mormon Hierarchy: Extensions of Power,* pp. 331–55; Lyman, "Tumultuous Interim to Statehood," chap. in *Political Deliverance;* Shipps, "Utah Comes of Age Politically"; Lyman, "Statehood, Political Allegiance, and Utah's First U.S. Senate Seats"; W. White, "Feminist Campaign for the Exclusion of Brigham Henry Roberts"; Bitton, "B. H. Roberts Case"; Iversen, "Resurgence of the Antipolygamy Controversy, 1898–1900," chap. in *Antipolygamy Controversy;* and *Salt Lake City Kinsman,* Sept. 1899–July 1900.

146. Arrington, "Aftermath," chap. in *Great Basin Kingdom.*

147. *Herald,* 25 July 1892.

148. C. Madsen, "Decade of Detente." For temperance activity, see *Tribune,* 2 Mar., 25 July 1892. The Utah WCTU was formed in 1883 (Madsen, p. 307).

149. Madsen, "Decade of Detente," p. 313; Derr, Cannon, and Beecher, *Women of Covenant,* pp. 137–40; and Parsons, *History of Fifty Years,* p. 88.

150. "Salt Lake City Council Minutes," Book O, p. 140, 18 Aug. 1892; *Tribune,* 19 Aug. 1892.

151. *Tribune,* 11 July 1892.

152. *Tribune,* 2 Sept. 1892.

153. *Tribune,* 22 Oct. 1892.

154. *Tribune,* 21 July 1894. For the movement to Franklin, see *Tribune,* 25 Feb. 1894; Polk, *Salt Lake City Directory* (1894–95). See also "Arrest Register, 1891–94," p. 274, 10 Jan. 1894; and p. 311, 18 June 1894; "Fire Insurance Map of Salt Lake City, 1895," sheet 41; and "Fire Insurance Map of Salt Lake City, 1898," sheet 113.

155. *Tribune,* 5, 15 Sept. 1892.

156. *Tribune,* 12 Oct. 1892. For Sarah Reed, see "Session Minutes," 30 Mar. 1872–17 Aug. 1886, in First Presbyterian Church Records, 1871–1983, JWM. On the matron, see *Tribune,* 30 Nov. 1892; 19 Dec. 1894; 27 Jan. 1895.

157. *Tribune,* 26 Oct. 1892.

158. On maternalism, see Baker, "Domestication of Politics"; Gordon, "Putting Children First"; Skocpol, *Protecting Soldiers and Mothers,* pp. 317–31; and Michel and Koven, "Womanly Duties." On home missions, see Pascoe, *Relations of Rescue,* pp. 3–10, 21–29, 36, 62–68, 76, 82.

159. *Tribune,* 8 Dec. 1891; Baskin, *Reminiscences,* p. 232.

160. *Tribune,* 12 Dec. 1892. See also *The Woman's Exponent* 19 (15 Feb. 1891); *Herald,* 13 Dec. 1892; and *Tribune,* 17 Dec. 1892.

161. *Deseret Evening News,* 18 Dec. 1894; *Tribune,* 11 May 1896.

162. *Tribune,* 26 Feb. 1893. See also *Tribune,* 19 Jan., 3 Apr. 1893; and *Proceedings of the National Conference of Charities and Corrections,* p. 416. Cornelia Paddock submitted Utah's report.

163. *Tribune,* 26 Feb. 1893; and *Utah Gazetteer* (1892–93).

164. For the fine proposal, see *Tribune,* 20 Mar. 1893; and "Salt Lake City Council Minutes," Book O, p. 710, 7 Apr. 1893. For the $100 appropriation, see "Salt Lake City Council Minutes," Book P, p. 138, 2 June 1893; and *Deseret Evening News,* 3 June 1893.

165. *Tribune,* 29 Mar. 1893. See also "Petition of Elijah Sells et al.," "Salt Lake City Council Minutes," Book O, p. 674, 28 Mar. 1893. Elijah Sells, whose name does not appear elsewhere in connection with the rescue effort, was a former secretary to the Utah Commission; see *Salt Lake City Directory* (1889). For the officers, see Polk, *Salt Lake City Directory* (1891–92); and *Utah Gazetteer* (1892–93).

166. *Tribune,* 26 Feb. 1893. On similar rescue ideology in Boston, see Hobson, *Uneasy Virtue,* pp. 75–76.

167. *Tribune,* 29 Mar. 1893.

168. John A. Mayer proposes a spectrum from "social" or wholly voluntary means to wholly coercive in "Notes Toward a Working Definition of Social Control in Historical Analysis."

169. See, for example, *Tribune,* 19 Dec. 1894.

170. *Tribune,* 26 May 1893; "Petition of Elijah Sells et al.," *Tribune,* 29 Mar. 1893; and Hobson, *Uneasy Virtue,* pp. 64–66.

171. "Salt Lake City Council Minutes," Book O, p. 763, 21 Apr. 1893.

172. *Tribune,* 23 Aug. 1893; and *Herald,* 23 Aug. 1893.

173. *Tribune,* 25 Mar. 1893.

174. *Tribune,* 25 June 1893.

175. *Tribune,* 3 May 1893. See also *Tribune,* 1 June, 27 Aug. 1893.

176. *Tribune,* 19, 20 Apr. 1893.

177. *Tribune*, 27 Mar. 1890, 8 Sept. 1894. For Sallie Davis's arrests, see SLCPC, "Book of Miscellaneous Offenses, 1893–5," p. 172, 11 May 1894; p. 183, 25 May 1894.

178. "Salt Lake City Council Minutes," Book V, p. 59, 28 Feb. 1899. See also *Tribune*, 1 Mar. 1899.

179. *Tribune*, 3 Nov. 1893. See also Arrington, "Utah and the Depression of the 1890s."

180. For the "visiting committees," see *Tribune*, 10 Nov. 1893. See also Van Wagenen, "Sister-Wives and Suffragists," pp. 404–73, passim.

181. *Tribune*, 26 Jan., 24 Oct., 1894.

182. *Tribune*, 19 Dec. 1894; Waters, "Pioneering Women Physicians, 1847–1900"; and Derr, Cannon, and Beecher, *Women of Covenant*, p. 109.

183. *Anti-Polygamy Standard* 2, no. 9 (1881). See also "Mormon Women Missionaries," *National Citizen and Ballot,* Sept. 1881, quoted in Van Wagenen, "Sister-Wives and Suffragists," p. 339; see also pp. 333–47.

184. On Ferguson, see Stone, "Dr. Ellen Brooke Ferguson."

185. *Deseret Evening News,* 19 Dec. 1894.

186. *Tribune*, 7 Nov. 1894; Polk, *Salt Lake City Directory* (1891–92, 1894–95, 1901).

187. *Tribune*, 3, 6 Jan. 1895; 15 Apr., 16 Nov. 1897.

188. *Deseret Evening News,* 18 Dec. 1894; and *Tribune*, 19 Dec. 1894.

189. *Tribune*, 14, 19 Dec. 1894.

190. "Salt Lake City Council Minutes," Book Q, p. 577, 16 Oct. 1894; and *Tribune*, 17–19 Oct. 1894.

191. *Tribune*, 24 Oct. 1894; and "Salt Lake City Council Minutes," Book Q, p. 586, 23 Oct. 1894.

192. *Tribune*, 28 Oct. 1894.

193. *Deseret Evening News,* 27 Nov. 1894.

194. Ibid.; see also *Tribune*, 28 Nov. 1894.

195. *Tribune*, 25 Dec. 1894.

196. *Tribune*, 5, 31 Dec. 1894, 4, 5, 6, 10 Jan. 1895. Pratt's quote is from 4 Jan.

197. *Deseret Evening News,* 5 Jan. 1895; and *Herald,* 16 Jan. 1895. For O. J. Salisbury, see Polk, *Salt Lake City Directory* (1891–92). For Gussie Blake (née Foote) in the Salt Lake Valley Loan Trust Co. building, see "Deed Book 4T," trustee's deed, pp. 517–18, filed 3 July 1895; and "Mortgage Book 3W," mortgage, pp. 30–33, 19 Dec. 1894. See also *Tribune*, 21 Aug. 1897.

198. *Herald,* 22 Jan. 1895. See also *Tribune*, 16, 22 Jan. 1895. For Watkins's move to 44 east Second South (former Flint property), see "Chattel Mortgage Book E," p. 601, 25 Feb. 1895.

199. See chap. 2.

200. *Tribune*, 20 Jan. 1895; *Herald,* 22 Jan. 1895; People v. Gussie Blake et al., cases no. 1227, 1228 (3d dist. criminal case files, 1895); and *Tribune*, 19, 21, 24 Feb. 1895.

201. *Tribune*, 19 May 1895.

202. *Tribune*, 1 Feb. 1895. See also *Tribune*, 2 Feb. 1895; Polk, *Salt Lake City Directory* (1896–1908).

203. *Tribune*, 3 Jan. 1895. See also *Tribune* 6, 19, 27 Jan., 17 Feb. 1895; and *Herald,* 6 Jan. 1895.

204. "Fourth Quarterly Report of the Woman's Home Association," *Tribune*, 24 Jan. 1896.

205. "Articles of Association of the Florence Crittendon [*sic*] Rescue Home," Weber County (Utah) County Clerk, *Articles of Incorporation Record Books,* 1871–1961. For Crittenton's visit, see *Deseret Evening News,* 13 Aug. 1895, in JH, 13 Aug. 1895; *Deseret Evening News,* 27, 29, 30 Jan. 1896, in JH, 27, 29 Jan. 1896; and Emmeline B. Wells Diary, 29 Jan. 1896, photocopy in Emmeline B. Wells Papers, JWM. On Charles Crittenton and the Florence Crittenton Missions, see Crittenton, *Brother of Girls;* Aiken, "National Florence Crittenton Mission"; Beard, *Woman's Work in Municipalities,* p. 123; Odem, *Delinquent Daughters,* p. 115; and Kunzel, "Maternity Home Movement," chap. in *Fallen Women, Problem Girls.* The "Florence Crittendon [*sic*] Rescue Home" of Ogden was incorporated on 18 Mar. 1897; see Weber County (Utah) County Clerk, Incorporation Case Files, file 80; and Weber County (Utah) County Clerk, *Articles of Incorporation Record Books,* 1871–1961, Book D, pp. 285–90.

206. *Tribune,* 25 Apr. 1896. That home, at 812 west Eighth South Street, was listed in 1898 as "Crittenton Home"; that label does not reappear. See Polk, *Directory of Salt Lake City,* 1898.

207. *Tribune,* 11 May 1896.

208. *Tribune,* 24, 28 Sept. 1895.

209. *Tribune,* 8 Feb. 1896.

210. *Herald,* 8 Feb. 1896.

211. *Tribune,* 22 May 1896. See also *Tribune,* 20 May 1896.

212. Rosen, *Lost Sisterhood,* pp. 102–8.

213. *Tribune,* 29 Dec. 1896, 1 Jan. 1897; *Herald,* 4 Jan. 1897. The Magdalen Home appears in Polk, *Salt Lake City Directory* (1897, 1898), but not after. On Good Shepherd rescue activities elsewhere, see Butler, *Daughters of Joy, Sisters of Misery,* pp. 65–67.

214. On moral progressivism, see Boyer, *Urban Masses and Moral Order in America;* Crunden, *Ministers of Reform;* and Keller, *Regulating a New Society.*

215. *Tribune,* 4 Nov. 1894. See also Van Wagoner and Van Wagoner, "Arthur Pratt, Utah Lawman," pp. 30–31; *Tribune,* 7, 18 Dec. 1894; and Gleason, "Salt Lake City Police Department," p. 85.

216. *Tribune,* 31 Jan. 1897.

217. *Tribune,* 7 Feb., 15 June 1897.

218. *Tribune,* 11 Jan. 1897.

219. *Tribune,* 18 Jan. 1897.

220. *Tribune,* 1 Feb. 1897.

221. *Tribune,* 12 Mar. 1897. On Lawrence, see *Tribune,* 16 Apr. 1897, Henry W. Lawrence Collection, JWM; Dimter, "Populism in Utah," pp. 129–31; Tullidge, *History of Salt Lake City,* pp. 168, 321, 379–80, 390–91, 401, 429–30, 506–7, 587, 590, 607–8, 611, and biographical supplement in same, p. 50; Griffiths, "Far Western Populism"; Walker, "When the Spirits Did Abound"; and McCormick, "Hornets in the Hive." See also Polk, *Salt Lake City Directory* (1897). For Corinne Allen, see Knudsen, *History of Utah Federation of Women's Clubs* in Utah Federation of Women's Clubs Records, JWM.

222. *Tribune,* 28 Mar. 1897.

223. For the "grand opening ball," see *Tribune,* 30 Mar. 1897. See also *Tribune,* 4 Jan., 31 Mar. 1897.

224. Anthon H. Lund Diary, 8 Apr. 1897, microfilm copy in CA; Brigham Y. Hampton Diary, p. 247; and Quinn, *Same-Sex Dynamics,* p. 319.

225. *Tribune,* 4 Jan. 1897. For Wilson, see "Chattel Mortgage Book E," entry no. 108660, p. 638, filed 15 Jan. 1897; "Fire Insurance Map of Salt Lake City, 1898," sheet 103; Polk, *Salt Lake City Directory* (1900–1903, 1905).

226. *Tribune,* 5 Apr. 1897.

227. Foster, "Open Letter to Angus M. Cannon."

228. *Tribune,* 1 Feb. 1897.

229. For Wilson at 33 Commercial (the Palace), see Polk, *Salt Lake City Directory* (1898–1908). For Wilson's arrests, see Salt Lake City Court Criminal Division, "Minute Book, 1905," passim; Salt Lake City Court Criminal Division, "Minute Book, 1908," passim.

230. *Tribune,* 15, 27 Apr. 1897.

231. *Tribune,* 25 June 1897.

232. *Living Issues,* 22 Oct. 1897.

233. Alexander and Allen, *Mormons and Gentiles,* p. 126; and *Tribune,* 17 Dec. 1897; 25 Feb. 1898. Clark's comment is from *Annual Message of the Mayor with the Annual Reports of the Officers of Salt Lake City, Utah, for the year 1897,* p. 19.

234. Beard, *Woman's Work in Municipalities,* p. 109; Boyer, *Urban Masses and Moral Order in America,* p. 192; Epstein, *Politics of Domesticity,* p. 125; Blocker, *American Temperance Movements,* pp. 82–83; and Odem, *Delinquent Daughters,* pp. 3, 8, 12, 30–38.

235. Age of Consent, in *Laws of the State of Utah, Passed at Special and First Regular Sessions of the Legislature;* Emmeline B. Wells Diary, 30 Jan. 1896.

236. *Tribune,* 10, 11 Oct., 22 Dec., 1897.

237. *Tribune,* 20 July 1896.

238. *Tribune,* 7, 17 Nov. 1896.

239. *Tribune,* 21 Sept., 16 Nov. 1897.

240. JH, 26 Jan. 1898; Salt Lake City Death Records, Certificate D8444; *Deseret Evening News,* 27 Jan. 1898; *Tribune,* 27, 28 Jan. 1898, 27 Nov. 1899; and *Herald,* 27 Jan. 1898.

241. *Tribune,* 7, 8, 14 Feb. 1898.

242. *Tribune,* 22, 23 Feb. 1898; and Emmeline B. Wells Diary, 29 Jan., 1, 3, 16, 21–23 Feb. 1898. For Shepard, see Polk, *Salt Lake City Directory* (1894–95, yearly thereafter until 1908).

243. Quote from *Tribune,* 6 Dec. 1898. See also "Report of 'Cornelia Paddock Rescue Home,'" *Tribune,* 11 July 1898; 20 Oct., 6 Dec. 1898; "Salt Lake City Council Minutes," Book V, p. 59, 28 Feb. 1899; and Polk, *Salt Lake City Directory* (1897–99).

244. *Tribune,* 19, 21 Jan. 1899; and Polk, *Salt Lake City Directory* (1899).

245. *Tribune,* 2 July 1899.

246. *Tribune,* 15 July 1899.

247. *Tribune,* 3, 27, 29 Nov. 1899; quote from 27 Nov. See also Polk, *Salt Lake City Directory* (1898).

248. Quotes from *Tribune,* 29 Nov. 1899; see also *Tribune,* 3 Dec. 1899.

249. *Tribune,* 29 Nov. 1899.

250. *Tribune,* 18 Nov. 1899; Epstein, *Politics of Domesticity,* pp. 125–29.

251. For the interview, see *Tribune,* 23 Nov. 1899. For Reed's response, see *Tribune,* 26 Nov. 1899.

252. *Tribune,* 18 Nov. 1899; and Bitton, "B. H. Roberts Case."

253. For the home at Gee's house, see *Tribune,* 14, 24 Jan. 1900. See also *Tribune,* 6, 8 Feb. 1900 and *Deseret Evening News,* 8 Feb. 1900; *Tribune,* 10 Feb. 1900; and *Deseret Evening News,* 27 Feb. 1900. Quotes from *Herald,* 1 Mar. 1900; see also *Deseret Evening News,* 1 Mar. 1900; and *Tribune,* 1 Mar. 1900.

254. For the final campaign against the WHA, see *Tribune,* 1, 5, 9, 13, 27 June 1900; and C. A. Doyle et al., petition 3723, "Salt Lake City Council Minutes," Book V, p. 216, 5 June 1900; and *Tribune,* 16 Oct., 12 Dec. 1900. For the closure, see *Herald,* 15 Jan. 1902.

255. The Crittenton Home in Ogden operated until 1933 and sometimes received women from Salt Lake City. See "Articles of Incorporation of the Florence Crittendon [*sic*] Home," Department of Commerce, Division of Corporations, Incorporation Case Files, Closed 1871–1974. See also *Herald,* 17 Feb. 1907.

256. *Herald,* 14–22, 24–25, 27–28, 30 Dec. 1902; 6, 18 Jan. 1903; *Deseret Evening News,* 19 Dec. 1902; and State v. Mary Jane Smith, case no. 988 (3d dist. criminal case files, 1903).

257. *Herald,* 18, 19 Dec. 1902.

258. *Herald,* 19 Dec. 1902.

259. *Herald,* 22 Dec. 1902.

260. *Herald,* 20, 27, 28, 30 Dec. 1902; 1, 3, 5, 6, 10, 25, 26, 27 Jan.; 23 May, 1903; and *Deseret Evening News,* 5 Jan. 1903.

261. *Herald,* 20, 22 Dec. 1902.

262. *Herald,* 20 Dec. 1902.

263. *Herald,* 10 Sept. 1907.

264. *Salt Lake City Inter-Mountain Republican,* 19 Dec. 1908; *Herald,* 18 Dec. 1908; and *Tribune,* 18 Dec. 1908.

265. *Herald,* 5–7 Sept. 1907; quote from 6 Sept.

4. "An Extremely Clever Woman"

THE 1903 ELECTION OF Reed Smoot to the United States Senate revived the battle over polygamy. The explicitly anti-Mormon "American" Party, which emerged from the controversy, controlled Salt Lake City's government from 1905 to 1911. The Smoot affair, with its revelations of continued Mormon polygamy, allowed the Americans to claim to be the champions of morality and the home.

But the Americans established the "Stockade," a new restricted district, and forced most of the city's prostitutes to work there. Dora B. Topham, better known as Belle London, managed the district with the open approval and protection of the municipal authorities. For the first time, a single person dominated the business of prostitution in the city instead of independent madams managing houses within the network of brothels. The high visibility of the Stockade allowed some Mormons and gentiles to claim the moral high ground against the Americans. The district became the leading issue in municipal elections, a point of contention in state politics, and the target of moral reformers across religious, political, and gender lines. After many failed attempts, reformers managed to convict Topham of pandering and she closed the Stockade. The women who sold sex there were thrown out of work, and the Americans were turned out of office. While prostitution was not eliminated, open regulation and political anti-Mormonism based on moral claims were discredited.

The B. H. Roberts episode first renewed the polygamy issue in 1898. The Salt Lake Ministerial Association, the Woman's Christian Temperance Union (WCTU), and Protestant women's home missionary groups helped deny Roberts his congressional seat. This campaign damaged the fragile detente

between gentiles and Mormons and caused divisions among purity reformers. The Roberts controversy, however, paled in comparison to the Smoot
brouhaha.[1]

By 1900, Republicans dominated Utah politics. Mining millionaire Thomas
Kearns, a gentile, was elected senator in 1901 with the approval of LDS leaders. Kearns purchased the *Salt Lake Tribune* and fired the paper's longtime
editor and antipolygamy crusader, C. C. Goodwin.[2] Kearns and Smoot, also
a Republican, had some type of understanding concerning Smoot's candidacy for the other Senate seat, but others had serious reservations. Smoot was
a member of the Quorum of Twelve Apostles, the second-highest leadership
group in the LDS Church. Many gentiles argued that his election by the state
legislature proved that Mormons still dominated Utah politics. They feared
that LDS leaders would direct Smoot's Senate vote and that he would wield
unacceptable authority over LDS constituents, while his loyalty would be to
church rather than country.[3]

The Ministerial Association again led the local opposition. In addition to
accusations of church influence, the ministers claimed that most apostles lived
in polygamy. Smoot had never been a polygamist, and was in fact a prominent voice for compliance with the Woodruff Manifesto. The controversy,
however, revealed that plural marriage was far from dead.[4] Thomas Kearns
weighed in against Smoot with his newspapers, the *Tribune* and afternoon
Telegram, after LDS leaders declined to support his reelection. Kearns's financial support and his newspapers would be crucial to the emerging political
movement.[5]

Opposition to Smoot quickly took organized form in Salt Lake City. Within
days of the legislature's vote, a group of citizens sent a protest to the president and the Senate. Its signatories included Presbyterian Rev. William M.
Paden, for the Ministerial Association; Edward B. Critchlow, an attorney and
a Republican; and Clarence E. Allen, Utah's first congressman, also a Republican. The protest claimed that Mormons "protect and honor those who
themselves violate the laws of the land and are guilty of practices destruc-
tive of the family and the home."[6] The protestors included several men who,
sometimes with their wives, had histories of opposing polygamy. Paden had
helped fight B. H. Roberts. C. C. Goodwin was among the best-known opponents of plural marriage and Mormon domination of politics. Clarence
Allen was a longtime Liberal, although he had cooperated with many Mormons in politics since 1890. His wife Corinne and Mary Willis (Mrs. E. B.)
Critchlow had been officers of the Industrial Christian Home Association.[7]

Many of these people were also active in the social purity movement. C. E.

Allen had challenged Liberal law enforcement in the early 1890s.[8] Corinne Allen was a trustee of the Municipal League in its fight against prostitution in 1897.[9] Paden was among those who tried to keep the rescue home alive after Cornelia Paddock's death.[10] At the time of the Smoot controversy, E. B. Critchlow was a member of the committee investigating Victoria Alley in the wake of the murder of Daniel Ryan. Critchlow led a group of Mormons and non-Mormons who requested that a grand jury investigate conditions in the alley.[11]

The latter effort, supported by the LDS First Presidency, the Ministerial Association, and the WCTU, was among the last cooperative reform ventures of the early 1900s. When the battle over polygamy erupted again, joint action against prostitution became difficult. Gentiles such as the Allens and Critchlows viewed polygamy and prostitution as similar threats to the home, just as reformers had in the 1880s.

While Smoot was allowed to take his seat, the Senate began an investigation that stretched from March 1904 to February 1907, but the most inflammatory evidence came early. LDS president Joseph F. Smith admitted that some plural marriages had been solemnized since the Woodruff Manifesto, and that he personally continued to cohabit with all of his wives. To quiet the resulting outcry and reaffirm the church's stance against plural marriage, Smith issued a "Second Manifesto" in April 1904, declaring that polygamists would be cut off from the church. A number of members were excommunicated, and the practice gradually faded in the mainstream LDS Church.[12]

The campaign to unseat Smoot became national, encompassing organizations that had fought polygamy before 1890 and had opposed B. H. Roberts in 1898. Once again, Protestant home mission women and other reform groups protested the corrupting effects of Mormonism, this time on national politics as well as on the home. The Utah Mothers' Assembly (or Congress), as its name indicates, stressed mothers' responsibility for protecting children and advocated maternalist solutions to such public problems as cigarettes, alcohol, and the presence of minors in saloons. The group was founded in 1898; early members included Mormons Emmeline B. Wells and Zina D. Young and gentiles Corinne Allen and Lulu Shepard.[13] During the Smoot controversy, Corinne Allen used her position as president of the Utah congress to bring the matter before the national congress, which formed an anti-Smoot coalition that conducted a massive campaign of petitions and speaking tours.[14]

The Smoot controversy particularly sparked the revival of anti-Mormon politics in Salt Lake City. On 14 September 1904, prominent gentiles launched the "American" Party, which promised to fight "Smootism" and to "free people from apostolic rule." The *Tribune* championed the new party; its managing editor was among the founders. While Thomas Kearns was not publicly among the founders, his influence was undoubtedly key.[15]

The Americans soon gained the support of a well-known figure. Frank J. Cannon, the son of the late LDS leader George Q. Cannon and a former U.S. senator, had become estranged from the LDS leadership following his father's death. He accused Joseph F. Smith of violating the Woodruff Manifesto and promises made during the statehood campaign that the church would not influence politics. In 1904, Cannon began writing *Tribune* editorials harshly critical of Smith and LDS Church interference in politics. In March 1905, he was excommunicated. The ex-Mormon would be an important player in the fight against polygamy for over a decade, writing a series of muckraking articles and becoming a sought-after speaker.[16]

Gentile women organized a ladies' auxiliary to the American Party, which heard from Angie F. Newman, the founder of the Industrial Christian Home.[17] In language that could have come from the *Anti-Polygamy Standard*, the *Tribune* issued a stirring call for female votes:

> The woman who believes in the home and family as God intended them to be, should . . . vote the American ticket. . . .
>   Let this woman bestir her benumbed faculties, send the joy-pulsing blood to the aching heart, and feel that she is a true woman—the most glorious creature that God ever created—and . . . file her solemn protest against the tyrant rule over woman and against church domination in politics.[18]

Mormons thought the Americans were reviving a dead conflict for partisan gain. The *Deseret Evening News* claimed that the party's name should be the "Amalgamated Order of Disgruntled Office Seekers"; the party was "Turning Back the Wheels of Progress Twenty Years." The participation of Frank J. Cannon, whose past indiscretions with prostitutes and alcohol were an open secret in Mormon circles, made the party's claims of moral superiority seem particularly hypocritical.[19]

In 1905, American cofounder Ezra Thompson, a former Republican mayor, won election as mayor along with American councilmen W. Mont Ferry, Arthur J. Davis, Lewis D. Martin, and Martin E. Mulvey.[20] Thompson's chief of police, George Sheets, was implicated in a bribery case. Although he was cleared, the chief resigned in July 1907; five days later, Thompson left office.[21] John S. Bransford finished Thompson's term and won reelection in 1907. Bransford, a mining partner of Thomas Kearns, seldom if ever indulged in anti-Mormon rhetoric and was respected by many Saints despite heading the American party.[22]

The Smoot controversy raged throughout this period, with some Salt Lake City women's groups lining up on opposite sides. The controversy split the Utah Mothers' Assembly, which temporarily disbanded.[23] Elizabeth Cohen, former president of the Woman's Democratic Club (which included many Mormons), led the Woman's American Club in attacks on senators who supported Smoot. When Cohen accused most LDS leaders from the bishop level up of practicing plural marriage, Mormon women charged that Cohen had unsexed herself by spreading lies.[24] Mormons complained that women's groups had become "the blind tools of certain political conspirators engaged in a relentless persecution of the Church of Jesus Christ of Latter-day Saints . . . to degrade American womanhood."[25]

The anti-Smoot forces were ultimately unsuccessful, as the Senate voted in February 1907 to seat the Utahn. Many people had come to view the campaign against him as an overreaction. Polygamy was obviously declining with the death of older Mormons and the LDS leadership's purging of recalcitrant polygamists. Theodore Roosevelt's support helped turn the tide in Smoot's favor.[26]

City politics continued to split along the religious divide, however. Another issue was Smoot's Republican organization. The "Federal bunch," as the *Tribune* named it for the number of federal offices filled by Smoot allies, regularly defeated the Americans for state and county offices, but the Americans managed to keep control in the city. One of the "Bunch's" chief tools was the *Inter-Mountain Republican* (later the *Herald-Republican*) newspaper under manager Edward H. Callister, a member of the "Federal bunch."[27]

Prostitution came to play a major role in the political debates of the early twentieth century, and eventually brought the American Party to grief. The origins of the party's policy on prostitution are cloudy, but the first public notice came from the police, always the most consistent advocates of regulation. In his 1907 annual report, American-appointed chief Thomas Pitt suggested that regulation, practiced informally since the 1870s, be formalized.

> Let the city set aside a piece of ground of sufficient size to accommodate several hundred of these prostitutes. Enclose same carefully with high fences; build cottages or houses to accommodate these inmates; charge them rent; license them and place them under control of the Police Department as to their safety and confinement, and to the Board of Health as to their cleanliness and sanitary conditions. In this way every person caught soliciting and working on the streets could be handled by the Police Court and run out of town or sent to the place where she belonged. In this way this Department would be in complete control of this element, and could also control the drug element and men who make a practice of living with this class of women.

Pitt's suggested district was part of a broad moral reform program that proposed limits on saloons, vagrancy, Sunday liquor sales, and gambling, and that advocated the creation of a juvenile detention home.[28]

Pitt's proposal was a logical extension of previous policy. The *Deseret Evening News* claimed it had first surfaced during Mayor Thompson's term, with "a fellow who found out that bad houses pay an enormous interest on the investment," but Thompson turned it down.[29] Police captain John Burbidge had expressed similar views after troubles on Victoria Alley in September 1907.[30]

The press response was immediate and dismissive. The *Deseret Evening News* declared that "nothing like it was ever before recommended by a chief of police in this city, and it is safe to say never will be again."[31] The *Inter-Mountain Republican* labeled the proposal a "Prison Home for Fallen Women" which the chief based on his experience as a sheepherder. The plan exposed Pitt as "brutal, nasty, vulgar, coarse, unfit for decency and he represents a party of pretended superior quality."[32] Reed Smoot's supporters seized on the idea as a political weapon. A letter to the editor of a newspaper that opposed Smoot noted that "the anti-Mormon political party, . . . advocates a stockade for the fallen women of the town,—a stockade maintained by the City, within which all the bad women shall be kept—a municipal bawdy house."[33] The American's own organ also attacked the plan, foreshadowing fatal divisions in the party. The *Tribune* denounced the "indecent proposition" as "so absolutely grotesque and impossible as to be astounding in its hardihood and lack of common decency and moral perception, to say nothing of common sense." The American paper, however, carefully attributed the idea to Burbidge, perhaps to insulate the Bransford administration from the proposal.[34]

The stockade[35] plan did not at first arouse much public interest. The Women's League (later the Women's Welfare League), a social purity group formed in February 1908, proposed a reform agenda that resembled Pitt's, except for the prostitution district. The league's directors included Lulu Shepard, who addressed the founders on "The Social Evil." Shepard made "an earnest plea for the women of the streets whose lives of shame are made still more sordid and shameful by the exorbitant rents demanded by landlords." While she did not specifically mention the stockade proposal, Shepard insisted "fifty determined men with a band of good women behind them can paralyze any tenderloin that ever existed."[36]

The *Tribune* used the Woman's League to attack polygamy. The American paper noted that to purify the city, the women would have to overcome "a low standard of morality, an execrable rule, as to the relations of the sexes;

an evil rule and a blight at the root of purity that elsewhere is not encountered."[37] The league quickly allied with the revived antipolygamy movement. Lulu Shepard introduced the league to the American Woman's Club, and the American women under their president, Elizabeth Cohen, enthusiastically joined the movement for social purity.[38]

Meanwhile, the proposed district moved forward. By late May 1908, agents were quietly purchasing large sections of Block 64, between 100 and 200 South and 400 and 500 West. "A notorious woman of Ogden" reportedly led the project and invested $20,000. Mayor John Bransford did not fully explain his participation, but endorsed the plan on business, law enforcement, and moral grounds.

> "If the resorts of Commercial streett [*sic*] were compelled to seek new locations, Commercial street would become a desirable wholesale district.
>
> "Scattered as the tenderloin resorts now are, it is difficult for the police to give them proper supervision. In the new district arrangements could be made so that the police could preserve order. . . .
>
> "I have gone to [Commercial] street to study the conditions reported to me, and, day and night, I have found boys either loitering or passing through the street. What a passer may see in Commercial street must certainly have a demoralizing effect upon the young and the doing away with such a spot in the center of the city would be a step in the right direction."[39]

When the district was near completion in December, Bransford publicly revealed his role. He insisted "I would prefer to see the city in a condition where there would be no such houses at all. That is, of course, the ideal which, I am sorry to say, is at present unattainable." The mayor had visited eastern cities with three councilmen, including Mulvey, to investigate methods of regulating prostitution. Upon returning, the officials consulted with unnamed "prominent residents" and "business men of all parties and former city officials" and decided on Block 64 as the best location for a restricted district. Bransford asked Mulvey to find investors, and "we got into communication with the Ogden people [Dora Topham and her associates]." Bransford reported that he promised the investors "I would see to it that the women of the downtown district were removed to the new location." The mayor boasted that he had helped create "one of the very best regulated districts of its kind in the country." Bransford did not propose to legalize prostitution, but he was committing his administration to open defiance of the law.[40]

The choice of Block 64 was both pragmatic and steered by class and ethnic biases. Councilman L. D. Martin explained that the block was already partially isolated by railroad tracks, and no children would pass it on the way to school. Besides, "most of the better class of residents were leaving that vicinity anyway, because of the influx of Italians and Japs."[41]

The authorities' reasoning, however, was not publicly known when work on the district began. In June, a group of "West Side Citizens" organized to defend their neighborhood. They condemned the plan by "some of the most influential capitalists of our town" to move the tenderloin. These "poor but honest" citizens wondered how those capitalists would enjoy having their children exposed to "that class of people."[42] The group's leaders included Elias C. Ashton, an attorney, and Alice Butterworth, a grocer. The other members were mostly residents and small business people.[43]

The West Siders were not necessarily against regulated prostitution. One member argued that the tenderloin should stay where it was, since "it would take half a century to put Commercial street on its feet as a business street, . . . Franklin alley, Plum alley, Victoria and the other alleys now inhabited by this class, will never amount to anything." Alice Butterworth was more concerned with moral corruption:

> "Keep them back!" exclaimed Mrs. Butterworth, . . . "I would rather have a nest of rattlesnakes in our midst than this class, for I would know how to deal with rattlesnakes.
> "If they must be sent somewhere, send them to the north end of Salt Lake, and then every man who visits them would be known.
> "Talk about polygamy! It's nowhere compared with this horror, this form which has not even ceremony."[44]

The West Side group continued its campaign against the district for months.

By the end of June, most of the details of the Stockade were publicly known. The "notorious woman from Ogden" was revealed to be Dora B. Topham, or Belle London, for two decades the leading madam in Ogden. Why officials did not choose a Salt Lake madam is unclear. Several women, including Emma DeMarr, Helen Blazes, Ada Wilson, and Beatrice "Bee" Bartlett, had been operating houses with the connivance of the authorities for years. Perhaps the district's backers felt that Topham had the political skills and financial savvy necessary to keep an illegal business thriving in the face of opposition, or perhaps the local women passed on the venture.[45]

Topham created the innocuous-sounding Citizens' Investment Company to manage the project. The company issued 2,500 shares of stock, valued at $100 each, and granted the Salt Lake Security and Trust Company a trust deed for $200,000 to secure four hundred bonds of $500 each to provide the necessary capital. The corporation was virtually a one-woman show: Topham was president, treasurer, and general manager, with 1,260 shares outright and the control of 1,200 more as trustee. Four other officers received ten shares each. While the company and its officers were named in early legal actions, opponents of the district quickly focused on two targets, one political and one legal: John S. Bransford and Dora B. Topham, respectively.[46] While Bransford risked only his political future, Topham's freedom and livelihood were at stake.

Construction work commenced in late summer 1908. Eventually, the district covered about one-third of block 64, from 100 to 200 South, and from about 530 to 560 West. Some existing buildings were converted into parlor houses, while others were demolished. Rows of cribs were constructed along the west, north, and east edges. The outside of the district featured stores and storage buildings, and a ten-foot wall surrounded the enclosure, with gates at the northern and southern ends (the northern gate was apparently sealed off at some point). About 150 cribs were built, although the frame partitions could easily be moved to accommodate more or fewer women. The parlor houses could accommodate between three and six women each (see figure 3).[47]

Opposition intensified as construction progressed. The West Side citizens met with the city council in July but complained that the majority of the councillors either favored the scheme or claimed the council had no say in the matter. Councilman T. R. Black, representing the Fifth Ward, which included the traditional brothel district, claimed a remarkable ignorance of the social realities of his constituency: "As far as I am concerned, I do not know that [prostitutes] live here. . . . The mayor and the chief of police are the ones to appeal to in regard to this matter. The council has no power to order these women to remain on Commercial street any more than we have the authority to order a man to build a butcher shop when he wants to build a grocery store."[48] One of the leading proponents of the plan, in fact, was former councilman Augustus R. Carter, who sold part of the land to the Citizens Investment Company. A sitting councilman, L. D. Martin, was the architect for the project, while Martin Mulvey was among its creators and most enthusiastic boosters.[49]

The man who publicly broached the idea, however, now expressed reservations. Chief Pitt declared that he could not support a district in a residential neighborhood. Why Pitt changed his mind is unclear. Publicly, he cited a desire for strict adherence to the law, which earned ridicule from those who noted that he had long tolerated prostitution. Perhaps the reason lay closer to home, as Pitt's wife was an officer in the WCTU.[50]

Other organizations joined in the opposition. The city Board of Education called the district "pernicious and subversive to the interests of the school children."[51] The Women's Democratic Club protested to the council, with

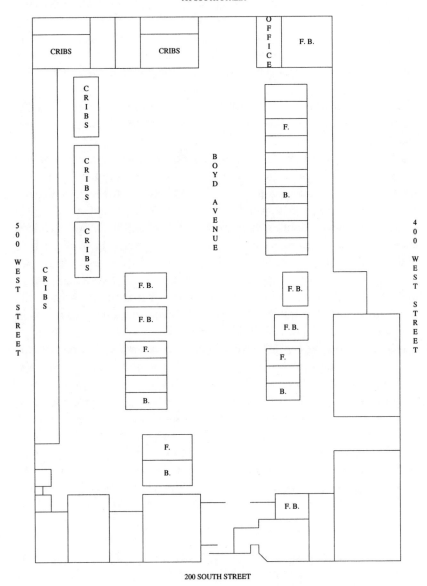

Figure 3. The Stockade. "F. B." is "female boarding." Other buildings shown are stores and storerooms; the remainder of the block on the east and west is not shown for clarity. Based on "Fire Insurance Map of Salt Lake City, 1911."

all councilmen present, including L. D. Martin, concurring in the protest. The Westminster Presbyterian church, located in the same block as the Stockade, also filed a complaint.[52]

Some "Americans" also opposed the plan. The city's American Club understood that the district belied the party's moral pretensions and could damage it politically. The club members declared that "the principles of 'Americanism' demanded that a vigorous stand be taken for the 'purity of the home in every form' and that this was a signal opportunity to prove that they were for decency and morality."[53] They asked Republican governor John C. Cutler to rescind the charter of the Citizens' Investment Company. Cutler sharply accused the American Club of "the rankest piece of hypocrisy that has come to my attention for a long time." The governor noted that the American administration had profited from prostitution fines for three years. He called on city officials to eliminate brothels and promised the assistance of county and state officials in repressing the new district should it begin operations.[54]

Salt Lake County sheriff C. Frank Emery did not wait for the new district to open. In September his sheriffs raided brothels on Commercial Street.[55] Although Emery, a Republican, denied any political motives, county and state elections were only weeks away. The Democratic *Herald* insisted the raid was a blatant effort to deprive the Americans of tenderloin support.[56] While the American county and state platforms denounced the Stockade, they characterized Emery's campaign as "both an imposture and a pretense, . . . his purpose is not for the betterment of moral conditions, but rather to advance the interests of the political party with which he is affiliated."[57] At an American rally, one campaign sign read: "Emery's deputies are working for Belle London's cribs!"[58] The *Deseret Evening News* cast the elections in stark terms, urging its readers to "vote against immorality" by rejecting the American ticket. Whatever Emery's motives, the Republicans swept the 1908 elections.[59]

By late December, the Stockade was ready. Chief Pitt refused to move prostitutes to the new district and stated flatly that it would not open. Bransford fired him, with the council's backing, and publicly declared his sponsorship of the new district.[60] Now that it was nearly a reality, reactions grew warmer. Many of the city's clergy sermonized against the Stockade. While two called for eradication of prostitution, another suggested a rescue home instead of a municipal brothel. W. M. Paden called prostitution and polygamy related vices that were equally "violations of the laws of God and the laws of man." Paden visited the district and noted that "if the hundred or so cubby holes, cribs or white slaves of this 'establishment' had been planned by a pimp [which, of course, they had been] they could not have been more evidently, impudently and brutally planned for the most degraded type of prostitution." An LDS leader called on Mormons "to raise their voices against the contemplated outrage."[61]

The West Side citizens began legal action in November 1908, a month before the Stockade opened. A group of nearby property owners charged that the buildings being erected were suitable only for prostitution and that the area was already being referred to as "the redlight district." If the Stockade opened, the plaintiffs' property values would be adversely affected. Plaintiffs' attorneys asked for a temporary restraining order to prevent the use of the property for the purpose alleged. Judge C. W. Morse issued the order on 22 December, as the district began to fill, and made it permanent on 15 February 1909.[62]

Public reaction, however, was not wholly negative. Several businessmen told the *Deseret Evening News* that prostitution should be segregated, preferably beyond the city's limits. The reporter may not have known that one of those businessmen was president of the bank that had loaned Topham her capital.[63] The *Herald* characterized the call for a crackdown on prostitutes as unchristian. As for a rescue home, the *Herald* reminded readers that "the 'home' experiment has been tried right here in Salt Lake. . . . A pest-house could not have been regarded with more horror—and this in a Christian community."[64] The *Herald* stopped short of endorsing the Stockade but declared that "sound policy still calls for [prostitutes'] restriction to some district where they can be kept under supervision and control."[65] That paper published two letters of support for the Stockade, one from "A WEST SIDE WOMAN." The second, signed by some fifty persons and businesses, argued that the district would clean up "vice and immorality" on West Second South Street. Some of the signatories may have believed that, but others may have expected jobs or increased business from the Stockade.[66]

The press also cast the issue in Mormon-gentile terms. The *Tribune* condemned the Stockade and predicted that it would never open, since "powerful interests in the dominant church are vitally concerned in protecting and retaining their Commercial street tenants because of the enormous revenue derived therefrom."[67] The *Telegram* claimed that a district had existed for decades without Mormon opposition.[68] The *Deseret Evening News* replied by likening the gentile clergy's opposition to the district to the reformers of 1890 who protested the Liberal regime they had helped elect.[69]

The *Inter-Mountain Republican* adopted the harshest tone. The Stockade promoters had "crucified John Bransford and damned the American party. . . . STOP! LOOK! LISTEN! Don't play further with fire!"[70] Governor Cutler said "I do not believe that it is for any financial gain that [Bransford] has taken the stand he has, and I admire the man for coming out in the open . . . , but I believe he has made a mistake."[71] No newspaper called for abolition. The press seemed to imply that while regulation was the best policy, the Stockade was unacceptable because it made explicit official toleration.

Some members of Bransford's administration opposed the project. City Attorney Harper J. Dininny, a founder of the American Party, promised to prosecute women in the new district. Bransford replied that "it does not make any difference to me what the opinion of the city attorney may be or what his pre-election promises may have been."[72] A historian of the Americans concludes: "For the American Party, the announcement of Mayor Bransford's considered position on the stockade was the beginning of the end."[73]

The plan moved forward. On 17 December, policemen visited the city's brothels and told the managers they must close and would not be allowed to reopen. The women were reportedly not told where to go, as that would imply official approval of their illegal activities (a familiar if rather absurd pretense), but the police made clear that prostitutes could either leave town or move to the Stockade.[74] The *Inter-Mountain Republican* reported that Dora Topham had amassed a $25,000 fund to lure women into her brothels:

> Yesterday Belle London sent for three women inmates of the closed houses and offered them free boarding and rooms for a week if they would enter one of her parlor houses.
>
> "There is no danger," she told them. "I will protect you with my life, if need be. I know what I am talking about and want you women to show the others in Salt Lake that this place will not be molested." That shows the vice queen's confidence in Mayor Bransford and his councilmen.[75]

Topham offered houses to several established madams, including Cleo Starr, a keeper at 222 south State Street and Commercial Street; Madge Daniels, of the Palace and other Commercial Street addresses; Lou Sheppard, a Commercial Street veteran; Irene McDonald, of Commercial Street and Topham's Ogden brothels; and Rose Bartlett, of 243 south Main Street.[76] All but Sheppard accepted the offer.[77]

Some madams refused to move. One unidentified woman defended her financial independence: "I own property here and the chief of police, the mayor nor anyone else will drive me away. I'll not go into any district or stockade and any woman who does, that is one who owns a house, is a fool. They can't bluff me. I'll stay where I am."[78] Interestingly, Salt Lake County sheriff Joseph C. Sharp cited antitrust as another reason to oppose the Stockade: "The segregated district controlled by one woman, to whom tribute is paid on all the drugs, liquors, laundry and almost everything else used by the inmates, is a monopolistic institution and wrong in theory and fact."[79]

Ada Wilson apparently left town.[80] Helen Blazes leased 7 Victoria Alley to Edna Prescott (formerly of 243 south Main) in February 1908 and left the business, possibly because she foresaw the Stockade move.[81] Prescott managed 7 Victoria and 222 south State Street successively throughout the life of the new district.[82] Bee Bartlett operated 7 Victoria from early 1910 through at least June 1911, defying repeated attempts by the police and Dora Topham to force her into the Stockade.[83] The persistence of the older district testified to the desire of many women to retain some independence and control over their work. Their tenacity would prove embarrassing to the Bransford administration, which promised that one of the benefits of the Stockade would be the "cleansing" of the old district. In general, however, the Stockade period marked the end of the era of the independent house-owning brothel operator and saw the departure from the scene of a number of long-term madams. By early spring 1909, the district was in full operation. The *Inter-Mountain Republican* sarcastically congratulated the Americans. "The unexpected has happened. The stockade has been built. The red-light women have been ordered down there, and they are going as rapidly as the most sanguine of the promoters could have expected. The order of the court, faithfully served by the sheriff, is ignored, the injunction disregarded by the Citizens' Investment company, and the black word 'TRIUMPH!' has been written across the Kearns party's effort to make a municipal bawdy house there in the new stockade."[84]

The experienced Dora Topham may have trusted the mayor's promise of protection, but she also prudently insulated herself from most direct responsibility. She acted as the overall manager and leased parlor houses to madams who furnished the brothels and procured inmates, while she apparently controlled the crib women herself. The population of the Stockade varied, but between 60 and 170 women worked there at any given time.[85] Most women evidently came from elsewhere, although a handful had worked in established houses in Salt Lake City.[86] At least one woman, Ray Woods, had long worked in a Victoria Alley crib.[87] Topham reportedly advertised for women in other cities and towns.[88]

The residents of the Stockade were a heterogeneous lot. The new tenderloin, like the old, acknowledged differences in race and class. The parlor houses were generally for higher-status white prostitutes, although at least one had a black keeper and inmates and black and white women worked together in two others. Black women reportedly worked in cribs along the north side, and Japanese women on the west.[89] Two inmates were identified as "Spanish," although they probably were Latin American. The men who provided ancillary services also reflected the city's variety: Koreans, Greeks, and Japanese liquor servers; a Hungarian piano player; and Chinese opium vendors all worked in the district and sometimes lived in the parlor houses.[90]

The Stockade, purpose-built for prostitution and related businesses, was considerably more self-contained and segregated from the outside world than the older district. Customers could mingle with women in the dance hall and patronize saloons, opium dens, restaurants, and cigar stores. Liquor and food storehouses ensured that those necessaries were plentiful. Dora Topham's office was located just inside the northern entrance, while a small jail cell for unruly patrons was built at the south end. "Special policemen," sometimes off-duty city patrolmen, provided security. The buildings were electrically wired for ordering food and liquor and to warn of police raids. An "immense indicator" in the main saloon tallied calls for beer at one dollar per bottle. While the Stockade had only one acknowledged entrance, with a guard to keep minors out, there were reportedly "several secret openings in the walled enclosure, known to the inmates and most of the incorrigible young males of the fair city."[91]

In court and sometimes out, women talked about the conditions of employment at the Stockade. Their working lives were evidently tightly controlled, and women probably had less independence and less financial opportunity than outside the district. Topham claimed that every woman underwent a physical examination before she was hired and every ten days afterward, and that many refused or failed the exam.[92] The woman whose case eventually closed the Stockade testified that a doctor examined her but only after she had already worked one night.[93] Topham knew the high turnover rate in the prostitution trade, and therefore charged daily for rent. Ray Woods moved from a parlor house to a crib in 1910 for unknown reasons; possibly she could earn more money there by servicing more customers in a night. First she had to obtain the consent of her "landlady" to leave the house, then see "Miss Belle" to obtain a key to the crib. Woods paid $2.50 daily rent for the crib to "Mrs. Lee"; if Lee was absent, she paid Topham. Medical examinations and hospital fees cost $1 each per week.[94] A year later, parlor house inmates were reportedly paying $7 nightly for rooms and $3 a week to the physician, while crib women paid $3 a night.[95]

These fees and rents were not the only expenses. Crib women were not allowed (and probably did not want) to sleep in their tiny quarters but rather occupied rooming houses surrounding the district at $5 per week, especially the Washington just outside the south entrance, which Topham owned, and the Plumas, which Mayor Bransford owned.[96] Inmates were also forced to patronize Stockade businesses.[97] One woman complained that she was constantly dunned, including for a fund to buy off the police.[98] Eva Edwards, who lived at the Plumas, told a disguised reporter that she "had to surrender most of her earnings to landladies, politicians, policemen and others."[99]

In return, women enjoyed virtual immunity from arrest. Arrests for prostitution-related offenses, which numbered over one thousand in 1908, dwindled to practically nothing from 1909 through 1911.[100] City Attorney Dininny complained that Dora Topham even issued "passes" allowing inmates to solicit on outside streets without interference. When inmates began selling or giving such passes to other women, Topham told the police that her "mark of approval" would henceforth be a nontransferable piece of cloth sewn to the skirt of each Stockade woman.[101] Little wonder that the police favored the Stockade—Dora Topham had solved their old dilemma of recognizing prostitutes by providing a fail-safe visual cue.

Judge Morse's injunction remained in effect throughout the Stockade's life, but enforcing it was another matter. Bransford replaced his dissenting police chief with the more amenable Samuel Barlow.[102] Barlow took no action on the injunction and effectively protected the district from prosecution for almost three years. The Republican county sheriff did attempt to enforce the injunction. County sheriffs arrested some forty Stockade women in April 1909, but few were brought to trial. County Attorney Job Lyon treated the women in accordance with traditional regulationist practice. He set bail at $10, the standard amount for prostitutes. The Republican paper accused Lyon of "introducing" Ogden's system of monthly fines and urged the authorities to ignore "the miserable women" and instead to go after "the people higher up."[103] Apparently no one seriously suggested arresting the district's patrons, nor taking legal action against the authorities who built and protected the Stockade. Just as before, women bore the brunt of legal responsibility for prostitution; the only "higher up" in real jeopardy was Dora Topham.

The 1909 state legislature deliberately took aim at the Stockade by stiffening laws against owning, leasing, or acting as the agent of property used for prostitution.[104] The Civic Betterment League filed complaints under the revised law against Topham and the Citizens' Investment Company in May 1909.[105] The league, founded in 1906, included many of the city's business and political elite and addressed a variety of concerns, including civic beautification and structural reform of municipal government. Members included both advocates of regulated prostitution, such as Frank B. Stephens and W. Mont Ferry, and some dedicated to abolition. Brigham Frederick Grant of the latter faction headed a committee fighting the Stockade. Grant was a Mormon businessman, the son of Salt Lake City's first mayor, and a member of the Salt Lake Stake High Council. He had worked as a "special policeman" concentrating on disorderly rooming houses and saloons. Other committee members included Lorenzo (Lon) J. Haddock, another Mormon businessman; George Q. Morris, a Mormon officer of a stone products company; and Elias Woodruff, bishop of the LDS Fourteenth Ward. Gaurdello Brown, probation officer of the juvenile court and a Mormon, was also involved.[106] Haddock explained the group's motives for fighting the Stockade: "It is simply a case of whether Salt Lake shall be known as the most depraved city in the country with regard to its fostering and protecting the social evil or whether we shall have a city that is known as moral and decent and law abiding."[107]

These men visited the district, where women solicited them. They filed dozens of complaints against individual women, the Citizens' Investment Company, and Dora Topham. At least two women were convicted on the group's testimony, but the real target remained Topham.[108] Judge Morse issued an order to show cause why she should not be cited for contempt of court for violating his injunction.[109]

While these cases pended, opposition to the Stockade widened. Attendees at a June 1909 meeting in the LDS Fifteenth Ward house adopted resolutions demanding its closure and sent them to the city council, Governor William Spry, and the state attorney general. B. F. Grant acknowledged that Mayor Bransford might have had altruistic motives in establishing the Stockade, but he noted that the promised cleanup of the older district had not materialized and that even more prostitutes now worked in the city.[110]

F. S. Fernstrom, an LDS member of the city council, moved that the council adopt the reformers' resolutions. He "had listened to hot air from the manageress of the Stockade, but did not at the time think that it would convert anyone to a belief that the thing should be tolerated." L. D. Martin employed the timeworn polygamy issue to defend the district. Martin told Fernstrom "your high ecclesiastics are living in violation of the laws of the country. . . . Suppose we insisted upon prosecuting President Smith every day, wouldn't you get tired of it?" Nevertheless, the council adopted the resolutions.[111] The American organ also rang the familiar changes on this theme. The *Tribune* claimed that Mormons "have a favorite vice very much akin . . . to the vice of the Stockade, and yet they are the ones that are most loud-mouthed in denouncing the Stockade and all its works." Both polygamy and prostitution, "kindred forms of the same vice," needed to be abolished.[112]

The Salt Lake County sheriff continued to apply pressure on the Stockade's women. On 18 June, deputies arrested thirty-one crib workers, whose bonds were fixed at $750 each, remarkably high for such a minor charge. Dora Topham reportedly refused to put up the bonds as she had in the past. The court quickly reverted to standard practice, however; the judge reduced the charges to vagrancy and gave all the women "floaters."[113] Ten days later, deputies accompanied by Lon J. Haddock and Gaurdello Brown raided the parlor houses at 3 A.M. They kicked in doors and forced windows to capture forty-two women.[114] On 29 June 1909 Dora Topham surrendered, announcing that the Stockade was closed and that all women must leave.[115] Significantly, she declared her intention to keep an office at the site. The women forced out of work scattered to rooming houses throughout the city or left Salt Lake entirely, and all furniture other than Topham's personal belongings was sold. A reporter interviewed Topham, who claimed that her motives for opening the Stockade were both altruistic and commercial.

> "I saw there would be money in such an investment. I'm a business woman; I'm a good manager. . . .
> "I don't like [the business of prostitution]—I abhor it. My conscience—yes, I have a conscience—has troubled me about it a good many times. . . .
> ". . . I can do this much: I can make this business as clean as it is possible for such a business as this to be, and I can persuade a great many girls who are just starting in to lead a life of shame to travel other paths. . . .
> "I still think that the city has turned down a good thing—the only possible solution of this social evil; and I think that before many weeks a good many people will realize this. There were 170 women here, who are now scattered about the city in rooming houses, in hotels, in the residence parts of the city. They are running wild, and they are going after the money."[116]

When the Stockade apparently closed, Judge Morse dismissed the contempt of court charges against Topham.[117]

The closing of the Stockade resulted from citizen pressure in the form of the betterment committee and legal pressure in the form of county prosecution. The campaign also had a strong political element. The Republicans (much stronger at the time than the Democrats) stood to gain by attacking the Stockade. Conversely, the district made the American Party potentially vulnerable. With the 1909 municipal campaign on the horizon, the Republicans vigorously employed the issue despite the closure. They opened with traditional charges of political exploitation, claiming that Martin Mulvey used the police to force "negroes and women of the under-world" to register to vote.[118] A woman in a downtown brothel reportedly confirmed the action and complained that the police demanded frequent bribes.

> These policemen told us that we could expect no mercy at all unless we registered. . . .
> Of course the women of our class who are located in houses don't have to dig up so much as those who work on the streets. I've got a friend who has a beat that takes in one block on Main street, one block on Third South and a

block on State street. In making the round she tells me that often in one night she is stopped by three policemen, one on each beat, and told that she must give up part of what she makes or to jail she must go.[119]

The Republicans expressed respect for John Bransford, who remained popular, but worried about the women in the Stockade.

> How in the name of all that is clean, can [Bransford] declare before the world that the scheme of a great commercial enterprise for the exploitation of women is his own scheme; that he believes it right and proper to aid the herding of women; that he can even in the smallest way lend aid or comfort to a business so utterly abhorrent? And how can he have the hardihood to declare—as he has done—that he would use all the power of his official position as mayor to compel the women to live in his walled prison, and guarantee material profit should be provided for the shareholders, and immunity should be assured by preventing the operation of law? . . .
> How can he so bemean himself as to invite the Belle of Ogden to transplant her cyprian empire to the town in which he has his home?[120]

The *Herald-Republican* insisted that the closure was a ruse and that Bransford and Topham would reopen in the event of victory.[121] Prostitution became the centerpiece of the paper's campaign. A long series of cartoons featured "The Red-Light Triplets"—Bransford, Mulvey, and Chief of Detectives George Sheets—in a variety of comic situations. The "triplets" were accused of running a "wide-open" town, with all vices tolerated. Interestingly, Topham does not appear in these cartoons, probably because she was not running for office, although in one drawing Bransford rides a horse labeled "Midnight Belle." The paper repeatedly published the mayor's December 1908 acknowledgment of his sponsorship of the Stockade in the weeks prior to the election.[122]

The antiprostitution material proved ineffective, as Bransford outpolled his Democratic, Republican, and Socialist rivals combined. The Americans won all city offices save two councilmen.[123] The result may indicate not only Bransford's popularity but the depth of resentment and fear of LDS Church domination into which the Americans had tapped. The victory also showed the weakness of the Stockade as a campaign issue. Many voters probably agreed that regulation was the best solution. The *Herald-Republican* dropped its anti-Stockade campaign and its concern for the law and the women of the district. The paper explained that since voters had overwhelmingly chosen the Americans, that meant they supported the Stockade, so it "was a dead issue so far as the Republican party was concerned."[124]

Republican charges of plans to reopen the district proved true. By March 1910, Dora Topham was back in operation, and citizens again rose in protest.

The West Side committee filed a petition with the city council, which called on city officers to enforce the law.[125] Topham met the renewed action with a curious public relations campaign. She tried and failed to gain an audience with the juvenile court judge and an unnamed LDS Relief Society worker, but did meet with several unnamed "prominent Salt Lake women," one of them the wife of a Protestant minister. The party of women visited Topham's "palatial apartments" in Ogden, and the madam took them on a tour of her parlor houses and cribs. Topham also met with an unnamed juvenile court officer (Gaurdello Brown?) with whom she promised to cooperate in keeping girls under eighteen out of her brothels. She bragged to her guests that she was "the greatest woman reformer in the world," because she warned every woman of "the awful shame, degradation, and misery that is invariably the final result of seamy life in the underworld. But if, in spite of my persuading efforts toward conversion, a woman wilfully [sic] insists upon throwing her life away, then I receive her into my district." The madam personally lived a life of "absolute chastity of body and purity of soul," and she wanted her daughter to "continue the grand work that I am trying to do." The visitors claimed not to be fooled by the "mistress of satanic vice."[126]

This remarkable interview raises many questions. The *Deseret Evening News* might have fabricated the incident for political or legal purposes, but that seems unlikely; the *Deseret News* was never very concerned with the Stockade. If it was authentic, Topham must have had her own reasons. The madam may have sincerely believed that she could convince reformers that she shared their goals and that her system was a practical means to minimize the harmful effects of prostitution. She showed easy fluency with the language of true womanhood and the stereotype of the fallen woman. Topham almost certainly *was* careful about the women she hired, especially underage girls, since enticing minors or women "of previous chaste character" into brothels carried severe penalties. Perhaps she was flaunting her ill-gotten wealth and political clout while enjoying a private laugh at the expense of her fascinated and horrified audience. Harold Ross, a young *Tribune* reporter who went on to found the *New Yorker* magazine, recalled years later that he had accompanied Topham on an inspection of the Stockade before it opened. "Belle had been represented in print as a 'friend of the fallen woman,' and so on—their benefactor. There was never a hint that she was in the game for profit and, by God, I was so young then that I fell for the publicity and assumed she was an old Methodist. I asked the old girl a lot of questions that dazed her. . . . She stood the high-level conversation as long as she could, and then said, 'Jesus Christ, kid, cut the honey. If I had a railroad tie for every trick I've turned x x [sic] I'd build a railroad from here to San Francisco.'"[127]

The threatened campaign against Topham did not materialize. A frustrated F. S. Fernstrom pushed another in a series of resolutions ordering the police to suppress the district.[128] Chief Barlow, presumably at the mayor's orders, refused to act. City Attorney Dininny took advantage of Barlow's and Bransford's absence to launch his own campaign, nicknamed by the papers the "Stockade war." On 15 June 1910, Dininny filed nine complaints against Topham for conducting houses of prostitution and selling liquor without a license. The acting chief of police served the complaints and claimed to be dedicated to closing the district.[129]

Dininny also moved against the women who sold sex. A police squad, supposedly acting on secret orders and armed with Jane Doe warrants, descended on the district but found it in darkness. The inmates had evidently been tipped off by a friendly policeman and had removed their valuables the day before, then returned and operated until 8:30 P.M., about forty-five minutes before the raid. Patrolmen staking out the empty district arrested six women who returned to get belongings they had forgotten, but they were given "floaters." This raid set the pattern for the ersatz "war."[130] The city attorney broadened the campaign to include the embarrassing downtown brothels, resulting in the arrest of "eighteen women of the silken plane of the demimonde."[131]

The prosecution of Topham ran into immediate difficulties. The jury selection process in the city court demonstrated the popularity of regulation. Several prospective jurors insisted they believed the laws should be enforced but also favored a restricted district. Chief Barlow followed instructions and claimed ignorance of the Stockade; he reportedly testified that "he knew only from hearsay" that Topham operated brothels. The jury was unconvinced that she was responsible for the liquor sales; upon her acquittal on the first charge, the others were dismissed.[132]

The city fared no better on the prostitution charges. An attorney reportedly testified that he had acted as the agent for one Herman J. Mundt of Washington State, who purchased the property when the Stockade temporarily closed. Mundt, whom the attorney admitted having never met, suggested that a "Mrs. Lee" be made manager of the district. The prosecutor was unable to produce other witnesses, including prostitutes and (presumably) "Mrs. Lee," and Topham was acquitted. Topham had made it very difficult for those authorities who desired to prosecute her. Her tactics of transferring ownership, inserting a layer of management between herself and day-to-day operations, and using prostitutes' traditional anonymity and mobility had foiled legal action.[133]

Dininny asked the city court justice to investigate the police for obstructing prosecution. He noted that he had issued hundreds of warrants in the weeks previous, but only the six stragglers had been arrested. Nearly all efforts to serve the warrants had come between 10:00 and 11:00 P.M. Newspaper reports confirmed that the district ran as normal until watchmen, some of them off-duty patrolmen probably in contact with police headquarters, warned of the impending raids. The district then closed and officers were unable to serve the warrants. "Five minutes after the officer had gone the lights were turned on, pianos started drumming, girls were disporting themselves and the Stockade was again running full blast." American officials, worried that Dininny would damage the party, reportedly telephoned Mayor Bransford to return to the city immediately.[134]

Bransford's return ended the "war" and proved that Dininny lacked either the desire or the clout to close the district. Bransford reportedly met with Barlow, Dininny, and several councilmen, including Mulvey, who in turn conferred with Topham. They agreed to some changes: Topham was to remove herself from direct management; all cribs were to be closed; no liquor or drugs were to be sold; and all brothels outside the Stockade were to be suppressed. The city court justice's investigation of the police was delayed (later dismissed). The *Herald-Republican* viewed the agreement cynically: "The old ruse of 'closing the stockade' is re-enacted, for this is the second time that matters have been forced to such an issue, and in each case Belle London has announced that she will quit. Likewise, in both instances, she started up again and the stockade ran as before."[135] The last condition—the only one that would improve the Stockade's business—was the only one carried out. Police staked out Bee Bartlett's brothel at 7 Victoria Alley and reportedly took down patrons' names. The madam was convicted in city court of keeping a house of ill fame, but appealed. Barlow reported that other downtown houses would also be closed.[136] The papers claimed Topham directed the police to suppress the downtown brothels, which would give her a monopoly on prostitution. (Of course, those same sources had also condemned the Americans for allowing those houses to continue to operate.) As for the rest of the deal, the cynics were proved correct. Dora Topham remained in charge, and opened makeshift cribs in the back of the parlor houses.[137]

With county elections looming, the Americans' opponents again used prostitution as a political weapon. The *Deseret Evening News* offered a campaign song for Chief Barlow, to the tune of "Tammany":

> Incompetency, Incompetency.
> Crooks and gamblers run the town,
> Miss Belle London keeps them round,

Incompetency, Incompetency,
I know nothing, I see nothing,
Incompetency.[138]

At the request of Governor Spry, the county sheriff launched new raids on the Stockade. Deputies arrested most of the women for vagrancy and gave them "floaters."[139] The Americans were accused of attempting to extort $225 from each remaining downtown brothel.[140] The Republicans did not, however, stress the Stockade as much in 1910 as they had a year earlier, probably because of its proven weakness as an issue.

Not everyone believed that Republicans wanted the Stockade closed. B. F. Grant of the Civic Betterment League, nominally a Republican, assailed Governor Spry, a member of the "Federal bunch" and a fellow Mormon, before a Democratic audience. Grant claimed that Spry "begged" the sheriff to cancel a planned raid, then telephoned Dora Topham to assure her that she was safe.[141] Despite these charges, the Republicans swept the county offices.[142]

Within ten days after the election, H. J. Dininny again attempted to prosecute the women of the Stockade. Chief Barlow again delayed serving the warrants, arguing that they had not been properly signed. Dininny accused Barlow of protecting the district and threatened legal action.[143] Mayor Bransford's use of the police to protect the Stockade drew increasing fire from within the party. An American meeting in early 1911 called on Barlow to clean up his department. Bransford himself was reportedly nearly thrown out of the party.[144]

The city attorney waited until Bransford again left town in February 1911 before he tried one more time to prosecute Topham and other women. These cases proved no more successful. The city court justice ruled that the city had not proven that Topham owned the property and directed a verdict of not guilty. After three inmates were acquitted, Dininny moved that all but liquor charges be dropped, stating that "I am satisfied that we cannot secure convictions of women in the Stockade by a jury in this court. I do not know of any way but to get a grand jury to enforce the law."[145] The city council, still dominated by Americans, also attempted to force Chief Barlow to carry out his duty. The chief denied that he had impeded past prosecutions and promised to cooperate with the city attorney.[146]

Bee Bartlett's appeal reached the Third District court in May 1911, and she revealed details of Topham's efforts to monopolize prostitution with the backing of the authorities. Bartlett testified that in April 1909 Chief Barlow and Tom Matthews, Dora Topham's lieutenant (and perhaps her lover)[147] visited her at 222 south State Street. While Barlow sat silently, Matthews told

Bartlett that she must move to the Stockade; she refused. Another visit from Matthews and a meeting with Topham did not change her mind, and the latter warned Bartlett that she would be "pulled." Police officers admitted that Bartlett's house had been particularly targeted, while others were unmolested. While the judge upheld her conviction, her testimony convinced him that the Bransford administration illegally protected the Stockade. The court fined Bartlett one dollar, noting that "this court will not permit itself to be used as an implement to aid the police or anyone in forcing women into the stockade."[148]

Change loomed that further threatened the Americans. The Civic Betterment League, like similar organizations around the country, had long argued that a commission form of government would be more efficient and businesslike. Such a change would likely doom traditional ward politicians like Martin Mulvey. The state legislature approved a commission measure to take effect on 1 January 1912. While Mayor Bransford professed to be in favor of the change, the reform tide was moving against him.[149]

The same legislature passed another bill that ultimately proved fatal to the Stockade. Lawmakers strengthened Utah's pandering statute, almost certainly as a direct weapon against the district.[150] "Inveigling" or "enticing" a woman into a house of ill fame had long been a crime, although the offense depended on the woman being "of previous chaste character."[151] That clause put the onus on a woman to prove her virginity; the obvious implication was that "fallen" women were no longer of concern. Nellie Davis, a Franklin Avenue brothel keeper, was convicted of abducting a woman for the purposes of prostitution in 1895, but the case was appealed and dismissed because the woman was not "of previous chaste character."[152] The 1911 law removed the chastity provision, and provided for imprisonment for up to twenty years.

On 22 July, one Helen Lofstrom invoked this law against Dora Topham. She swore a complaint that Topham did "by promises and threats, and by divers devices and schemes cause, induce, persuade and encourage one Dogney Gray, being then and there an inmate of a certain house of prostitution, to remain therein as such inmate."[153] The wording of this complaint, taken directly from the statute, would prove problematic for the prosecution.

Helen Lofstrom initially told a dramatic story through the newspapers. Dogney Gray, née Lofstrom, was Helen's sixteen-year-old daughter. Helen operated a rooming house, and claimed "when I found it hard to get along in conducting a rooming house from an absolutely honorable standpoint, in which I had placed a ban on liquor or women of questionable character, I advised my daughter to find work somewhere."[154] Dogney[155] went to work at a laundry, where she met a woman later identified as Lillian Evans. Evans took Dogney to dinner on 8 May. The girl noticed that her coffee tasted bitter just before she lost consciousness. When she came to, she found herself in No. 140, the Stockade, a brothel operated by one Ethel Clifford. Her clothing was gone, and she was dressed in the Stockade uniform, described by Helen Lofstrom as "a short red dress, only to her knees, the neck was cut very low and she had red stockings. Her cheeks were covered with pink powder, her lips had been painted very red and her eye-lashes and eye-brows blackened." Dogney begged to be allowed to call her mother but was prevented from contacting anyone or leaving the Stockade. Finally she convinced Dora Topham to call Helen, who armed herself with a revolver and, accompanied by one T. J. Gray, stormed the madam's office and confronted her. When all involved lived in Ogden, Topham had reportedly broken up Lofstrom's marriage to a tailor who made uniforms for Topham's inmates. For some reason, Topham had supposedly sworn vengeance against Helen Lofstrom. The madam told her "now, I am getting even with you. I have got your daughter in a house of ill fame." Helen rescued her frantic daughter, who then married Gray, and lodged the complaint against the Stockade madam.[156]

This lurid tale appears to be pure fantasy, concocted by the Lofstroms, the prosecution, or the *Herald-Republican*. A reporter for that paper managed to combine maternal courage with two of the era's foremost concerns—white slavery and monopoly—in a single sentence: "Bringing tears to the eyes of attorneys and spectators . . . , Mrs. Helen Lofstrom, mother of the girl, told a heart-rending story of unflinching mother's love, in which she had valiantly dashed into the maw of Salt Lake's 'white slave' trust and snatched her daughter from a life of shame which enveloped her."[157]

The fragmentary evidence paints a different picture. Helen Lofstrom apparently did have a history with Dora Topham in Ogden. In 1906 she rented "furnished rooms" at 250 25th Street, a house later under Topham's management.[158] At the trial, Dogney testified that Topham vaguely remembered her; she told the madam they had been acquainted in Ogden when she was a child. The Utah Supreme Court later concluded that Dogney entered the Stockade voluntarily, was allowed to come and go as she pleased, and that Topham did not even know she was there until the following day.[159] She apparently sought work there for mundane economic reasons, as she had lost her $5 per week job in a laundry strike.[160]

The case against Topham boiled down to statements she had allegedly made to Dogney on 9 May 1911. Dogney had entered the Stockade the night before, and according to the Supreme Court decision "voluntarily prostituted her person to divers men, some of whom had roomed at her mother's rooming house and with whom she was acquainted." The next day she reported to Topham's office for her medical examination and met the madam. Topham thought she recognized her, but Dogney gave the madam a false name. The next few fragments of conversation were crucial. Dogney testified that she told Topham she was sixteen years old. "I asked her if I was not too young to be down there, and she said 'No, you are just the right age.' She said I was a blonde and could make good money down there; that there were several calls for blondes. She said I could make good money and I could get me some good clothes." When pressed for the exact words Topham had used, Dogney declared that the madam said "'if your mother don't object I'll buy you a nice suit of clothes and send you to Ogden,' or 'if your mother don't object she would send me to Ogden and give me some clothes.'" "A night or two thereafter" the young woman spoke to Topham in the dance hall. "'I asked her if she would telephone to my mother and she said yes. Then she told me to get in and hustle.'" A day or so later "the husband of the inmate's sister, . . . who was a piano player in one of the houses, informed the defendant who the inmate was." Dogney's sister may have also been in the Stockade. She testified that Topham told her "'I don't know why your mother should have any objections for you to do a little sporting when you have had one sister down here who has been doing sporting.'"[161]

Dora Topham realized the seriousness of the case against her and evidently tried to keep the Lofstroms from testifying. She reportedly sent Norman Mathews, Helen Lofstrom's piano-playing son-in-law, to Lofstrom's rooming house with an offer of money and tickets to Sweden if she disavowed Dogney's story. Lofstrom rejected the offer but may have reconsidered. Another Topham confederate approached her during the trial and was arrested. Helen Lofstrom herself was arrested, reportedly to prevent her from leaving the state, and charges were lodged against Dogney to keep her in custody. The Supreme Court suggested that Topham might have influenced the mother's and daughter's testimony.[162]

Some local authorities were willing to attest to Topham's character and reform credentials. Ogden chief of police Thomas Browning reportedly testified that she had a good reputation for truth and veracity, and like Chief Barlow, "he didn't know whether she was interested in the red light district in Ogden or not."[163] If the newspapers reported his testimony accurately, Browning perjured himself, since he is recorded as having personally arrested Belle London almost a dozen times for keeping a house of prostitution.[164] A parole officer at the state industrial school claimed that he "had found Belle London always ready to help him in any way she could in getting young girls away from lives of shame." Topham herself testified that she had tried for two hours to convince Dogney not to enter the Stockade.[165]

The jurors, however, had heard enough; they concluded that Dogney had been induced to remain in the Stockade. On 23 September 1911, they found Topham guilty. The verdict brought congratulations from the papers for the prosecution team and the anti-Stockade reformers. Gaurdello Brown reportedly "secured practically all of the evidence that went to convict Mrs. Topham," although his role was not further explained.[166] The anti-Stockade activists could rejoice that the "mistress of satanic vice" had finally been brought to justice.

With a possible twenty-year sentence hanging over her head, Topham issued a statement on 27 September declaring that the Stockade would close permanently at noon the next day. The madam denied all wrongdoing and expressed confidence that she would be exonerated. She credited female moral reformers with her conviction and offered her assistance to purify Salt Lake City.

> I hope that my course in this regard will be an encouragement to the women to whom I refer to continue their work, and that the alleys and streets, the rooming houses and hotels, and the secret dens of vice of uptown Salt Lake will be made clean. I am aware that my action will turn upon the streets a large number of women who will not know where to go. Now that it will not be necessary for the women to wage war upon me, I sincerely hope and trust that these women will extent [sic] a helping hand to the women who will find themselves homeless when I close. In this work, which is a charitable and Christian work, I will gladly aid any and all of my sex who are willing to extend a helping hand to their fallen sisters.[167]

On 20 October, Topham was sentenced to eighteen years at hard labor. Her attorneys filed immediate notice of appeal.[168]

The reforming women to whom Topham referred included the Women's Welfare League. Just before the trial, Elizabeth Cohen and Corinne Allen addressed the WCTU about the need to eradicate the Stockade.[169] Several women attended the trial, including Allen and Georgiana McMahon, president of the Utah Federation of Women's Clubs.[170] The day before Topham's announcement, Cohen chaired a meeting that resolved to work for the abolition of prostitution in the Stockade, downtown rooming houses, and cheap hotels. Elmer O. Leatherwood, the district attorney who prosecuted Topham, addressed this group. He declared that her conviction was the beginning of moral reform in the city and congratulated the women in the courtroom for influencing the verdict. Leatherwood soon declared his candidacy for mayor on a "good government" platform.[171]

Topham's attribution of the Stockade's closure to the Woman's Welfare League was almost certainly disingenuous. The pandering conviction forced her to close the district, while the league had apparently become involved only after her arrest. Reformers did offer aid to the women thrown out of work and home by the closure of the Stockade. The adjutant of the Salvation Army told Dora Topham that the army would house any girls "with a determination to live decent lives." Elizabeth Cohen opened a "bureau of information and assistance" at St. Paul's Episcopal church, where she proposed to offer women help in finding employment or transportation back to their families. The *Herald-Republican* described the prostitutes' response in unlikely language: "The outcasts were told that Christian women were downtown waiting to receive them. The straw was grasped eagerly at first, then each asked the other: 'What can they do—these Christian women; what can they do for women whose lives have been devoted to the scarlet kimono?' Hope was killed by the question. Of the three score whose lives had been designated to the 'under half,' many would have welcomed a suggestion pointing the way to the straighter path, but what could that suggestion be?"

When no inmates had visited the bureau by lunchtime, a Women's League committee headed to the Stockade. Corinne Allen, Kate Hilliard, and Ruth May Fox interviewed the inmates in Dora Topham's now-famous office, where they took down each woman's name, age, former residence, name of parents, and future plans. The reformers did not impress the Stockade women. "With ribald jests and coarse laughter, the human derelicts swarmed into the room where the three good women, on an errand of mercy and sister love, awaited them. Nor did the presence of the three motherly-looking matrons serve to awe their erring sisters into respect. The inmates of the place appeared to take delight in covert remarks of offense without openly showing their contempt for the visitors."[172]

The Woman's League offered the same kind of work that the city's previous rescue homes had: domestic labor, cooking, and sewing, none of which paid well nor carried much status. The majority of women recognized the dim prospects offered and "declared their aversion to 'slaving in a kitchen for twelve or fourteen hours every day.'" One woman, who gave her age as thirty-eight, declined to be a servant but "if she could enter a home as a daughter, she might consider such a proposition. Another said she might cook for a husband, but she'd like to see herself cooking for anybody else." Dora Topham claimed to empathize with the women's predicament.

"These poor women in the houses here are absolutely helpless," she said. "They earned their living in the only way they knew how, and now they are homeless. . . .

"All of the girls are on the street; at least they told me that was where they were going. They called upon the women of the organization this afternoon, but they offered them nothing except scrubbing, washing and ironing, and those girls will not do that kind of work."[173]

Five women accepted the committee's aid. Two were offered unspecified medical treatment, two were "placed in good homes," and one asked for help to reach her family. With the reformers offering unsatisfactory alternatives, forty women reportedly marched on the county commissioners' office and insisted they be provided with rooms. The county officials disavowed any responsibility and referred them back to the rescue committee.[174]

Dora Topham faced a long prison term and had undoubtedly lost a great deal of money (although she claimed neither circumstance bothered her). The other women who had worked in the Stockade were in much less dire circumstances, and most were probably used to sudden and frequent moves. But in the short run, they faced hardships as well: no home and no income. Many had reportedly paid Topham in advance for their rent, but she refused to return any money. Reformers were not the only ones interested in their futures. One reporter watched two "white slavers" approach Topham and ask to take some of the "'prettiest' girls" to brothels in other states; Topham reminded them of her legal predicament. Hotel runners competed to offer women inexpensive lodging. Topham predicted that the women "will stream the streets and rob and plot and commit every possible crime. They ask me what they are going to do. I tell them frankly to go to the streets or do what they please."[175]

Many women probably left the city, but as advocates of regulation had always warned, many others scattered to hotels and rooming houses. The rescue committee recognized its failure and looked to government for a solution, this time a coercive one. Since most of the women refused to perform respectable labor, Elizabeth Cohen and her fellow workers called on the police to force the women to return to their home towns.[176]

While the committee offered little to tempt the Stockade women, it was noteworthy for a different reason. The rescue attempt united gentiles and Mormons in a common reform effort. Elizabeth Cohen and Corinne Allen had been major figures in the campaign against Reed Smoot and Mormon polygamy just a few years prior. Cohen's actions especially elicited the scorn and anger of Mormon women, while Allen's antipolygamy activism continued for decades.[177] The committee also included Mormons Ruth May Fox, a prominent leader in the Young Ladies Mutual Improvement Association, and Emily Richards.[178] The decline of polygamy conflict allowed some Mormon and gentile women to put aside their differences. Institutionalized, government-supported and -protected prostitution so egregiously violated the tenets of true and Mormon womanhood that it united erstwhile enemies and allowed respectable, middle-class Mormons and non-Mormons to feel comfortable offering rescue to fallen women.

The political campaign of 1911 also brought people together. John Bransford faced a storm of criticism, including accusations that he benefited financially from the Stockade. The *Herald-Republican* disclosed that the mayor owned the Plumas rooming house on 200 South Street, across from the Stockade's entrance, and had refurbished it just before the district's opening to house Stockade inmates and their "macquereaux."[179] The mayor also owned a single share of stock in a company that sold a rooming house to Dora Topham, who used it to house crib workers.[180] Bransford's opponents dismissed the closure of the Stockade as the same political ruse that had fooled voters twice previously. If the Americans won, they warned, the district would open again. The continued presence of a few prostitutes within the Stockade's walls seemed to support this prediction.[181]

The timing of the Topham case could not have been worse for the city's Americans, facing reelection in November. Some of their earliest supporters were now deserting. Rev. William M. Paden cited prostitution as grounds to oust Bransford.[182] The American Club resolved to work for the Stockade's abolition, while prominent party members including H. J. Dininny mulled challenges to Bransford.[183] The reform women entered the contest with a list of questions soliciting candidates' positions on the suppression of prostitution in general and a restricted district in particular.[184] Bransford grudgingly replied that he would bow to the reformers' will.[185]

The reform women endorsed E. O. Leatherwood for mayor.[186] While the *Tribune* dismissed him as the "Federal bunch" candidate,[187] Senator Reed Smoot was cautious. Smoot was confident that the Americans were doomed, but he cautioned E. H. Callister to ease the attacks on Bransford in the *Herald-Republican* "as I believed it was creating sympathy for him." The emergence of a "Citizen's Non-Partisan" ticket, headed by Samuel R. Park, a gentile businessman, further complicated the situation. Smoot advised Callister to wait until the primaries, and then support whichever ticket emerged opposite the Americans. Perhaps because of antipathy toward Elizabeth Cohen, the senator advised two women not to support any ticket "proposed by the Woman's Purity League."[188]

Samuel Park defeated Leatherwood and faced Bransford in the general election. Republicans supported Park and again accused the Americans of colonizing voters and coercing prostitutes' votes.[189] If true, those efforts were in vain. According to the *Herald-Republican,* on 7 November 1911 the city was

"Redeemed From Bransford Rule by a Great Avalanche of Ballots." The paper did not mention the Stockade in its congratulatory editorial, perhaps an indication that the issue had been a tactical expedient. The *Deseret Evening News* exulted "NOW FOR PEACE, PROGRESS AND REFORM," since the victory had eliminated "religious strife" from local politics. Predictably, the *Tribune* saw "THE CHURCH VICTORIOUS." The American Party would never again be a major force in Utah politics.[190]

Meanwhile, Dora Topham's appeal proceeded. Her attorneys complained of the confluence of law, politics, and reform that they claimed had led to her conviction. Several of the major players in the trial had close political ties. Judge Frederick Loofbourow was the ex-chairman of the Republican city committee and part of the convention that nominated District Attorney Leatherwood for mayor. Senator Reed Smoot met with Loofbourow, Leatherwood, Governor Spry, *Herald-Republican* manager Callister, and Sheriff Sharp shortly before the trial began to, in Smoot's words, plan "the best way to handle the coming city election as far as the Republican Party is concerned." No evidence suggests they discussed the trial. The Women's Welfare League also figured in Topham's appeal. Another affidavit noted that Loofbourow had invited "fifteen or twenty" women, including Corinne Allen, to sit within the bar of the court in sight of the jury, prejudicing the case against the madam. Yet another affidavit complained of Leatherwood's statement to the league that the reformers' presence contributed to Topham's conviction. The Supreme Court apparently did not credit these implications of conflict of interest or undue influence.[191]

The madam's optimism proved well-founded, however. On 4 May 1912, the Utah Supreme Court reversed her conviction. The court ruled that the information (based on the statute's precise wording) did not spell out the alleged crime in sufficient detail that Topham could prepare an adequate defense. The court further held that Topham's promise to get Dogney new clothes was based solely on her mother's approval and did not constitute an inducement.[192]

While some people feared that Topham's victory could mean the reopening of the Stockade, the city and county authorities declared they would not tolerate it.[193] The *Tribune* took the overturned verdict philosophically. "Salt Lake City has suffered nothing, . . . either morally or in any other way, by the ruling of the Supreme Court; but the law has been vindicated, and definite public effort in morality and penalty has been crowned. The chief offender has not been punished, true, but she is not in the least likely to repeat her offensive efforts within the jurisdiction of the Third District Court. The proposition or scheme for a red-light district in Salt Lake is absolutely dead."[194] The *Herald-*

Republican expressed remarkable respect for Topham's managerial skills and suggested that just as a prostitute could reform through respectable work, Topham could also reform—indeed, had a duty to reform—through legitimate commercial enterprise. "Mrs. Topham is an extremely clever woman. . . . She is known to have executive ability of a high order, to be gifted with business acumen above that of many men and of most women. Should she turn her talents to legitimate use she could accomplish much constructive work that would be of benefit to society, and it behooves her to remember that, because of her ability, much is required of her."[195] Dora Topham returned to her properties in Ogden, although she quietly continued to lease a brothel in the southwest corner of the Stockade until early 1913.[196] By 1920, she was living in California under another name.[197] The Stockade did not reopen, although a few women were occasionally arrested in buildings there.[198]

Dora Topham had played an unwitting role in reconciling old antagonisms in Salt Lake City and in creating a new reform alliance. The campaign against the Stockade resembled other contemporary fights against urban problems such as political machines and corrupt franchises. Regulated prostitution, however, could be put to rhetorical uses that other issues could not. A reformer could not, for example, easily argue that a suspect streetcar franchise was inherently immoral, or that it violated the sanctity of the Christian home. By particularly targeting prostitution, however, a progressive LDS reformer like B. F. Grant could draw on a traditional and widely respected (if often impotent) body of argument about prostitution's violation of the Victorian and Mormon moral codes. By this process he gained powerful allies among the gentile clergy and other opponents of prostitution like Elizabeth Cohen and Lulu Shepard. The alliance between progressives and moralists could then mobilize public opinion through the popular press, and more importantly effective legal action through the courts, to abolish the Stockade.

By firmly associating John Bransford's administration with regulated prostitution (and conveniently ignoring the long tradition of that practice before the Americans took office), opponents united moralists with progressive supporters of commission government and prohibition across religious, political, and gender lines in a moral reform effort that for some also served political ends. The victory must have been particularly sweet for Mormons. Reversing the gentiles' use of polygamy as a political tool against them in the 1880s, Mormons had used accusations of immorality to help defeat anti-Mormonism. In effect, B. F. Grant and his betterment committee succeeded where B. Y. Hampton's clumsy effort had failed.

However expedient it might have been for some, the antiprostitution alliance represented both a real sense of reconciliation between Mormons and gentiles and a mutual moral vindication. The "Second Manifesto," the LDS Church's vigorous purge of recalcitrant polygamists, and the inevitable passing of the older generation convinced most people that polygamy would soon be part of the Mormon past.[199] Some of polygamy's staunchest opponents conceded that the mainstream LDS Church was leaving the practice behind.[200] The American Party (with help from its opponents) had discredited anti-Mormonism based on claims of gentile moral superiority. Since some gentiles had joined in the fight against prostitution, they no longer appeared hypocritical and unfair in the eyes of Mormons. After 1911, "prostitution" lost its rhetorical value as a weapon in a war over comparative morality that appeared over.

As plural marriage gradually (and never wholly) faded as an issue of contention, many conservative gentiles and Mormons realized they shared much of the same moral code, and many of the same concerns about the changing morality of young people. In effect, they worried about the preservation of what historian Mark Connelly calls "the code of civilized morality": an insistence on premarital chastity, an emphasis on companionate marriage, an abhorrence for extramarital sexuality (especially prostitution), and respect for the pure, selfless wife and mother within the Christian home.[201] Historian Joan Iversen notes that the first federal morals legislation was the Morrill Anti-Bigamy Act of 1862, deliberately aimed at Mormon polygamy.[202] The Saints stoutly resisted federal pressure to change their marital system until the government brought effective coercive measures to bear by 1890. After the turn of the century, however, many Mormons welcomed and helped lead state-sponsored efforts to eradicate prostitution, ban alcohol, and curb immoral recreation.

The conviction of Dora B. Topham and the defeat of the Americans marked the beginning of the end of regulated prostitution in Salt Lake City. While some future governments practiced regulation, no administration dared to openly plan and help build a district and then use its police force to protect its operations. The turn away from regulation made it harder for those women who sold sex. Although reporters and reformers often deplored the supposed plight of the exploited women in the Stockade and those thrown onto the streets by its closure, they offered few realistic alternatives to prostitution. When women rejected those alternatives and continued to sell sex in unregulated venues, most respectable citizens viewed them as a dangerous plague to be eliminated. Inspired by the reform climate sweeping the nation, self-styled progressives turned to campaigns to stamp out all forms of urban immorality. Ironically, reformers would also discover that without a regulated district and its easily identifiable inhabitants, the control of prostitution would become even more complex and difficult.

Notes

1. On Roberts, see the previous chapter and Merrill, *Reed Smoot,* pp. 13–16.

2. On Kearns, see Larsen, "Life of Thomas Kearns," pp. 57, 72. See also Malmquist, *First 100 Years,* pp. 178–205; Merrill, *Reed Smoot,* pp. 17–18.

3. Holsinger, "For God and the American Home"; Merrill, *Reed Smoot,* pp. 18–22.

4. For the ministers' protest, see *Salt Lake City Herald,* 24 Nov. 1902, in JH, 24 Nov. 1902. On Smoot and polygamy, see Merrill, *Reed Smoot,* pp. 37–39, and 56–59; and Brudnoy, "Of Sinners and Saints."

5. Larsen, "Life of Thomas Kearns," pp. 110–14; and Malmquist, *First 100 Years,* pp. 238–41.

6. U.S. Congress, Senate, *Proceedings Before the Committee on Privileges and Elections of the United States Senate in the Matter of the Protests Against the Right of Hon. Reed Smoot, A Senator from the State of Utah, to Hold His Seat,* 1:1; cited in Merrill, *Reed Smoot,* p. 30.

7. Iversen, *Antipolygamy Controversy,* pp. 186–87; *Salt Lake City Deseret Evening News,* 29 July 1899, in JH, 29 July 1899; and Roberts, *Comprehensive History: Century I,* 6:390. For Paden, see Iversen, *Antipolygamy Controversy,* pp. 188–89.

8. *Salt Lake City Daily Tribune,* 13 Jan. 1891.

9. *Tribune,* 26 Mar. 1897.

10. *Tribune,* 24 Jan. 1896, 8 Feb. 1898, 18 Jan. 1899, 8 Feb. 1900.

11. *Herald,* 20, 30 Dec. 1902. See also chap. 3.

12. Merrill, *Reed Smoot,* pp. 47–50; Callister, "Political Career of Edward Henry Callister," p. 55; and Iversen, *Antipolygamy Controversy,* p. 216. On the "Second Manifesto," see Alexander, *Mormonism in Transition,* pp. 64–65; Quinn, *Mormon Hierarchy: Extensions of Power,* pp. 182, 193–94; and Quinn, "LDS Church Authority and New Plural Marriages."

13. For the Utah Mothers' Assembly/Congress, see "Minutes of Utah State Mothers' Congress," 1898–1902, USHS. For membership, see pp. 4–19; for constitution, pp. 22–23.

14. Iversen, *Antipolygamy Controversy,* pp. 216–17.

15. *Tribune,* 15 Sept. 1904. On the creation of the party, see R. Snow, "American Party in Utah," pp. 60–78.

16. Larsen, "Life of Thomas Kearns," pp. 123–25; Malmquist, *First 100 Years,* pp. 236–38; K. Godfrey, "Frank J. Cannon"; *Tribune,* 15 Mar. 1905; and chap. 2 of this study. See also F. Cannon and O'Higgins, *Under the Prophet in Utah.*

17. *Tribune,* 29 Sept. 1904; and R. Snow, "American Party in Utah," p. 87.

18. *Tribune,* 10 Oct. 1904.

19. *Deseret Evening News,* 15, 17 Sept. 1904. For accusations against Cannon, see *Salt Lake City Herald-Republican,* 7, 21 Apr. 1911.

20. *Tribune,* 18 Oct., 7, 8 Nov. 1905.

21. *Herald,* 3, 10 Jan. 1906, 1, 6 Aug. 1907; and R. Snow, "American Party in Utah," pp. 154–57.

22. Alexander and Allen, *Mormons and Gentiles,* p. 142; Larsen, "Life of Thomas Kearns," pp. 23, 133–34; *Herald,* 14 Aug., 6 Nov. 1907.

23. Iversen, *Antipolygamy Controversy,* pp. 247–48.

24. *Tribune,* 18 Oct. 1906, in JH, 16 Oct. 1906; *Deseret Evening News,* 27 May 1908, in JH, 27 May 1908; and *Tribune,* 2 June 1906, in JH, 2 June 1906. For the Mormon response, see *Deseret Evening News,* 15 June 1908.

25. *Deseret Evening News,* 22 June 1905, in JH, 22 June 1905.

26. Merrill, *Reed Smoot,* pp. 96–99; Iversen, "Masculine Backlash, 1903–1912," chap. in *Antipolygamy Controversy.*

27. On the "Federal bunch," see Merrill, *Reed Smoot,* pp. 177–86; Callister, "Political Career of Edward Henry Callister," pp. 45–49; and Thompson, "Utah's Struggle for Prohibition," p. 6. For the founding of the *Salt Lake City Inter-Mountain Republican,* see Callister, p. 70. On the merging of the *Herald* and the *Inter-Mountain Republican,* see Callister, p. 73, and *Herald-Republican,* 14 Aug. 1909.

28. *Annual Message of the Mayor with the Annual Reports of the Officers of Salt Lake City, Utah, for the year 1907,* p. 375.

29. *Deseret Evening News,* 21 Aug. 1908, in JH, 21 Aug. 1908.

30. See *Herald,* 5, 6 Sept. 1907. Chief Roderick McKenzie expressed almost identical sentiments; see *Herald,* 7 Sept. 1907.

31. *Deseret Evening News,* 21 Jan. 1908.

32. *Inter-Mountain Republican,* 21, 23 Jan. 1908.

33. LeRoy Armstrong to the editor, apparently of the *Chicago Interior,* 8 Feb. 1908, Mormonism file, Westminster College Archives. See also Merrill, *Reed Smoot,* pp. 91, 179.

34. *Tribune,* 22 Jan. 1908.

35. The first use of "stockade" which I could locate was *Inter-Mountain Republican,* 23 Jan. 1908. See also McCormick, "Red Lights in Zion."

36. *Herald,* 21 Feb. 1908; *Tribune,* 21 Feb. 1908.

37. *Tribune,* 22 Feb. 1908.

38. *Herald,* 3 Mar. 1908.

39. *Herald,* 30 May 1908.

40. *Herald,* 8 Dec. 1908.

41. *Herald,* 10 Dec. 1908. A similar quote appears almost verbatim in McCormick, "Red Lights in Zion," p. 178. McCormick, however, identifies the speaker as Councilman Martin Mulvey, speaking of "Italians and Greeks"; he cites the *Herald,* 18 Dec. 1908, p. 2. The proposed district was in the heart of "Greektown"; see Papanikolas, "Exiled Greeks."

42. *Herald,* 7 June 1908.

43. *Herald,* 12 June 1908; *Inter-Mountain Republican,* 12 June 1908; and Polk, *Salt Lake City Directory* (1907).

44. *Herald,* 12 June 1908.

45. *Tribune,* 27 June 1908; and *Herald,* 27, 29 June 1908. The first mention of Topham found was Ogden Police Court, "Justice's Docket, 1889," 14 Aug. 1889, p. 387. According to the 1900 census, Topham was born in Illinois in 1866. See U.S. Bureau of the Census, Twelfth Census (1900), Weber County, Enumeration District No. 187, sheet 8, line 1. See also U.S. Bureau of the Census, Thirteenth Census (1910), Weber County, Enumeration District No. 226, sheet 8, line 69; and Polk, *Ogden City Directory* (1903–16); Barnes, "Ogden's Notorious 'Two-Bit

Street,'"; Twenty-fifth Street, vertical file, Archives and Special Collections, Stewart Library, Weber State University, Ogden, Utah. Topham may have worked in Denver: "Belle London" reportedly operated a house in Denver called the "Fashion" at some point in the 1880s or 1890s; Topham managed a house in Ogden called the "Fashion." See Parkhill, *Wildest of the West*, p. 15. See also Held, *Most*, p. 100.

46. Articles of Incorporation of the Citizens Investment Company, file no. 6976, Corporation Files, Salt Lake County Clerk; Plaintiff's Exhibit C, State of Utah v. Citizens Investment Company, case no. 2135 (3d dist. criminal case files, 1909). For the trust deed, see SLCR, "Book of Mortgages" 6J, trust deed, pp. 108–12, 25 June 1908. The bonds bore the date 20 June 1908, came due on 1 July 1918, and paid 10 percent annually.

47. See "Fire Insurance Map of Salt Lake City, 1911"; *Herald*, 24 July, 13, 20 Aug. 1908; and U.S. Bureau of the Census, Thirteenth Census (1910), Salt Lake County, Enumeration District No. 120, sheets 13B, 15A, 15B, supplemental.

48. *Herald*, 11 July 1908.

49. *Herald*, 30 May, 27, 29 June 1908; and *Tribune*, 27 June 1908.

50. *Herald*, 30 May, 27 June, 3 July 1908. For Mrs. Thomas D. Pitt, see *Herald*, 15 Mar. 1908; and *Herald-Republican*, 16 Oct. 1909.

51. *Herald*, 6 Sept. 1908.

52. For the Democratic Club petition, see petition number 1031, "Salt Lake City Council Minutes," p. 642, 14 Sept. 1908. For the Westminster protest, see *Herald*, 14 Sept. 1908.

53. *Herald*, 9 Sept. 1908.

54. For the letter to Cutler, see *Herald*, 13 Sept. 1908. For his response, see John C. Cutler to Trustees of "American" Club of Utah, 12 Sept. 1908, in *Herald*, 14 Sept. 1908.

55. *Deseret Evening News*, 23 Sept. 1908, in JH, 23 Sept. 1908; *Herald*, 24, 25, 26, 29 Sept., 8 Oct. 1908; and *Deseret Evening News*, 25 Sept. 1908.

56. *Herald*, 9 Oct. 1908.

57. For the American county and state platforms, see *Herald*, 29 Sept. 1908.

58. *Deseret Evening News*, 31 Oct. 1908, cited in R. Snow, "American Party in Utah," p. 187.

59. *Deseret Evening News*, 31 Oct. 1908; *Herald*, 4 Nov. 1908; and R. Snow, "American Party in Utah," p. 190.

60. *Herald*, 8, 9, 15 Dec. 1908; *Inter-Mountain Republican*, 8 Dec. 1908; *Deseret Evening News*, 8 Dec. 1908; and *Tribune*, 9 Dec. 1908.

61. See *Deseret Evening News*, 14 Dec. 1908. For Paden, see *Herald*, 14 Dec. 1908.

62. Exhibit "A," John Lloyd et al. v. Dora P. [*sic*] Topham et al., case no. 10741 (3d district civil case files, 1909). See also *Herald*, 15 Nov. 1908; *Deseret Evening News*, 22 Dec. 1908; *Herald*, 23 Dec. 1908; *Inter-Mountain Republican*, 29, 31 Dec. 1908; *Herald*, 13, 14, 15 Jan. 1909; *Inter-Mountain Republican*, 13, 14 Jan. 1909; *Deseret Evening News*, 13 Jan. 1909, in JH, 13 Jan. 1909.

63. The banker was Frank McGurrin. See *Deseret Evening News*, 9 Dec. 1908; Polk, *Salt Lake City Directory* (1908).

64. *Herald*, 15 Dec. 1908.

65. *Herald*, 9 Dec. 1908.

66. *Herald*, 13 Dec. 1908; Polk, *Salt Lake City Directory* (1908).

67. *Tribune*, 9 Dec. 1908. The paper undoubtedly referred to the Clayton Investment

Company, the successor to the Brigham Young Trust Company; see Brigham Young Trust Company Records, file no. 853, Corporation Files, Salt Lake County Clerk.

68. *Salt Lake City Telegram,* 12 Dec. 1908, in JH, 12 Dec. 1908.

69. *Deseret Evening News,* 16 Dec. 1908, in JH, 16 Dec. 1908.

70. *Inter-Mountain Republican,* 17 Dec. 1908, in JH, 17 Dec. 1908.

71. *Inter-Mountain Republican,* 22 Dec. 1908.

72. *Herald,* 9 Dec. 1908.

73. R. Snow, "American Party in Utah," p. 193.

74. *Deseret Evening News,* 18 Dec. 1908; *Tribune,* 18 Dec. 1908; *Herald,* 18 Dec. 1908; and *Inter-Mountain Republican,* 19 Dec. 1908.

75. *Inter-Mountain Republican,* 19 Dec. 1908.

76. See subpoenas in Lloyd et al. v. Topham et al., and *Inter-Mountain Republican,* 14 Jan. 1909. For McDonald in Ogden, see Ogden Police, "Arrest Records, 1902–1904," 17 May 1902, p. 11.

77. For Starr, McDonald, and Daniels in the Stockade, see *Herald,* 28 June 1909. Starr returned to 222 south State Street; see *Herald-Republican,* 25 June 1910. For Bartlett, see State v. Dora Topham, case no. 2710 (3d dist. criminal case files, 1911).

78. Quote from *Deseret Evening News,* 18 Dec. 1908. See also *Inter-Mountain Republican,* 20 Dec. 1908.

79. *Deseret Evening News,* 7 May 1912.

80. See Lloyd et al. v. Topham et al.; *Inter-Mountain Republican,* 13 Jan. 1909; *Deseret Evening News,* 13 Jan. 1909.

81. Helen Smith v. H. J. Robinson et al., case no. 11444 (3d dist. civil case files, 1909); and *Herald,* 6, 9 June 1909.

82. *Deseret Evening News,* 9 Mar. 1911; 27 May 1910. For Prescott at 243 south Main, see Rose Bartlett v. Edna Prescott, case no. 10905 (3d dist. civil case files, 1909); for 7 Victoria, see *Deseret Evening News,* 13 Jan. 1909 and Helen Smith v. H. J. Robinson et al.; for 222 State, see Salt Lake City v. Edna Prescott, case no. 2979 (3d dist. criminal case files, 1912).

83. U.S. Bureau of the Census, Thirteenth Census (1910), Salt Lake County, Enumeration District No. 145, sheet 2b, line 61; *Herald-Republican,* 25 May, 10 June 1911.

84. *Inter-Mountain Republican,* 18 Apr. 1909.

85. *Herald,* 1 July 1909; *Inter-Mountain Republican,* 16 June 1909; *Herald-Republican,* 5 Aug. 1911; and U.S. Bureau of the Census, Thirteenth Census (1910), Salt Lake County, Enumeration District No. 120, sheets 13B, 15A, 15B, supplemental.

86. Only five women have been identified before and in the Stockade: Irene McDonald, a brothel keeper; see Salt Lake City Court Criminal Division, "Minute Book, 1908," 22 Apr. 1908, p. 155; 24 Aug. 1908, p. 364; 1 Oct. 1908, p. 428; and *Herald,* 28 June 1909. Florence or Flossie Devine; Salt Lake City Court Criminal Division, "Minute Book, 1908," 3 Aug. 1908, p. 331; *Herald,* 27 May 1909. Bessie Richmond, U.S. Bureau of the Census, Thirteenth Census (1910), Salt Lake County, Enumeration District No. 120, sheet 15A, line 35; Salt Lake City Court Criminal Division, "Minute Book, 1908," 2 July 1908, p. 280. Lillie Wilson, U.S. Bureau of the Census, Thirteenth Census (1910), Salt Lake County, Enumeration District No. 120, supplemental, line 7; Salt Lake City Court Criminal Division, "Minute Book, 1908," 26 Feb. 1908, p. 76. Ray Woods, see below.

87. For arrests of Woods, see Salt Lake City Court Criminal Division, "Minute Book,

1905," 23 Jan. 1905, p. 37; 21 Aug. 1905, p. 479; 20 Dec. 1905, p. 746; Salt Lake City Court Criminal Division, "Minute Book, 1908," 24 Apr. 1908, p. 157; 16 June 1908, p. 252; 17 July 1908, p. 302. For Woods on Victoria Alley, see State of Utah v. Ray Woods, case no. 1843 (3d dist. criminal case files, 1907). See also *Deseret Evening News,* 12, 14 July 1910; and *Herald-Republican,* 15 Sept. 1910.

88. *Deseret Evening News,* 15 June 1909, in JH, 15 June 1909; *Inter-Mountain Republican,* 16 June 1909; *Herald,* 16 June 1909; and *Herald-Republican,* 30 Sept. 1911.

89. For the black inmates and keeper, see *Herald-Republican,* 4 Sept. 1910; for houses with black and white women, see U.S. Bureau of the Census, Thirteenth Census (1910), Salt Lake County, Enumeration District No. 120, sheets 13B, lines 53–55; 15A, lines 24–28; 15B, lines 69–71. For the cribs, see *Deseret Evening News,* 18 Dec. 1908; *Inter-Mountain Republican,* 16, 24 May 1909.

90. For the "Spanish" inmates, see *Herald,* 11 Apr. 1909, and U.S. Bureau of the Census, Thirteenth Census (1910), Salt Lake County, Enumeration District No. 120, sheet 15A. For Korean, Greek, and Japanese liquor servers, see *Herald-Republican,* 8 July 1910; and *Deseret Evening News,* 12 July 1910. For the Hungarian piano player, see *Deseret Evening News,* 13 Jan. 1909, in JH, 13 Jan. 1909. For Chinese opium sellers, see *Herald-Republican,* 16, 17, 18, 20 July 1911. For men in Stockade houses, see U.S. Bureau of the Census, Thirteenth Census (1910), Salt Lake County, Enumeration District No. 120, sheets 13B, lines 32, 38; 15A.

91. This description is taken from a number of sources; conditions probably changed over time. The "Fire Insurance Map of Salt Lake City, 1911," shows stores and storehouses outside of the district but does not specify their purposes. For Topham's office, see Polk, *Salt Lake City Directory* (1910). For the dance hall, see *Herald-Republican,* 5 May 1912. For saloons and restaurants, see *Inter-Mountain Republican,* 23 May 1909. For the "immense indicator," see *Inter-Mountain Republican,* 22 May 1909. For opium dens, see *Herald-Republican,* 16, 17, 18 July 1911. For the liquor and food storehouses and "indicators and bells," see *Herald-Republican,* 7 July 1910. For the jail, see *Deseret Evening News,* 18 Dec. 1908. For the "special policemen," see *Herald-Republican,* 8 July 1910; 16 May 1911. For the "secret openings," see Held, *Most,* pp. 100–101.

92. *Herald,* 1 July 1909.

93. State v. Topham, case no. 2710.

94. *Deseret Evening News,* 12 July 1910.

95. *Herald-Republican,* 5, 17 Aug. 1911.

96. *Inter-Mountain Republican,* 22 May 1909; *Deseret Evening News,* 24 May 1910; *Herald-Republican,* 30 Aug. 1910, 12, 13 Aug. 1911; and U.S. Bureau of the Census, Thirteenth Census (1910), Salt Lake County, Enumeration District No. 120, sheets 13B, 15A, supplemental.

97. *Herald-Republican,* 5 Aug. 1911.

98. *Herald-Republican,* 24 May 1910.

99. *Herald-Republican,* 13 Aug. 1911.

100. For 1908 figures, see *Annual Message of the Mayor with the Annual Reports of the Officers of Salt Lake City, Utah, for the year 1908,* p. 485. In 1909, two persons were convicted for keeping; eight for prostitution, and ten for resorting; see *Annual Reports, 1909,* p. 23. In 1910, three persons were arrested for keeping; three for prostitution; and three

for resorting; see *Annual Reports, 1910*, pp. 15–16. In 1911, twelve were arrested for keeping (ten for "allowing house of ill fame on premises"); eight for prostitution; and two for resorting; see *Annual Reports, 1911*, pp. 16–17, 334. In 1912, after the closure of the Stockade, seventy-nine prosecutions were made for keeping; eighteen for prostitution; and 184 for resorting. Chief B. F. Grant usually charged prostitutes with vagrancy; 1,680 vagrants were prosecuted. See *Annual Reports, 1912*, p. 89.

101. *Herald-Republican*, 27, 28 Aug. 1911.

102. *Herald*, 22 Dec. 1908; *Deseret Evening News*, 23 Dec. 1908, in JH, 23 Dec. 1908.

103. *Herald*, 11 Apr. 1909; *Tribune*, 17 Apr. 1909, in JH, 17 Apr. 1909; and *Inter-Mountain Republican*, 16 May 1909. Quotes from *Inter-Mountain Republican*, 18 May 1909.

104. "An Act to Amend Section 4251, Compiled Laws of Utah, 1907, Relating to Owning or Renting Buildings, Keeping, Residing in, or Resorting to Houses of Ill-fame," in *Laws of the State of Utah, Passed at the Eighth Regular Session of the Legislature*. For debate on this bill, see *Herald*, 13 Mar. 1909; and *Inter-Mountain Republican*, 13 Mar. 1909.

105. State of Utah v. Citizens Investment Company, cases no. 250, 251, 2135, and 2152 (3d dist. criminal case files, 1909); State of Utah v. Dora B. Topham, cases no. 2146 and 2147 (3d dist. criminal case files, 1909); *Inter-Mountain Republican*, 23, 29 May 1909; *Herald*, 23 May, 5, 13 June 1909; and *Deseret Evening News*, 1 June 1909, in JH, 1 June 1909.

106. See Polk, *Salt Lake City Directory* (1908); *Deseret Evening News*, 28 June 1902, in JH, 28 June 1902; and *Inter-Mountain Republican*, 19, 20 May 1909. On the Improvement/Betterment League/Union, see Alexander and Allen, *Mormons and Gentiles*, pp. 142–50, 155, 164–72; *Herald*, 8 Apr. 1906. For Stephens, see *Herald*, 17 Mar. 1908. For Grant and Woodruff, see Appendix G, "High Council of Salt Lake Stake, 1847–1972"; and Appendix H, "List of Wards of Salt Lake Stake with their Bishops, 1847–1972," in Hilton, *Story of Salt Lake Stake*.

107. *Inter-Mountain Republican*, 18 May 1909.

108. *Inter-Mountain Republican*, 21, 22, 25 May 1909.

109. "Order to Show Cause," 27 May 1909, in Lloyd et al. v. Topham et al.

110. *Deseret Evening News*, 15 June 1909, in JH, 15 June 1909; *Inter-Mountain Republican*, 16 June 1909; and *Herald*, 16 June 1909.

111. *Herald*, 22 June 1909.

112. *Tribune*, 25 June 1909, in JH, 25 June 1909.

113. *Herald*, 19, 20 June 1909.

114. *Herald*, 28 June 1909.

115. *Herald*, 30 June 1909; and *Inter-Mountain Republican*, 30 June 1909, in JH. See also *Tribune*, 30 June 1909, in JH.

116. *Herald*, 1 July 1909.

117. *Herald*, 7 July 1909.

118. *Herald-Republican*, 13 Oct. 1909; see also 16 Oct.

119. *Herald-Republican*, 19 Oct. 1909.

120. *Herald-Republican*, 16 Oct. 1909.

121. *Herald-Republican*, 20 Oct., 1 Nov. 1909.

122. For the p. 1 cartoons, see *Herald-Republican*, 17, 19, 20, 21, 22, 23, 27 Oct. 1909. "Midnight Belle" appears on 20 Oct. For Bransford's statements, see *Herald-Republican*, 17, 20, 25, 26 Oct. 1909.

123. R. Snow, "American Party in Utah," p. 201. For election results, see R. Snow, pp. 209–11; and *Herald-Republican,* 3 Nov. 1909.

124. *Herald-Republican,* 24 Sept. 1910.

125. *Deseret Evening News,* 2 Mar. 1910, in JH, 2 Mar. 1910; J. W. Ure et al., petition no. 228, "Salt Lake City Council Minutes," p. 143, 7 Mar. 1910; and *Herald-Republican,* 12, 13, 18 Mar. 1910.

126. *Deseret Evening News,* 19 Mar. 1910, in JH, 19 Mar. 1910.

127. Harold Ross to John Held, Jr., undated, Held Papers, Archives of American Art, in Carmack, "Before the Flapper," p. 317. See also Rosen, *Lost Sisterhood,* p. 102.

128. *Herald-Republican,* 22 Mar. 1910.

129. *Herald-Republican,* 16, 18, 22 June 1910; *Deseret Evening News,* 16 June 1910; and *Deseret Evening News,* 22 June 1910, in JH, 22 June 1910.

130. *Herald-Republican,* 24, 25 June 1910.

131. *Herald-Republican,* 25, 26, 27 June 1910; quote from 25 June. See also *Deseret Evening News,* 27 June 1910, in JH, 27 June 1910.

132. *Deseret Evening News,* 6, 7, 8 July 1910; and *Herald-Republican,* 7, 8, 9 July 1910. Barlow quote is from 8 July.

133. *Herald,* 30 June 1909; *Deseret Evening News,* 12, 13 July 1910; *Herald-Republican,* 13 July 1910; 10 Feb. 1912. On the mobility of present-day prostitutes, see James, "Mobility as an Adaptive Strategy."

134. *Herald-Republican,* 14 July 1910. For Dininny's affidavit, see *Herald-Republican,* 17 July 1910. For the warnings, see *Deseret Evening News,* 14 July 1910; quote from *Herald-Republican,* 15 July 1910.

135. *Herald-Republican,* 23 July 1910. See also *Herald-Republican,* 8 Sept. 1910; *Deseret Evening News,* 22 July 1910.

136. State v. B. Bartlett, case no. 2482 (3d dist. criminal case files, 1911); *Deseret Evening News,* 1 Aug. 1910; and *Herald-Republican,* 1 Aug. 1910.

137. *Herald-Republican,* 9, 19, 21 Aug. 1910; *Deseret Evening News,* 3 Sept. 1910.

138. *Deseret Evening News,* 21 Oct. 1910.

139. *Deseret Evening News,* 18 Oct. 1910. See also *Herald-Republican,* 19, 20 Oct. 1910.

140. *Herald-Republican,* 5 Nov. 1910.

141. *Tribune,* 6 Nov. 1910, in JH, 6 Nov. 1910. See also *Deseret Evening News,* 4 Nov. 1910, in JH, 4 Nov. 1910.

142. R. Snow, "American Party in Utah," pp. 126–27; and *Herald-Republican,* 9 Nov. 1910.

143. *Herald-Republican,* 18, 21 Nov. 1910.

144. R. Snow, "American Party in Utah," pp. 238–39; and *Herald-Republican,* 20 Jan., 2 Feb. 1911.

145. Salt Lake City v. Dora B. Topham et al., case no. 2640 (3d dist. criminal case files, 1911); *Herald-Republican,* 9, 18 Feb.; 7, 8, 10, 12 Mar. 1911; and *Deseret Evening News,* 9, 10 Mar. 1911. Quote from *Herald-Republican,* 10 Mar. 1911.

146. *Herald-Republican,* 24 Mar. 1911. For the resolutions, see "Salt Lake City Council Minutes," p. 205, 3 Apr. 1911; *Herald-Republican,* 14, 25, 31 Mar., 4 Apr. 1911.

147. *Herald-Republican,* 27 May 1911. See also chap. 2.

148. State v. B. Bartlett; *Herald-Republican,* 25, 26, 27 May, 10 June 1911. Quote from 10 June.

149. *Herald,* 27 Sept. 1906; 27 Feb. 1907; *Herald-Republican,* 21 Mar. 1911. See also Humphrey, "Commission Government in Salt Lake City"; Reed Smoot to Ed Callister, 26 Dec. 1910; quoted in Callister, "Political Career of Edward Henry Callister," pp. 127–28. On commission government elsewhere, see E. Anderson, "Prostitution and Social Justice"; and Hayes, "Politics of Reform in Municipal Government."

150. "Pandering," in Utah, *Compiled Laws* (1911), p. 178. See also *Senate Journal, Ninth Session of the Legislature of the State of Utah, 1911,* pp. 279, 410, 510.

151. Utah, *Compiled Laws* (1876), sec. 138.

152. On "presumption of chastity clauses," see Hobson, *Uneasy Virtue,* p. 68. For Nellie Davis, see People v. Nellie Davis, case no. 1190 (3d dist. criminal case files, 1894); People v. Nellie Davis, case no. 183 (3d dist. criminal case files, 1894); and SLCPD, "Criminal Record," 1892–1920, p. 280, 9 Sept. 1894. Several other persons were charged with pandering before 1911; see People v. Elizabeth Metz and Anna Baumgarten, case no. 1262 (3d dist. criminal case files, 1895); and *Tribune,* 28 Dec. 1894; 28 Feb., 3 Mar., 1 June, 8 Sept. 1895. For other cases, see *Tribune,* 2, 3, 12, 16 Oct. 1895; *Herald,* 14, 21 Feb. 1902.

153. State v. Topham, case no. 2710. The case file contains the original complaint, the information, affidavits, the defendant's demurrers and motions, subpoenas, instructions to the jury, notice of verdict, notice of appeal, and the Utah Supreme Court's remitter overturning the conviction and ordering dismissal. No testimony exists in the case file. Testimony has been re-created using newspapers, especially the *Herald-Republican,* 5 May 1912; and State v. Topham, 41 Utah 39 (1912).

154. *Herald-Republican,* 27 July 1911.

155. To avoid confusion between "Gray" and "Lofstrom," I will hereafter refer to the young woman as "Dogney."

156. *Herald-Republican,* 23, 26, 27 July 1911. Quote re Dogney's clothing is from 27 July; purported Topham quote is from 23 July.

157. *Herald-Republican,* 27 July 1911.

158. The 1906 Ogden directory lists "Helen Lofstrom" offering "furnished rooms" at 250 25th Street. Thomas Topham, Dora's husband, is listed at that address in 1903–4. From 1907 through 1912, Dora B. Topham is listed as the proprietor of the Palace Rooming House at 250 25th Street. See Polk, *Ogden City Directory* (1906–12).

159. State v. Topham, 41 Utah 60.

160. Ibid., pp. 55–60; and *Herald-Republican,* 26 July, 7 Aug. 1911.

161. State v. Topham, 41 Utah 55–60; and *Herald-Republican,* 5 May 1912. The stockade physician testified he overheard Dogney tell Topham she was nineteen; see *Herald-Republican,* 1 Aug. 1911. Dogney denied her sister was a prostitute; see *Herald-Republican,* 26 July 1911.

162. *Deseret Evening News,* 20 Sept. 1911; and *Herald-Republican,* 1 Aug., 19, 20 Sept. 1911, 5 May 1912. One Leona H. Lofstrom married Norman S. Mathews on 23 May 1910; see Salt Lake County Probate Court, Record of Marriage Certificates, license no. A010218.

163. *Herald-Republican,* 22 Sept. 1911. See also 23 Sept. 1911.

164. Ogden's regulation system, like Salt Lake City's, relied on monthly fines. "Belle London" was arrested monthly along with approximately two dozen women; "Chief Browning" is listed as the arresting officer. See Ogden Police, "Arrest Records, 1902–1904," 17 May 1902, p. 11, arrest no. 69; 17 June 1902, p. 31, no. 192; 18 Aug. 1902, p. 72, no. 434; 17

Sept. 1902, p. 93, case no. 551; 16 Oct. 1902, p. 114, case no. 565; 17 Nov. 1902, p. 114, case no. 683; 17 Dec. 1902, p. 145, no. 869; 17 Jan. 1903, p. 165, no. 1002. See also Ogden Police, "Record of Prisoners, 1904–1909," 15 Sept. 1905, p. 81; 17 Oct. 1905, p. 88; 17 Nov. 1905, p. 95.

165. *Herald-Republican*, 22 Sept. 1911.

166. State v. Topham, case no. 2710; *Deseret Evening News*, 23 Sept. 1911; and *Herald-Republican*, 23, 24 Sept. 1911. The Brown claim is from 24 Sept. See also *Tribune*, 24 Sept. 1911. The cases against Evans and Clifford were dismissed; see State of Utah v. Ethel Clifford, case no. 2711 (3d dist. criminal case files, 1911) and State of Utah v. Lillian Evans et al., case no. 2718 (3d dist. criminal case files, 1911).

167. *Herald-Republican*, 28 Sept. 1911.

168. State v. Topham, case no. 2710; and *Herald-Republican*, 21 Oct. 1911.

169. *Herald-Republican*, 8, 9 Sept. 1911.

170. State v. Topham, case no. 2710; and Knudsen, *History of Utah Federation of Women's Clubs*, in Utah Federation of Women's Clubs Records, JWM.

171. *Deseret Evening News*, 28 Sept. 1911; *Salt Lake City Goodwin's Weekly*, 30 Sept. 1911, in JH, 30 Sept. 1911. For Leatherwood's candidacy, see *Herald-Republican*, 13 Oct. 1911.

172. *Herald-Republican*, 29 Sept. 1911.

173. *Tribune*, 29 Sept. 1911.

174. *Herald-Republican*, 2 Oct. 1911.

175. *Herald-Republican*, 29 Sept. 1911.

176. *Tribune*, 2 Oct. 1911. See also *Herald-Republican*, 3 Oct. 1911.

177. Joan Iversen calls Corinne Allen "The Last Antipolygamist"; see *Antipolygamy Controversy*, pp. 246–53.

178. See Ruth May Fox Diary, 21 Oct. 1911, photocopy in Ruth May Fox Papers, JWM. For Richards, see Van Wagenen, "Sister-Wives and Suffragists," pp. 404–11, 416, 464, 471–72. For the Council of Women, see Polk, *Salt Lake City Directory* (1906).

179. *Herald-Republican*, 12, 13 Aug. 1911.

180. *Herald-Republican*, 19, 20 Aug. 1911.

181. *Tribune*, 29 Sept. 1911; and *Herald-Republican*, 29 Sept., 5, 18 Oct. 1911.

182. *Herald-Republican*, 25 Sept. 1911.

183. *Herald-Republican*, 14 Sept., 1 Oct. 1911.

184. *Herald-Republican*, 15, 16 Oct. 1911.

185. *Herald-Republican*, 22 Oct. 1911.

186. *Herald-Republican*, 23, 24 Oct. 1911.

187. *Tribune*, 13 Oct. 1911.

188. Reed Smoot Diary, book 9 (hereafter "Reed Smoot Diary"), typescript in Reed Smoot Papers, JWM. For Callister advice, see 1 Sept. 1911; for advice about endorsing a ticket, see 13 Oct. 1911; for advice to women, see 19 Oct. 1911.

189. *Herald-Republican*, 25 Oct., 5 Nov. 1911; and Reed Smoot Diary, 26 Oct. 1911.

190. *Herald-Republican*, 8 Nov. 1911; *Deseret Evening News*, 8 Nov. 1911; and *Tribune*, 8 Nov. 1911. On a brief revival of the American party in 1923, see Alexander, *Mormonism in Transition*, p. 56.

191. Quote from Reed Smoot Diary, 5 Sept. 1911. See also State v. Topham, 41 Utah 39; and State v. Topham, case no. 2710.

192. State v. Topham, 41 Utah 39; State v. Topham, case no. 2710; and *Herald-Republican,* 5 May 1912.

193. *Deseret Evening News,* 7 May 1912, in Samuel C. Park Scrapbooks, USHS.

194. *Tribune,* 8 May 1912.

195. *Herald-Republican,* 7 May 1912.

196. Polly A. Boyd v. Dora B. Topham, case no. 16565 (3d dist. civil case files, 1913).

197. See chap. 2.

198. *Herald-Republican,* 28 Feb. 1913, 3 Aug. 1915.

199. Alexander, *Mormonism in Transition,* pp. 64–66.

200. See, for example, Cullom, "Reed Smoot Decision."

201. Connelly, *Response to Prostitution in the Progressive Era,* p. 6.

202. Iversen, *Antipolygamy Controversy,* p. 99.

5. "The Future Occupants of the Houses of Ill-Repute"

REFORMERS CONSIDERED the closing of the Stockade a great victory, but it was only one battle in an ongoing war against urban immorality. The war exhibited some unique elements but also mirrored progressive national trends. Citizens across the nation believed that cities posed many moral dangers for young people. Reformers considered prostitution an anachronism of the corrupt, immoral, and inefficient nineteenth-century city and demanded it be abolished instead of regulated. Prostitution was only the most obvious and extreme form of illicit sexuality, however. New patterns of work, residence, and recreation also seemed to lure young people, especially women, into dangerous behaviors. Many citizens called on the state to use its power to control urban immorality, resulting in legislation that often proved intrusive and repressive.

In Salt Lake City, the progressive effort to make the city purer and more moral began before the Stockade and picked up momentum with the campaign against it. Gentiles and Mormons took action against alcohol, immoral entertainment, and venues where young people of both sexes met. The Samuel Park administration suppressed prostitution and prevented the reestablishment of a restricted district. Women moved to cheap hotels and rooming houses to sell sex, without the degree of predictability and protection that regulation had offered. City authorities and reformers attempted to crack down on those new venues, further entangling the control of prostitution with intervention into the sex lives of the young and the working class. The subsequent administration's veiled attempt to allow prostitutes to return to the old district aroused determined opposition. Many Utahns welcomed federal intervention in the control of prostitution, first in the form of "white slavery" prosecutions. With the entry of the United States into World War I, many residents enthusiastically supported the federally enforced zone of exclusion around army training posts such as Fort Douglas.

Progressive reform in Salt Lake played out in a time of great change. From 1880 to 1910 the population increased nearly fivefold to 92,777 inhabitants. The downtown physical environment was transformed as well. One- and two-story adobe and frame buildings gave way to brick, stone, and steel structures, some of them of ten stories or more. The few adobe buildings remaining by 1911 included the Victoria Alley cribs and 222 south State Street (both still housing prostitutes) and the now-vacant 243 south Main Street. Paved streets, sidewalks, electrical power, sewer systems, street cars, and automobiles gave the city a distinctly "modern" atmosphere.[1]

Urban residents nationwide boasted of their cities' rapid growth and modern amenities. Some perceived a dark side, however. One nationally known muckraker wrote that "the City—from scarlet Babylon to smoky Chicago—has always been the great marketplace of dissipation."[2] Utah's reformers agreed that city life broke down traditional, family-based society, since so many residents lived alone or with virtual strangers, surrounded by temptations. They especially feared for unprotected young women who left rural areas to come to the city to work and play.[3]

Rapid economic growth opened up retail, clerical, and secretarial jobs for women.[4] These jobs brought young women into public spaces, often without supervision and in the same neighborhoods where prostitutes worked. As more women took urban jobs, many persons expressed concerns about their moral well-being. Governor John C. Cutler offended several of the city's major employers when he suggested that manufacturing jobs "demoralized" girls.[5]

Even more disturbing were the new forms of public amusement. Saltair, a bathing resort on the Great Salt Lake, and other venues drew large crowds of men and women who danced, swam, and drank together. Saltair reportedly sold 9,180 quarts of beer in one night, sparking fights among men and "Commercial street ladies," including Helen Blazes.[6] A disgusted Lulu Shepard witnessed the scene and enlisted the Ministerial Association to plead with LDS authorities to bar alcohol from the church-owned resort.[7] Reformers also worried about dance halls, saloons, wine rooms, and cheap rooming houses where men and women congregated. The secretary of the local YMCA claimed that "saloons, dance halls, pleasure resorts, [and] houses of ill-fame" were "dragging men and women down to destruction."[8] Shepard warned of moral and racial threats to young (implicitly white) women: saloons where even "well dressed women" got drunk; moving pictures shown in total darkness where girls were "subjected to insults from libertines," including black men; dance halls that sold liquor; and cheap rooming houses. Shepard called for "legislation, vigilance and better mothers" to protect young women.[9] Mayor Samuel Park complained that girls were being allowed to "go to theatres unattended and go to expensive cafes—places where girls meet their undoing."[10]

New music and dance styles outraged some people, especially "ragging," where partners held each other close and executed vigorous steps to ragtime, music created by African Americans and often associated with prostitution.[11] Another source of worry was the cheap cafés or "chili parlors," described as "a new sort of saloon . . . for the special benefit of the gentler sex" and condemned by chief of police B. F. Grant as "the most dangerous and law defying we have in the city."[12] Gaurdello Brown agreed that "if we could eliminate the evil of the cafés, the most serious problem with which the juvenile court has to deal would be gone, for more cases of delinquency among young girls and young men and boys have their source in such places than in any other place in the city."[13] One reformer cautioned parents and police to pay attention to higher-class resorts as well. "No one who has designs on the innocence of a young woman will visit with her those places which disgust and repel. They would take her to those places of amusement operating under the guise of respectability where music and decoration and light and song disarm the mind and open gradually the door to importunity. Places of this sort, where the glamour and tinsel abound and fascinate, and the atmosphere hypnotically lulls to sleep the sterner centers of resistance, are far more dangerous than the resorts of dissolute orgies. They are the recruiting grounds, the preserves where the game is hunted."[14]

Such complaints indicated at least two related worries. First, reformers expressed conservative middle- and upper-class fears for the virtue of women in public. Unmarried or unchaperoned women in saloons, theaters, and other public spaces were considered in constant danger of "falling" to the corrupting influences of alcohol, immoral entertainment, and lascivious men. Those influences were so strong, and women so weak and passive, that sex was almost inevitable. In past decades, the only women in such places had supposedly already fallen. But in the early twentieth century, the sharp line between the places where respectable and fallen women could be found had blurred.

The problem went beyond the geography of respectability. Many women seemed to be dressing like prostitutes; in the logic of many reformers, that meant they were acting like them too. Mayor Samuel Park condemned parents who "let their girls over-dress, let them adopt dress styles that are not in good taste, let them use rouge and cosmetics."[15] Juvenile court officials complained of "peekaboo waists, slit skirts, low neck dresses and the 'shuffling' walk styles. . . . The prevailing styles in feminine attire . . . [are] not only indescent [*sic*] in themselves, but extremely dangerous to the welfare of the girls and the boys." LDS president Joseph F. Smith claimed modern dress was "derived from the lowest classes of life, and not such as to be adopted by women and girls possessing respect for morals and character."[16]

These developments were symptoms of a changing code of behavior, feared and fought by many conservative Americans but created and welcomed by a younger generation. Historian Mary Odem argues that young people, especially women, enjoyed the economic opportunities and relative social freedom of the modern city. After long days working behind shop counters or in offices, they demanded the diversions of dance halls, amusement parks, vaudeville shows, cafés, and cabarets. Since they often had no kitchen facilities in their rooms, they necessarily ate in inexpensive restaurants. When they could afford to, women indulged in fashionable clothing and cosmetics for nights out. Many young people, free of parental supervision, enjoyed greater social contact with the other sex in these public venues. As they always had, some working women indulged in occasional prostitution to supplement their legitimate earnings.[17] Others adopted a more open sexual ethic, sometimes sleeping with boyfriends or dates. One evidence of this change is a climb in the national rate of premarital pregnancy from approximately 10 percent in the mid-nineteenth century to 23 percent by 1910.[18]

To many observers, the new sexual ethic resembled prostitution. A Salt Lake City reformer advocated criminalizing all extramarital sex. "Prostitution in the dictionary sense is 'commercialized vice,' 'selling the body for hire.' Broadly speaking it does not mean that there is always a fee directly paid. It may be the price of a supper, or a ride in a taxi; or if one can believe his eyes, in Salt Lake's Louvre, Maxim's or Saltair, it may be the buying of a few drinks or a couple of railroad fares. . . . Illigitimate [*sic*] sexual intercourse should be considered as prostitution, no matter where practiced—nor for what returns."[19]

Reformers demanded and often got governmental action. In 1902 the city council banned separate wine rooms or screens "where women can be hidden."[20] A year later, the council began requiring keepers of rooming houses with ten or more rooms to keep registers in an effort to discourage prostitution and fornication.[21] In 1905 the chief of police closed the Utahna park dance hall, which he labeled "a rendezvous for disorderly women, a place where street walking and divorces are started."[22]

Related concerns for children and juvenile offenders began in the late nineteenth century. Citizens and elected officials concurred that minors convicted of crimes should not be exposed to hardened adult criminals in jails and penitentiaries but rather rehabilitated through schooling, industrial training, and moral instruction. Cornelia Paddock had included the need for an "industrial school for young girls" in an 1886 article outlining the planned Industrial Christian Home for polygamous wives.[23] The Utah legislature established a "Territorial Reform School" in Ogden in 1888. Any boy or girl under eighteen convicted in district court of a crime other than murder could be ordered to the reform school; a justice of the peace could hold a convict in his court to the district court for similar disposition. Students would be "instructed in correct principles of morality and in such branches of useful knowledge as are adapted to their age and capacity." Commitment could range from six months to the achievement of majority. One trustee explained that the school's atmosphere would be homelike, with "the boys comprising one family and the girls another." A "family father and mother" would have charge of each division.[24]

The State Industrial School, as it was officially named, became the institution of choice for the control of wayward minor females. A young girl in an Ogden brothel swore that she merely served drinks, but her mother testified that the girl was "incorrigible" and the judge committed her to the industrial school. One observer felt the precedent would allow the police court justice "to dispose of the girls who are from time to time brought to his attention by distracted parents."[25] Police courts sometimes treated the industrial school and rescue homes as alternatives for the disposition of girls accused of chastity offenses. For example, one woman wanted her thirteen-year-old daughter committed to the school for spending the night with Fort Douglas soldiers; the judge sent her instead to the rescue home.[26] Another mother charged her fifteen-year-old daughter with incorrigibility "in the hope that she would be committed to the Reform School, but a Christian woman now has her in charge and is attempting to teach her the error of her ways."[27] The industrial school was not always popular, nor successful in its reform mission. Minerva Reeves, committed to the school in 1901, allegedly attempted to burn down the facility a year later. By 1906, she was an inmate of 243 south Main Street.[28]

Concern for juveniles led to other institutions in the new century. The Utah Federation of Women's Clubs pushed for a juvenile court system and detention homes for juveniles awaiting trial.[29] The Utah state legislature adopted a juvenile court in 1905. Children could be judged delinquent for a wide variety of offenses, including violating any law, "growing up in idleness or crime," visiting or entering a house of ill repute, or "immoral conduct." A child's home circumstances could also result in an appearance in juvenile court, if the only surviving parent was perceived as "a person of notorious and scandalous conduct, or a reputed thief or prostitute" or the child was "found in the custody of vicious, corrupt, or immoral people, or surrounded by vicious, corrupt, or immoral influences."

Juvenile law permitted the court broad latitude in the disposition of a child. The court could allow the parents to continue custody or it could commit the child to another family home or to any state, county, or state-chartered institution "for care, correction, or advancement of children" or to the state industrial school. In fact, the court could dispose of the child in any way (except to commit him or her to jail or prison) "that may in the discretion and judgment of the court . . . be for the best interest of the child, to the end that its wayward tendencies shall be corrected and the child be saved to useful citizenship."[30] The juvenile court system gave the state another means of dealing with young women accused of prostitution or other sexual behavior.

These moral reform efforts had a strong element of social control to them, as reformers and the state attempted to convince or coerce young, mostly working-class women to conform to their notion of gender-appropriate behavior. Most of Salt Lake City's moral reformers could be broadly categorized as middle class: professionals, business people, ministers, schoolteachers, and their spouses. However, such reform efforts may have been as much about generational as class control. Working-class parents also used the new apparatus to deal with unruly daughters. Susannah Blundell, for example, lodged a charge of incorrigibility against her sixteen-year-old daughter Elizabeth in October 1898. Elizabeth promised that she would reform, and was allowed to go to the WHA Rescue Home. The girl ran away in December, however; her parents and a WHA officer testified "they could do nothing with her." Upon her parents' request, Elizabeth was sentenced to the reform school until she achieved majority.[31]

Christian Nyborg used the system to break up a romance between his daughter and a black man. He charged sixteen-year-old Ragna with incorrigibility because she refused to stop seeing her black lover. Ragna testified that a white man she refused to name had "accomplish[ed] her downfall" and wanted her to enter a house of ill fame. Ragna broke with him over this and met her new lover, who "proceeded to take up the white man's burden [a child?]." She was sentenced to the industrial school.[32]

Citizens sometimes protested too-vigorous attempts to impose moral control over young working-class women. In May 1900 police confronted three girls eating dinner in a restaurant and brought them to the station where they were examined to determine their virginity and possible infection with ve-

nereal disease. In the course of newspaper publicity and a city council investigation, their names and the examinations' results were published. All three
were reportedly found uninfected, while two were found "virtuous" and the
third "immoral."[33] The press unanimously declared that the examinations
violated the girls' civil rights. One paper noted that none of the girls had fathers or brothers to protect them from police abuse. The *Deseret Evening News*
argued that the incident threatened all women:

> If such proceedings are permitted in their case, what is to hinder similar assaults
> upon anybody's daughter or sister, who through thoughtless or unseemly con-
> duct may be suspected of unchastity? . . .
>
> [S]upposing they were known without a doubt to be bad and vicious in the
> lowest sense. Where do the police find their authority to take such a course? . . .
>
> It is an invasion of the rights and the liberties of individuals that is subver-
> sive of the freedom of the citizen, and it ought not to be passed by as a trivial
> thing. It is an outrage and a shame.[34]

The *Herald* editorialized that "the commonest street-walker of the city ought
to be immune from such indignities."[35]

The outcry bewildered the police, who claimed to be protecting the community's morality, health, and racial hierarchy. Chief Thomas Hilton explained the girls had often been seen on the streets after curfew and that police
had shadowed them to their rooms in the company of black men. Hilton
claimed that he had received complaints about their immoral conduct and
that rumors abounded that they carried "a loathsome disease."[36] Detective
George Sheets, who arrested the three, argued that "the girls were a bad lot
all through, and had been brought in several times. . . . Sheets thought the
police had the right to act as they had, and that the action was solely in the
interest of morality and for the good of the girls."[37]

City officials condemned the examinations but stopped short of dismiss-
ing the officers. The council censured Chief Hilton, but a motion to include
Sheets and the city physician failed. Hilton took responsibility for the action
and apologized, which seemed to satisfy the officials. The girls' mothers,
however, were not so easily mollified and fought to restore their daughters'
reputations. One produced a sworn document from the city physician denying that he had found her daughter to be not "virtuous." All three mothers filed lawsuits against the officers but quickly dropped them.[38]

The uproar indicates that the public acknowledged limits on the actions
it was willing to sanction in pursuit of moral order. If the authorities followed
accepted processes, however, few people seemed to object. A year after the
examinations, two of the same girls were before a judge to show cause why

they should not be sent to reform school. Despite an impassioned defense by one mother, the girls were judged "incorrigible" and committed to the school with no public outcry.[39]

The apparent emergence of a new sexual ethic concerned many Mormons and non-Mormons alike. In past years, such comments as B. F. Grant's, Gaurdello Brown's, or Joseph F. Smith's quoted above might have triggered gentile attacks on Mormon morality. But the informal antiprostitution alliance that had emerged during the anti-Stockade fight continued to strengthen. The new sense of common cause was demonstrated in 1913 when an Illinois purity reformer urged a fight against "Mormonism, white slavery, cocaine, morphine and other institutions of evil." Mormons and many Utah gentiles condemned her remarks. The Salt Lake Commercial Club protested the statement, as did the secretary of the Salt Lake City WCTU, a Methodist. C. C. Goodwin dismissed the comments and claimed that "in Illinois there are more men confessing one wife and supporting two than ever have been in Utah."[40] After decades of conflict, many gentiles and Mormons realized that when it came to the protection of young women from alarming new developments, they were on common ground. Some Mormons congratulated progressives for apparently accepting long-held LDS moral positions. When the New York Bureau of Social Hygiene concluded that segregation of prostitutes was a failed policy, the *Deseret Evening News* noted archly that "it is well known that the 'Mormon' Church was assailed on all sides as seeking the impossible when it took a stand against segregation and toleration in Salt Lake City."[41]

By 1912, antiprostitution activism was peaking across the nation. Reformers demanded abolition and attacked vice districts in virtually every city. A Salt Lake reformer argued that regulation was illogical in an imaginary dialogue between "Segregation" and "Extirpation." "Extirpation" believed "segregation isolates the individual from society for the very purpose of allowing a regulated continuance of evil conduct. Segregation admits an evil and then strives to regulate it instead of annihilate it. How preposterous! How terribly fatal to the ideal which humanity holds and must maintain, that evil is eradicable!"[42]

Prostitution increasingly seemed not only a moral threat but also a disturbing symptom of urban cultural change. Progressive-era reformers often linked prostitution to the vast influx of immigrants who brought alien and supposedly licentious cultures. Many activists also worried about "social hygiene" or the general sexual health of the population. They feared that prostitutes were infecting men with venereal diseases, who in turn were passing on hereditary weaknesses to their children.[43]

Some researchers concluded that prostitutes were "feeble-minded" and dangerous to the race. George Snow Gibbs, a Utah reformer, claimed that "the formidable quartette of social evil—alcoholism, pauperism, prostitution, and criminality—are shown by definite investigations of recent years to be problems much more nearly within possible solution since it has been found that about 50 per cent of the cases are those of the feeble-minded." Gibbs advocated confining the feeble-minded to institutions to prevent them from reproducing "as the public mind is not yet ready to use sexual sterilization."[44]

Prostitutes still received some qualified public sympathy. LDS president Joseph F. Smith argued that

> it is a deplorable fact that society persists in holding woman to stricter account than man in the matter of sexual offense. . . .
> It would be manifestly unjust to sweepingly condemn every fallen woman as of equal culpability with the rest of her degraded class. . . . many a woman who offers her body for hire entered into this dreadful commerce when she found herself despoiled and betrayed through undue confidence in man.[45]

Most activists, however, demanded repressive legislation to combat the "social evil." Smith went on to note that "while her despairing and desperate condition must be considered as an element of cause if not of mitigation, she is nevertheless a criminal under the secular law and a grievous [sic] offender against the mandate of the Almighty."[46] Amey B. Eaton, a University of Utah sociologist and a representative of the American Vigilance Association, insisted that only abolition could end prostitution.[47]

The confluence of nativism and social purity resulted in the campaign against white slavery, defined by one scholar as "the enslavement of white women or girls by means of coercion, trick, or drugs by a non-white or non-Anglo-Saxon man for purposes of sexual exploitation."[48] The white slavery issue first emerged in England in the 1880s, but the uproar in the United States really began around 1907, when George Kibbe Turner and other muckrakers wrote magazine exposés of urban conditions. White slavery fed on fear of the city and growing disquiet among native-born Americans over undesirable immigrants.[49]

The term was used in Salt Lake City, but often simply as a synonym for "prostitution." A 1908 newspaper recalled Kate Flint and "the white slaves whom she owned."[50] Another referred to "Belle London, the Cyprian Queen, and Her White Slaves."[51] The first version of Dogney Lofstrom's tale, with its accusations of drugs and coercion, is a classic white slavery story. Indeed, her testimony at Dora Topham's preliminary hearing was described as "a chapter out of the 'House of Bondage,'" a popular 1910 white slave novel. Like anti-Mormon fiction, white slave stories drew from nineteenth-century captivity narratives.[52]

The federal government took action against "white slavers," including in Utah. In July 1908, an immigration inspector removed a French woman from a Commercial Street brothel, where a French procurer had reportedly placed her.[53] By 1910, concern over white slavery became so intense that Congress passed the White Slave Traffic or Mann Act to punish trafficking in women across state or national borders.[54] One Salt Lake paper looked to the Mann Act as a solution to prostitution. "At the present time in Salt Lake a greater part of the women engaged in shameful occupations are of foreign birth. Many have secured citizenship papers, but these papers were secured during the time when they were engaged in the lawless occupation and consequently according to the recent laws which are enacted they can be deported at the expense of the companies who brought them to this country. When the enforcement of the law starts it is estimated that one-third of the underworld population of this city will be transported across the Atlantic."[55] In reality, over 90 percent of Salt Lake prostitutes claimed to be U.S.-born.[56] While federal officials prosecuted a handful of cases in Utah under the Mann Act, including at least two people accused of placing women in the Stockade, the federal effort did not affect the district.[57] Salt Lakers praised the campaign, but noted that it only applied to interstate cases. They called on local officials to display the same kind of energy and efficiency against prostitution that marked the federal effort.[58]

By 1914, the national outcry over white slavery had largely died down. Most reformers had come to realize that no single "ring" of alien conspirators existed which placed women in brothels; rather, the same general economic and social conditions that obtained in past years caused women to turn to prostitution. Clifford Roe, the Chicago district attorney and muckraker who became a national reform figure, told a Utah crowd "there has been too much hysteria over white slavery. . . . Everything that pertains to the social evil has been classed as white slavery. The idea that women are being forced against their will to become inmates of immoral houses after being drugged and by coercion is preposterous. The real white slaver is the man who profits through commercialized vice or the women who run the houses in which commercialized vice is permitted."[59]

Despite the easing of the white slavery scare, social purity reformers across the country convinced municipal and state governments to take vigorous action against prostitution. Scores of cities and three states created special vice commissions that universally condemned regulation and called for erad-

ication to eliminate the many dangers that prostitution posed.[60] The advocates of regulated prostitution were everywhere in retreat.

When Samuel Park ran against John S. Bransford in 1911 in the wake of the
Dora Topham conviction, both men promised to eliminate restricted vice districts. Park won and embarked on a tour of western cities, where he studied
how those municipalities managed prostitution. Several commissioners-elect
visited Des Moines, Iowa, the model for Salt Lake City's new commission government. The Salt Lakers were impressed by the lack of public prostitution and
expressed confidence that similar results could be obtained in Utah. The new
administration began with a self-consciously "progressive" agenda that emphasized the control of vice.[61]

Park chose as his chief of police Brigham F. Grant of the Betterment League,
which had played the leading role in closing the Stockade. Grant declared his
fitness for the job, since his "particular hobby [was] to guard the young from
disreputable and demoralizing influences."[62] Grant replaced nearly the entire police force and instituted new standards of discipline and training.[63]
Mayor Park and Chief Grant explicitly rejected the regulationist argument
and declared a policy of "no necessary evils."[64] The new chief told an audience at the YMCA that he supported a single sexual standard and that prostitutes deserved Christian sympathy: "When they are turned out on the streets
they have no home to go to; no father, no mother, no brother, no sister to
whom they may apply for help. I have gone to some citizens and asked them
to give these girls employment, but they were stricken with horror at the
thought of taking them into their homes."[65]

Grant moved against brothels at the commission's direction in April 1912.
Police officers visited houses on State Street, Victoria Alley, West Temple
Street, Commercial Street, and elsewhere and told the operators they had
thirty-six hours to cease operations. The chief later claimed that some women
who had managed houses for years were impressed. "They looked at me in
surprise and asked if this was only another political spasm, but I told them
no. They said that word had come to them that this all would blow over and
things would open up again. 'You can't stop prostitution. You will scatter it
all over the residence section of your city,' they told me. But the houses were
closed. When the women were ready to leave the city they came to me, some
of them did, and said, 'Chief, if you really intend to stop this business, this is
the only way.'" Grant's crackdown even forced women out of the remaining longtime parlor houses in Block 57.[66] Women continued to sell sex, but
they no longer worked in established houses under a de facto licensing system that provided a minimum of predictability and protection. Some moved
elsewhere in the city and sold sex; undoubtedly some took other jobs, while

many reportedly left the city. City authorities had adopted suppression of prostitution in earnest for the first time since the 1870s.

While Chief Grant was pledged to stamp out the prostitution district, he showed leniency toward the women involved. Most were arrested as vagrants and given "floaters." Grant allowed prostitutes anywhere from a few days to two weeks to save enough money and arrange their affairs so that they could leave the city permanently. He claimed that most women could be trusted to take the "floater," but those who remained were arrested again.[67]

The crackdown scattered the remaining prostitutes throughout downtown. Without regulated brothels, many women who sold sex had to use hotels or rooming houses, many owned or managed by men. While "white slavery" gained headlines, Salt Lake officials moved against these more realistic, if more difficult, targets. The authorities had always worried about sex (commercial and otherwise) in venues other than regulated brothels, but the concern peaked in the 1910s. Differentiating between legitimate and "disorderly" houses was often as problematic as telling respectable from fallen women. A house could gain an unsavory reputation just as a woman could, with legal consequences for those who lived or visited there. During the era of regulation, women listed their brothels in city directories as "rooming houses" and called themselves "housekeepers" and their inmates "boarders" or "lodgers." The prostitution district always contained numerous legitimate houses that rented rooms on a daily, weekly, or monthly basis. As the city's population grew, the number of rooming houses followed suit. In 1910, the city contained over three hundred rooming houses providing cheap lodging for newly independent young women and men working in downtown businesses. Precisely because of that independence, reformers and authorities saw them as locales for illicit sex. The crackdown on brothels meant that women living in rooming houses were even more suspect.[68]

In June 1912 the city commissioners enacted ordinances stipulating that rooming house license applications be referred to the police department, which created a "purity squad" to investigate for liquor or moral violations.[69] Chief Grant explained that new officers were usually assigned to undercover work in rooming houses, as prostitutes and keepers did not yet recognize them as policemen.[70] While the authorities promoted these measures as antiprostitution devices, they also represented state intrusion into the private morality of working-class citizens as a response to the new sexual ethic.

The new laws and the purity squad's actions encountered resistance. Attorney William Newton, who had represented women charged with vagrancy and prostitution-related offenses for years, complained that the ordinances violated constitutional guarantees against warrantless searches.[71] Some pro-

prietors resisted in a variety of ways. Veteran detective Hugh L. Glenn headed the "purity squad." His chief targets were Kenneth and Ingeborg Martin,
who operated the Norge rooming house. Glenn was convinced that the Norge
was a brothel, and over the course of two years he charged the Martins with
dozens of liquor, prostitution, and register ordinance violations, but the couple managed to parry most of his efforts.[72] When the detective charged Ingeborg Martin with conducting a disorderly house, the commission revoked
her license. She obtained a court order restraining Glenn from arresting her
on the grounds that the commission lacked legal authority over rooming
houses and continued to run the Norge. She accused Glenn of attempting
to ruin her reputation by sending women of ill repute to stay in her house
and then arresting her. The city attorney eventually ruled that proprietors
were entitled to a hearing before the commission.[73]

Rooming house hearings nearly swamped the city government. Owners
and tenants of suspect houses and detectives testified for much of January
1913. Among the witnesses for the city were Nellie Elder and Lucille Walker,
"women detectives" hired by Glenn (undoubtedly the "women of ill repute"
of whom Ingeborg Martin complained). Elder and Walker testified that they
had stayed at hotels and rooming houses throughout the city and had sometimes been approached by tenants for sex. At one hotel, they arranged with
the manager to be introduced to men.[74]

The commission was equally concerned about noncommercial sex. Lulu
Shepard told of a young woman who was "induced" to share a room with a
man. Shepard investigated with two plainclothes detectives and attempted
to charge the man under the Mann Act, but he fled the city. The matron of
the county detention home testified of "orgies and disgraceful scenes in
rooms when girl performers from a theatre and drunken men were the prin-
cipals."[75]

The hearings discouraged some women from attempting to run houses that
might have been brothels. Irene McDonald, who had kept houses in the Stockade and before, gave up and withdrew her application. Belle Clark, another
Stockade veteran, also fell under suspicion and apparently abandoned her
effort.[76] The commission eventually denied eleven licenses. Several proprietors followed the Martins' lead, however, and obtained restraining orders
until the district court could rule on the legality of the rooming house ordinances.[77] The "purity squad" continued its vigorous work, sometimes flout-
ing the courts. Lucy Walker charged one man with attempting to recruit her
for prostitution at his hotel, which had already been denied a license. The
hotelier's lawyers attempted to prove that both Walker and Elder had been
arrested for soliciting and were promised immunity from prosecution if they

worked for the city. Although Walker denied those charges, the hotelier was acquitted.[78] Glenn's squad also arrested some of the proprietors who had obtained restraining orders, opening the city to contempt of court citations.[79] The Utah Supreme Court finally ruled in May 1914 that the city commission had legal authority to deny licenses to disorderly rooming houses, but some proprietors had managed to stall the process and continue to offer venues where women could sell sex.[80]

While the rooming house campaign hung fire, new citizens' groups joined the purity effort. In June 1911, Episcopal bishop Franklin Spalding created a "Social Service Commission" under Rev. Ward Winter Reese. Its duties were "to encourage the study of moral and economic conditions within the District and to tabulate and publish their findings, . . . [and] to suggest methods of social work and encourage movements of social reform."[81] Reese joined the Women's Welfare League in its protests against the Stockade in September 1911. Reese and many of his fellow reformers, however, moved beyond the traditional tactics of clubwomen and voluntary associations and their petitions and protests. In November 1912, a group of "citizens interested in checking the spread of social evil" called for a statewide "social service conference" at which professionals would plan systematic investigation and action. The founders of this movement, from which the Social Service Society of Utah emerged, included Dr. Ephraim G. Gowans of the state industrial school, Rev. Reese, Judge Alexander McMaster of the juvenile court, Elizabeth Cohen, and Amey B. Eaton. Many participants differed from their reform predecessors in their positions within relatively new state institutions and in their self-consciously scientific approach to urban problems. Rev. Reese, for example, advocated a favorite progressive-era tool, the social survey, to obtain data upon which to base reforms.[82]

In October 1912, the Social Service Commission began investigating "the moral condition of Salt Lake." Reese asked Chief Grant to furnish the names, dates, and addresses of all women and men arrested "on charges of immorality" and the disposition of those cases.[83] Grant, who could be sensitive to criticism, reportedly did not respond. As a Mormon, he may have harbored resentments against the Episcopal clergy. Bishop Spalding had authored "Joseph Smith as a Translator," which purported to expose the fraudulent origins of the *Book of Mormon*. Some people may have disapproved of Spalding and Reese's Christian Socialist sympathies.[84]

Grant was convinced that his antiprostitution tactics were succeeding. He declared in his annual report in January 1913 that "we have not now one known public house of prostitution." That claim was misreported or misinterpreted by some to read "we have not now one disorderly resort," a rather different statement. Grant was more emphatic in the official *Municipal Record*, where he claimed to have achieved "the complete elimination of all houses of prostitution."[85] The chief's report came out just before the rooming house hearings began, embarrassing Grant and inspiring the Social Service Commission to carry on its own investigations. The commission's first report demonstrates how broad the campaign against immorality had become. The report cited nine "disorderly resorts." These ranged from no. 85 Stockade place, where a woman had recently been arrested for running a house of ill fame (apparently the last such arrest in the Stockade), to a house where women reportedly solicited passers-by, to several cafés "fitted up with stalls wherein girls and young men were drinking and very hilarious, contrary to city ordinance."[86] Reese and his commission viewed rowdy, mixed-sex cafés as the first step on a path that led to the brothel. The *Herald-Republican* agreed that there was an inevitable progression:

> From the resort to the rooming house, from innocence to bitter knowledge and a compunction of conscience that is only dulled by further excesses and a complete surrender to immorality, it is only a step. . . .
> The young girls that are learning their first alluring lessons in the resorts that this community permits will be the future occupants of the houses of ill-repute, the new generation of underworld habitues.[87]

The commission's second report of similar conditions at six more "resorts" prompted a testy open letter from Chief Grant, who wondered where Reese had been during the "days that tried the souls of would-be reformers." The chief boasted that he had destroyed the brothel district. "Any fair minded citizen who will contrast conditions of today with those of four years ago or two years ago, who will walk at night through Commercial street or Victoria alley, or the Stockade, or any of the well-known haunts of immorality and note the change, cannot conscientiously deny that there has been some progress made, cannot censure without laying his motives open to question." While Grant resented Reese's criticisms, he had nothing but praise for other reformers. "The women of Salt Lake, especially the club women, have given loyal support to the city and to this department in its efforts to enforce the slot machine ordinance, the rooming house ordinance, the crusade against wine rooms and closed restaurant booths, against houses of ill-fame, against gambling and opium selling, until their work has become our work and their cause our cause."[88]

Indeed, the chief claimed to be explicitly carrying out the will of women reformers. When state Senate president W. Mont Ferry reportedly sneered that Grant was "a Sunday school chief, who is trying to remodel Salt Lake to suit the women's clubs"; Grant answered "I only wish it were possible to do this."[89] Grant undoubtedly meant the members of the Women's Welfare League, the Utah Mothers' Congress, the Utah Federation of Women's Clubs, and Salt Lake's Association of City Clubs (after 1915, the Salt Lake City Federation of Clubs). Some clubwomen had also adopted new reform tactics, with notable success. Elizabeth Cohen chaired the Utah federation's "Industrial and Legislative Committee," which lobbied the state legislature for a wide variety of legislation to protect women and children.

Cohen praised the cooperation she received from the LDS women's auxiliaries, the Relief Society and the Young Ladies' Mutual Improvement Association, as well as the WCTU and YWCA.[90] The women of the Relief Society expressed many typical progressive concerns, although they carefully couched their activism within Mormon doctrine. For instance, the society's officers "upheld" LDS president Joseph F. Smith's counsel to observe the Word of Wisdom, which included shunning alcohol. Similarly, while non-Mormon reformers condemned revealing female dress, the Relief Society promised to "show reverence for the sacred garment of the holy Priesthood by refusing to wear short sleeves or low-necked dresses."[91]

Social purity reformers welcomed a new and potentially powerful weapon in May 1913. Betterment groups and women's clubs successfully lobbied the state legislature to pass an injunction and abatement of nuisances law. Such "red light" abatement laws defined any premises where prostitution was carried on as a nuisance and allowed any citizen or law enforcement official to petition a court for an injunction against the site. Testimony of the place's general reputation was admissible evidence. If the court concurred, it issued an order of abatement directing the sale of the premises' contents and closing the place for up to one year, in addition to levying a fine of up to $1,000 and/or six months imprisonment for the person judged responsible. These laws allowed private reformers to take the initiative against houses of prostitution, rather than relying on reluctant police forces. These laws became some of the most powerful weapons in the nationwide campaign against restricted vice districts.[92]

The Utah law, however, proved ineffective. Detective Hugh Glenn immediately invoked it against his nemeses, Kenneth and Ingeborg Martin. Glenn notified the Martins that they were in violation of prostitution and liquor laws and had three days to abate those violations. When no changes were made, he arrested the Martins and two lodgers.[93] While one lodger was convicted of resorting to a house of ill fame, the judge ruled that the city had failed to prove its case against the Martins and refused to grant an injunction.[94] While the law remained on the books, authorities wielded it more as a threat than a reality. Chief Grant considered the law unworkable and seldom used it.[95] Glenn, however, did not give up; he filed pandering charges against Kenneth Martin, then followed with charges of violating the register ordinance and keeping a house of ill fame. Once again, the Martins won acquittal or dismissal in all cases.[96]

Other reformers' efforts were also stymied. The Ministerial Association complained to Governor William Spry of "cabaret shows" where women performed in violation of city ordinances. Spry replied that the association should gather specific evidence of their charges and present them to law enforcement officials; if they neglected their duties, he would take action.[97] When the association sent a delegation to Mayor Park and the city and county attorneys, they were rebuffed. Those officials asked for specific evidence. City attorney Harper Dininny also claimed that the ordinances had been enacted to control "hurdy-gurdies," which no longer existed, and that no court would convict based on those statutes.[98]

Having gotten nowhere with the authorities, the ministers appealed to the public: "We only ask of our fellow citizens that they judge the movement we are undertaking according to their own ideals of civic righteousness . . . , so that the children of the other man's family may have the same protection you wish for your own."[99] The Ministerial Association and the Social Service Commission soon gained LDS allies. The parents' classes of the Sunday schools of the Liberty Stake, under Dr. Joseph H. Grant Jr. and Orson Hewlett, a veteran of the Stockade fight, formed the Liberty Stake Betterment League in summer 1914, and other stakes soon followed suit. The Liberty Stake league presented a petition with over three thousand signatures to the city commission protesting women performers in cabarets and sale of liquor to minors. As they had with the previous petitioners, however, the mayor and county attorney told the stake representatives that the laws they cited were obsolete, and suggested they gather more evidence for the district court.[100]

In September 1914 reformers established a countywide betterment league. The league continued to pressure officials on the issue of cafés and wine rooms.[101] The associated leagues promoted "betterment days" on which citizens were asked to act on a dizzying list of moral reforms: "the liquor habit; public dance halls; dangers and temptations of cabarets; wine and beer gardens; roadhouse resorts; care in conduct of resorts and parks; cigarette smoking; swearing habit; observing the Sabbath; good influence of home life; election of good men to public office, men who will enforce the laws; vaudeville and picture shows should be clean and not suggestive; pride in city, home and surroundings, and encouragement of others to do likewise."[102]

The league concentrated its campaign against cafés on the Semloh-Louvre and its manager, E. L. Wille. They accused Wille of selling liquor to an underage girl who was later "guilty of immoral conduct" with two men. Reformers and representatives of state institutions united to condemn the café. A young telephone operator claimed "she became a woman of the underworld through the influence exerted over her by men she met in the Louvre cafe, and as a result of liquor she first tasted there." Once again, reformers were frustrated; although Wille was convicted in city court, he was acquitted on appeal.[103]

Although convictions on morals charges remained elusive, the fight against cafés showed the extent of cooperation between Mormon and gentile voluntary associations. One newspaper noted that the demands of the Ministerial Association, Social Service Commission, and the LDS Betterment Leagues were virtually identical.[104] Writing on progressive legislation in the Social Service Commission's *Utah Survey,* Lily Munsell Ritchie noted in 1914 that reconciliation across the religious divide had happened since 1911 (by implication, since the defeat of the "American" Party).[105] The *Survey*'s editor noted the "Marvelous Coincidentility" [*sic*] between citizens' campaigns and government responsiveness. When the non-Mormon Ministerial Association attacked cafés, for example, the county attorney investigated; when the LDS Mutual Improvement Association attacked a disorderly club, the authorities quickly closed it. The demands for cabaret reform promised to yield similar positive results. The editor of the Episcopal service newspaper concluded that "in the long run, it is not the saloon or cafe man who will advance our interests, but the sober and home-loving citizen. In this particular we are indebted to the strict principles of many of our old Mormon families, whose example newcomers may well regard with profit."[106] "Betterment" formally became a shared Mormon and gentile concern in April 1917. Officers of the Civic Betterment League and the LDS Betterment Leagues organized the nonsectarian Civic Betterment Union, reportedly numbering over two thousand members from twenty-five churches and civic organizations.[107]

A closely related area of cooperation that resulted in successful legislation was prohibition. Prohibitionists blamed alcohol for causing or exacerbating a myriad of health and social problems, including prostitution. Some reformers expected prohibition to kill the brothel as well as the saloon.[108] The issue gained urgency within the LDS Church at the same time as the national campaign grew to critical strength. Joseph Smith Jr. reported an 1833 revelation that counseled abstinence from alcohol, tobacco, and "hot drinks." Nineteenth-century Mormons generally treated this "Word of Wisdom" as advisory rather than doctrinal, but by the early twentieth century, LDS leaders were preaching strict abstinence. Some high officials, especially Apostle

Heber J. Grant (half-brother of B. F. Grant), urged Church support for state-wide prohibition. LDS president Joseph F. Smith hesitated to align the LDS Church with prohibition forces, however. His reasons were political, and Senator Smoot shared them. Smoot argued that a strong Republican stance on prohibition would alienate many gentiles and renew accusations of LDS political interference. Instead of prohibition, Smoot's "Federal bunch" advocated local option legislation. Governor Spry, at Smoot's urging, opposed statewide prohibition but signed a local option law in 1911. The great majority of Utah towns voted to go "dry," while Salt Lake City and Ogden, with substantial gentile populations, remained "wet." By 1916, Smoot and Smith decided that prohibition had broad enough support among gentiles to make it safe to support a statewide bill.[109]

Secular and non-Mormon reformers also supported prohibition. The Ministerial Association declared that its members "almost to a man were thorough prohibitionists."[110] Orson Hewlett invited the Ministerial Association to join "in the work of obtaining legislation on the prohibition question and enforcing the already existing liquor laws."[111] Lulu Shepard of the WCTU, of course, enthusiastically advocated a statewide ban.[112] When the "Federal bunch" delayed such legislation, however, she decided that the LDS Church was in league with the saloon and became an outspoken anti-Mormon.[113]

Cooperation and constant activism paid off in 1916. Both gubernatorial candidates, Democrat Simon Bamberger, a Jew, and Republican Nephi L. Morris, a Mormon, supported prohibition. Bamberger won, and after close consultation with Heber J. Grant and betterment organizations, signed a statewide prohibition bill on 8 February 1917.[114] Prohibition legislation gave authorities another weapon to use against brothels, since so many brothel patrons and prostitutes alike considered alcohol almost indispensable.

Of course, not all Salt Lake residents favored antivice efforts. The city's prostitution policy came under attack from opposite sides. On one side were abolitionist reformers like W. W. Reese and the Betterment Leagues, who complained that Chief Grant's tactics were tentative and ineffective. On the other side were the advocates of regulation—brothel keepers, businessmen with direct investments, and a few civil libertarians—who, while they no longer dominated the argument, still wielded considerable influence.

In 1914, Chief Grant gave his second annual report, in which he stressed the success that his department had achieved against prostitution in the face of determined legal opposition. Grant reiterated his claim that "not a known house of prostitution is running in this city."[115] Some citizens and city officials rejected Grant's assurances. C. C. Goodwin, a longtime advocate of regulation, wrote that "you are either willfully misrepresenting the facts or else you are too ignorant of local conditions to occupy the position of chief of police," although he offered no contradictory evidence.[116] Councilman Henry W. Lawrence, a veteran antiprostitution activist, objected when the chief recommended that a license be granted to Mae Donnelly's Brunswick rooming house. Grant later admitted that "I have had men and women planted in Mae Donnelly's place for a week at a time, but she is smooth enough to get onto my game and prevent them from getting evidence. I am satisfied right now that Mae Donnelly is not running a straight house, but I can't get the evidence to close her up. I have tried and tried hard, but she is a shrewd woman and I can't get the evidence."[117] Lawrence hired a private investigator who found Donnelly running "a full-fledged house of ill fame of the sort that once flourished within the stockade."[118]

Detective Hugh Glenn bore the brunt of criticism from both sides. His tactics were understandably wearing thin with rooming house keepers, but some city officials also sought his dismissal.[119] On 29 January 1914, the day after Lawrence reported on his investigation of Mae Donnelly's house, Mayor Park submitted Glenn's letter of resignation. The detective insisted he was resigning because "I have incurred the ill will of some of the most persistent lawbreakers in the state as well as some of their friends who happen to be among the active politicians who are now asking for my removal as the price of their work in the last city campaign."[120] Just who the "active politicians" were, Glenn did not specify. Park noted vaguely that Glenn had "incurred enmities and brought upon himself censure and a large degree of unpopularity" and claimed to be submitting the resignation "in order to relieve the commissioners of persistent complaints from certain quarters."[121]

Chief Grant was outraged that his valued detective had been forced out by "rooming house keepers, prostitutes and panderers."[122] Glenn, however, now claimed that Grant and/or Park had fired him. The detective explained that his letter was simply a precautionary measure taken before the November 1913 city elections. He feared that commission candidates Heber M. Wells and William Shearman would, if elected, demand that he be fired, and he wanted to save the mayor that embarrassment. Wells and Shearman won, but did not call for the detective's head. Instead, Glenn claimed the mayor and chief used his letter as a pretext to rid themselves of a controversial subordinate.[123]

One day after Glenn's resignation, Commissioner Shearman proposed an alternative to the rooming house campaign that would supposedly lift the control of prostitution above petty politics. He suggested a vice commission composed of "a minister, a lawyer, a doctor, a business man and possibly a newspaper man"; later, he suggested that "five of the very best men and women" be chosen. The commission would employ an independent force of detectives and officers to investigate and act against prostitution. Shearman argued that such a body could handle the "moral situation" more efficiently and fairly than the current police force, while eliminating the temptation to graft. In any event, two commissioners opposed delegating any of the commission's powers to such a body, and Shearman dropped the proposal.[124]

In summer 1915, scandal erupted in the police department concerning alleged extortion and graft. In a lengthy series of hearings, reporters, current and former police officers, attorneys, and alleged brothel keepers testified about prostitution. Ex-detective Hugh Glenn swore that a "real estate combination" protected immoral rooming houses. The "combination" had pressured the city commission to ease the pressure on favored houses since "[t]he business district wants prostitution and a wide-open town."[125] The ex-detective hinted that the combination was behind his dismissal. Several former and current police officers corroborated that claim, some stating that their superiors, including the veteran Benjamin Siegfus, had ordered them to ignore certain houses.[126]

Other witnesses refuted these assertions. The Martins' attorney, S. P. Armstrong, was accused of working for the "real estate combination" but insisted "it would not be possible for two real estate men to combine on everything." Chief Grant agreed and praised several "big business interests" and real estate men who had assisted the police in keeping their properties free of prostitution. As for the supposed commission plot against Glenn, Grant was equally dismissive. The chief acknowledged that some women still sold sex, but he maintained that the policy of "no necessary evils" had resulted in a cleaner city than ever before.[127] Several reformers affirmed the department's effectiveness. Orson Hewlett praised Grant and blamed defendants and lawyers who employed traditional tactics to delay the prosecution of prostitutes. "We found that the chief of police made the arrests, but that the cases were appealed and would never be brought to trial. We found when the appeals were called in the district court that the witnesses were either spirited away or had left the state. If a man had a few dollars to hire an attorney, he could take an appeal and the case would hang fire for two years. After our investigation we did not feel that we could criticize the police."[128] E. T. Ashton, who supported the West Side citizens' league against the Stockade, thanked Grant for helping to close that district.[129]

The hearings sputtered to an ambiguous conclusion. Glenn refused to name those he accused of hampering his work but promised to tell a grand jury.[130] The commissioners' report, with two dissensions, concluded that nearly all of the testimony consisted of rumor, hearsay, or suspicion, and that no substantive charges could be made.[131] No grand jury was impaneled, and Glenn moved on to other reform campaigns.[132]

The hearings provided one of several indications of the continuing strength of regulationist sentiment and the determination of prostitutes. Keepers like Mae Donnelly attracted enough customers to stay in business and skillfully managed to avoid being caught for at least two years until early 1916, when she reportedly closed her house.[133] Whether a "real estate combination" existed or not, rooming house keepers had successfully parried legal efforts and perhaps pressured the city government to fire a vigorous antivice crusader. Prostitution continued to be more profitable for some property owners and landlords than legitimate business. The failure to obtain convictions may indicate that many citizens on juries continued to favor regulation.

Some people resented what they considered paternalistic and repressive reforms. As usual, C. C. Goodwin was among these critics. The vice commission proposal invited his scorn, as did the Ministerial Association:

> Nobody can make a Sunday school of this town, but unquestionably the city can be made better. Its betterment however, does not rest in the hands of narrow, bigoted, little men who know nothing whatever of real vice conditions or the way to handle them, and who cause only turmoil and heartburnings and never offer a real remedy for any bad condition. . . .
> . . . It is about time that they ceased to intrude in the business of other people, and begin their personal advertising campaign in some other way.[134]

Attorney William Newton told the city commission "the utility of the police department has been almost destroyed because it has been compelled to follow out the fool sanctimonious notions of such sapheads as Orson Hewlett, Sam Park and Upstart George [George Startup, a Mormon prohibitionist and advocate of the abatement act]." Newton claimed that the police could not enforce vice laws with fifteen hundred officers, and suggested that they ignore prostitution unless it became obnoxious: "I am in favor of blowing off the lid and let a man get anything he wants as long as he can lay the money down for value received."[135] "I believe that decent people with common sense don't have to have a lot of pinheads try to legislate morals into them. It can't be done."[136]

Some who held or sought political power shared Newton's views. A self-described progressive candidate for the city commission declared, "I believe in a restricted district with close police supervision. I am opposed to having the residents of the underworld scattered through the hotels and residential districts, as at the present time."[137] The candidate lost, but another regulation advocate won. W. Mont Ferry, a former American Party city councilman and one-time owner of 243 south Main Street, was elected mayor in 1915. Ferry had headed the Civic Betterment League in 1908, but he did not share all of its goals, as his "Sunday school chief" swipe at B. F. Grant indicated.[138] His election aroused speculation that the "lid would be tilted." Ferry denied those rumors, although he stopped well short of promising to abolish prostitution.

> Neither Commercial street nor any other street, nor any portion of any other street, or any house or building in any part of the city will be opened, or reopened as a centralized or decentralized vice district during the present administration with the knowledge, consent or co-operation of the department of public safety, . . .
> . . . I am heartily in favor of controlling and minimizing this evil to the last possible degree. I am satisfied that the condition of this evil as well as of every other evil in this community, will be no worse in the future than it has been in the immediate past.[139]

B. F. Grant would not be the man to enforce this policy, as Ferry removed him within weeks of taking office. The *Deseret Evening News* condemned the move, arguing that those who favored "a morally clean city" supported Grant.[140] Grant reported that the new mayor promised him he would follow a policy of "no necessary evils" but suggested that houses of ill fame would exist "until we have raised a generation of people that does not believe they are necessary to a community."[141]

Grant's successor lasted fewer than four months before it was discovered that he was ineligible for office. Some welcomed his departure, claiming that prostitution had risen sharply under his brief tenure.[142] Reformers could at least celebrate the appointment of the city's first policewoman in April 1916. The Salt Lake City Federation of Clubs extracted a promise from each candidate for mayor and commission in 1915 that he would appoint "two police women or 'street mothers' whose duty shall be the supervision and protection of the welfare and morals of our young girls, boys, and children in all places of amusement as well as the public streets." The clubwomen reasoned such a "street mother" could provide needed maternal influence and discipline for youths threatened by urban dangers (she reported she spent most of her time on "mashers, loafers, and spitters").[143]

Mayor Ferry settled on J. Parley White as his police chief. White immediately declared his intention to "drive gamblers, immoral women and undesirables from town."[144] Within months, however, prostitutes were working openly on Commercial Street. The chief insisted "his orders to his men were as to where the women should not be permitted to be or live, but that no orders were issued as to where they would be permitted to stay." The boundaries

White informally established—State Street to the east, West Temple to the west, South Temple to the north, and Third South to the south—encompassed the traditional district. White implied that discreet brothels would once again be tolerated when he explained that women would not be allowed to solicit on the streets or advertise their establishments and that his men had broken red and green lights outside some Commercial Street houses.[145] Mayor Ferry claimed that these developments were part of an evolving policy. The police had already forced prostitutes out of the residential districts, rooming houses, cafés, cabarets, and streets. Now the police were "gathering evidence, names, pictures and other data in relation to all these women and men of the city" so that they could be forced out of the city under the vagrancy laws.[146]

If that was ever actually Ferry's plan, he did not get the chance to carry it through. In September 1916, county attorney H. J. Mulliner threatened to order the sheriff to raid Commercial Street if the city authorities did not take action against prostitutes within the week. Two days later, Ferry declared that he intended to close all houses of prostitution permanently.[147] Police arrested some twenty-one proprietresses and eighty inmates of Commercial Street brothels. Those who pleaded not guilty were released on $25 bail for inmates and $100 for keepers. The court released the majority who pleaded guilty on their own recognizance. Chief White addressed them:

> You will not be allowed to go back to your old resorts, and I advise you to take up other and better lines of business. You will not be allowed to ply your trade on the streets. . . . I do not intend to persecute you girls. I am sorry for you and I do not believe that you are here of your own volition or that you follow this business of your own will. . . .
>
> But hereafter I shall wage a ceaseless war against the plying of your business in cafes, on the streets, in the rooming houses or wherever I shall find it.[148]

To ensure that Commercial Street remained free of undesirable tenants, Mulliner issued abatement notices to five property owners, including the Clayton Investment Company and the Joseph J. Snell estate. A week later, Mulliner declared that he was satisfied with the actions of the landowners and would take no further legal steps.[149]

Chief White's campaign caused frustration and hardship for several madams. Edna Black claimed that police captain John Hempel had told her during the summer that she must move her brothel from West Temple to Commercial Street (which he denied). Black and three other women told the city commission they had moved to Commercial expecting to operate regulated brothels with the authorities' approval. With brothels now under ban, several Commercial Street rooming house keepers applied for legitimate licenses.

The commission eventually denied licenses to any women who had previously pleaded guilty to keeping a brothel.[150]

Despite the spectacular raid, Commercial Street did not stay free of prostitution for long. A traveling evangelist declared two months later that resorts were openly operating. The Mormon press agreed that the situation was deplorable and suggested that the civic and betterment leagues were shirking their duties.[151] Chief White responded with another raid, taking in 136 women and men and seizing pianos, paintings, furniture, and $2,500 worth of liquor.[152]

Once again, the crackdown proved temporary and prostitutes returned to Commercial Street. The police did finally move against female entertainers in cabarets, using the same laws the authorities had dismissed as obsolete three years earlier.[153] The apparent resurgence of prostitution and the impending statewide ban on alcohol on 1 August prompted the April 1917 formation of the Civic Betterment Union from the Civic Betterment League and the LDS stake Betterment Leagues. The union presented Chief White with a list of twenty-five houses of prostitution and demanded he take action.[154]

By this point, reformers throughout the nation had another overriding concern. With Congress's declaration of war in April 1917, thousands of American men prepared to go overseas. Fort Douglas became a training camp for the American Expeditionary Force. Secretary of War Newton Baker, determined that the American forces be kept "pure," created the Commission on Training Camp Activities and sought protective legislation. Military authorities quickly forbade serving alcohol to uniformed soldiers.[155]

Some reformers expressed concerns about young women attracted to the uniformed men at Fort Douglas. A traveling lecturer suggested "the forces of evil follow the camps" and warned young women away from training posts.[156] Patriotic civilians and military officials leapt to the defense of the troops. The commanding officer at Fort Douglas declared that his men "are as a class clean, moral young men" and that "it is for the women of Salt Lake to see that their daughters are protected by the ordinary usages which society throws about all young women."[157] Governor Bamberger agreed that the soldiers were not to blame for any untoward activity, but rather the young women for abandoning proper gender roles: "Girls should not run around unchaperoned at night, and . . . should dress modestly. They should spend more of their leisure hours at their homes, learning housekeeping."[158] The Forty-second Regiment barred women from their cantonment without a special permit.[159] A local woman established a "hostess house" where "under proper chaperonage, men in uniform are given an opportunity to become acquainted with young women and to join them in wholesome social activities."[160]

The Civic Betterment Union joined those worried about the moral health of soldiers. The union charged that prostitutes were pouring in from towns that were suppressing their vice districts.[161] A CBU committee met with the mayor, chief of police, city attorney, and head of the "purity squad." In a scene reminiscent of the Grant police regime, the city authorities welcomed the CBU's interest but insisted on the correctness of their own policy while suggesting that the betterment group seek more evidence. Ferry did agree to appoint six members of the CBU as special police officers.[162] Not all reformers agreed that the city had a major problem, however. The Zion Aid Society hired a former police matron to investigate. She reported that "the morality of Salt Lake is far above the average, in my opinion. As a matter of happy fact, the absence of social evil is easily noticeable. My inquiries proved the rumors to be absolutely unfounded."[163]

The CBU remained unmollified, and during the autumn 1917 election campaign, they determined to seek a grand jury if city officials did not crack down on prostitution. The CBU's Orson Hewlett told commissioners that many citizens believed "that the police and some of the commissioners want a wide-open city." After the election, the CBU called on the new board to replace J. Parley White with a union member.[164]

Federal action preempted the CBU campaign against prostitution. In January 1918 city officials received notice that by federal order, prostitution was barred within a five-mile radius of any military facility. The order, part of the Selective Service Act, had actually been issued the previous May but had not been enforced. Now, a U.S. district attorney and a special agent from the Department of Justice were directed to work with Salt Lake City officials in carrying out the ban.

The Civic Betterment Union and other opponents of prostitution rejoiced over the order. The secretary of the state board of health welcomed the move as an antivenereal disease measure. Some CBU members wondered if they should disband since the federal government would now enforce their goals.[165] One national correspondent explained that a vigorous federal government was using modern scientific techniques to eliminate a source of contagion against which earlier reformers had been powerless.

> There is scarcely an American city which has not passed through successive waves of reform and vice crusading, which have always subsided without eliminating the evil, because they were not sincerely and scientifically conducted. . . . The very words reformer and vice crusader have become jokes, and all per-

sons proposing to eliminate vice have been regarded either as insincere dema-
gogues or as prudes. . . .

. . . Redlight districts are removed in the same spirit and for the same reason that stagnant puddles in which mosquitoes breed are removed. Scattering
cases are followed up and cured, just as are scattering cases of malaria, in the
canal zone. No claim is made that human nature can be altered, or that all vice,
so called, can be eliminated. But the claim is made that by these measures the
efficiency of the army can be increased by a considerable percentage, and much
death and suffering can be prevented.[166]

Newly appointed commissioner of public safety Karl Scheid and Chief
White promised to cooperate with the federal government. White's critics
noted that the federal government was forcing him to enforce state and municipal laws that had long existed. The chief retorted that the reformers' own
publicity was responsible for the city's prostitutes, since disorderly women
had heard from the reformers that Salt Lake was a "wide-open" town. Commissioner Scheid vowed to drive prostitutes and bootleggers from the city if
it meant hiring a new police force. Apparently that proved necessary. Veterans Benedict D. Siegfus, John Hempel, and five other officers were fired. The
first two, with decades of experience in regulation, may have balked at the new
abolitionist policy. The head of the purity squad was named captain of police, and longtime antiprostitution reformer Gaurdello Brown was appointed to head the purity squad.[167]

The authorities turned the full weight of city, state, and federal prosecution against prostitution. Chief White authorized the arrest of all "immoral
women" and announced that the nuisance abatement law would be invoked
against any house or resort after the second complaint of liquor or moral violations. County sheriffs arrested women under state laws and threatened to
invoke the new federal statutes as well. A U.S. attorney warned owners of
property used for immoral purposes that they would be prosecuted under
federal law. Any woman living alone was suspect. White suggested that unmarried women residing in lodging houses should be made to supply a detailed accounting of their means of support. He added that the federal government should draft prostitutes and put them to work in munitions factories.
Although White's drastic measures were ignored, dozens of women reportedly left the city within days of the commencement of the campaign.[168] Constant pressure kept most prostitutes from operating. By midsummer 1918,
police raids were yielding so few prostitutes and so little liquor that the *Herald* declared Salt Lake City "practically free of bootleggers, women of the
underworld and other law violators."[169] Salt Lake City's purity reformers and

authorities on the municipal, county, state, and federal level had joined forces to drive prostitution underground, at least temporarily.

The intervention of the federal government in the control of prostitution in Salt Lake City demonstrated a remarkable culmination of efforts to implement social policy. In some ways, the process mirrored that occurring nationally. Across the country, reformers forced municipal authorities to abandon regulation and abolish restricted districts, a development that historian John Burnham calls the single largest tangible change in American urban social life in the Progressive Era.[170] Much of the credit for that change must go to female moral reformers who had long worked for a single standard of morality. Historian Paula Baker argues that throughout the nineteenth century, women pursued moral reform efforts mostly through voluntary associations.[171] These activists necessarily used mostly nonelectoral means, often achieving attention and respect but limited results. In the Progressive Era, however, women's social concerns became state concerns as electoral politics became less local and women began to gain suffrage rights.[172] Women in Salt Lake City did much more than vote, however. Female activists turned from individual rescue work to influencing state mechanisms and made some of their reform concerns the subject of legislation. Eventually male-dominated associations such as the Civic Betterment League took up their reform concerns. In Baker's term, politics had become "domesticated."

Notes

1. For population, see table 21, *Statistical Abstract of Utah*, pp. 27–28. On physical changes, see Alexander and Allen, *Mormons and Gentiles*, pp. 107–9, 123, 131, 153–54; and McCormick, *Salt Lake City*, pp. 44–51, 63–73.

2. Turner, "City of Chicago."

3. Boyer, *Urban Masses and Moral Order in America*, pp. 121–251 passim; Meyerowitz, "Women and Migration"; Meyerowitz, "Introduction" to *Women Adrift*; and Odem, *Delinquent Daughters*, pp. 19–24.

4. Kessler-Harris, "Women's Choices in an Expanding Labor Market," chap. in *Out to Work*; Benson, *Counter Cultures*, pp. 177–78.

5. *Salt Lake City Herald*, 17 May 1907. See also Kessler-Harris, "'Why Is It Can a Woman Not Be Virtuous If She Does Mingle With the Toilers?'" chap. in *Out to Work*.

6. *Salt Lake City Daily Tribune*, 31 May 1900; for the beer, see *Tribune*, 2 June 1900.

7. *Tribune*, 2 June 1900.

8. *Herald*, 11 Feb. 1902. See also *Tribune*, 2 June 1900; and *Herald*, 17 Sept., 11 Dec. 1901. On national concerns over women's new freedom, see Meyerowitz, *Women Adrift*.

9. *Salt Lake City Herald-Republican*, 13 Jan. 1913.

10. *Herald-Republican*, 18 Mar. 1913, in SCP.

11. *Herald-Republican,* 10 Apr. 1912; Berlin, *Ragtime,* pp. 21–31, 32–60; Leonard, "Reactions to Ragtime."

12. *Annual Message of the Mayor with the Annual Reports of the Officers of Salt Lake City, Utah, for the year 1913,* p. 262.

13. *Herald-Republican,* 24 Mar. 1914.

14. "Beginning of the Descent."

15. *Herald-Republican,* 18 Mar. 1913, in SCP.

16. *Herald-Republican,* 5 Oct. 1913.

17. On sexual attitudes, see D'Emilio and Freedman, *Intimate Matters,* pp. 171–200. On nightlife, see Nasaw, *Going Out.*

18. Odem, *Delinquent Daughters,* pp. 22–24; Meyerowitz, *Women Adrift,* pp. 102–94.

19. "Commercialized Prostitution," p. 2. This paper, in the Ralph Taylor Richards Papers, JWM, is anonymous and is stamped "Timpanogos Club, 1913." See also *Herald-Republican,* 24 Nov. 1916. The Louvre and Maxim's were Salt Lake City cafés.

20. *Herald,* 9 Dec. 1902.

21. Utah, *Revised Ordinances,* sec. 449; *Herald,* 22 May 1903.

22. *Tribune,* 31 Jan. 1905.

23. Paddock, "Industrial Home for Mormon Women." See also Odem, *Delinquent Daughters,* pp. 115–18, 128–56; Hobson, *Uneasy Virtue,* pp. 130–36; Platt, *Child Savers;* Brenzel, "Domestication as Reform"; and Lindsey and O'Higgins, *Beast,* pp. 80–83.

24. Reform School, in Utah, *Compiled Laws* (1888).

25. *Tribune,* 21 May 1891.

26. *Tribune,* 26, 27 July 1893.

27. *Tribune,* 19 Aug. 1893. See also *Tribune,* 24 Sept. 1895; *Tribune,* 18 Dec. 1898.

28. State v. Eva Curtis, Maggie Curtis, Minerva Reeves, case no. 838 (3d dist. criminal case files, 1901); *Herald,* 30 Nov., 8 Dec. 1901, 9 Mar. 1903; Salt Lake City Court Criminal Division, "Minute Book, 1905," p. 750, 21 Dec. 1905; and *Deseret Evening News,* 23 Jan. 1906.

29. See Utah Federation of Women's Clubs Records, especially Knudsen, *History of Utah Federation of Women's Clubs,* p. 5, in Utah Federation of Women's Clubs Records, JWM.

30. "Juvenile Courts," in *Laws of the State of Utah, Passed at the Sixth Session of the Legislature,* p. 182; and "Juvenile Courts," in Utah, *Compiled Laws* (1907).

31. *Tribune,* 31 Jan. 1905. See State v. Elizabeth Blundell, case no. 389 (3d dist. criminal case files, 1898); and *Tribune,* 30 Oct., 3 Dec. 1898; 22 Jan. 1899. See also Odem, *Delinquent Daughters,* pp. 128–56.

32. *Tribune,* 3 Mar. 1899. See also State v. Ragna Nyborg, case no. 434 (3d dist. criminal case files, 1899); and *Tribune,* 2, 8 Mar. 1899.

33. For the examinations, see Committee on Police and Prison Department report 5311, "Salt Lake City Council Minutes," Book V, p. 195, 16 May 1900. See also *Deseret Evening News,* 7, 8, 11 May 1900; "virtuous" from 8 May. *Herald,* 11 May 1900; and *Tribune,* 8, 10, 13, 15, 17, 20, 21 May, 2 June, 1900; "immoral" from 10 May.

34. *Deseret Evening News,* 8 May 1900.

35. *Herald,* 11 May 1900.

36. *Tribune,* 8 May 1900.

37. *Tribune,* 11 May 1900.

38. *Tribune,* 12, 20, 21 May 1900.

39. State v. Pearl Kessler, case no. 743 (3d dist. criminal case files, 1901); *Tribune,* 29 May 1901; and *Herald,* 2 June 1901.

40. For the reformer's remarks, see *Herald-Republican,* 11 Oct. 1913. For responses, see *Herald-Republican,* 15 Oct. 1913, and *Deseret Evening News,* 15 Oct. 1913, in JH, 10 Oct. 1913. For Goodwin, see *Salt Lake City Goodwin's Weekly,* 18 Oct. 1913, in JH, 18 Oct. 1913. On the WCTU's campaign against polygamy, see Iversen, *Antipolygamy Controversy,* pp. 218–19, 248.

41. *Deseret Evening News,* 31 Jan. 1914, in JH, 31 Jan. 1914.

42. J. H. W., "Dialogue. Segregation vs. Extirpation."

43. Boyer, *Urban Masses and Moral Order in America,* p. 191; Hobson, *Uneasy Virtue,* pp. 150–59; Connelly, *Response to Prostitution in the Progressive Era;* Keller, *Regulating a New Society;* Rosen, *Lost Sisterhood,* pp. 111–40; Lubove, "Progressive and the Prostitute"; Feldman, "Prostitution, the Alien Woman and the Progressive Imagination"; and D'Emilio and Freedman, *Intimate Matters,* pp. 202–15.

44. Gibbs, "Need of a State Institution for Feeble-Minded"; and *Herald-Republican,* 2 Dec. 1912.

45. J. Smith, "Unchastity the Dominant Evil of the Age," pp. 6–9.

46. Ibid., p. 9.

47. *Tribune,* 16 Dec. 1912.

48. Grittner, *White Slavery,* p. 5. See also Cordasco and Pitkin, *White Slave Trade and the Immigrants;* Feldman, "Prostitution, the Alien Woman and the Progressive Imagina-tion"; Connelly, "American Dilemma: Prostitution and Immigration," chap. in *Response to Prostitution;* Odem, *Delinquent Daughters,* pp. 11–13, 96–98; and Boyer, *Urban Masses and Moral Order in America,* pp. 191–218. On international white slavery, see E. Bristow, *Vice and Vigilance;* Evans, "Prostitution, State and Society in Imperial Germany"; and Walkowitz, "Politics of Prostitution."

49. Turner, "City of Chicago." Turner inspired, among others, Jane Addams; see her *New Conscience and an Ancient Evil.* On this literature, see E. Anderson, "Prostitution and Social Justice," p. 205.

50. *Tribune,* 26 Sept. 1908.

51. *Salt Lake City Inter-Mountain Republican,* 16 May 1909. See also *Deseret Evening News* 24, 25, 26, 27 May 1910.

52. For the "chapter" see *Herald-Republican,* 26 July 1911. See also Kauffman, *House of Bondage;* de Young, "Help, I'm Being Held Captive!"; and Grittner, *White Slavery,* pp. 18–32.

53. *Herald,* 7, 21 July 1908.

54. Langum, *Crossing over the Line;* Boyer, *Urban Masses and Moral Order in America,* pp. 191–94; Grittner, *White Slavery,* pp. 70–73, 83–106; Addams, *New Conscience and an Ancient Evil,* pp. 23–24; and Beard, *Woman's Work in Municipalities,* pp. 114–18.

55. *Herald-Republican,* 20 Aug. 1910.

56. Of likely prostitutes who reported a birthplace in the 1910 census (N=85). U.S. Bu-reau of the Census, Thirteenth Census (1910), Salt Lake County, Enumeration District No. 120, sheets 13B, 15A, 15B; Enumeration District No. 145, sheets 2A, 2B.

57. *Herald-Republican,* 9 Jan., 24 Feb., 6, 10, 13, 15, 26, 30 Apr., 16, 23 May, 18 June, 14 July, 28 Sept., 26 Nov. 1911, 30 Jan., 21 Nov. 1912, 18, 19 Feb. 1913; and *Tribune,* 22 Dec. 1913.

58. *Herald-Republican,* 7 Apr., 10 June 1911.

59. *Herald-Republican,* 30 Jan. 1914. On the waning of concerns, see Grittner, *White Slavery,* pp. 72–75. On Roe, see E. Anderson, "Prostitution and Social Justice."

60. Boyer, *Urban Masses and Moral Order in America,* pp. 193–98; E. Anderson, "Prostitution and Social Justice"; Felt, "Vice Reform as a Political Technique"; and Hass, "Sin in Wisconsin." For contemporary views, see "Organized Vice as a Vested Interest"; and "Putting Out the Red Lights."

61. *Herald-Republican,* 26 Nov., 3, 6 Dec. 1911; Alexander and Allen, *Mormons and Gentiles,* p. 163.

62. *Tribune,* 10 Dec. 1911, in SCP.

63. *Herald-Republican,* 25, 30 Dec. 1911; 12 Jan., 14 Feb. 1912; "Manual of the Salt Lake City Police Department," passed and adopted by Board of Commissioners, 16 Dec. 1912. On police reform, see Fogelson, *Big-City Police,* pp. 93–116.

64. *Herald-Republican,* 28 July 1915.

65. *Tribune,* 8 Mar. 1912, in SCP.

66. *Herald-Republican,* 6 Apr. 1912; *Herald-Republican,* 28 July 1915; quote from latter.

67. *Herald-Republican,* 16 Jan. 1912.

68. Polk, *Salt Lake City Directory* (1900, 1910). On rooming houses, see Groth, *Living Downtown,* pp. 57, 90–130; Meyerowitz, *Women Adrift,* pp. 44–112.

69. Salt Lake City, *Revised Ordinances* (1913), secs. 849, 861. See also *Deseret Evening News,* 22 May, 4 June 1912, in SCP; *Herald-Republican,* 23 May 1912; and "For Moral Betterment," *Municipal Record* 1, no. 5 (1912): 14.

70. *Herald-Republican,* 28 July 1915.

71. *Deseret Evening News,* 4 June 1912, in SCP. For Newton as prostitutes' lawyer, see *Tribune,* 22 May 1891; 12 July 1892; *Deseret Evening News,* 20 Oct. 1910; State of Utah v. Ray Woods, case no. 1843 (3d dist. criminal case files, 1908); State of Utah v. Babe Rivers, case no. 2523 (3d dist. criminal case files, 1910); Salt Lake City v. Ethel Cockron, case no. 2595 (3d dist. criminal case files, 1910); and Salt Lake City v. Margaret Duran, case no. 2598 (3d dist. criminal case files, 1910). Newton allegedly tried to blackmail Dora Topham into hiring him; see *Herald-Republican,* 27 June 1910.

72. State v. Kenneth Martin et al. (3d dist. criminal case files, 1913).

73. For the restraining order, see *Herald-Republican,* 15 Dec. 1912. For the ruling, see *Herald-Republican,* 8 Jan. 1913.

74. *Herald-Republican,* 11, 14, 15 Jan., 23, 24 May 1913.

75. For Shepard, see *Herald-Republican,* 11, 13 Jan. 1913. For the hearings, see *Herald-Republican,* 17, 22, 25, 28, 29 Jan., 1 Feb. 1913. Quote from 29 Jan.

76. *Herald,* 28 June 1909; *Herald-Republican,* 29 Jan. 1913.

77. *Herald-Republican,* 31 Jan., 1 Feb. 1913.

78. *Herald-Republican,* 1 Feb., 11, 12 Apr. 1913.

79. *Herald-Republican,* 17, 18 Feb. 1913.

80. *Herald-Republican,* 2 May 1914.

81. *Journal of the Proceedings of the Fourth Annual Convocation of the Protestant Episcopal Church in the Missionary District of Utah* (1911), pp. 14, 22; and *Journal of the Proceedings of the Fifth Annual Convocation of the Protestant Episcopal Church in the Missionary District of Utah* (1912), p. 14.

82. *Herald-Republican,* 27 Oct., 23, 24, 26 Nov. 1912.

83. *Herald-Republican*, 27 Oct. 1912.

84. On Spalding, see Melish, *Franklin Spencer Spalding*. For "Joseph Smith as a Trans-lator," see Melish, pp. 171–74. For his Christian Socialism, see Melish, pp. 236–56. See also *Missionary District of Salt Lake, Journal of Convocation* (1907); Mercer, "Joseph Smith as an Interpreter and Translator of Egyptian"; *Goodwin's Weekly*, 30 Sept. 1911, in JH, 30 Sept. 1911; and Scholefield, "Social Service Commission—Why?"

85. *Annual Message of the Mayor with the Annual Reports of the Officers of Salt Lake City, Utah, for the year 1912; Tribune*, 12 Jan. 1913. For "not now one disorderly resort," see *Herald-Republican*, 28 Jan. 1913. For "complete elimination," see *Municipal Record* 1, no. 12 (1912): 11.

86. *Herald-Republican*, 6 May 1913.

87. *Herald-Republican*, 20 May 1913.

88. For the commission's second report, see *Herald-Republican*, 11 May 1913; for Grant's letter, see *Herald-Republican*, 13 May 1913. See also "Appendix XIV. Report of the Social Service Commission," in *Journal of the Proceedings of the Seventh Annual Convocation of the Protestant Episcopal Church in the Missionary District of Utah* (1914), pp. 46–47; No-ble Warrum to Rev. W. W. Reese, 9 Oct. 1913, *Utah Survey*, 1, no. 2 (Oct. 1913): 1–4.

89. *Deseret Evening News*, 26 Feb. 1913, in SCP.

90. See "Report of Industrial and Legislative Committees," in *Utah Federation of Wom-en's Clubs Yearbook*, 1910–11; and Knudsen, *History of Utah Federation of Women's Clubs*, pp. 3–5; both in Utah Federation of Women's Clubs Records, JWM; Ritchie, "What Utah Women Have Done with the Vote"; "Book One Association of City Clubs 1912–1917," in Salt Lake Council of Women Records, JWM; "List of Officers of the Board of Directors of the YWCA, 1906–1934," in Young Women's Christian Association of Salt Lake City Records, JWM.

91. "Resolutions passed by the Officers and Members of the Relief Society of the Church of Jesus Christ of Latterday Saints, Oct. 7, 1912," quoted in Derr, Cannon, and Beecher, *Women of Covenant*, p. 185. On general reform, see Derr, Cannon, and Beecher, pp. 183–90. On auxiliary organizations, see Alexander, *Mormonism in Transition*, pp. 125–53; Scott, "Mormon Women, Other Women."

92. Mackey, *Red Lights Out*, pp. 8, 121, 124–30. For Utah's law, see Startup, *Effective Li-quor and Vice Law;* "Commercialized Vice and the Remedy," in JH, Aug. 1914; Knudsen, *History of Utah Federation of Women's Clubs*, pp. 3–4, in Utah Federation of Women's Clubs Records, JWM. For the actual law, see "Abatement of Common Nuisances," in Utah, *Compiled Laws* (1917).

93. *Herald-Republican*, 28 May, 1 June 1913.

94. *Herald-Republican*, 24, 27 June, 6 July 1913.

95. *Herald-Republican*, 9 Jan., 2 July 1914; 18, 23 Sept., 1 Oct. 1916. For Grant on the law, see *Tribune*, 28 July 1915.

96. For pandering, see State v. Kenneth Martin, case no. 3308 (3d dist. criminal case files, 1913). For the register, see City v. Kenneth and I. Martin, case no. 3341 (3d dist. criminal case files, 1913). For keeping, see City v. Kenneth and I. Martin, case no. 3343 (3d dist. crim-inal case files, 1913); *Herald-Republican*, 12 Nov. 1913.

97. For the first letter, see *Herald-Republican*, 3 Feb. 1914; for the second, 6 Mar. 1914. For Spry's answer, see *Deseret Evening News*, 16 Mar. 1914, in JH, 14 Mar. 1914.

98. *Herald-Republican,* 8 Apr. 1914; and *Tribune,* 8 Apr. 1914. See also "Ministers and Ministrators."

99. *Herald-Republican,* 29 Apr. 1914.

100. *Herald-Republican,* 1, 2, 8 July 1914.

101. *Herald-Republican,* 22 July, 18 Sept. 1914.

102. *Deseret Evening News,* 7 Jan. 1915, in JH, 7 Jan. 1915. See also *Deseret Evening News,* 10 Aug. 1914, in JH, 10 Aug. 1914.

103. For "guilty of immoral conduct" see *Herald-Republican,* 26 Dec. 1914. For reformers, see *Herald-Republican,* 28 Dec. 1914. For the *Herald-Republican* on prohibition, see 27, 28 Dec. 1914. For the league affidavit, see *Herald-Republican,* 29 Dec. 1914. For Wille's case, see State of Utah v. E. L. Wille, case no. 3858 (3d dist. criminal case files, 1915).

104. *Herald-Republican,* 2 July 1914.

105. Ritchie, "What Utah Women Have Done with the Vote," p. 8.

106. "Marvelous Coincidentility," "Hurting the Town."

107. *Herald-Republican,* 25 Apr., 25 May 1917; *Deseret Evening News,* 29 June 1917, in JH, 29 June 1917.

108. *Herald-Republican,* 14 Oct. 1916.

109. Thompson, "Utah's Struggle for Prohibition"; Shipps, "Utah Comes of Age Politically"; Nelson, "Utah Goes Dry"; and Alexander, "Adoption of a New Interpretation of the Word of Wisdom," chap. in *Mormonism in Transition.*

110. *Herald,* 13 Jan. 1903.

111. *Herald-Republican,* 5 Jan. 1915.

112. *Deseret Evening News,* 3 Sept. 1913, in JH, 2 Sept. 1913.

113. See, for example, Shepard, "Utah Dry in November"; and "Mormonism Militant."

114. Thompson, "Utah's Struggle for Prohibition," pp. 83–89.

115. *Annual Message of the Mayor with the Annual Reports of the Officers of Salt Lake City, Utah, for the year 1914.*

116. *Goodwin's Weekly,* 24 Jan. 1914, in SCP.

117. *Herald-Republican,* 28 July 1915.

118. "Salt Lake City Commission Minutes," 29 Jan. 1914, 73. See also *Herald-Republican,* 29, 30 Jan. 1914.

119. *Tribune,* 7 Aug. 1913; and *Herald-Republican,* 7 Aug., 1 Oct. 1913.

120. "Salt Lake City Commission Minutes," 29 Jan. 1914, p. 74; and *Herald-Republican,* 30 Jan. 1914.

121. *Herald-Republican,* 30 Jan. 1914.

122. *Herald-Republican,* purporting to quote *Deseret Evening News* of 29 Jan. 1914.

123. *Herald-Republican,* 19, 27 Mar. 1914.

124. *Herald-Republican,* 30 Jan., 11, 17, 20 Feb. 1914. Quotes are from 30 Jan. and 17 Feb.

125. *Herald-Republican,* 10 July 1915. See "Salt Lake City Commission Minutes," pp. 8, 9, 12–16, 19, 20, 26–28, 30 July, 2 Aug. 1915.

126. *Tribune,* 10 July 1915; and *Herald-Republican,* 13, 17 July 1915.

127. *Herald-Republican,* 28 July 1915.

128. *Herald-Republican,* 10 July 1915.

129. *Deseret Evening News,* 11 Aug. 1915, in SCP.

130. *Herald-Republican,* 10, 13 July 1915; State of Utah ex rel. the Board of Commissioners

of Salt Lake City v. Hugh L. Glenn, case no. 20166 (3d dist. civil case files, 1915); and State of Utah ex rel. the Board of Commissioners of Salt Lake City v. Guy La Coste, case no. 20115 (3d dist. civil case files, 1915).

131. *Herald-Republican,* 12 Nov. 1915.

132. *Herald-Republican,* 14 Oct. 1916; 24 May 1917.

133. For Donnelly, see *Herald-Republican,* 22 July 1915; 17, 29 Mar. 1916.

134. *Goodwin's Weekly,* 7 Feb. 1914, in SCP. See also *Goodwin's Weekly,* 11 Apr. 1914, in SCP.

135. *Herald-Republican,* 10 July 1915.

136. *Tribune,* 10 July 1915.

137. *Herald-Republican,* 9 Oct. 1913.

138. *Herald,* 29 Aug. 1908; and Alexander and Allen, *Mormons and Gentiles,* p. 144.

139. *Herald-Republican,* 6 Jan. 1916.

140. *Deseret Evening News,* 18 Jan. 1916, in JH, 18 Jan. 1916.

141. *Herald-Republican,* 29 Jan. 1916.

142. *Herald-Republican,* 7, 9 May 1916.

143. "Book One Association of City Clubs 1912–1917," in Salt Lake Council of Women Records, pp. 26–28, 47, 94–95, in JWM. See also *Herald-Republican,* 21, 25 Apr. 1916; for "mashers, etc.," see *Herald-Republican,* 24 May 1916; *Municipal Record* 5, no. 12: 7.

144. *Herald-Republican,* 10 June 1916.

145. *Herald-Republican,* 12 Aug. 1916. See also *Tribune,* 4 Aug. 1916; and *Herald-Republican,* 4 Aug. 1916.

146. *Herald-Republican,* 14 Sept. 1916; see also 15, 17 Sept. 1916.

147. *Herald-Republican,* 18, 20 Sept. 1916. See also Alexander and Allen, *Mormons and Gentiles,* pp. 166–67.

148. *Tribune,* 21 Sept. 1916; and *Herald-Republican,* 21 Sept. 1916.

149. *Herald-Republican,* 23 Sept., 1 Oct. 1916. Snell had died two months prior; see "Salt Lake County Probate Record Book 60," p. 92, 47; and Salt Lake City Death Records, Death Certificate No. L890. See also *Deseret Evening News,* 11 July 1916; in JH, 10 July 1916; and *Tribune,* 14 July 1916, in JH, 13 July 1916.

150. *Herald-Republican,* 4, 11 Oct. 1916.

151. *Herald-Republican,* 19 Nov. 1916; and *Deseret Evening News,* 21 Nov. 1916, in JH, 21 Nov. 1916.

152. *Tribune,* 27 Nov. 1916; and *Herald-Republican,* 26, 27, 28, 29 Nov. 1916.

153. *Herald-Republican,* 22, 23, 24 May 1917.

154. *Herald-Republican,* 25 Apr., 25 May 1917.

155. N. Bristow, *Making Men Moral,* pp. 98–113; Keller, *Regulating a New Society,* pp. 123–24; and Odem, *Delinquent Daughters,* pp. 121–27.

156. *Herald-Republican,* 10, 11 Sept. 1917. Quote is from 11 Sept. On national concerns, see N. Bristow, *Making Men Moral,* 113–36.

157. *Herald-Republican,* 11 Sept. 1917.

158. *Herald-Republican,* 12 Sept. 1917.

159. *Herald-Republican,* 7 Sept. 1917.

160. *Herald,* 16 Aug. 1918.

161. *Deseret Evening News,* 10 Mar. 1917, in JH, 10 Mar. 1917; *Deseret Evening News,* 29 June 1917, in JH, 29 June 1917; and *Herald-Republican,* 25 May, 30 June 1917.

162. Alexander and Allen, *Mormons and Gentiles*, pp. 166–71; and *Herald-Republican*, 3 July 1917.

163. *Herald-Republican*, 21 Oct. 1917.

164. *Herald-Republican*, 8, 9, 12, 13 Oct. 1917. Quote is from 9 Oct. For the chief, see *Herald-Republican*, 28 Dec. 1917; 22 Feb. 1918. See also Alexander and Allen, *Mormons and Gentiles*, pp. 166–68.

165. *Herald-Republican*, 31 Jan., 1 Feb. 1918. See also Odem, *Delinquent Daughters*, pp. 121–27.

166. Frederic J. Haskin, "Federal Cleanup of American Cities," in *Tribune*, 19 Mar. 1918, in JH, 15 Mar. 1918.

167. *Tribune*, 8 Feb. 1918; and *Herald-Republican*, 8, 12 Feb. 1918. Siegfus had been on the force since at least 1890; Hempel, 1903. See Polk, *Salt Lake City Directory* (1890, 1903).

168. *Herald-Republican*, 4, 10, 11, 12, 13 Feb. 1918. Quote from 13 Feb.

169. *Herald*, 5 Aug. 1918.

170. Burnham, "Progressive Era Revolution in American Attitudes toward Sex."

171. Baker, "Domestication of Politics." See also Ethington, "Recasting Urban Political History"; Flanagan, "Gender and Urban Political Reform"; and McGerr, "Political Style and Women's Power."

172. For an explanation by a prominent Mormon woman, see Susa Young Gates to Arthur W. Page, *Deseret Evening News*, 18 Oct. 1913, in JH, 18 Oct. 1913.

Conclusions

THE LONG TRANSITION from regulated prostitution to abolition was complicated by issues and ironies that dated from the mid-nineteenth century. People in Salt Lake City found many uses and meanings for prostitutes, prostitution, and reform over those decades, and people have continued to do so ever since.

One of the first ironies concerned the changes in the city that initially attracted substantial numbers of prostitutes. The gentile men who demanded a share of economic and political power saw railroads and mining as essential for Utah's future. Patrick Edward Connor viewed these industries not only as the keys to prosperity but also as weapons to break Mormon hegemony by attracting overwhelming numbers of gentiles. Female activists like Cornelia Paddock also promoted economic development as an indirect means of purifying Utah's moral climate and saving women from plural marriage. By encouraging miners and railroad workers to come to Utah, those activists abetted a different violation of their vaunted moral code, since those same men provided a customer base for the prostitutes that arrived with them. While Mormons and some gentiles, especially women, professed horror at the presence of prostitutes, some gentile and probably some Mormon men actually welcomed prostitution as a sign the city was becoming more modern and American.

Women like Kate Flint and those who worked in her brothel were almost certainly indifferent toward the polygamy conflict except for the few times when it directly affected them. Most women who resorted to prostitution probably did so temporarily, out of desperation and lack of options, but some saw financial opportunity in the developing city. Women like Flint, Emma

DeMarr, and Sadie Noble established a network of brothels and cribs in the heart of the business district that lasted for decades. They provided sexual services much in demand while they earned profits for themselves and a broad spectrum of businesspeople. Those women who sold sex contributed to the economic, political, and social life of the community and, in a very real sense, the "Americanization" of Salt Lake City. While gentile and Mormon activists used prostitution as a weapon against each other, the antipathies created during the struggle over polygamy may have made it somewhat easier for women to sell sex by hampering effective cooperation against prostitution.

The responses to prostitution were also marked by multiple ironies and uses. The relatively few non-Mormon female activists in 1870s and 1880s Salt Lake were far more concerned about the supposed threat licentious Mormon males posed to pure womanhood and the Christian home than that posed by a handful of prostitutes on Commercial Street. Mormons were also more concerned about the antipolygamy campaign, although they condemned prostitution as a corrupting influence upon their virtuous community brought by those who opposed their marital practices. After an early attempt at abolishing prostitution, however, LDS city authorities adopted a regulationist policy similar to that in cities across the nation. Brigham Young Hampton's seriocomic effort to use prostitutes to discredit antipolygamists embarrassed Mormons and probably further entrenched regulation. The Saints concentrated on enforcing their moral code within their membership while they parried gentile attacks on LDS morality by constructing a myth of Salt Lake City's former purity under all-Mormon rule. Some Mormons may have also realized that prostitution provided them with a convenient pretext: they could blame gentiles for introducing and supporting immoral women (who had proved difficult to eliminate at any rate), while at the same time those Mormons could share in the economic and social benefits of prostitution.

The "Americanization" of Salt Lake City after 1890 included the Mormon retreat from plural marriage, a successful gentile attempt to share political and economic power, and the increasing participation of Mormons in capitalistic business practices. These changes had an ironic dual effect upon prostitution: first, regulation was strengthened, as businessmen and municipal authorities of all descriptions defended the profits prostitution earned and the social order regulation supposedly protected. Prostitutes and madams welcomed regulation, although the system only benefited those of the highest status and respectable society still considered them criminals and undesirables.

But "Americanization" also eventually allowed some Mormons and gentiles to leave the polygamy conflict behind and make common cause against prostitution. The effort to rescue prostitutes was part of some women's attempts to construct their version of a moral community. Reformers' efforts to rescue individual women from brothels or to fight the institution of prostitution were largely unavailing. The women who operated rescue homes did succeed in aiding a small number of individual women. In fact, they were the only reformers who combined sympathy for prostitutes with sustained (albeit largely ineffective) action to improve their lot. The rescue effort barely made a dent in prostitution, however, and was constantly plagued by a shortage of funds and the opposition of respectable neighbors. More and more reformers abandoned the hands-on rescue effort in favor of repressive state action to abolish prostitution.

Those reformers who demanded abolition also had little success until the campaign against the Stockade. Prostitutes and madams effectively shaped the regulation system and used techniques of mobility and anonymity to stay in business. Male economic and political elites provided powerful support for regulation. Salt Lake's would-be social purity activists also kept splitting along Mormon-gentile lines over the polygamy issue. For example, when activists were seemingly poised to take united action (however limited and ineffective it likely would have been) in the wake of the murder on Victoria Alley, the election of Reed Smoot reopened old wounds.

The reemergence of polygamy as an issue in Salt Lake City politics during the Smoot controversy led to yet another ironic dual effect. First, an influential madam, Dora Topham, created a new restricted prostitution district—the apotheosis of regulation—at the behest of an avowedly anti-Mormon political party. But Topham's Stockade and the waning of polygamy spurred the emergence of an effective, broad-based abolition alliance that brought down the district and the party. Gentile and Mormon reformers in the new century gradually came to believe that a modern, American city must be free of sexual immorality, especially prostitution. Some Mormons, consciously or not, used the fight against regulated prostitution to prove their mainstream moral credentials. Reformers used both traditional moral arguments and newer scientific ones to demand an end to regulation. Many reformers no longer considered fallen women the victims of lustful men to be rescued and converted back into "true women." Instead, the victim was society itself, and the solution was abolition. The needs or circumstances of the women who sold sex were largely ignored.

The abolition alliance helps demonstrate the degree to which Mormons and gentiles had reconciled by 1918 and how far the state's "peculiar people"

had come into the mainstream of American society. Female progressive reformers were instrumental in this fight, but they fell well short of achieving
everything they wanted. While they helped create new institutions and pass
legislation to repress prostitution, they certainly did not succeed in imple-
menting a single standard of morality. Nor did they achieve the economic
gains for women that might have made prostitution unnecessary.

The change from regulation to abolition had largely negative effects upon
prostitutes. While their lives and livelihoods had never been easy and were
often dangerous, regulation offered some advantages. With the end of regulation, prostitutes found that although demand for their services remained
strong, they had to bear the burdens of prostitution without those advantages. The end of regulation forced underground (or to the streets) the wom-
en who sold sex, but it probably did not significantly lessen their numbers.[1]
The slow pace of improvement in genuine economic opportunities for wom-
en (or working-class persons of either gender, for that matter) guaranteed
that there would always be women desperate enough to sell sex.

The arguments surrounding prostitution and polygamy established in the
nineteenth century are still evident today. Despite the antipolygamy campaign, the LDS Church's repeated and highly public renunciations of plural
marriage, and the Church's extensive efforts to eliminate the practice among
its members, some people still live in polygamy. An unknown number of
"fundamentalists," not associated with (and condemned by) the mainstream
LDS Church, practice polygamy in Utah and surrounding states. After a flurry
of prosecutions and publicity in the 1940s and 1950s and violence within
polygamist circles in the 1980s, the issue seemed to subside. Polygamy resurfaced in 1998 when a young woman accused her father of beating her when
she refused to become the plural wife of a relative.[2] The arrest and conviction of Tom Green, the self-described husband of five wives, ignited a highly public debate that features arguments virtually identical to those from the
nineteenth-century contest.[3] The rhetorical link between polygamy and prostitution seems to have withered, however, despite an occasional letter to the
editor arguing that both practices constitute only slightly different forms of
illicit sex.[4]

The cycles of police raid and prostitute persistence established long ago
are also still evident. In an example reminiscent of century-old patterns,
women from throughout the West reportedly came to Salt Lake to take advantage of lax enforcement in 1995. "Asha" and "Unique" told a reporter that
they were in San Francisco when they heard that Salt Lake had no jail room
for prostitutes, so they quickly made the trip.[5] Salt Lake city and county officers declared a joint campaign against prostitution (less than ten days before

a mayoral election). The campaign included targeting patrons, although the officers complained that prosecuting customers was much more difficult and expensive.[6] While the antiprostitution campaign seemed to bear some short-term fruit, within a month police and citizens complained that the "circuit" prostitutes were back.[7] Women still use traditional tactics to stay in business and face familiar risks (as well as deadly newer ones such as AIDS) while authorities in Salt Lake City continue to wrestle with their responses to prostitution.

These events indicate that the contested meanings and uses of prostitutes, prostitution, and reform are still with us, and will likely be for many years. Hundreds of women will make a more or less voluntary choice to sell sex in Salt Lake City and will face the dangers of abusive customers, disease, and legal prosecution. Men will use them for sex; men and sometimes women will use them for profits and votes. Respectable society will treat prostitutes as criminal threats and will offer them little empathy or assistance. The roles prostitutes played in building the community and closing the Mormon-gentile gap will continue to be overlooked. And despite their lack of power, prostitutes will persevere.

Notes

1. On similar processes throughout the country, see Hobson, *Uneasy Virtue,* pp. 156–59; Rosen, "Epilogue," in *Lost Sisterhood;* and Shumsky and Springer, "San Francisco's Zone of Prostitution," p. 73. See also Groth, *Living Downtown,* pp. 120–21.

2. Van Wagoner, *Mormon Polygamy,* pp. 177–217; Alexander, *Utah, the Right Place,* pp. 391–92; and *Salt Lake City Deseret Evening News,* 5 Aug. 1998.

3. For the verdict, see *Deseret Evening News,* 19 May 2001.

4. *Deseret Evening News,* 26 Aug. 1998.

5. *Deseret Evening News,* 29 Oct. 1995.

6. *Deseret Evening News,* 25, 27 Oct. 1995.

7. *Deseret Evening News,* 30 Nov. 1995.

References

Manuscript Collections

Family and Church History Department, Church of Jesus Christ of Latter-day Saints, Salt Lake City, Utah Church Archives
  Mary Katherine Keemle Field. "The Mormon Monster." Lecture, Congregational Church, Washington, D.C., 15 Dec. 1886
  Brigham Young Hampton Papers, 1870–1901
  Anthon H. Lund Diary
  Levi James Taylor Diary
  Church History Library
    Journal History of the Church of Jesus Christ of Latter-day Saints
    Newman, Angie F. "To the Members of the Senate and House of Representatives of the 50th Congress." N.d. [probably 1889]
First Baptist Church of Salt Lake City, Salt Lake City, Utah
  "Record and Roll Book of the Salt Lake City Baptist Church"
  "Minutes" of First Baptist Church
L. Tom Perry Special Collections and Manuscripts Library, Harold B. Lee Library, Brigham Young University, Provo, Utah
  Ann Gordge Lee Autobiography
Manuscripts Division, University of Utah Marriott Library, Salt Lake City, Utah
  Abraham Hoagland Cannon Diaries, 1879–1896, MS 3
  Henry Dinwoodey Family Papers, Accn. 880
  Episcopal Diocese of Utah Records, Accn. 426
  First Presbyterian Church Records, Accn. 1049
  Ruth May Fox Papers, MS 443
  Ladies' Literary Club Papers, MS 439
  Henry W. Lawrence Collection, MS 309
  Ralph Taylor Richards Papers, MS 258

Salt Lake Council of Women Records, Accn. 1069

Reed Smoot Papers, MS 449

Utah Federation of Women's Clubs Records, MS 558

Emmeline B. Wells Papers, Accn. 1520

Young Women's Christian Association of Salt Lake City Records, MS 550

Special Collections, Stewart Library, Weber State University, Ogden, Utah

Twenty-fifth Street, Vertical File

Utah State Historical Society, Salt Lake City, Utah

Historicus [Amos Milton Musser], "Offences in 1882. Percentage in every 1,000 souls." Transcript in the hand of L. Weihe

Minutes of Utah State Mothers' Congress

Mormon Manuscripts and Broadsides

Samuel C. Park Scrapbooks

Rockwood, Albert P. "A Report with Extracts from the Congressional Acts of the United States Congress, the Legislative Journals and Laws of the Territory of Utah and A Concise History of Utah Penitentiary Its Inmates and Officers, From the Year 1855 to 1878." Compiled for and by the request of Mr. H. H. Bancroft, by A. P. Rockwood. Salt Lake City, 4 Jan. 1878

Westminster College Archives, Giovale Library, Salt Lake City, Utah

LeRoy Armstrong to the Editor. 8 Feb. 1908. Mormonism file

Public Documents

The Annual Message of the Mayor with the Annual Reports of the Officers of Salt Lake City, Utah. 1889–95, 1897–1900, 1904–5, 1907, 1909–15.

Commonwealth of Massachusetts, Office of the Secretary of State. "Copy of Record of Birth." Susan Norton, no. B 000897.

Ogden Police Court. "Justice's Docket, 1889." Utah State Archives series 13300.

Ogden Police Department. "Arrest Records, 1902–1904." Utah State Archives series 13300.

———. "Record of Prisoners, 1904–1909." Utah State Archives series 13300.

Salt Lake City. *Revised Ordinances and Resolutions of the City Council of Salt Lake City, 1875.* Salt Lake City: Deseret News Printing, 1875.

———. *Revised Ordinances of Salt Lake City, Utah, 1892.* Salt Lake City: Authority of the City Council of Salt Lake City, 1893.

———. *Revised Ordinances of Salt Lake City, Utah, 1903.* Salt Lake City: Deseret News, 1903.

———. *Revised Ordinances of Salt Lake City, Utah, 1913.* Salt Lake: Arrow Press, 1913.

———. Salt Lake City Commission Minutes.

———. Salt Lake City Council Minutes.

———. Salt Lake City Council Ordinances, 1851–91.

———. Salt Lake City Council Reports of Committee. Utah State Archives series 5556.

———. Salt Lake City Death Records.

Salt Lake City Court Criminal Division. "Minute Book, 1905." Utah State Archives series 5364.

———. "Minute Book, 1908." Utah State Archives series 5364.

———. "Minute Book, 1 January 1910–25 February 1914." Utah State Archives series 5364.

Salt Lake City Fifth Precinct Court. "J. P. Docket Book, February 1880–January 1884." Utah State Archives series 4669.

Salt Lake City Police Court. "Book of Miscellaneous Offenses, 1891–93." Utah State Archives series 4618.

———. "Book of Miscellaneous Offenses, 1893–5." Utah State Archives series 4618.

———. "Book of Miscellaneous Offenses, 1897–99." Utah State Archives series 4618.

———. "Book of Miscellaneous Offenses, 1899–1901." Utah State Archives series 4618.

Salt Lake City Police Department. "Arrest Register, 1891–1894." Utah State Archives series 4611.

———. "Arrest Register, 1896–1899." Utah State Archives series 4611.

———. "Criminal Record, 1892–1920." Salt Lake City Police Department Museum.

———. "Manual of the Salt Lake City Police Department," 1912.

———. "Record Commencing July 7, 1871–June 8, 1875." Utah State Archives series 4639.

———. "Record Commencing July 1, 1875–October 23, 1878." Utah State Archives series 4639.

Salt Lake County Clerk. Articles of Incorporation Record Books, 1870–1952. Utah State Archives series 3884.

———. Incorporation Case Files. Utah State Archives series 3888.

———. Record of Marriage Certificates.

Salt Lake County Probate Court. "Estate Registers, 1876–1979." Utah State Archives series 3927.

———. "Probate Record Books, 1852–1966." Utah State Archives series 3372.

Salt Lake County Recorder. "Abstract Books."

———. "Chattel Mortgage Books."

———. "Deed Books."

———. "Liens and Leases Books."

———. "Mortgage Books."

Senate Journal, Ninth Session of the Legislature of the State of Utah, 1911. Salt Lake City: Century Printing Company, 1911.

State of California. Department of Health Services. "Certificate of Death," Ethel Topham, no. 86-174183.

State of Iowa. Department of Health Records and Statistics Division. "Certification of Birth," Free, no. 23-87-264.

Third District Civil Case Files, 1851–96. Utah State Archives series 9802.

Third District Civil Case Files, 1896– . Utah State Archives series 1622.

Third District Criminal Case Files, 1896–1970. Utah State Archives series 1471.

Third District Territorial Criminal Case Files, 1882–96. Utah State Archives series 6836.

U.S. Bureau of the Census. *Compendium of the Eleventh Census: 1890.* Part 1: *Population.* Washington: Government Printing Office, 1892.

———. *Ninth Census of the United States.* Vol. 1: *Population and Social Statistics.* Washington: Government Printing Office, 1872.

———. Ninth Census of the United States, 1870.

———. Tenth Census of the United States, 1880.

———. Eleventh Census of the United States, 1890.

———. Twelfth Census of the United States, 1900.

———. Thirteenth Census of the United States, 1910.

———. *Thirteenth Census of the United States: Abstract of the Census.* Washington: Government Printing Office, 1913.

———. Fourteenth Census of the United States, 1920.

———. *Fourteenth Census of the United States Taken in the Year 1920.* Vol. 3: *Population.* Washington: U.S. Department of Commerce, Bureau of the Census, 1921.

U.S. Congress. House. Committee on the Judiciary. *Polygamy in the Territories* [*sic*] *of the United States (to accompany Bill H.R. No. 7).* House Report no. 83. 36th Cong., 1st sess., 1860.

———. Senate. *Woman Suffrage in Utah.* Petition of Mrs. Angie F. Newman. 49th Cong., 1st sess., 8 June 1886, S. Misc. Doc. 122.

———. Senate. *Proceedings Before the Committee on Privileges and Elections of the United States Senate in the Matter of the Protests Against the Right of Hon. Reed Smoot, A Senator from the State of Utah, to Hold His Seat.* 4 vols. Washington: Government Printing Office, 1904–7.

Utah. *The Compiled Laws of the Territory of Utah, 1876.* Salt Lake City: Deseret News, 1876.

———. *The Compiled Laws of Utah, 1888.* Salt Lake City: Herbert Pembroke, 1888.

———. *The Compiled Laws of the State of Utah, 1907.* Salt Lake City: Skelton Publishing Co., 1908.

———. *The Compiled Laws of the State of Utah, 1917.* 2 vols. Salt Lake City: Century Printing Co., 1919.

———. *Laws of the State of Utah, Passed at Special and First Regular Sessions of the Legislature of the State of Utah.* Salt Lake City: Deseret News Publishing Company, 1896.

———. *Revised Statutes of the State of Utah, 1898.* Lincoln, Neb.: State Journal Co., Printers, 1897.

———. *Laws of the State of Utah, Passed at the Sixth Regular Session of the Legislature of the State of Utah.* Salt Lake City: Star Printing Co., 1905.

———. *Laws of the State of Utah, Passed at the Eighth Regular Session of the Legislature of the State of Utah.* Salt Lake City: Skelton Publishing Company, 1909.

Utah Constitutional Convention, 1895. *Official Report of the Proceedings and Debates.* 2 vols. Salt Lake City, 1898.

Utah Department of Commerce. Division of Corporations. Incorporation Case Files, Closed 1871–1974.

Weber County (Utah) County Clerk. Articles of Incorporation Record Books, 1871–1961. Utah State Archives series 5079.

———. Incorporation Case Files, 1871–1961. Utah State Archives series 5297.

Books, Articles, Theses, and Papers

Acton, William. *The Functions and Disorders of the Reproductive Organs in Youth, in Adult Age, and in Advanced Life: Considered in Their Physiological, Social, and Psychological Relations.* Philadelphia, 1865.

———. *Prostitution Considered in its Moral, Social and Sanitary Aspects in London and Other Large Cities; with Proposals for the Mitigation and Prevention of its Attendant Evils.* 2d ed. London: J. Churchill and Sons, 1870.

Addams, Jane. *A New Conscience and an Ancient Evil.* New York: Macmillan Company, 1912.

Aiken, Katherine Gertrude. "The National Florence Crittenton Mission, 1883–1925: A Case Study in Progressive Reform." M.A. thesis, Washington State University, 1980.

Alexander, Thomas G. "Charles S. Zane, Apostle of the New Era." *Utah Historical Quarterly* 34, no. 4 (1966): 290–314.

———. *A Clash of Interests: Interior Department and Mountain West, 1863–1896.* Provo: Brigham Young University Press, 1973.

———. "An Experiment in Progressive Legislation: The Granting of Woman Suffrage in Utah in 1870." *Utah Historical Quarterly* 38 no. 1 (Winter 1970): 20–30.

———. "'Federal Authority versus Polygamic Theocracy': James B. McKean and the Mormons." *Dialogue* 1 (Autumn 1966): 85–100.

———. *Mormonism in Transition: A History of the Latter-day Saints, 1890–1930.* Urbana: University of Illinois Press, 1986.

———. *Things in Heaven and Earth: The Life and Times of Wilford Woodruff, a Mormon Prophet.* Salt Lake City: Signature Books, 1991.

———. *Utah, the Right Place: The Official Centennial History.* Rev. ed. Salt Lake City: Gibbs Smith, 1996.

Alexander, Thomas G., and James B. Allen. *Mormons and Gentiles: A History of Salt Lake City.* Boulder: Pruett Publishing Company, 1984.

Anderson, Amanda. *Tainted Souls and Painted Faces: The Rhetoric of Fallenness in Victorian Culture.* Ithaca: Cornell University Press, 1993.

Anderson, Eric. "Prostitution and Social Justice: Chicago, 1910–1915." *Social Service Review* 48, no. 2 (1974): 203–28.

Armitage, Shelley. *John Held, Jr.: Illustrator of the Jazz Age.* Syracuse: Syracuse University Press, 1987.

Armitage, Susan, and Elizabeth Jameson, eds. *The Woman's West.* Norman: University of Oklahoma Press, 1987.

Arrington, Leonard J. "Abundance from the Earth: The Beginnings of Commercial Mining in Utah." *Utah Historical Quarterly* 31, no. 3 (1963): 192–219.

———. *Brigham Young: American Moses.* New York: Alfred A. Knopf, 1985.

———. "The Commercialization of Utah's Economy: Trends and Developments from Statehood to 1910." In Leonard J. Arrington and Thomas G. Alexander, *A Dependent Commonwealth: Utah's Economy from Statehood to the Great Depression,* ed. Dean May, pp. 3–34. Provo: Brigham Young University Press, 1974.

———. *Great Basin Kingdom: An Economic History of the Latter-day Saints, 1830–1900.* Cambridge: Harvard University Press, 1958.

———. "Utah and the Depression of the 1890s." *Utah Historical Quarterly* 29, no. 1 (1961): 318.

Arrington, Leonard J., and Thomas G. Alexander. *A Dependent Commonwealth: Utah's Economy from Statehood to the Great Depression.* Edited by Dean May. Provo: Brigham Young University Press, 1974.

Arrington, Leonard J., and Davis Bitton. *The Mormon Experience: A History of the Latter-Day Saints.* 2d ed. Urbana: University of Illinois Press, 1992.

Arrington, Leonard J., Feramorz Y. Fox, and Dean L. May. *Building the City of God: Com-*

munity and Cooperation among the Mormons. 3d ed. Urbana: University of Illinois Press, 1992.

Arrington, Leonard J., and Jon Haupt. "Intolerable Zion: The Image of Mormonism in Nineteenth-Century American Literature." *Western Humanities Review* 22, no. 3 (1968): 243–60.

Baker, Paula. "The Domestication of Politics: Women and American Political Society, 1780–1920." *American Historical Review* 89, no. 3 (1984): 620–47.

Barnes, Lyle J. "Ogden's Notorious 'Two-Bit Street,' 1870–1954." M.S. thesis, Utah State University, 1969.

Barnhart, Jacqueline Baker. *The Fair but Frail: Prostitution in San Francisco, 1849–1900.* Reno: University of Nevada Press, 1986.

Barth, Gunther. *Bitter Strength: A History of the Chinese in the United States, 1850–1870.* Cambridge: Harvard University Press, 1964.

———. *Instant Cities: Urbanization and the Rise of San Francisco and Denver.* New York: Oxford University Press, 1975.

Baskin, Robert N. *Reminiscences of Early Utah.* Salt Lake City: Tribune-Reporter Printing Co., 1914.

Beard, Mary Ritter. *Woman's Work in Municipalities.* New York: D. Appleton and Company, 1915. Reprint, New York: Arno Press, 1972.

Beecher, Maureen Ursenbach. "Eliza R. Snow." In *Mormon Sisters: Women in Early Utah,* ed. Claudia L. Bushman, pp. 25–41. Cambridge, Mass.: Emmeline Press Limited, 1976.

Beecher, Maureen Ursenbach, and Lavina Fielding Anderson, eds. *Sisters in Spirit: Mormon Women in Historical and Cultural Perspective.* Urbana: University of Illinois Press, 1987.

Beeton, Beverly. "Woman Suffrage in the American West, 1869–1896." Ph.D. diss., University of Utah, 1976.

"The Beginning of the Descent." *Utah Survey* 1, no. 5 (1914): 1–2.

Beless, James W., Jr. "The Episcopal Church in Utah: Seven Bishops and One Hundred Years." *Utah Historical Quarterly* 36, no. 1 (1968): 77–96.

Bennion, Sherilyn Cox. "The *Woman's Exponent:* Forty-Two Years of Speaking for Women." *Utah Historical Quarterly* 44, no. 3 (1976): 222–39.

Benson, Susan Porter. *Counter Cultures: Saleswomen, Managers, and Customers in American Department Stores, 1890–1940.* Urbana: University of Illinois Press, 1986.

Berlin, Edward A. *Ragtime: A Musical and Cultural History.* Berkeley: University of California Press, 1980.

Bitton, Davis. "The B. H. Roberts Case of 1898–1900." *Utah Historical Quarterly* 25, no. 1 (1957): 27–46.

———. *The Ritualization of Mormon History and Other Essays.* Urbana: University of Illinois Press, 1994.

Blair, Karen J. *The Clubwoman as Feminist: True Womanhood Redefined, 1868–1914.* New York: Holmes and Meier, 1980.

Bliss, Jonathan. *Merchants and Miners in Utah: The Walker Brothers and Their Bank.* Salt Lake City: Western Epics, 1983.

Blocker, Jack S., Jr. *American Temperance Movements: Cycles of Reform.* Boston: Twayne Publishers, 1989.

Bordin, Ruth. *Women and Temperance: The Quest for Power and Liberty, 1873–1900*. Philadelphia: Temple University Press, 1981.

Boyce, Ronald R. "An Historical Geography of Greater Salt Lake City, Utah." M.A. thesis, University of Utah, 1957.

Boyer, Paul. *Urban Masses and Moral Order in America, 1820–1920*. Cambridge: Harvard University Press, 1978.

Brands, H. W. *The Reckless Decade: America in the 1890s*. New York: St. Martin's Press, 1995.

Brandt, Allan M. *No Magic Bullet: A Social History of Venereal Disease in the United States since 1880*. New York: Oxford University Press, 1985.

Brenzel, Barbara M. "Domestication as Reform: A Study of the Socialization of Wayward Girls, 1856–1905." *Harvard Educational Review* 50, no. 2 (1980): 196–213.

Bringhurst, Newell G. *Saints, Slaves, and Blacks: The Changing Place of Black People within Mormonism*. Westport, Conn.: Greenwood Press, 1981.

Bristow, Edward J. *Vice and Vigilance: Purity Movements in Britain since 1700*. Dublin: Gill and Macmillan, 1977.

Bristow, Nancy K. *Making Men Moral: Social Engineering during the Great War*. New York: New York University Press, 1996.

Brown, Richard Maxwell. *Strain of Violence: Historical Studies of American Violence and Vigilantism*. New York: Oxford University Press, 1975.

Brudnoy, David. "Of Sinners and Saints: Theodore Schroeder, Brigham Roberts, and Reed Smoot." *Journal of Church and State* 14, no. 2 (1972): 261–78.

Buel, J. W. *Metropolitan Life Unveiled: Sunlight and Shadow of America's Great Cities*. Philadelphia: West Philadelphia Publishing Company, 1891.

Burgess-Olson, Vicky, ed. *Sister Saints*. Provo: Brigham Young University, 1978.

Burnham, John C. "The Progressive Era Revolution in American Attitudes toward Sex." *Journal of American History* 59, no. 4 (1973): 885–908.

———. "The Social Evil Ordinance: A Social Experiment in Nineteenth-Century St. Louis." *Missouri Historical Society* 27 (1971): 203–17.

Burton, Richard Francis. *The City of the Saints, and Across the Rocky Mountains to California*. London: Longman, Green, Longman and Roberts, 1861.

Bush, Lester E. Jr. "Mormonism's Negro Doctrine: An Historical Overview." In *Neither White nor Black: Mormon Scholars Confront the Race Issue in a Universal Church*, ed. Lester E. Bush, Jr., and Armand L. Mauss, pp. 53–129. Midvale, Utah: Signature Books, 1984.

Bushman, Claudia L., ed. *Mormon Sisters: Women in Early Utah*. Cambridge, Mass.: Emmeline Press Limited, 1976.

Butler, Anne M. *Daughters of Joy, Sisters of Misery: Prostitutes in the American West, 1865–1890*. Urbana: University of Illinois Press, 1985.

Callister, Ellen Gunnell. "The Political Career of Edward Henry Callister, 1885–1916." M.A. thesis, University of Utah, 1967.

Campbell, Eugene E. "The Government of Utah, 1847–51." M.A. thesis, University of Utah, 1940.

Cannon, Charles A. "The Awesome Power of Sex: The Polemical Campaign against Mormon Polygamy." *Pacific Historical Review* 43, no. 1 (1974): 61–82.

Cannon, Frank J., and Harvey J. O'Higgins. *Under the Prophet in Utah: The National Menace of a Political Priestcraft.* Boston: C. M. Clark, 1911.

Cannon, George Q. *A Review of the Decision of the Supreme Court of the United States in the Case of George Reynolds vs. the United States.* Salt Lake City, 1879.

Carmack, Noel A. "Before the Flapper: The Utah Beginnings of John Held, Jr." *Utah Historical Quarterly* 66, no. 4 (1998): 292–319.

Carpenter, George E. *Souvenir History of the Salt Lake Fire Department, 1852 to August, 1901.* Salt Lake City: Deseret News, 1901.

Charles, Melodie Moench. "Precedents for Mormon Women from Scriptures." In *Sisters in Spirit: Mormon Women in Historical and Cultural Perspective,* ed. Maureen Ursenbach Beecher and Lavina Fielding Anderson, pp. 37–63. Urbana: University of Illinois Press, 1987.

Cheney, Thomas, ed. *Mormon Songs from the Rocky Mountains.* Austin: University of Texas Press, 1968.

Cheng, Eric Yuan-Chin. "Chinese." In *Asian Americans in Utah: A Living History,* comp. John H. Yang, pp. 49–53, 64–66. Salt Lake City: State of Utah Office of Asian Affairs, 1999.

Clark, Michael James Tinsley. "A History of the Twenty-Fourth United States Infantry Regiment in Utah, 1896–1900." Ph.D. diss., University of Utah, 1979.

Cohen, Stanley, and Andrew Scull, eds. *Social Control and the State: Historical and Comparative Essays.* Oxford: Martin Robertson, 1983.

Coleman, Ronald Gerald. "Blacks in Utah History: An Unknown Legacy." In *The Peoples of Utah,* ed. Helen Z. Papanikolas, pp. 115–40. Salt Lake City: Utah State Historical Society, 1976.

———. "A History of Blacks in Utah, 1825–1910." Ph.D. diss., University of Utah, 1980.

Conley, Don C. "The Pioneer Chinese of Utah." In *The Peoples of Utah,* ed. Helen Z. Papanikolas, pp. 251–77. Salt Lake City: Utah State Historical Society, 1976.

Connelly, Mark Thomas. *The Response to Prostitution in the Progressive Era.* Chapel Hill: University of North Carolina Press, 1980.

Cook, Mrs. Joseph. "Face to Face with Mormonism." Paper read at the Semi-Annual Meeting of the Woman's Home Missionary Association, 27 Mar. 1884. Boston: Thomas Todd, 1887.

Cooley, Everett L. "Carpetbag Rule: Territorial Government in Utah." *Utah Historical Quarterly* 26, no. 2 (1958): 107–29.

Corbin, Alain. *Women for Hire: Prostitution and Sexuality in France after 1850.* Translated by Alan Sheridan. Cambridge: Harvard University Press, 1990. Originally published as *Les filles de Noce: Misère Sexuelle et Prostitution aux 19th et 20th Siècles.* Paris: Aubier Montaigne, 1978.

Cordasco, Francesco, and Thomas Monroe Pitkin. *The White Slave Trade and the Immigrants: A Chapter in American Social History.* Detroit: Blaine Ethridge, 1981.

Cott, Nancy F. "Passionlessness: An Interpretation of Victorian Sexual Ideology, 1790–1850." *Signs* 4 (Winter 1978): 219–36

Cresswell, Stephen. "The U.S. Department of Justice in Utah Territory, 1870–1890." *Utah Historical Quarterly* 53, no. 3 (1985): 204–22.

Crittenton, Charles Nelson. *The Brother of Girls: The Life Story of Charles Nelson Crittenton as Told by Himself.* Chicago: World's Events Co., 1910.

Crofutt, Geo A., comp. *Crofutt's Salt Lake City Directory for 1885–6.* Salt Lake City: Herald Job Department, 1885.

Crunden, Robert M. *Ministers of Reform: The Progressives' Achievement in American Civilization, 1889–1920.* New York: Basic Books, 1982.

Cullom, Shelby M. "The Reed Smoot Decision." *North American Review* 611 (15 Mar. 1907): 572–76.

Darling, Dee Richard. "Cultures in Conflict: Congregationalism, Mormonism and Schooling in Utah, 1880–1893." Ph.D. diss., University of Utah, 1991.

Davidson, Cathy N. *Revolution and the Word: The Rise of the Novel in America.* New York: Oxford University Press, 1986.

Davis, David B. "Some Themes of Counter-Subversion: An Analysis of Anti-Masonic, Anti-Catholic, and Anti-Mormon Literature." *Mississippi Valley Historical Review* 47 (1960): 205–24.

Degler, Carl. *At Odds: Women and the Family in America from the Revolution to the Present.* New York: Oxford University Press, 1980.

D'Emilio, John, and Estelle Freedman. *Intimate Matters: A History of Sexuality in America.* New York: Harper and Row, 1988.

Derr, Jill Mulvay. "Sarah Melissa Granger Kimball: The Liberal Shall be Blessed." In *Sister Saints,* ed. Vicky Burgess-Olson, pp. 21–40. Provo: Brigham Young University, 1978.

———. "'Strength in Our Union': The Making of Mormon Sisterhood." In *Sisters in Spirit: Mormon Women in Historical and Cultural Perspective,* ed. Maureen Ursenbach Beecher and Lavinia Fielding Anderson, pp. 153–207. Urbana: University of Illinois Press, 1987.

Derr, Jill Mulvay, Janath Russell Cannon, and Maureen Ursenbach Beecher. *Women of Covenant: The Story of Relief Society.* Salt Lake City: Deseret Book Company, 1992.

De Voto, Bernard. "Sin Comes to Ogden." In *Among the Mormons: Historic Accounts by Contemporary Observers,* ed. William Mulder and A. Russell Mortensen, pp. 446–54.

de Young, Mary. "Help, I'm Being Held Captive! The White Slave Fairy Tale of the Progressive Era." *Journal of American Culture* 6, no. 1 (1983): 96–99.

Dimter, Lauren H. "Populism in Utah." M.A. thesis, Brigham Young University, 1964.

Dubois, Frederick T. *Fred T. Dubois' The Making of a State.* Edited by Louis J. Clements. Rexburg, Idaho: Eastern Idaho Publishing, 1971.

Dudden, Faye E. *Serving Women: Household Service in Nineteenth-Century America.* Middletown, Conn.: Wesleyan University Press, 1983.

Duke, James A. *CRC Handbook of Medicinal Herbs.* Boca Raton, Fla.: CRC, 1985.

Dwyer, Robert Joseph. *The Gentile Comes to Utah: A Study in Religious and Social Conflict, 1862–1890.* Salt Lake City: Western Epics, 1971.

Dykstra, Robert R. *The Cattle Towns.* Lincoln: University of Nebraska Press, 1968.

Embry, Jessie L. *Black Saints in a White Church: Contemporary African American Mormons.* Salt Lake City: Signature Books, 1994.

Encyclopedia of Mormonism: The History, Scripture, Doctrine, and Procedures of the Church of Jesus Christ of Latter-day Saints. New York: Macmillan, 1992.

Epstein, Barbara Leslie. *The Politics of Domesticity: Women, Evangelism, and Temperance in Nineteenth-Century America.* Middletown, Conn.: Wesleyan University Press, 1981.

Erickson, Velt G. "The Liberal Party of Utah." M.A. thesis, University of Utah, 1948.

Ethington, Philip J. "Recasting Urban Political History: Gender, the Public, the Household, and Political Participation in Boston and San Francisco during the Progressive Era." *Social Science History* 16, no. 2 (1992): 301–33.

Evans, Richard J. "Prostitution, State and Society in Imperial Germany." *Past and Present* 70 (Feb. 1976): 106–29.

Feldman, Egal. "Prostitution, the Alien Woman and the Progressive Imagination." *American Quarterly* 19 (1967): 192–206.

Felt, Jeremy P. "Vice Reform as a Political Technique: The Committee of Fifteen in New York, 1900–1901." *New York History* 54, no. 1 (1973): 24–51.

Finnegan, Frances. *Poverty and Prostitution: A Study of Victorian Prostitutes in York.* Cambridge: Cambridge University Press, 1979.

"Fire Insurance Map of Salt Lake City, 1884." New York: Sanborn Map and Publishing Co., 1884.

"Fire Insurance Map of Salt Lake City, 1889." New York: Sanborn-Perris Map Company, 1889.

"Fire Insurance Map of Salt Lake City, 1895." New York: Sanborn Map Company, 1895.

"Fire Insurance Map of Salt Lake City, 1898." New York: Sanborn-Perris Map Company, 1898.

"Fire Insurance Map of Salt Lake City, 1911." New York: Sanborn Map Co., 1911.

Firmage, Edwin Brown, and Richard Collin Mangrum. *Zion in the Courts: A Legal History of the Church of Jesus Christ of Latter-day Saints, 1830–1900.* Urbana: University of Illinois Press, 1988.

Fishbein, Leslie. "Harlot or Heroine? Changing Views of Prostitution, 1870–1920." *Historian* 43, no. 1 (1980): 23–35.

Flanagan, Maureen A. "Gender and Urban Political Reform: The City Club and the Woman's City Club of Chicago in the Progressive Era." *American Historical Review* 95, no. 4 (1990): 1032–50.

Fogelson, Robert M. *Big-City Police.* Cambridge: Harvard University Press, 1977.

Foster, Lawrence. *Religion and Sexuality: The Shakers, the Mormons, and the Oneida Community.* Oxford: Oxford University Press, 1981.

———. *Women, Family, and Utopia: Communal Experiments of the Shakers, the Oneida Community, and the Mormons.* Syracuse: Syracuse University Press, 1991.

Foster, Warren. "Open Letter to Angus M. Cannon." *Living Issues,* 29 Dec. 1899.

Furniss, Norman F. *The Mormon Conflict, 1858–1859.* New Haven: Yale University Press, 1960.

Gage, Matilda. "Mormon Women Missionaries." *National Citizen and Ballot,* Sept. 1881.

Gerlach, Larry R. "Justice Denied: The Lynching of Robert Marshall." *Utah Historical Society Quarterly* 66 (Fall 1998): 355–64.

———. "Ogden's 'Horrible Tragedy': The Lynching of George Segal." *Utah Historical Society Quarterly* 49, no. 2 (1981): 157–72.

———. "Vengeance vs. the Law: The Lynching of Sam Joe Harvey in Salt Lake City." In *Community Development in the American West: Past and Present, Nineteenth and Twentieth Century Frontiers,* ed. Jessie L. Embry and Howard A. Christy, pp. 201–37. Provo: Charles Redd Center for Western Studies, Brigham Young University, 1985.

Gibbs, George Snow. "The Need of a State Institution for Feeble-Minded in Utah." *Utah Survey* 2, no. 4 (1915): 5–10.

Gibson, Mary. *Prostitution and the State in Italy, 1860–1915.* New Brunswick: Rutgers University Press, 1986.

Givens, Terryl L. *The Viper on the Hearth: Mormons, Myths, and the Construction of Heresy.* New York: Oxford University Press, 1997.

Gleason, Herbert Lester. "The Salt Lake City Police Department, 1851–1949: A Social History." M.S. thesis, University of Utah, 1950.

Godfrey, Audrey M. "Housewives, Hussies, and Heroines, or the Women of Johnston's Army." *Utah Historical Quarterly* 54, no. 2 (1986): 157–78.

Godfrey, Kenneth W. "Frank J. Cannon: Declension in the Mormon Kingdom." In *Differing Visions: Dissenters in Mormon History,* ed. Roger D. Launius and Linda Thatcher, pp. 241–61. Urbana: University of Illinois Press, 1994.

Goldman, Marion S. *Gold Diggers and Silver Miners: Prostitution and Social Life on the Comstock Lode.* Ann Arbor: University of Michigan Press, 1981.

Goodson, Stephanie Smith. "Plural Wives." In *Mormon Sisters: Women in Early Utah,* ed. Claudia L. Bushman, pp. 89–112. Cambridge, Mass.: Emmeline Press Limited, 1976.

Gordon, Linda. "Putting Children First: Women, Maternalism, and Welfare in the Early Twentieth Century." In *U.S. History as Women's History: New Feminist Essays,* ed. Linda K. Kerber, Alice Kessler-Harris, and Kathryn Kish Sklar, pp. 63–86. Chapel Hill: University of North Carolina Press, 1995.

———. *Woman's Body, Woman's Right: A Social History of Birth Control in America.* New York: Grossman, 1976.

Griffiths, David B. "Far Western Populism: The Case of Utah, 1893–1900." *Utah Historical Quarterly* 37, no. 4 (1969): 396–406.

Grittner, Frederick K. *White Slavery: Myth, Ideology, and American Law.* New York: Garland Publishing, 1990.

Groth, Paul. *Living Downtown: The History of Residential Hotels in the United States.* Berkeley: University of California Press, 1994.

Grow, Stewart L. "A Study of the Utah Commission, 1882–1896." Ph.D. diss., University of Utah, 1954.

Gusfield, Joseph R. *Symbolic Crusade: Status Politics and the American Temperance Movement.* 2d ed. Urbana: University of Illinois Press, 1986.

Haller, John S., Jr., and Robin M. Haller. *The Physician and Sexuality in Victorian America.* Urbana: University of Illinois Press, 1974.

Haller, Mark H. "Historical Roots of Police Behavior: Chicago, 1890–1925." *Law and Society Review* 10, no. 2 (1976): 303–23.

Hansen, Klaus. "Mormon Sexuality and American Culture." *Dialogue: A Journal of Mormon Thought* 10, no. 2 (1976): 45–56.

———. *Quest for Empire: The Political Kingdom of God and the Council of Fifty in Mormon History.* East Lansing: Michigan State University Press, 1967.

Hardy, B. Carmon. *Solemn Covenant: The Mormon Polygamous Passage.* Urbana: University of Illinois Press, 1992.

Harring, Sidney L. *Policing a Class Society: The Experience of American Cities, 1865–1915.* New Brunswick: Rutgers University Press, 1983.

Harsin, Jill. *Policing Prostitution in Nineteenth-Century Paris.* Princeton: Princeton University Press, 1985.

Hass, Paul H. "Sin in Wisconsin: The Teasdale Vice Committee of 1913." *Wisconsin Magazine of History* 49 no. 2 (1965–66): 138–51.

Hathaway, Jim. "A History of the American Drinking Place." *Landscape* 29, no. 1 (1986): 1–9.

Hayes, Samuel P. "The Politics of Reform in Municipal Government in the Progressive Era." *Pacific Northwest Quarterly* 55, no. 4 (1964): 157–69.

Hayward, Barbara. "Utah's Anti-Polygamy Society, 1878–1884." M.A. thesis, Brigham Young University, 1980.

Held, John, Jr. *The Most of John Held, Jr.* Brattleboro, Vt.: Stephen Greene Press, 1972.

Hibbard, Charles G. "Fort Douglas, 1862–1916: Pivotal Link on the Western Frontier." Ph.D. diss., University of Utah, 1980.

Hilton, Lynn M., ed. *The Story of Salt Lake Stake of the Church of Jesus Christ of Latter-day Saints.* Salt Lake City: Salt Lake Stake, 1972.

Himes, Norman E. *Medical History of Contraception.* New York: Gamut Press, 1963.

Hirata, Lucie Cheng. "Free, Indentured, Enslaved: Chinese Prostitutes in Nineteenth-Century America." *Signs* 5, no. 1 (1979): 3–29.

Hobson, Barbara Meil. *Uneasy Virtue: The Politics of Prostitution and the American Reform Tradition.* New York: Basic Books, 1987.

Holsinger, M. Paul. "For God and the American Home: The Attempt to Unseat Senator Reed Smoot, 1903–1907." *Pacific Northwest Quarterly* 60, no. 3 (July 1969): 154–160.

Hoop, O. W. "Recollections of Fort Douglas at the Turn of the Century." *Utah Historical Quarterly* 21, no. 1 (1953): 57–66.

Hubbard, Lester, ed. *Ballads and Songs from Utah.* Salt Lake City: University of Utah, 1961.

Hulse, James W. "C. C. Goodwin and the Taming of the *Tribune.*" *Utah Historical Quarterly* 61, no. 2 (1993): 164–81.

Humphrey, Isaac B. "Commission Government in Salt Lake City, Utah." M.A. thesis, University of Utah, 1936.

"Hurting the Town." *Utah Survey* 1, no. 10 (1914): 6–7.

Iversen, Joan. *The Antipolygamy Controversy in U.S. Women's Movements, 1880–1925: A Debate on the American Home.* New York: Garland Publishing, 1997.

———. "Feminist Implications of Mormon Polygyny." *Feminist Studies* 10 (Fall 1984): 505–22.

Ivins, Stanley S. "A Constitution for Utah." *Utah Historical Quarterly* 25, no. 2 (1957): 95–116.

———. "Notes on Mormon Polygamy." In *The New Mormon History: Revisionist Essays on the Past,* ed. D. Michael Quinn, pp. 169–76. Salt Lake City: Signature Books, 1992.

James, Jennifer. "Mobility as an Adaptive Strategy." *Urban Anthropology* 4 no. 4 (1975): 349–64.

Jeffrey, Julie Roy. *Frontier Women: "Civilizing" the West?* Rev. ed. New York: Hill and Wang, 1998.

Johnson, Claudia J. "That Guilty Third Tier: Prostitution in Nineteenth-Century American Theaters." *American Quarterly* 27, no. 5 (1975): 575–84.

Journal of Discourses. 26 vols. Liverpool, Eng.: Latter-day Saints Book Depot, 1854–86.

Journal of the Proceedings of the Fourth Annual Convocation of the Protestant Episcopal Church in the Missionary District of Utah (1911).

Journal of the Proceedings of the Fifth Annual Convocation of the Protestant Episcopal Church in the Missionary District of Utah (1912).

Journal of the Proceedings of the Seventh Annual Convocation of the Protestant Episcopal Church in the Missionary District of Utah (1914).

Kasai, Alice. "Japanese." In *Asian Americans in Utah: A Living History,* comp. John H. Yang, pp. 125–31. Salt Lake City: State of Utah Office of Asian Affairs, 1999.

Katzman, David M. *Seven Days a Week: Women and Domestic Service in Industrializing America.* New York: Oxford University Press, 1978.

Kauffman, Reginald Wright. *The House of Bondage.* New York: Moffat, Yard and Co., 1910. Reprint, Upper Saddle River, N.J.: Gregg Press, 1969.

Keller, Morton. *Regulating a New Society: Public Policy and Social Change in America, 1900–1933.* Cambridge: Harvard University Press, 1994.

Kerber, Linda K., Alice Kessler-Harris, and Kathryn Kish Sklar, eds. *U.S. History as Women's History: New Feminist Essays.* Chapel Hill: University of North Carolina Press, 1995.

Kessler-Harris, Alice. *Out to Work: A History of Wage-Earning Women in the United States.* Oxford: Oxford University Press, 1982.

Knudsen, Mrs. Ernest E., comp. *History of Utah Federation of Women's Clubs, 1893 to 1952.* N.d., n.p., 1952. (Utah Federation of Women's Clubs Records, JWM.)

Kunzel, Regina G. *Fallen Women, Problem Girls: Unmarried Mothers and the Professionalization of Social Work 1890–1945.* New Haven: Yale University Press, 1993.

Langum, David J. *Crossing over the Line: Legislating Morality and the Mann Act.* Chicago: University of Chicago Press, 1994.

Larsen, Kent Sheldon. "The Life of Thomas Kearns." M.A. thesis, University of Utah, 1964.

Larson, Gustive O. *The "Americanization" of Utah for Statehood.* San Marino, Calif.: Huntington Library, 1971.

———. "An Industrial Home for Polygamous Wives." *Utah Historical Quarterly* 38, no. 3 (1970): 263–75.

Lee, Ann Gordge. "Autobiography." Ca. 1900. Variant given to Salt Lake City policeman, ca. 1915. Copy in author's possession.

Lender, Mark Edward. *Dictionary of American Temperance Biography: From Temperance Reform to Alcohol Research, the 1600s to the 1980s.* Westport, Conn.: Greenwood Press, 1983.

Leonard, Neil. "The Reactions to Ragtime." In *Ragtime: Its History, Composers, and Music,* ed. John Edward Hasse, pp. 102–13. New York: Schirmer Books, 1985.

Liestman, Daniel. "Utah's Chinatowns: The Development and Decline of Extinct Ethnic Enclaves." *Utah Historical Quarterly* 64, no. 1 (1996): 70–95.

Lindsey, Judge Ben B., and Harvey J. O'Higgins. *The Beast.* New York: Doubleday, Page & Company, 1910.

Lobb, Ann Vest, and Jill Mulvay Derr. "Women in Early Utah." In *Utah's History,* ed. Richard D. Poll, Thomas G. Alexander, Eugene E. Campbell, and David E. Miller, pp. 337–41. Provo: Brigham Young University Press, 1978.

Lubove, Roy. "The Progressive and the Prostitute." *Historian* 24, no. 3 (1962): 308–30.

Lyman, Edward Leo. *Political Deliverance: The Mormon Quest for Utah Statehood.* Urbana: University of Illinois Press, 1986.

———. "Statehood, Political Allegiance, and Utah's First U.S. Senate Seats: Prizes for the National Parties and Local Factions." *Utah Historical Quarterly* 63, no. 4 (1995): 341–56.

Lyon, Thomas Edgar. "Evangelical Protestant Missionary Activities in Mormon Dominated Areas, 1865–1900." Ph.D. diss., University of Utah, 1962.

———. "Religious Activities and Development in Utah, 1847–1910." *Utah Historical Quarterly* 35, no. 4 (1967): 292–306.

Mackey, Thomas C. *Red Lights Out: A Legal History of Prostitution, Disorderly Houses, and Vice Districts, 1870–1917.* New York: Garland Publishing, 1987.

Madsen, Brigham D. *Corinne: The Gentile Capital of Utah.* Salt Lake City: Utah State Historical Society, 1980.

———. *Glory Hunter: A Biography of Patrick Edward Connor.* Salt Lake City: University of Utah Press, 1990.

———. *Gold Rush Sojourners in Great Salt Lake City, 1849 and 1850.* Salt Lake City: University of Utah Press, 1983.

Madsen, Carol Cornwall. "'At Their Peril': Utah Law and the Case of Plural Wives, 1850–1900." *Western Historical Quarterly* 21, no. 4 (1990): 425–443.

———. "Decade of Detente: The Mormon-Gentile Female Relationship in Nineteenth-Century Utah." *Utah Historical Quarterly* 63, no. 4 (1995): 298–319.

———. "A Mormon Woman in Victorian America." Ph.D. diss., University of Utah, 1985.

Malmquist, O. N. *The First 100 Years: A History of the Salt Lake Tribune, 1871–1971.* Salt Lake City: Utah Historical Society, 1971.

"Marvelous Coincidentility." *Utah Survey* 1, no. 10 (1914): 5–6.

Matthews, Glenna. *The Rise of Public Woman: Woman's Power and Woman's Place in the United States, 1630–1970.* New York: Oxford University Press, 1992.

Mauss, Armand L. *The Angel and the Beehive: The Mormon Struggle with Assimilation.* Urbana: University of Illinois Press, 1994.

May, Dean L. *Three Frontiers: Family, Land, and Society in the American West, 1850–1900.* Cambridge: Cambridge University Press, 1994.

———. *Utah: A People's History.* Salt Lake City: University of Utah Press, 1987.

Mayer, John A. "Notes toward a Working Definition of Social Control in Historical Analysis." In *Social Control and the State: Historical and Comparative Essays,* ed. Stanley Cohen and Andrew Scull, pp. 17–38. Oxford: Martin Robertson, 1983.

McCormick, John S. "Hornets in the Hive: Socialists in Early Twentieth-Century Utah." *Utah Historical Quarterly* 50, no. 3 (1982): 236–37.

———. "Red Lights in Zion: Salt Lake City's Stockade, 1908–11." *Utah Historical Quarterly* 50, no. 2 (1982): 168–81.

———. *Salt Lake City: The Gathering Place.* Woodland Hills, Calif.: Windsor Publications, 1980.

McGerr, Michael. "Political Style and Women's Power, 1830–1930." *Journal of American History* 77, no. 3 (1990): 864–85.

McLaren, Angus. *A History of Contraception: From Antiquity to the Present Day.* Oxford: Basil Blackwell, 1990.

McLaws, Monte. *Spokesman for the Kingdom: Early Mormon Journalism and the Deseret News, 1830–1898.* Provo: Brigham Young University Press, 1977.

Melish, John Howard. *Franklin Spencer Spalding: Man and Bishop.* New York: Macmillan Company, 1917.

Mercer, Samuel A. B. "Joseph Smith as an Interpreter and Translator of Egyptian." *Utah Survey* 1, no. 1 (1913): 4–36.

Merrill, Milton R. *Reed Smoot: Apostle in Politics.* Logan: Utah State University Press, 1990.

Messages of the First Presidency of the Church of Jesus Christ of Latter-day Saints, 1833–1964. 4 vols. Edited by James R. Clark. Salt Lake City: Bookcraft, 1965.

Meyerowitz, Joanne. *Women Adrift: Independent Wage Earners in Chicago, 1880–1930.* Chicago: University of Chicago Press, 1988.

———. "Women and Migration: Autonomous Female Migrants to Chicago, 1880–1930." *Journal of Urban History* 13, no. 2 (1987): 147–68.

Michel, Sonya, and Seth Koven. "Womanly Duties: Maternalist Politics and the Origins of Welfare States in France, Germany, Great Britain, and the United States, 1880–1920." *American Historical Review* 95, no. 4 (1990): 1076–1108.

"Ministers and Ministrators." *Utah Survey* 1, no. 8 (1914): 2–4.

Missionary District of Salt Lake, Journal of Convocation (1907).

Monkonnen, Eric H. *Police in Urban America, 1860–1920.* Cambridge: Cambridge University Press, 1981.

Moorman, Donald R., with Gene Sessions. *Camp Floyd and the Mormons: The Utah War.* Salt Lake City: University of Utah Press, 1992.

Morgan, Dale L. *The State of Deseret.* Logan, Utah: Utah State University Press with the Utah State Historical Society, 1987.

"Mormonism Militant." *Christian Statesman,* Jan. 1917: 33–35.

Murphy, Mary. "The Private Lives of Public Women: Prostitution in Butte, Montana, 1878–1917." In *The Women's West,* ed. Susan Armitage and Elizabeth Jameson, pp. 193–205. Norman: University of Oklahoma Press, 1987.

———. "Women on the Line: Prostitution in Butte, Montana, 1878–1917." M.A. thesis, University of North Carolina, 1983.

Murphy, Miriam B. "The Working Women of Salt Lake City: A Review of the *Utah Gazetteer,* 1892–1893." *Utah Historical Quarterly* 46, no. 2 (1978): 121–35.

Nasaw, David. *Going Out: The Rise and Fall of Public Amusements.* New York: Basic Books, 1993.

Nelson, Larry E. "Utah Goes Dry." *Utah Historical Quarterly* 41, no. 4 (1973): 340–57.

Newby, I. A. *Jim Crow's Defense: Anti-Negro Thought in America, 1900–1930.* Baton Rouge: Louisiana State University Press, 1965.

Nichols, Jeffrey. "African-American Soldiers and Civilians in the News: Salt Lake City, 1896–1898." Paper presented at the annual meeting of the Utah State Historical Society, 15 July 1994, Price, Utah.

Noel, Thomas J. *The City and the Saloon: Denver, 1858–1916.* Lincoln: University of Nebraska Press, 1982.

Odem, Mary E. *Delinquent Daughters: Protecting and Policing Adolescent Female Sexuality in the United States, 1885–1920.* Chapel Hill: University of North Carolina Press, 1995.

"Organized Vice as a Vested Interest." *Current Literature* 52, no. 3 (1912): 292–94.

Paddock, Mrs. A. G. *The Fate of Madame La Tour: A Tale of Great Salt Lake.* New York: Fords, Howard, and Hulbert, 1881.

———. "An Industrial Home for Mormon Women." *Christian Register,* 7 Jan. 1886.

———. *In the Toils; or, Martyrs of the Latter Days.* Chicago: Shepard, Tobias and Co., 1879.

———. *Saved at Last from among the Mormons.* Springfield, Ohio: Farm and Fireside Company, 1881.

Painter, Nell Irvin. *Standing at Armageddon: The United States, 1877–1919.* New York: W. W. Norton, 1987.

Papanikolas, Helen Z. "The Exiled Greeks." In *The Peoples of Utah,* ed. Papanikolas, pp. 409–35. Salt Lake City: Utah State Historical Society, 1976.

———, ed. *The Peoples of Utah.* Salt Lake City: Utah State Historical Society, 1976.

Papanikolas, Helen Z., and Alice Kasai. "Japanese Life in Utah." In *The Peoples of Utah,* ed. Helen Z. Papanikolas, pp. 333–62. Salt Lake City: Utah State Historical Society, 1976.

Parent-Duchatelet, Dr. Alex. J. B. *De la prostitution dans la ville de Paris.* 3d. ed. 2 vols. Paris: J. B. Baillière, 1836. Completed with new documents by MM. A. Trébuchet, Poirat-Duval, 2 vols. Paris: J. B. Baillière et frères, 1857.

Parkhill, Forbes. *The Wildest of the West.* New York: Holt, 1951.

Parsons, Katherine Barrette. *History of Fifty Years: Ladies' Literary Club, Salt Lake City, Utah, 1877–1927.* Salt Lake City: Arrow Press, 1927.

Pascoe, Peggy. *Relations of Rescue: The Search for Female Moral Authority in the American West, 1874–1939.* New York: Oxford University Press, 1990.

Peiss, Kathy. *Cheap Amusements: Working Women and Leisure in Turn-of-the-Century New York.* Philadelphia: Temple University Press, 1986.

Peterson, Paul Henry. "The Mormon Reformation." Ph.D diss., Brigham Young University, 1981.

Petrik, Paula. "Capitalists with Rooms: Prostitution in Helena, Montana, 1865–1900." *Montana* 31 no. 2 (spring 1981): 28–39.

Pivar, David J. *Purity Crusade: Sexual Morality and Social Control, 1868–1900.* Westport, Conn.: Greenwood Press, 1973.

Platt, Anthony. *The Child Savers: The Invention of Delinquency.* Chicago: University of Chicago, 1969.

Polk, R. L., comp. *Ogden City Directory, 1904–1916.* Ogden: R. L. Polk and Company, 1904–16.

———. *Salt Lake City Directory, 1890, 1891–2, 1894–5, 1896–1918.* Salt Lake City: R. L. Polk and Company, 1890–1918.

Poll, Richard, Thomas G. Alexander, Eugene E. Campbell, and David E. Miller, eds. *Utah's History.* Provo: Brigham Young University Press, 1978.

Proceedings of the National Conference of Charities and Corrections. Boston: Geo. H. Ellis, 1893.

"Putting Out the Red Lights." *Literary Digest* 51 (13 Nov. 1915): 1086–87.

Quinn, D. Michael. "LDS Church Authority and New Plural Marriages, 1890–1904." *Dialogue: A Journal of Mormon Thought* 18, no. 1 (1985): 9–105.

———. *The Mormon Hierarchy: Extensions of Power.* Salt Lake City: Signature Books in association with Smith Research Associates, 1997.

———. *The Mormon Hierarchy: Origins of Power.* Salt Lake City: Signature Books in association with Smith Research Associates, 1994.

————. *Same-Sex Dynamics among Nineteenth-Century Americans: A Mormon Example.* Urbana: University of Illinois Press, 1996.

————, ed. *The New Mormon History: Revisionist Essays on the Past.* Salt Lake City: Signature Books, 1992.

Raynes, Marybeth. "Mormon Marriages in an American Context." In *Sisters in Spirit: Mormon Women in Historical and Cultural Perspective,* ed. Maureen Ursenbach Beecher and Lavina Fielding Anderson, pp. 227–48. Urbana: University of Illinois Press, 1987.

Reed, James. *The Birth Control Movement and American Society: From Private Vice to Public Virtue.* New York: Basic Books, 1978.

Reherd, Herbert Ware, comp. and ed. *An Outline History of the Protestant Churches of Utah.* Salt Lake City: Salt Lake Ministerial Association, 1948. Reprinted in *Utah: A Centennial History,* ed. Wain Sutton. New York: Lewis Historical Publishing Company, 1949.

Ritchie, Lily Munsell. "What Utah Women Have Done with the Vote." *Utah Survey* 1, no. 8 (1914): 8–13.

Roberts, Brigham H. *A Comprehensive History of the Church of Jesus Christ of Latter Day Saints: Century I.* 6 vols. Salt Lake City: Deseret News Press, 1930. Reprint, Provo: Brigham Young University Press, 1965.

Rosen, Ruth. *The Lost Sisterhood: Prostitution in America, 1900–1918.* Baltimore: Johns Hopkins University Press, 1982.

Ryan, Mary P. *Cradle of the Middle Class: The Family in Oneida County, New York, 1790–1865.* Cambridge: Cambridge University Press, 1981.

Salmon, Lucy Maynard. *Domestic Service.* New York: Macmillan, 1897. Reprint, New York: Arno Press, 1972.

Salt Lake City Directory, 1889. N.p., n.d.

Sanger, William W. *The History of Prostitution: Its Extent, Causes, and Effects Throughout the World.* New York: Harper and Brothers, 1858. Reprint, New York: Eugenics Publishing Company, 1937.

"Saved from the Mormons." *Galaxy: A Magazine of Entertaining Reading* 14, no. 5 (1872): 684–85.

Schindler, Harold. *In Another Time: Sketches of Utah History.* Logan, Utah: Utah State University Press, 1998.

Scholefield, J. B. "The Social Service Commission—Why?" *Utah Survey* 1, no. 2 (1913): 19–21.

Scott, Anne Firor. "Mormon Women, Other Women: Paradoxes and Challenges." *Journal of Mormon History* 13 (1986–87): 13–20.

Seligman, Edward R. *The Social Evil, with Special Reference to Conditions Existing in the City of New York.* New York: G. P. Putnam's Sons, 1912.

Sheldon, Carrel Hilton. "Mormon Haters." In *Mormon Sisters: Women in Early Utah,* ed. Claudia L. Bushman, pp. 113–21. Cambridge, Mass.: Emmeline Press Limited, 1976.

Shepard, Lulu Loveland. "Utah Dry in November." *Christian Statesman,* June 1916: 271–72.

Shipps, Jan. "Utah Comes of Age Politically." *Utah Historical Quarterly* 35, no. 2 (1967): 91–111.

Shumsky, Neil Larry, and Larry M. Springer. "San Francisco's Zone of Prostitution, 1880–1934." *Journal of Historical Geography* 7 no. 1 (1981): 71–82.

Sillito, John R., ed. *From Cottage to Market: The Professionalization of Women's Sphere.* Salt Lake City: Utah Women's History Association, 1983.

Sklar, Kathryn Kish. *Catharine Beecher: A Study in American Domesticity.* New Haven: Yale University Press, 1973.

Skocpol, Theda. *Protecting Soldiers and Mothers: The Political Origins of Social Policy in the United States.* Cambridge: Belknap Press of Harvard University Press, 1992.

Smith, Daniel Scott. "Family Limitation, Sexual Control, and Domestic Feminism in Victorian America." In *Clio's Consciousness Raised: New Perspectives on the History of Women,* ed. Mary Hartman and Lois W. Banner, pp. 119–36. New York: Harper and Row, 1974.

Smith, Joseph F. "Unchastity the Dominant Evil of the Age." Written for and at request of The Newspaper Enterprise Association. San Francisco, n.d.

Smith-Rosenberg, Carroll. *Disorderly Conduct: Visions of Gender in Victorian America.* New York: Oxford University Press, 1985.

Snow, Eliza R. "Decision of the Supreme Court of the United States in the Reynolds Case." *Deseret Evening News,* 21 Jan. 1879.

Snow, Reuben Joseph. "The American Party in Utah: A Study of Political Party Struggles during the Early Years of Statehood." M.A. thesis, University of Utah, 1964.

"Special Conference at Great Salt Lake City." *Millenial Star,* supplement to vol. 15 (1853): 24–25.

Stanton, Elizabeth Cady. *Eighty Years and More.* New York: European Publishing, 1898.

Startup, George A. *Effective Liquor and Vice Law.* Provo: "Betterment or Booze?" Pub. Co., n.d.

Statistical Abstract of Utah. Salt Lake City: Bureau of Economic and Business Research, David Eccles School of Business, University of Utah, 1996.

Stenhouse, Fanny. *A Lady's Life among the Mormons.* New York: American News Company, 1872.

———. *"Tell It All": The Story of a Life's Experience in Mormonism.* Hartford: A. D. Worthington, 1874.

Stenhouse, T. B. H. *The Rocky Mountain States: A Full and Complete History of the Mormons.* Salt Lake City: Shepard Book Company, 1904.

Stone, Ann Gardner. "Dr. Ellen Brooke Ferguson: Nineteenth-Century Renaissance Woman." In *Sister Saints,* ed. Vicky Burgess-Olson, pp. 325–39. Provo: Brigham Young University Press, 1978.

Stout, Hosea. *On the Mormon Frontier: The Diary of Hosea Stout, 1844–1861.* Salt Lake City: University of Utah Press and Utah State Historical Society, 1964.

Sutherland, Daniel E. *Americans and Their Servants: Domestic Service in the United States from 1800 to 1920.* Baton Rouge: Louisiana State University Press, 1981.

Tanner, Annie Clark. *A Mormon Mother: An Autobiography by Annie Clark Tanner.* Salt Lake City: Tanner Trust Fund and University of Utah Library, 1991.

Thompson, Brent Grant. "Utah's Struggle for Prohibition 1908–1917." M.A. thesis, University of Utah, 1979.

Tone, Andrea. *Devices and Desires: A History of Contraceptives in America.* New York: Hill and Wang, 2001.

Tong, Benson. *Unsubmissive Women: Chinese Prostitutes in Nineteenth-Century San Francisco.* Norman: University of Oklahoma Press, 1994.

Travis, Marilyn Reed. "Social Stratification and the Dissolution of the City of Zion in Salt Lake City, 1847–1880." Ph.D. diss., University of Utah, 1995.

Tullidge, Edward W. *History of Salt Lake City and Its Founders.* Salt Lake City: E. W. Tullidge, 1886.

———. *The Women of Mormondom.* New York: Tullidge and Crandall, 1877.

Turner, George Kibbe. "The City of Chicago: A Study of the Great Immoralities." *McClure's Magazine* 28, no. 6 (1907): 575–92.

Tuttle, Daniel Sylvester. *Reminiscences of a Missionary Bishop.* New York: T. Whittaker, 1906.

Twain, Mark. *Roughing It.* Berkeley: University of California Press, 1996.

Tyrrell, Ian. *Woman's World, Woman's Empire: The Woman's Christian Temperance Union in International Perspective, 1880–1930.* Chapel Hill: University of North Carolina Press, 1991.

Utah Gazetteer, 1892–93. Salt Lake City: Stenhouse & Co, 1892.

Van Wagenen, Lola. "Sister-Wives and Suffragists: Polygamy and the Politics of Woman Suffrage, 1870–1896." Ph.D. diss., New York University, 1994.

Van Wagoner, Richard S. *Mormon Polygamy: A History.* 2d ed. Salt Lake City: Signature Books, 1989.

Van Wagoner, Richard S., and Mary Van Wagoner. "Arthur Pratt, Utah Lawman." *Utah Historical Quarterly* 55, no. 1 (1987): 22–35.

W., J. H. "A Dialogue. Segregation vs. Extirpation." *Utah Survey* 1, no. 3 (1913): 18–24.

Walker, Ronald W. "When the Spirits Did Abound: Nineteenth-Century Utah's Encounter with Free-Thought Radicalism." *Utah Historical Quarterly* 50, no. 4 (1982): 319–23.

Walkowitz, Judith R. "The Politics of Prostitution." *Signs* 6, no. 1 (1980): 123–35.

———. *Prostitution and Victorian Society: Women, Class, and the State.* Cambridge: Cambridge University Press, 1980.

Warner, Sam Bass, Jr. *The Urban Wilderness: A History of the American City.* Berkeley: University of California Press, 1972.

Waters, Christine Croft. "Pioneering Women Physicians, 1847–1900." In *From Cottage to Market: The Professionalization of Women's Sphere,* ed. John R. Sillito, pp. 47–61. Salt Lake City: Utah Women's History Association, 1983.

Welter, Barbara. "The Cult of True Womanhood: 1820–1860." *American Quarterly* 18, no. 2 (1966): 151–74.

West, Elliott. *The Saloon on the Rocky Mountain Mining Frontier.* Lincoln: University of Nebraska Press, 1979.

White, Jean Bickmore. "Woman's Place Is in the Constitution." *Utah Historical Quarterly* 42, no. 4 (1974): 344–69.

White, Richard. *"It's Your Misfortune and None of My Own": A New History of the American West.* Norman: University of Oklahoma Press, 1991.

White, William Griffin Jr. "The Feminist Campaign for the Exclusion of Brigham Henry Roberts from the Fifty-Sixth Congress." *Journal of the West* 17, no. 1 (1978): 45–52.

Whitney, Orson F. *History of Utah.* 4 vols. Salt Lake City: George Q. Cannon & Sons, 1904.

Williamson, Joel. *The Crucible of Race: Black-White Relations in the American South since Emancipation.* New York: Oxford University Press, 1984.

Wunsch, James. "The Social Evil Ordinance." *American Heritage* 33, no. 2 (1982): 50–55.

Yang, John H., comp. *Asian Americans in Utah: A Living History.* Salt Lake City: Asian American Advisory Council, 1999.

Young, Ann Eliza Webb. *Wife No. 19, or The Story of a Life in Bondage.* Hartford: Dustin, Gilman, 1875.

Young, Kimball. *Isn't One Wife Enough?* New York: Holt, 1954.

Zane, Charles S. "The Death of Polygamy in Utah." *Forum* 12 (Nov. 1891): 368–75.

Index

156; on Victoria Alley, 57, 63–64, 68, 93–
94, 122–23, 179
Critchlow, Edward B., 136–37
Critchlow, Mary Willis, 136
Crittenton, Charles Nelson, 114
Cutler, John C., 145, 146–47, 179

Dance halls, 179–81
Daniels, Madge, 147
Davenport, Fanny, 33, 34
Davis, Arthur J., 138
Davis, Nellie, 64, 158
Davis, Sallie, 109
Davis Deaconess Home, 111
"Declaration of Grievances and Pro-
tests," 32
Defense of landlord provision, 61, 90
DeMarr, Emma (aka Matilda Turncross,
Emma Whiting): alternate identities of,
60–61, 90; business dealings of, 54–56; as
madam, 1, 53–57, 68, 69, 89–90, 142, 213–14
D'Emilio, John, 12
Democratic Party, 97–98, 104
De Voto, Bernard, 30
Dickson, William H., 22, 32, 44n.189
Dininny, Harper J., 147, 150, 155–57, 164, 194
Dinwoodey, Henry, 59–60
Doctrine and Covenants, 10
Domestic feminism, 15
Donnelly, Mae, 197, 199
Drugs, 63, 70, 156
Drummond, Willis W., 26, 41n.125
Dubois, Fred T., 14–15

Eaton, Amey B., 186, 191
Edmunds Act (1882), 21, 31–32, 98
Edmunds-Tucker Act (1887), 98
Edwards, Eva, 149–50
Elder, Nellie, 190
Emery, C. Frank, 145
Empey, Nelson A., 104
Englebrecht, Paul, 27, 29, 33
Evans, Lillian, 93, 158–59

Fairchild, Catherine (aka Kitty Hicks), 60,
77n.95
Fate of Madame La Tour (Paddock), 19
"Federal Bunch," 139, 157, 164, 196
Federal government, 15, 179, 203–5; officials
in, 1, 10, 26, 29, 30, 32, 204
Feeble-mindedness, 185–86
Ferguson, Ellen B., 110

Fernstrom, F. S., 151, 155
Ferry, William Montague (W. Mont): as
American councilman, 138; and Civic
Betterment League, 150; as mayor, 199–
201, 203; and reform, 192–93; and 243
south Main, 54–55
Fields, S. J., 1, 33, 34
Flint, Kate: alternate identity of, 60; busi-
ness dealings of, 59; in Corinne, 27–28, 52;
and 1872 abatement, 28–30, 33, 34, 86, 97;
as folk figure, 30, 31, 42–43n.154; and
Frank J. Cannon, 65; as madam, 1, 27–30,
33, 34, 52–53, 56, 186, 213
Foote, Gussie, 66
Fort Douglas: founded, 10–11, 26; and World
War I, 202; mentioned, 30, 48, 64, 94, 95,
179, 182
Foster, Warren, 93, 117
Fox, Ruth May, 162, 163
Franklin Avenue: African Americans on, 47;
prostitution on, 47, 48, 57, 62, 93, 100–102,
105–6, 112–13; Variety Theater on, 63, 99–
100. *See also* Prostitution: district
Free, John Finley, 56
Free, Susie. *See* Noble, Sadie
Freed Furniture and Carpet Company, 60
Freedman, Estelle B., 12
Frogtown (Dobeytown, Fairfield), 26
Froiseth, Jennie, 19, 20

Gardiner, F., 112
Gee, Henrietta, 121
Gee, W. W., 121
Gentiles: and crime, 85–86; defined, 7n.1;
gender system of, 5, 11, 15; moral code of,
5, 11, 166; settlement of, in Salt Lake City,
10, 20, 25. *See also* Antipolygamy; Con-
flict, Mormon-gentile
Gibbs, George Snow, 186
Glendinning, James, 92, 97, 107, 115–16
Glenn, Hugh L., 190–91, 193–94, 197–99
Godbe, William S., 15
Godbeites, 15–16, 18
Goldman, Marion, 4
Goodwin, Charles Carroll (C. C.): on polyg-
amy, 14, 25, 33, 185; on prostitution, 33, 87,
97, 196–97, 199; and *Salt Lake City Daily
Tribune*, 16, 136
Gospel Relief Mission, 117
Gowans, Ephraim G., 191
Grant, Brigham F.: as chief of police, 180,
188–89, 191–92, 194, 196–97, 198–200; and

Mathews, Norman, 160
Mathis, Charlotte, 121
Matthews, Glenna, 12–13
Matthews, Thomas, 157
McCornick, William S., 60
McDonald, Irene, 147, 190
McKay, William, 116–17
McKean, James B., 27, 29
McMahon, Georgiana, 161
McMaster, Alexander, 191
McNiece, Rev. R. G., 110
McNiece, Sara, 107
Meyerowitz, Joanne, 4
Miles, Luella, 119
Miller, Rose, 101, 103
Mining, 11, 20, 213
Ministerial Association, 122, 135–37, 179, 194–96, 199
Mormons: and African Americans, 47; and alcohol, 27, 195–96; and American Party, 138–39; and antipolygamy, 14, 21, 22, 28, 29, 32–36; defined, 1; gender system of, 5, 10, 12, 15; and Liberal Party, 98–99, 104; moral code of, 5, 10, 25, 111, 166, 185, 193, 214; and prostitution, 2, 5, 13, 23–36, 83–87, 98–99, 146, 214; "reformation," 26, 84; and Stockade, 151. *See also* Antipolygamy; Church of Jesus Christ of Latter-day Saints; Conflict, Mormon-gentile; Polygamy
Morrill Anti-Bigamy Act (1862), 15, 21, 24, 27, 167
Morris, George Q., 151
Morris, Nephi L., 196
Morse, C. W., 146, 151, 152
Mortimer, Madeline, 67
Mulliner, H. J., 201
Mulvey, Martin: as politician, 98, 158; and Stockade, 138, 141, 143, 152, 153, 156
Mundt, Herman J., 155
Municipal League, 116–18, 137
Murphy, Mary, 4
Murray, Eli H., 22, 44n.189
Musicians, 65, 149, 160
Musser, Amos Milton (pseud. Historicus), 30–31, 85

National Florence Crittenton Mission, 114
Nauvoo, 25
Newman, Angie, 21–23, 35, 138
New Movement (Godbeites), 15–16, 18

Newton, William, 189, 199
New York Bureau of Social Hygiene, 185
Noble, Sadie (aka Susie Free): alternate identities of, 56, 60; business dealings of, 56, 60; as madam, 1, 55–56, 60, 66, 101, 113, 214
Noble, Worden P., 116
Non-Mormons. *See* Gentiles
Nyborg, Ragna, 183

Odem, Mary, 4, 181
Ogden, Nellie, 69
Ogden, Utah, 30, 62, 70; Dora Topham in, 141–42, 154, 159–60; industrial school in, 182
Opium, 63
Owens, Caroline, 18–19

Paddock, Algernon Sidney, 21
Paddock, Alonzo G., 18, 20
Paddock, Cornelia: death of, 119, 137; *Fate of Madame La Tour,* 19; *In the Toils,* 19–20; and moral reform, 182, 213; and polygamy, 18–22, 105; on relief committee, 110; and rescue, 110–12, 113–15, 118–19
Paden, Rev. William, 120, 136, 137, 145, 164
Palace, the, 63, 66, 117
Panic of 1893, 56, 109–10
Parent-Duchatelet, Alexandre-Jean-Baptiste, 88
Park, Samuel R., 164, 178, 188, 194, 197, 199
Parker, William B., 100–101
Pascoe, Peggy, 4
Pearl of Great Price, 10
People's Party, 31, 104–5
Petrik, Paula, 4
Pitt, Thomas, 139–40, 143, 145
Plum Alley, 47–48, 66, 102
Plumas rooming house, 149–50, 164
Plummer, Anna C., 119
Plural marriage. *See* Polygamy
Police: all-Mormon, 31, 65, 85; arrests of prostitutes by, 28, 30–31, 32–33, 35, 85–86, 87–88, 91–92, 94, 99, 150, 155–56; conflicts and scandals among, 100–104, 115–16, 183–84, 198–99; court and, 33, 85, 92–93, 97, 182; justice and, 27, 32–33, 85, 93, 101–2; matron of, 106, 112; "purity squad," 189–91, 203, 204; and regulation, 6, 27–28, 88, 91, 93, 105–6, 112, 123, 139–40; and relations with prostitutes, 100–103; and res-

21–22, 97, 98, 110; "true," 5, 11, 13, 15, 21, 88,
106, 108, 154, 163–64, 215; work and, 11, 49–
50, 179, 181, 204, 216
Woodruff, Elias, 151
Woodruff, Wilford, 36, 87
Woodruff Manifesto, 36, 104, 121, 136, 137, 138
Woods, Ray, 148, 149
Word of Wisdom, 193, 195. *See also* Prohibi-
tion; Reform: of alcohol use
World War I, 179, 202–5

Young, Brigham, 14, 15, 27, 28, 30
Young, Brigham, Jr., 90
Young, Zina D., 137
Young Ladies' Mutual Improvement Associ-
ation, 193, 195
Young Women's Christian Association
(YWCA), 193

Zane, Charles S., 22, 31–32, 33–35, 89
Zion Aid Society, 203

JEFFREY NICHOLS is an assistant professor of history at Westminster College in Salt Lake City. Born in New York State, he served nine years in the United States Navy as an antisubmarine warfare officer before earning his Ph.D. from the University of Utah.

The University of Illinois Press
is a founding member of the
Association of American University Presses.

Composed in 10.5/13 Minion
with Minion display
by Celia Shapland
for the University of Illinois Press
Designed by Paula Newcomb
Manufactured by Thomson-Shore, Inc.

University of Illinois Press
1325 South Oak Street
Champaign, IL 61820-6903
www.press.uillinois.edu